PC Card/PCMCIA Software Developer's Handbook Second Edition

Steven M. Kipisz

Brian E. Moore

Dana L. Beatty

Peer-to-Peer Communications, Inc.

Published by Peer-to-Peer Communications, Inc.
P.O. Box 689
Menlo Park, CA 94026-0689 U.S.A.
Phone: 1 650-325-4080
Fax: 1 804-975-0790
E-mail: *info@peer-to-peer.com*
World Wide Web: *http://www.peer-to-peer.com/*

Peer-to-Peer offers discounts on this title when purchased in bulk quantities. For information, please contact the Sales Department at an address above.

10 9 8 7 6 5 4 3 2 1

Front Cover: Beth Morgan, Southern Pines, NC
Printing: Data Reproductions, Auburn Hills, MI

Printed in the United States of America

Library of Congress Cataloging-in-Publication Data

Kipisz, Steven M.
PC Card/PCMCIA software developer's handbook / Steven M. Kipisz, Brian E. Moore, Dana L. Beatty
p. cm.
Includes index.
ISBN 1-57398-015-3 (pbk.)
1. Computer software—Development. I. Moore, Brian E. II. Beatty, Dana L. III. Title.
QA76.76.D47K5617 1998
005.1—dc21 98-39278
CIP

TRADEMARKS AND COPYRIGHTS

DISCLAIMER

Dedications

To my parents and my brother for their support of all my unique endeavors.
Steven

To my wife, Barbara, and my children, Brian Jr., Betsy, and Robert. I also want to thank my parents, John and Doris. Without your support and love during the last few years, I couldn't have done it.
Brian

To my parents for those ruby red slippers, which came in handy this year.
Dana

Contents

Foreword ... ix
Acknowledgments ... xi
Obtaining the source code for this book ... xiii

CHAPTER 1: INTRODUCTION ... 1

The Purpose of This Book ... 1
How To Use This Book ... 2

CHAPTER 2: WHAT IS PCMCIA? ... 5

Terminology Conventions ... 5
The Association ... 6
The PC Card Standard Goals ... 6
Organization of the Standard ... 7
PC Card Hardware Elements ... 7
PC Card Types ... 8
Handheld PC Devices ... 17
PC Card Sockets ... 18
16-bit PC Card Adapters ... 21
32-bit PC Card Adapters ... 21
The PC Card Evolution ... 22
PC Card 2.X Software Elements ... 22
Card Services (CS) ... 23
Socket Services (SS) ... 23
Client Device Drivers (CDD) ... 24
How PC Card Software Works: The Chain of Events ... 26
PC Card Advantages ... 26
PC Card Pitfalls ... 28
What Does the Future Hold? ... 28

CHAPTER 3: UNDERSTANDING TRADITIONAL CLIENT DRIVERS ... 29

Why Do We Need Client Drivers? ... 29
What Is A Client Driver? ... 30
What Are Super Client Drivers? ... 30
Types of Client Drivers ... 31
Memory Technology Driver (MTD) ... 31
Implementing Client Drivers ... 32
DOS Application Program Client Drivers ... 32
DOS TSR Client Drivers ... 33
Client Device Drivers ... 33

How Client Drivers Work 35
Card Services API 35
Using the Card Services API 37
Detecting Card Insertion: A Sample Client Driver 38
Card Services Function Codes 39
Determining Card Services Presence 41
Registering as a Card Services Client 43
Fielding a Callback Event 46
Card Insertion Event 48
Deregistering a Card Services Client 49
Power Management for PC Cards 50
Summary 54

CHAPTER 4: PC CARDS AND HOST SYSTEM RESOURCES 57

16-bit PC Cards 57
16-Bit Function Configuration Registers 59
CardBus PC Cards 61
Card Information Structure (CIS) 64
CIS Development 67
CIS Sample Source Code for a 16-bit PC Card 68
Parsing the CIS: A Sample Client Driver 81
Accessing PC Card Address Space 83
Mapping PC Card Memory to System Memory 83
Decoding I/O Address Space 86
Obtaining System IRQs 86
Assigning System Resources to a PC Card 88
Management of System Resources: The Chain Reaction 91
Summary 92

CHAPTER 5: DOS/ WINDOWS 3.1 93

DOS 93
Microsoft Windows 93
DOS Client driver template 94
Device Driver Entry Point 95
Terminate-Stay-Resident (TSR) Entry Point 98
Registration Complete 112
Card Insertion 112
Card Removal 124
Client Info 126
Request Exclusive 129
Debugging Tips and Techniques 133

CHAPTER 6: OS/2 135

IBM OS/2 2.1 135
OS/2 WARP 138
Client Driver Template and Sample 139
THE TEMPLATE 139
THE SAMPLE TOKEN-RING CLIENT DEVICE DRIVER 147
ENHANCEMENTS 161
DEBUGGING TIPS AND TECHNIQUES 163
SUMMARY 164

CHAPTER 7: WINDOWS 95/ 98 165

WINDOWS 95 PC CARD INSTALLATION 168
WINDOWS 95 PC CARD IDENTIFICATION 169
WINDOWS 95 CLIENT DEVICE DRIVERS 172
WINDOWS 95 PC CARD REMOVAL 172
WINDOWS 95 CARD SERVICES (PCCARD.VXD) 173
WHY DEVELOP SOFTWARE WITH CARD SERVICES CALLS? 174
TEMPLATE FOR CALLING CARD SERVICES FUNCTIONS FROM A DEVICE DRIVER 174
WINDOWS 95/98 PC CARD CONFIGURATION 175
WINDOWS 95 SOCKET SERVICES 178
Multi-Function PC Card Support 179
CardBus PC Card Support 182
Application Notifications 184
SUMMARY 185

CHAPTER 8: WINDOWS NT/CE 187

WINDOWS NT 187
Registry Keywords 188
Multi-Function PC Cards 192
CardBus PC Cards 196
Application Notifications 197
WINDOWS CE 201
Windows CE Device Driver Architecture 201
Windows CE Registry Structure 202
Windows CE Application Notifications 206
SUMMARY 206

CHAPTER 9: LINUX PCMCIA PROGRAMMER'S GUIDE 209

INTRODUCTION 209
ACKNOWLEDGMENTS 210
BASIC PC CARD CONCEPTS 210
THE PC CARD SOCKET INTERFACE 210
THE 16-BIT PC CARD SOCKET ADAPTER 211
CARD SERVICES SUBFUNCTION DESCRIPTIONS 212

Client Management Functions 212
BindDevice 215
Socket State Control 215
I/O Card Configuration Calls 219
Card Information Structure (CIS) calls 229
Memory Window Control 233
Bulk Memory Services 237
Miscellaneous Calls 244
Card Information Structure Definitions 248
CIS Configuration Registers 262
Card Services Event Handling 265
Memory Technology Drivers 268
Driver Services Interface 272
The CardBus client interface 275
Card Services Event Notifications 278
Anatomy of a Card Services Client Driver 281
The PC Card Event Handler 283
Where to Go for More Information 284

CHAPTER 10: PC CARD DEVELOPMENT UTILITIES 285

A Utility For Parsing the Card Information Structure (CIS) 287
A Utility to Display Card Insertion/Removal 307
A Utility That Shows Application Notifications 313
A Modem Detecting Utility 319
Debugging Tips and Techniques 320
A Socket Controller Examination Tool 321
Standard Information provided by the PCIC Tools 322
Summary 331

APPENDIX A: WHERE TO GO FOR MORE INFORMATION 333

GLOSSARY 339

INDEX 361

WINDOWS 2000 VS. WINDOWS NT 5.0 367

Foreword

The PC Card Standard was conceived in 1989 to provide a method by which portable and mobile computers could load and run programs from IC Cards without the need for floppies. They were designed as memory expansion and file formatted memory cards. The organization formed to develop this standard was appropriately named the Personal Computer Memory Card International Association (PCMCIA). Subsequent releases of the standard included Release 2.0, which added I/O capability and in February 1995 which added DMA, 3.3 volts, multifunction and CardBus (32bit/33MHz capability). In the recent past PCMCIA has added Zoom Video capability which allows a card to talk directly to the video controller in the host bypassing the system local bus. Today, PC Card sockets are standard equipment on mobile computers and moving into the desktop arena.

The rapid development of the PC Card Standard did not leave time for the association to write any comprehensive programmer's manual to go along with the standard. The standard is largely written for engineers and software architects rather than the average programmer or end user. This second edition of "PCMCIA Software Developer's Handbook" bridges this information gap and gives the reader an easy to understand, step-by-step explanation of the PC Card Standard and how to program to it. IT provides insight into the reasoning behind some of the seemingly confusing requirements of the standard. This edition includes chapters on Windows 95/98, Windows NT, and Windows CE. It also includes information on multi-function and CardBus PC Cards. Some new utility programs for development purposes have also been added.

As the chairman of the PCMCIA technical committee from 1990-1993, and chairman of the board from 1993-1994 & 1997-1998, I recommend this well organized and informative book for anyone interested in PC Card technology. I have known the authors, Dana Beatty, Steven Kipisz, and Brian Moore from my days at IBM. Dana from her days in Boca Raton and Steven and Brian from the development of PCMCIA LAN products from IBM RTP.

Respectfully,
Anthony Wutka
Texas Instruments, Senior Member Technical Staff, PCIbus Solutions.

Acknowledgments

I would like to thank Rick Morris at IBM for getting me involved in LAN PC Card development. I would also like to thank Dean Walker, Billy Moon, and Mike Fehnel at Ericsson for keeping me involved in PC Card development. With their help I am able to continue working on PC Card products.

(SMK)

My thanks to Steve and Dana for their support all through the PC Card development efforts we were involved in. As always, John Beidl provided moral and technical support that was second to none. I will never forget his insight and patience.

(BEM)

My thanks to both Steve and Brian for their insanity in pursuing yet another edition of this book. I'm certain to keep learning from their involvement in PC Card. And a special thanks to Russ Gordon for giving me the set of legitimate excuses to tell Steve and Brian.

(DLB)

Lastly, the authors extend their sincere thanks to David A Hinds for kindly allowing us to reprint his Linux PCMCIA Programmer's Guide in this book as Chapter 9.

Obtaining the source code for this book

The source code featured in this text is available from the Peer-to-Peer Web site via FTP. The address is ftp.peer-to-peer.com/pubs/pc-card. The file is called handbook.zip. Unzip this file into any subdirectory you wish. Be sure to use an option that preserves the directory structure in the file when you unzip it. The subdirectories will match the chapter where the software was referenced.

In the root directory of handbook.zip is a README.TXT file. This file contains information about the overall contents of the zip file.

Chapter 1: Introduction

PCMCIA. It initially catches your eye because of its size. It's hard to believe something the size of a credit card could actually be a modem or a LAN card. The circuitry is all self-contained inside a molded casing. Some cards come with cables or connectors; some even come with antennas. The smallest PC Cards are a mere 3.3mm thick; the largest, a whole 10.5mm thick.

While size certainly is a big benefit, some of the other key advantages aren't quite so obvious at first. Things like the absence of jumpers or DIP switches to toggle, no complicated installation or configuration instructions, and lower power consumption (consequently, a longer system battery life) all result from this amazing technology. Better still, these little wonders can be inserted or removed from the system while it is powered on. Try doing that with your desktop adapter cards. PC Cards are a whole new way of computing. However, like all new technology, it takes a little getting used to. That's where this book can help.

The Purpose of This Book

PC Cards, like the personal computer, have made the transition from a nifty gadget for an executive willing to pay the price, to something sold from the back of trade magazines. Unfortunately, a lot of the trade advertisement claims are too good to be true. This book is designed to quickly bring you up to speed on the PC Card Standard so you can rapidly put this technology to work. It will help you understand the standard and guide you in learning to use PC Card technology so you can dodge some of the incompatibility bullets.

For the more experienced user, this book serves as a reference and guide. Developers wishing to write either applications or device drivers to control or exploit PC Card features will want to pay particular attention to the actual program code templates.

Who Should Read This Book

PC Card/ PCMCIA Developer's Software Handbook assumes nothing about your previous experience with the PC Card Standard. You will find it useful whether you are new to the PC Card Standard, need to program to the interfaces or just want a handy reference. Those searching for an understanding of the PC Card Standard and products may want to take a look at Chapter 2 while Chapter 4 will broaden your knowledge on configuring these devices. Software developers who need some background on the standard should start with Chapter 3, while those with more experience may want to jump straight to the chapter that discusses the Operating System you are interested in. Chapter 5 discusses PCMCIA in the DOS/ Windows 3.1 environment. Chapter 6 discusses OS/2 and it's implementation of PCMCIA. Chapter 7 covers Windows 95 and it's successors. Chapter 8 covers Windows NT and Windows CE. Chapter 9 covers Linux and how it implements the PCMCIA architecture. Finally, Chapter 10 presents some utility programs and debug tools that operate under the various operating systems.

For the software developer, this book presents the concepts of the PC Card Standard in a way that is simple and easy to comprehend. By focusing on the elements that are pertinent to the development of PC Card "aware" software and through the use of actual source code templates, you will gain knowledge that can quickly be put to use. Couple that with actual source code templates included in this book, you will have the tools to assist you in developing client driver or application software. Tools for examining the PCMCIA hardware allow the user to examine the settings for further understanding .

For the consumer, this book will teach the significant end-user aspects of the PC Card Standard. This book demystifies PC Cards. It explains the terminology and concepts that are important to understand, not only for making an informed PC Card purchase, but for using it as well. This book also educates you on some of the pitfalls and compatibility problems that can be avoided simply by understanding the key components of this standard: card and socket types, PC Card software, and interaction with existing application software.

How To Use This Book

Chapter 1 through Chapter 4 of the book bring you up to speed on the PC Card terminology, concepts, software and hardware products that exist in the marketplace today. This portion of the book is ideally suited to the reader who wants a thorough introduction to the PC Card Standard.

Chapter 5 through chapter 9 get to the core of the PC Card architecture that is important for software developers to grasp. These chapters of the book examine the information that is relevant to the development of PC Card software and include program source code listings. Chapter 10 contains sample utility and debug programs.

Chapter Summary

Chapter 2 familiarizes first time users of PC Cards with the fundamentals of the standard. Starting with an overview about the committee that governs the PC Card Standard, it quickly moves to the end-user elements that are integral to the standard, including card Types, the different kind of cards, and how all these pieces interact to make PC Cards work. It also discusses the advantages of this technology, as well as the pitfalls that are out there with some of the products in the marketplace today. This chapter also gives you a quick list of key buying questions in case you're in the market for PC Card devices.

Chapter 3 describes the software that directly supports PC Cards. You'll learn not only what client drivers and super client drivers are, but why you need them. This is also the place where the programmer in you will describes the software that directly supports begin to see how client drivers use the card services API to support PC Card devices

Chapter 4 introduces you to the information stored on a PC Card that is critical to software development. You'll learn not only the terminology of attribute and common memory, tuples, and the all- important *Card Information Structure*, or CIS, but how to use the card services API to access it.

Chapter 5 discusses PCMCIA architecture in the DOS/ Windows 3.1 environments. It gives you a step-by-step approach to building a client driver either as a device driver or a Terminate-Stay-Resident program. Debugging tips and techniques are also discussed.

Chapter 6 discusses PCMCIA architecture in the OS/2 environment. It gives you a step-by-step approach to building a client device driver, including a Token-Ring device driver as an example. Debugging tips and techniques are also discussed.

Chapter 7 discusses PCMCIA architecture in the Windows 95/98 environments. It discusses how Windows 95/98 implements support for PC Cards.

Chapter 8 discusses PCMCIA architecture in the Windows NT environment. It discusses how Windows NT implements support for PC Cards.

Chapter 9 discusses PCMCIA architecture in the Linux environment

Chapter 10 discusses some PC Card Development tools that provide a variety of functions.

Typographical Conventions

In order to make the information as clear as possible, this book follows certain conventions. In the text section of this book, key words or phrases defined for the first time appear in *italics.* This is also an indication that the term is included in the glossary. Similarly, all card services functions such as ***RegisterClient()*** appear in boldface italics to better distinguish them from normal text.

Source code file names and program file names (including the file extension) appear in normal print, with all capital letters such as READCIS.C and PCMCIA.H. This is also an indication of the file name on the corresponding program diskette included with this book. System key files also appear in normal print and in all capitals, such as the AUTOEXEC.BAT, CONFIG.SYS, and COM.SYS files. Sample source code included within a chapter appears in `courier` print.

Card services parameters, sample source code subroutine names, operating system application programming interface functions, data structures, and variables all appear in roman print within the text.

Chapter 2: What is PCMCIA?

The Personal Computer Memory Card International Association (PCMCIA) is an alliance of computer companies that have joined together to create a nonproprietary software and hardware standard for plug-in computer devices. This nonprofit organization formed in 1989 to agree on a consistent form factor for add-on memory for handheld systems like the HP95LX. Since then, the charter has grown to include everything from the card dimensions and label to system hardware and software. Along the way, the PC Card Standard has gained ground, first with portable systems, then increasingly with desktop systems as a way to extend the usefulness of these older systems.

Terminology Conventions

The PCMCIA standard, including its terminology, has been evolving since its inception. Originally, the PCMCIA acronym encompassed everything: the specification, devices, and the association. The committee instituted a change whereby the term PCMCIA would be used to represent the association only, while the term PC Card would be a prefix for all the components associated with the hardware technology. For example, the document that describes the technology is now called the PC Card Standard. Every attempt has been made to adhere to this convention. When the term "PC Card" or the word "Card" appears by itself, it is referencing the physical adapter cards, such as a modem PC Card or a LAN PC Card.

A *PC Card adapter* is a chip that performs the interface conversion between the PC Card and the host system while an adapter (without the PC Card prefix) denotes an adapter card that is traditionally installed into a slot residing in a desktop computer system. With the addition of CardBus to the PC Card Standard, there are even distinct functional differences between the 16-bit PC Card adapter and the CardBus PC Card adapter. Every attempt has been made to clearly identify these differences either by calling out the PC Card Standard release levels (such as the PC Card Standard 2.X levels, which includes all specifications before the February, 1995 release) or by using the 16-bit prefix (such as 16-bit PC Cards).

Finally, a PC Card system is a computer system that supports PC Cards. That is, the system has one or more sockets that accept PC Cards. These terms are all discussed in more detail in the chapters that follow.

The Association

The PCMCIA ranks comprise over five hundred companies the world over, from all walks of the industry: system manufacturers, semiconductors, *BIOS* software developers, operating system architects, cable vendors.

To ensure acceptance of the standard, the PCMCIA organization works closely with other standards bodies, such as the Electronics Industry Association (EIA), which recognizes the electrical and physical aspects of the standard. Additionally, to ensure compatibility with Japanese standards, the committee works closely with the Japan Electronic Industry Development Association (JEIDA), and the Joint Electron Devices Engineering Council (JEDEC). However, because the organizations operate independently of one another, one group may take the lead in developing extensions to the standard.

Additionally, PCMCIA maintains offices throughout the world. The association maintains a United States headquarters in San Jose, California, and a European chapter in Brussels, Belgium. It also has district offices in Hong Kong, Taiwan, and Scandinavia as well. General membership meetings take place monthly from which meeting minutes are distributed to all members.

The association has three membership tiers: executive, associate, and affiliate. Membership privileges, such as attending meetings or voting on issues, vary based on the membership level. Executive members are companies that plan and influence the development and marketing of PC Card technology. Executive members, including representatives from companies such as IBM, Intel, Apple, and Compaq, hold nine of the fourteen board of director seats.

Associate members, like executive members, have voting rights on standard issues. Associate members hold the remaining five board of director seats. Associate members participate in setting the direction of the standard. Companies that design, manufacture, or resell PC Card products should, at a minimum, maintain an associate member level.

Affiliate members do not have voting privileges and are not permitted to attend the committee meetings. As such, affiliate members generally do not influence the direction of the standard, instead they receive meeting minutes and information about committee activities that keep them current on the evolution of PCMCIA.

The PC Card Standard Goals

The PC Card Standard is based on a 1985 Japanese integrated circuit (IC) card standard. This collaboration has resulted in a proliferation of devices with enormous popularity. In 1992, the sales of PC Card data/fax modems alone surpassed a million units.

The standard strives for consistency and compatibility across various manufacturer PC Cards and computer platforms (Motorola, Intel, Sun, etc.). Hence, a modem card built by IBM would work not only in IBM PC Card Intel-based systems, but Apple systems as well.

Organization of the Standard

To aid in this goal, the standard is partitioned into three key parts: *card physical*, *card interface*, and *card data format,* or software. Dividing the standard into major sections makes it easier for the relevant subcommittees and work groups to focus on appropriate parts.

The hardware components of the standard addresses PC Cards, systems and *sockets*, and PC Card *adapters* and chip sets. The card physical piece of the standard deals with the physical aspects of the card, such as its dimensions, pin lengths, connectors, reliability factors, and test methods. The card interface section covers signal definitions and pinouts, timing and function information, and the interpretation of card status information.

The software components of the standard address client drivers and card and socket services. The card services portion of the standard is the most important piece for software developers. This section covers the card data organization and PC Card software *application programming interfaces (APIs).* It specifies the methods for accessing card data as well as the format of that data. The later chapters of this book cover, in detail, the card services API and client drivers.

PC Card Hardware Elements

The three key elements of PC Card hardware are cards, sockets, and adapters. PCMCIA cards, or *PC Cards* as they are referred to in the February 1995 release of the PC Card Standard, are really a family of card types. Currently, there are three card types and two extensions, for a total of five distinct PC Card varieties. A PC Card type denotes two important facts. First, the type generally indicates its function (a memory or I/O). Second, the type indicates the dimensions of the card. Cards with an extension jut out of the system PC Card socket. The extension can be up to 40mm in length. The extension of a PC Card can prevent other PC Cards from operating with them simultaneously. For instance, a wireless communication PC Card may have an antennae that may prevent a pager card from residing in the PC Card socket above it. *Table 2-1*summarizes the PC Card types

PC Card Type	Dimensions (thickness x width)	Typical Implementation
Type I	3.3mm x 54.0mm	Memory cards
Type II	5.0mm x 54.0mm	I/O Cards (Network cards, modems)
Type III	10.5mm x 54.0mm	Hard Disks
Type I Extended	3.3mm x 54.0mm with up to 40mm of extended length	
Type II Extended	5.0mm x 54.0mm with up to 40mm of extended length	Pagers, Wireless communication adapters (with antennas)

Table 2-1 PC Card Types

Types are also used to delineate the type of PC Card socket on the system. For example, a system may be described as having a single Type II socket or having two Type II sockets. However, when PC Card types are used relative to a system, the definition is somewhat broadened. PC Card socket types are backward compatible. That is, a system with one Type II socket accepts a PC Card Type I or a PC Card Type II card (with or without the extension), while a system with a single Type I socket accepts only a Type I card. Finally, a system, such as the one shown in Figure 2-3, which has two horizontally stacked Type II sockets is equivalent to a single Type III socket. Therefore a system with this configuration accepts all PC Card types.

PC Card Types

Type I

Type I PC Cards are usually memory cards, such as a Static RAM (SRAM), Flash, or an SRAM/Flash combination card. A Type I card is the thinnest PC Card at 3.3mm thick and 54mm wide.

Figure *2-1* is a PC Card Type I. Memory cards are basically used for storage. Each of the various memory types has its advantages for certain uses, and disadvantages that make it less desirable for other uses.

Figure 2-1: Type I PC Card

SRAM

SRAM cards are typically used like floppy diskettes. However, SRAM cards have relatively small storage capacity, at just 1MB to 2MB. In order to maintain the data stored on these cards, SRAM cards require continual power. Because of this requirement, these cards have their own batteries. The battery must be replaced prior to being completely discharged or data loss will result. Some SRAM cards have both primary and secondary batteries. This allows the user to change the primary battery without losing data. Despite these limitations, SRAM has two advantages over Flash memory: price and speed. SRAM cards are faster and cheaper than Flash memory.

Flash

Flash cards use low-power, nonvolatile EEPROM memory modules. Flash cards are ideally suited for distribution of applications or data (such as a database). Some Flash cards are accessed as linear memory, meaning they require a special *Memory Technology Driver* (MTD) in order to read or write the device and a *Flash File Systems* (FFS) so that they may be used like a diskette. However, many of the FFS are incompatible with one another, meaning a card written by one FFS may be incapable of being read by another FFS.

Other Flash cards emulate *AT Attachment* (ATA) or *Integrated Drive Electronics* (IDE) interfaces, which make them appear as a hard drive. The ATA interface accesses data on a block basis instead of requiring direct addressing of each byte; therefore, only a small memory window or I/O space is required to access large amounts of data. Additionally, because these cards appear as a hard disk (and utilize the DOS FAT file system) they do not require a special MTD or file system.

Flash disks have several advantages over conventional hard drives. First, they have a much lower power consumption. This makes Flash cards ideally suited to handheld, battery operated computers. Second, Flash cards do not have any moving parts, which makes them more rugged and durable than a hard drive. They are also lighter weight. Finally, Flash cards do not incur the seek-time delays typically seen by hard drives. As such, they are ideally suited for applications that require a large number of random disk accesses.

Relative to SRAM memory, Flash cards have a large storage capacity, from 1MB to 40MB. While Flash cards support both read and write operations, it differs from SRAM in that once a byte is written to a Flash memory location, that location cannot be rewritten without erasing the entire memory chip. As the name implies, erasing this type of memory is a flash.

SRAM/Flash Combination

The SRAM/Flash card uses both types of memory. It is ideally suited fir situations in which both an application and its data must be resident on the same card. The application would be stored in the Flash region while the SRAM would store temporary data. Some operating system software companies discourage the use of these types of cards because the card requires multiple partitions that they feel confuse the user.

Type II

Type II PC Cards are usually I/O cards, such as a network adapter card (Token-Ring or Ethernet LAN cards or even an IBM 3270 or 5250 card) and data/fax modems. Unlike memory PC Cards, Type II cards generally come with a connector or cable. In the case of a LAN PC card, this would be the cable that is used to connect to the network. For a modem, this includes the telephone line connector. A Type II card is 5.0mm thick and 54mm wide with a raised substrate area 48mm wide.

Figure 2-2 is a Type II PC Card.

Type II PC Cards have many advantages over alternative solutions in the marketplace. Obviously PC Cards have a distinct size and weight advantage over traditional desktop adapter cards. A less obvious advantage is performance. For instance, LAN PC Cards offer up to two times the performance of an external, parallel port LAN adapter, which is limited by the speed of the parallel port. Similarly, PC Card modems contain their own UART, allowing a system with a lower speed UART to now take advantage of higher-speed communications.

Figure 2-2: Type II PC Card

Type III

Hard drives are typically implemented as Type III PC Cards. Unlike SRAM and Flash cards, these devices contain mechanical articulation. That is, they have moving parts and are true rotating media. As a result, they are somewhat more delicate than other PC Cards. Still, a PC Card version of a hard drive is more rugged than one would expect. The PC Card Standard requires PC Cards to adhere to an impact shock standard that is roughly equivalent to a six-foot drop onto a carpeted area.

One advantage of the Type III hard drive over the Flash drive is that the Type III hard drive offers far more storage capacity than the Flash PC Cards do today, and at roughly one-tenth of the cost. Today, Type III hard drives typically cost an average of \$5/MB while Flash devices average roughly \$50/MB. However, unlike the Flash cards, which have a low power consumption, Type III hard drives consume considerable power from the system.

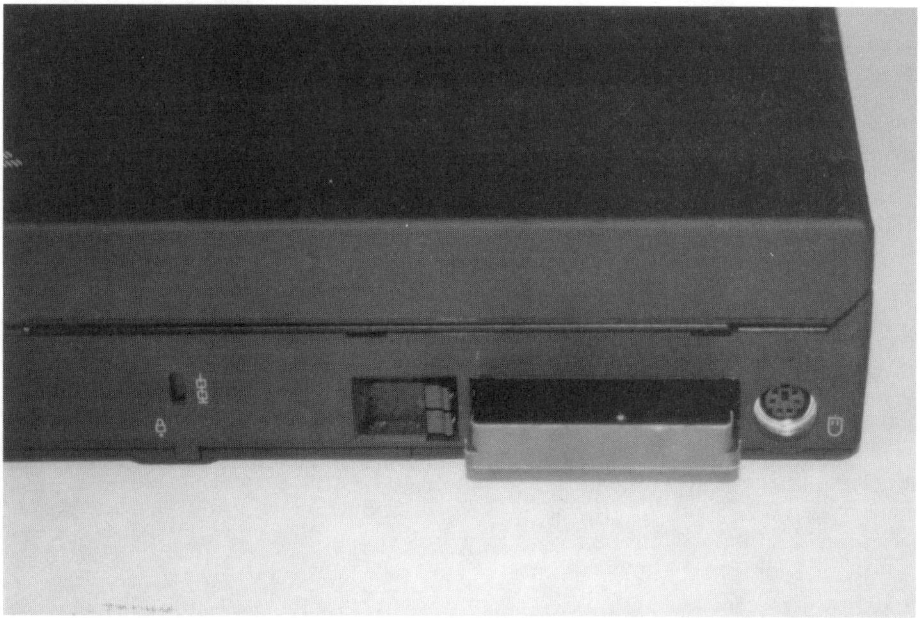

Figure 2-3: An IBM ThinkPad 770 with Two Type II Sockets, Accepting a Type III PC Card

Currently Type III cards are the thickest of the three PC Cards, at 10.5mm thick and 54mm wide with a raised substrate area of 51mm wide. The card shown in Figure 2-3 is a Type III PC Card. Because of the thickness of the card, a PC Card system must specifically state it will accept Type III PC Cards. In a stroke of engineering genius, however, some systems with two Type II PC Card sockets stacked vertically oftentimes accept a single Type III PC Card. System literature may refer to this configuration as a "2 x Type II" or "1 x Type III" or as a "2 x II" or "1 x III," where the first figure represents the number of cards the socket can simultaneously accept and the second figure represents the card Type. A system that is "1 x Type III" accepts a single PC Card of any Type (Type I, Type II, or Type III). Not all "2 x Type II" systems accept a single Type III card, so it is important to determine the capabilities of the system prior to buying Type II PC Cards.

"Type IV"

The PC Card Standard and committee do not support a "Type IV" socket or card. However, a consortium of companies are considering the release of a 14mm thick "Type IV" socket, nearly three times the thickness of a Type II socket. Should such a device appear in the marketplace, it is important to remember that it is not endorsed by the PCMCIA committee. As a result, devices conforming to Type IV dimensions are scarce and perhaps even proprietary.

On the other hand, the JEIDA standard has approved the Type IV card. This is one example of an area where the two standards diverge. However, most PC Card developers avoid implementing designs that are compatible under only one of the standards.

Extended PC Cards

The standard also allows for extended versions of all three card types. While the thickness of these cards remains the same, the card is permitted to have 40mm of extended length. The extension protrudes out of the PC Card system socket. A typical extended PC Card implementation is a PC Card that requires an antenna, or similar device, external to the host system.

Figure 2-4 shows a Type III extended PC Card.

Figure 2-4: Type III Extended PC Card

Multi-function PC Cards

Multi-function PC Cards are cards that perform more than one unrelated function. Although the PC Card version 2.00 and 2.10 specifications support memory-only combination devices, multi-function I/O PC Cards are available in the marketplace today. One such example is a PC Card that operates both as an Ethernet LAN card and as a modem. However, it was not until the February, 1995 that the PC Card Standard was extended to include multi-function I/O PC Card support. The standard outlines provisions including a Configuration Option register set for each function on the PC Card, a strict CIS format, and host PC Card software changes required to support these devices. As a result, multi-function devices that do not adhere to these requirements should be considered noncompliant.

Besides eliminating the need to carry or swap between separate PC Cards, multi-function PC Cards are extremely handy for systems with a single PC Card socket. They are also useful on systems whose socket configuration cannot simultaneously accommodate certain PC Cards. For example, on some PC Card systems the cable for the LAN card obstructs or prevents other PC Cards.

The standard was extended in February 1995 to support multi-function PC Cards. However, many cards appeared on the market prior to that date, hence multi-function PC Cards sold before then should be considered proprietary. Figure 2-5 shows an Ethernet/Fax/Modem multi-function PC Card.

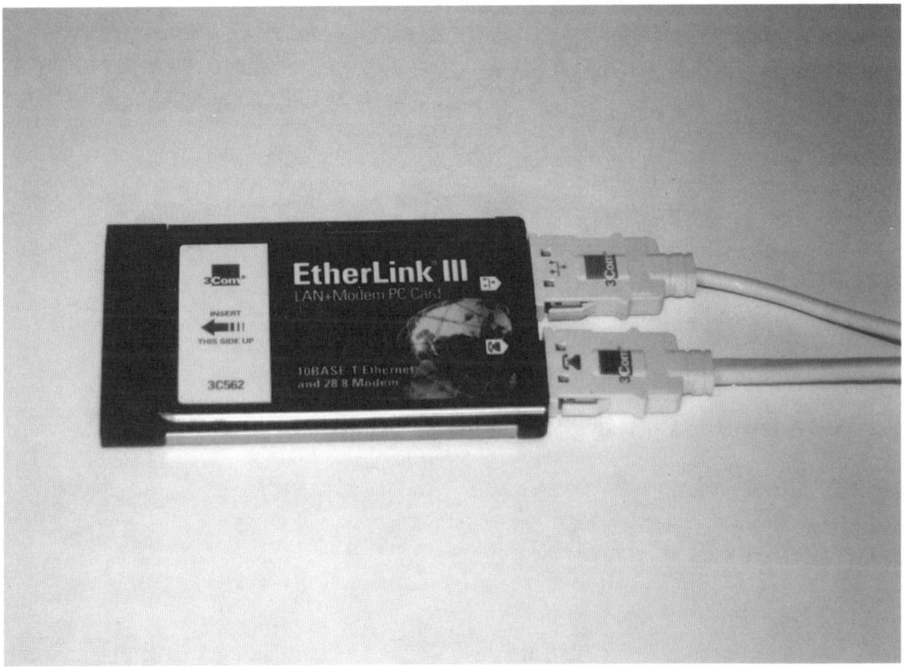

Figure 2-5 Multi-Function PC Card

CardBus PC Cards

The release of the PC Card 95 Standard included a 3.3volt, 32-bit PC Card CardBus definition. High-speed LANs, SCSI, and multimedia devices in the PC Card CardBus form factor are currently available. The standard outlines provisions including a *BAR* (Base Address Register) for the PC Card, a strict CIS format, and host PC Card software changes required to support these devices.

Figure 2-6 CardBus PC Card

Miscellaneous PC Card Devices

Miscellaneous other PC Card devices are available in the marketplace. Some of these devices extend the PC Card Standard to the desktop. One such device is an external PC Card drive designed to connect to the parallel port of a notebook or desktop system. Another device is an ISA, PCI, or Micro Channel adapter card that is installed in a desktop system. Currently these adapter cards are equipped with either two or four PC Card sockets.

While these devices achieve the same goal, there are some subtle differences. The performance of an external PC Card drive will be slower than an adapter that connects directly to the system bus. Additionally, some of these external PC Card drives have proprietary design deviations from the PC Card Standard that may cause incompatibilities with some hand-held systems.

Another method for retrofitting older systems is a *reader/writer* device. A reader/writer is a half-inch high floppy drive with one, two, or four PC Card sockets, designed to replace existing full-sized floppy drivers.

The most common PC Card options though are *docking stations* and *port replicators*. As the name implies, docking stations are designed to connect, or dock, with a portable computer. Port replicators, like the one shown in Figure 2-7, differ from docking stations in that they simply replicate the bus connectors of the portable system. This way all the office cables can remain attached to the port. The port replicator in Figure 2-7 also adds two more PC Card sockets.

Figure 2-7: A Port Replicator with PC Card Sockets

Handheld PC Devices

PC Card slots are not only found in notebook computers but can also be found in the newer Handheld PC (HPC). A HPC usually has one Type II slot and can accommodate modem or network PC Cards. Due to the low power of an HPC the PC Card may reduce battery life. Figure 2-8 shows an Ericsson MC12 HPC with an Ethernet PC Card inserted in its socket.

Figure 2-8 Ericsson MC12 Handheld PC

PC Card Sockets

The PC Card socket is the receptacle where the PC Card is inserted. Similar to a diskette drive, the socket contains guides on the side that help align the PC Card during insertion. Also like a diskette drive, the PC Card socket contains an ejection button. However, these mechanisms tend to vary from system to system. The most common ejection mechanism, shown in, Figure 2-9, is a small push-style button. Typically there is one of these buttons, usually in blue, for each PC Card socket. Another common ejection mechanism is a dual ejection slide switch, located on the bottom of the system. This mechanism forces PC Cards present in both sockets to be ejected simultaneously, which is often undesirable.

The quantity and arrangement of sockets also varies. Currently the most common configuration is to have two Type II sockets vertically stacked. The reason for this, as pointed out earlier, is that two vertically stacked Type II sockets are capable of accepting one Type III PC Card.

Table 2-2 shows the socket arrangements on various manufacturers' systems.

	1 x Type III -or- 2 x Type II -or- 2 x Type I	CardBus
Apple Mac Power Book 1400c	x	
Compaq Presario 1220	x	
Compaq Presario 1622		x
Gateway 9100XL		x
IBM ThinkPad 755, 365	x	
IBM ThinkPad 760, 770		x
Toshiba Tecra 780CDM		x

Table 2-2: Sample PC Card System Socket Arrangements

Figure 2-9: PC Card Ejection Button

Inserting a PC Card into a system is as easy as placing a diskette into a diskette drive. Like a diskette, the PC Card must be positioned correctly. First, the correct side must be facing up. Second, the PC Card connector end must be inserted into the system. As Figure 2-10 shows, some PC Card labels contain an orientation notation, such as an arrow, to assist with the insertion process. However, before inserting a PC Card into a system be sure to check the socket type. A system with a Type I socket will only accept Type I cards, while a system with a Type II socket will accept both Type I and Type II cards. Finally, when inserting a Type III PC Card into a system with two Type II sockets, both sockets must first be empty. Next, insert the Type III PC Card using the guide on the bottom most socket.

On most systems today, PC Cards may be inserted or ejected from a system while it is powered on. However, this feature requires specific software support. System documentation generally lists system capabilities and limitations.

Figure 2-10: PC Card with Orientation Indicator

16-bit PC Card Adapters

The term PC Card adapter should not be confused with the ISA or Micro Channel adapter cards installed in desktop computers. Rather, it is an interface controller chip typically implemented as a *Large Scale Integration (LSI)* circuit mounted on the system motherboard and connected to the PC Card sockets.

The PC Card adapter performs three important functions. First, it provides the conversion between the system bus and the PC Card expansion bus. The IBM ThinkPad 750 and 755 are ISA systems. Their PC Card adapter performs an ISA to PC Card conversion function. Secondly, the PC Card adapter is responsible for interfacing to the PC Card sockets; this includes all interrupt routing, power control, and access timing operations. The PC Card bus has a single interrupt signal from the PC Card to the PC Card adapter. Unbeknownst to the PC Card, the PC Card adapter routes this interrupt to the corresponding IRQ line. All PC Cards are capable of generating card status change interrupts, such as card detect, ready/busy, and battery low. The card status change interrupt is separate from and should not be confused with the normal, operational I/O interrupts that result from an I/O PC Card.

Finally, in the PC Card 2.X versions of the standard, the PC Card adapter is responsible for mapping the PC Card memory into system memory, either through memory mapping or I/O windows.

Most PC Card adapters are capable of supporting up to two sockets. Hence, a system with more than two sockets will have more than one PC Card adapter. In fact a PC Card system may have up to sixteen such PC Card adapters for a total of thirty-two sockets.

32-bit PC Card Adapters

The PC Card adapter for a 32-bit system is referred to as a PCI to CardBus bridge. It is an interface controller chip typically implemented as a *Large Scale Integration (LSI)* circuit mounted on the system motherboard and connected to the PC Card sockets. It performs the same basic function as the 16-bit PC Card adapter outlined above except that it connects a PCI bus to the CardBus bus. CardBus adapters do not map memory or I/O. Instead, it directly decodes access to the host system. The IBM Thinkpad 760 and above are PCI systems with CardBus PCI bridge adapters. 16-bit PC Cards will still function in a PC CardBus socket.

The PC Card Evolution

As the name implies, the Personal Computer Memory Card International Association was originally chartered with adopting a memory card standard. They reached an accord, and Release 1.0 of the PC Card Standard resulted, which detailed the requirements for a Type I and Type II memory cards. Shortly thereafter, PC Card memory cards and even a couple of data-only modems began to appear on the market. Computer system manufacturers began to take notice of this leading technology. Companies like Sharp and NCR rushed notebook systems to the market with a single PC Card Type I socket.

To support the memory and modem cards, a setup utility program was shipped with the systems. The setup utility would statically configure the system's PC Card socket. This created several problems. First, the socket was configured to only accept a single card type. For example, the socket could accept either an I/O PC Card, such as a modem, or a memory card. If the user had set the socket up to accept the modem and they now wanted to use a memory card, the modem had to be removed, the setup program rerun, and finally they rebooted the system. Often times an additional restriction was levied: the PC Card had to be inserted prior to turning the system on and it could not be removed until the system was turned off. This was known as *cold insertion*. Imagine having to power off your system every time you inserted or removed a floppy disk !

A less obvious problem with this approach is compatibility. Because the setup programs were specific to a system, inconsistencies abounded. One system might support only memory cards, while another supported memory cards and modems. This meant that cards would not readily operate from one system to another. Plus, the setup program quickly became outdated as new types of cards became available. In an effort to combat this, some PC Card manufacturers began to write their own setup programs, known as *point enablers,* for each system they wished to support. Without any point enabler guidelines, the environment was ripe for anarchy.

PC Card 2.X Software Elements

Realizing a need to safeguard its ease-of-use and cross-platform compatibility goals, the PCMCIA committee pushed forward with a new release of the standard in September of 1992. Release 2.0, which is backward compatible with Release 1.0, introduced three new software elements: *card services, socket services,* and *client drivers.* Driven by events, such as a PC Card being inserted into a system, these three components work to provide seamless management of the card.

Card Services (CS)

Card services (CS) is a common industry standard API for operating system-specific PC Card client device drivers. Through this API, clients request and receive system resources and are notified of events. This design eliminates the need for platform-specific point enablers. That is, a client has no need to understand the physical hardware on the system in order to support a PC Card. For example, a client driver written to work in OS/2 on an IBM ThinkPad would also work in OS/2 on a Compaq Concerto, regardless of the underlying system hardware.

Because CS is operating system-specific, it is ideally suited to ship with either an operating system as an embedded function or as a separate component such as a device driver. Card services follows a client/server model. That is, a client device driver (CDD) makes requests for resources and CS acts as a server, allocating available resources in response to these requests. To track available resources, CS maintains a *resource map*, sometimes with the help of a *resource manager*.

The job of the resource manager is to determine the resources already in use by the computer and to inform CS accordingly. For example, most computers have a communications port, or COM1, standard on the system planar. The resource manager would take note of this and inform CS that COM1 resources are unavailable. Thus, if a PC Card modem client driver requested COM1 resources from CS, the request would be rejected. This illustrates how CS is able to coordinate resources among its various clients. In addition, CS relies on Socket services (SS) to manage the PC Card system hardware.

Socket Services (SS)

Socket services, like CS, is an API but unlike CS, which have many clients, SS generally has few clients; namely card services and memory technology drivers. Because there are a variety of PC Card adapters in the marketplace today, SS implementations vary. For example, the SS that supports the Cardbus-based IBM ThinkPad 760 would be different from the SS that supports the ISA-based IBM ThinkPad 755, the reason being that the PC Card adapter that supports the PC Card socket is different on these two systems. If the PC Card adapter is different, in all likelihood the method for controlling the PC Card adapter is different. As a result, each PC Card adapter could require its own version of SS. This is why multiple-point enablers were required prior to the invention of card and socket services. Remember, point enablers interface directly with the PC Card adapter. So each system with a different PC Card adapter interface required a different point enabler.

Because SS deals directly with the PC Card system hardware, the intention is for SS to be implemented in system BIOS. However, this does not preclude it from being implemented as a device driver. At present, the device driver format is the most common.

As Figure 2-11 shows, more than one socket services driver loaded in a single system. This would be the case on a system that has two different PC Card adapter implementations. With the advent of the February 1995 PC Card Standard, a system could conceivably have a PC Card adapter that supports CardBus and another PC Card adapter that did not. This could require two different socket services implementations to be loaded; one to support the PC Card adapter with CardBus capabilities and another to support the PC Card adapter that did not support CardBus. Figure 2-11 also shows that a single card services implementation supports multiple socket services drivers. Only one card services implementation is ever present in a system at any given time.

Client Device Drivers (CDD)

Client device drivers, or client drivers, supersede point enablers. In many ways they are superior to point enablers because they contain no details about the system level hardware and because they rely on CS to coordinate system resources. As a result, client drivers can focus on the task at hand: supporting a PC Card. To support a PC Card, a client driver interfaces with CS in order to receive notification about PC Card events and to request or return system resources. It is important to note that neither card nor socket services are responsible for configuring the card: this is the role of the client driver.

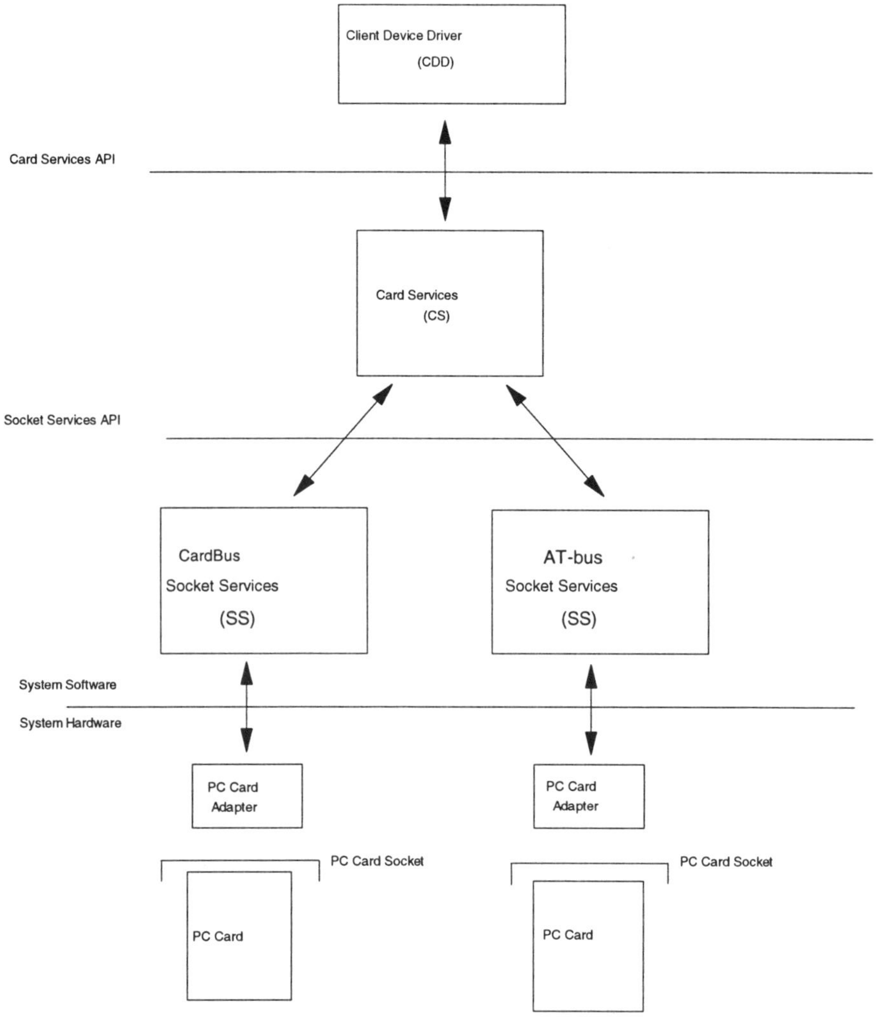

Figure 2-11: PC Card Software Trinity

How PC Card Software Works: The Chain of Events

Getting PC Cards to work takes a careful blending of software and hardware. When a PC Card is inserted into a PC Card socket, it sets off a chain of events. When inserted properly, the card is grounded, which results in the PC Card adapter detecting the card. The PC Card adapter then generates an interrupt that is, surprisingly, fielded by card services and not socket services. Although socket services is responsible for managing the PC Card adapter and socket, it has no built-in interrupt-handling capability. This design enables socket services to be implemented in BIOS.

When card services receives the interrupt, it calls socket services to investigate the cause of the interrupt. Socket services determines that a "card insertion" event occurred and dutifully informs card services of this. Card services checks its chain of registered client drivers, looking for parties interested in card insertion events. CS notifies each interested CDD of this event, starting with the first client driver in the chain, it continues this notification process until the event is claimed by a CDD or it reaches the end of the chain. Once a CDD has claimed an event, the sequence varies depending on the client and type of card inserted. For example, a Flash card could require formatting, while a modem card would require COM port resources.

A similar set of events occurs when the PC Card is ejected from the system. SS detects the card has been removed from the socket and interrupts CS with a "card ejection" event. CS proceeds to notify all interested CDDs until the event is claimed or it has reached the last CDD in line. Usually, when a card is ejected from a system, the CDD proceeds to free resources that had been allocated to that device. Because it is currently absent from the system, there is no need to tie up valuable system resources, such as IRQs. In all likelihood, another card will be inserted into the socket and it may need the IRQ that had been set aside for the previous PC Card.

PC Card Advantages

PC Cards differ significantly from traditional adapter cards. Many of these differences translate directly into advantages; the most striking is its miniaturization and packaging. PC Cards are compact, lightweight and more convenient than conventional adapter cards. Surprisingly, they are also incredibly rugged. The delicate circuitry is protected by a hard outer casing that keeps dust, water, static, and other potentially harmful matter away from the circuitry. Because of their diminutive size, PC Cards are sometimes called *credit card adapters*. The size and compactness of these cards often result in big power savings. Power conservation is critically important to battery powered systems.

In addition to the size difference, PC Cards are not Industry Standard Architecture (ISA), or Peripheral Component Interconnect (PCI) bus cards; rather the PC Card Standard is an entirely new expansion bus interface. Fortunately, it's an entirely new expansion bus interface with a twist: system hardware and software abstracts the differences from the end user. A PC Card purchased for use in the Cardbus-based IBM ThinkPad 760 would also work in an ISA bus PC Card notebook from another manufacturer. Together, packaging and bus abstraction result in a hardware installation revolution: there is none. Instead, PC Cards are inserted and ejected from a system while power is active to the system, much like a floppy disk.

Which brings up yet another benefit: configuration. Clearly configuration has to be simplified if these cards are going to be randomly inserted into and ejected from a system. Previously, adapter cards had jumpers and DIP switches that had to be set prior to installing the hardware. Then adapter resources, such as Interrupt Requests (IRQs), system memory, and I/O address spaces, were coordinated among all adapters installed in the system. Once installed into the system, the resources required by the adapter card were reserved each time the system was turned on, even if the card was not being used. The more adapter cards installed in the system, the harder it became to coordinate these resources.

PC Cards are configured by PC Card host software. System resources, such as I/O addresses and interrupt request levels, are managed by PC Card host software. This PC Card host software is responsible for coordinating the system resources. Early personal computer adapter cards relied on architected, or reserved, IRQs and memory address space. PC Card simplifies this task by allowing the PC Card to be mapped into any available address space on the host system. Unlike the older adapter cards that needlessly tie up resources, PC Card resources are allocated when the card is needed (usually when the card is inserted). Similarly, PC Card resources are freed when the card is no longer needed (usually when the card is ejected).

The potential also exists for PC Card-aware application software to automatically launch once the card is inserted. Using detailed information stored in the CIS, the application could then dynamically configure itself. Imagine a data/fax application determining for itself the COM port, speed, and other capabilities of the modem without asking the user for input. Likewise, the application could deactivate and free precious system resources when the card is removed. All of this and more is possible with PC Card.

Still another benefit is system expansion. Personal computer systems are limited by the number of sockets. For example, a system that has three sockets can take at most three add-on adapter cards. Likewise, a system with four sockets can have up to four adapters installed. PC Card systems are limited only to the simultaneous use of their *sockets.* For example, a system with two PC Card sockets could simultaneously use at most two PC Cards, such as a Flash card and a modem. In order to use a third PC Card, one of the cards occupying a socket would be ejected.

PC Card Pitfalls

Currently the PCMCIA committee has not outlined a certification program. As a result, proprietary designs, incomplete implementation of the PC Card Standard, or improper implementation of the standard (especially the CIS), and misinterpretations of the standard all contribute to incompatibility problems. Prominent examples exist in the industry including, glaring errors such as systems that permit PC Cards to be inserted backward into the socket, something the standard clearly safeguards against.

To reduce the cost of a system, some manufacturers limit the function of the socket adapter to support only a reduced set of PC Cards. PC Card LANs and modems are more ideally suited for higher end portable systems with more battery life. A handheld system running on small AA batteries may not be capable of even powering the card up.

What Does the Future Hold?

Spurred by the acceptance and demand for this amazing technology, the PC Card Standard has evolved quickly to become the defacto expansion-bus standard for computers. Where once there was just a handful of Type I memory cards and a couple of single-socket notebook systems, now more and more desktop function is migrating its way to the PC Card form factor. Already desktop function such as SCSI and multimedia devices have found their way into PC Cards.

Higher function, both in the form of multi-function PC Cards and advanced technology, is also migrating to PC Card form factor. Global positioning satellites, pagers, and wireless LANs have all become available today. Surprisingly, while function is increasing, prices are dropping. When PC Card was first introduced it often commanded a premium price tag. Now the demand for these devices has increased the production volumes, causing the prices to fall. PC Cards and systems can now be found in discount computer warehouses.

Chapter 3: Understanding Traditional Client Drivers

With the advent of Windows 95 and Windows NT, a different model for PC Card device drivers was introduced. This model does not require the need for an event callback handler or any of the Card Services API calls. This chapter focuses on the PC Card client driver model that utilizes card services API calls for event and resource management. Windows 95 and Windows NT PC Card device drivers will be discussed in Chapters 7 and 8, respectively.

When the PC Card Standard first appeared, few systems were capable of accepting even the Type I PC Cards. Memory PC Cards and data-only (Type I) modem PC Cards were the only variations of PC Cards available. To support these PC Cards, most system vendors provided a setup utility that configured the PC Card sockets to only accept either one PC Card type or the other.

As a result, when the system PC Card socket was configured for a modem and the user wanted to insert a memory PC Card, the modem had to be ejected, the setup utility rerun (to reconfigure the socket to accept a memory PC Card) then the system rebooted. Oftentimes, this approach required cold insertion and *cold ejection*; that is, the system had to be powered off prior to inserting or removing the PC Card ! This posed an incredible ease-of-use hurdle. Imagine if a similar restriction was in force when diskettes were first introduced. Having to power down prior to inserting or removing a diskette from a system would surely have adversely affected the acceptance of this media.

The problem did not lie in the standard; it supported hot insertion and ejection. However, in the rush to be first-to-market with this new hardware, the software required to support hot insertion lagged behind. Regardless, system vendors opted to ship systems along with these unwieldy setup utilities.

This approach presented an additional acceptance barrier. PC Cards would not readily operate from one system to the next. Furthermore, as new PC Cards entered the market, such as Type II LAN PC Cards, the utility quickly became outdated: it only knew how to support memory and data-only modems. The task of supporting new PC Cards on these systems became much more complex. Point enablers provided relief, but it was clear this was not the long term solution.

Why Do We Need Client Drivers?

The software trinity of client drivers working in conjunction with card and socket services solves these problems. Client drivers provide a way to retrofit PC Cards into a system. If a PC Card system has card and socket services support, all that is required to retrofit a new PC Card into the system is a client driver. How is this different from a point enabler? The key difference is that card services is an orderly approach. CS coordinates and manages the resources amongst all the client drivers. Point enablers do not work in unison with each other. Rather, they tend to arbitrarily allocating system resources, modify hardware states or registers, and generally view the system as solely their own.

What Is A Client Driver?

A traditional client driver is a program that interfaces with card services to manage either a set of similar PC Cards or a specific PC Card. For instance, one client driver may be capable of controlling a modem PC Card from any manufacturer, while another client driver may only be capable of controlling just the IBM PC Card modem. Regardless, each PC Card usually requires a client driver. The exception, as previously discussed in chapter 2, are Flash PC Cards that emulate the ATA. With the introduction of Windows 95, a client driver is no longer required to interface with card services.

In DOS, client drivers are implemented in a variety of ways. They may be written as an application program, a *terminate-stay-resident (TSR)* program, or as a device driver. However, under Windows 95, Windows NT, OS/2, and Linux, a client driver must be implemented as a device driver.

What Are Super Client Drivers?

A super client driver (SCD), or *universal card installer*, is a collection of client drivers bundled together. Some SCDs contain a database of known PC Cards. When a PC Card is inserted into the system, the SCD determines if the PC Card is in its database. If it is, it configures it. If it is not, the PC Card cannot be configured. Super client drivers should not be confused with point enablers. Point enablers bypass card services whereas super client drivers do not.

One benefit of the SCD approach is that the a can be tailored to take advantage of features on a particular PC Card. The drawbacks, though, include the fact that the database quickly becomes out-of-date as new PC Cards are introduced into the marketplace. Another drawback is the overhead of storing this database; especially if the database contains information for PC Cards that will never be used on that system.

Another approach is for the super client driver to take a more generic approach to configuring the PC Card. By processing information in the CIS, a well designed SCD can configure the PC Card according to the capabilities outlined in the CIS. However, not all generic SCDs are well designed. Instead, they simply enable a class of devices to a static configuration. For example, a generic modem SCD may not allow the IRQ value to be used by the modem to be altered.

Oftentimes a system, or an operating system, such as IBM PC DOS, includes a super client driver as a base feature. However, users still have the option of purchasing a separate PC Card software trinity implementation as an add-on feature from a BIOS vendor. Similar to a spreadsheet or a word processing package, the various implementations offer different features, including the number and types of different PC Cards that are supported as well as the different systems on which the software is warranted. However, it is usually best to stick with the software the system manufacturer provides because oftentimes the manufacturer has conducted compatibility testing of the PC Card software with various PC Cards.

Another point of caution, do not mix PC Card point enablers with the PC Card software trinity solutions provided by the system manufacturer. When in doubt, refer to system documentation or a system customer service help line before installing any PC Card software that does not specifically state it is a client driver.

Types of Client Drivers

Because the PC Card Standard encompasses both memory (Type I) and I/O (Type II and Type III) PC Cards, it also supports a variety of client drivers to handle these assorted devices. The task of a client driver is further defined by the different memory and I/O PC Card implementations. A client driver for a LAN PC Card will greatly differ from a client for a modem PC Card, both of which are I/O PC Cards. Likewise, a client driver for a SRAM PC Card will differ from a Flash client driver. In fact, while PC Card services provides bulk memory services to write and erase PC Cards, it cannot possibly implement all of the special programming algorithms that are sometimes required to write or erase a PC Card. To accommodate PC Cards that require special algorithms, the standard affords a *memory technology driver (MTD)* interface.

Memory Technology Driver (MTD)

A memory technology driver is a hybrid client driver. The purpose of many client drivers, such as a modem client driver or a LAN client driver, is to simply configure the PC Card. Once configured, application programs access the PC Card oftentimes without even knowing it is a PC Card. MTDs on the other hand, have intimate knowledge of the PC Card hardware, including the special programming algorithms that are required to accommodate that device.

MTDs can be implemented as a client of card services or as part of card services. When implemented as a client, an MTD registers with card services. It configures the PC Card via the CS API and depends on CS for event notification. However, it also directly accesses specific programming hardware on the PC Card. A card services implementation may include a set of default MTDs. For instance, all PC Cards can be read as if they contained SRAM. As a result, a card services implementation could then recognize a region as SRAM and install a default MTD that supports read-and-write requests. When a client makes a read request, card services invokes the default MTD to service the request. However, if a client makes an erase request, a failure is returned by card services because a special programming algorithm may be required to erase the PC Card. A specialized MTD would be required to service such a request.

Implementing Client Drivers

Under DOS, a PC Card client driver can be written as either a TSR, a device driver, or as a command-line executable application program (such as a utility). Each of these types of client drivers serves a particular purpose.

DOS Application Program Client Drivers

A client driver written as an application program, executes once and terminates. Typically a utility program, such as a client driver designed to read and display the CIS, is written as an application program. However, because it is written as an application program, a key limitation is imposed. The application is constrained by virtue of the fact that DOS is single tasking. As a result, it can either require that the PC Card whose CIS it is supposed to read to be inserted prior to executing the program, or it can simply tie up the system waiting for the PC Card to be inserted. When it finishes reading the CIS, the program could either wait for another PC Card to be inserted and tie up the system further or it could terminate.

Once the program terminates, like any other application program, the associated system memory is freed. This is an advantage to this design. Precious DOS memory is only utilized when the end user needs the program to execute. Another advantage is simplicity. Implementing a client driver as an application program is easier than writing and debugging a TSR or a device driver. Still, an improved implementation is to write the client driver as a TSR.

DOS TSR Client Drivers

A client driver written as a DOS TSR combines the features of an application program with the features of a device driver. Like an application program, a TSR is loaded from a command line or via the AUTOEXEC.BAT file. Once it is loaded, it generally stays loaded into system memory like a device driver.

Using this approach, a utility program designed to read and display the CIS could be triggered by a PC Card event such as card insertion. Each time a PC Card is inserted into the system, the utility program could display a message to the user asking if they want to view the CIS. After completing this task, the program would lie dormant waiting for the next PC Card to be inserted.

While this is an improvement over the application program approach, the TSR design has a few drawbacks of its own. When a client driver is implemented as a TSR, the order of application program execution becomes important. For instance, if a PC Card modem client driver is written as a TSR, care must be taken to ensure that the TSR is executed prior to any communication programs that wish to use the modem PC Card. For example, prior to using the terminal emulator program that is included with Windows, the modem client driver TSR program must be run. If Windows is invoked via the AUTOEXEC.BAT file, than this can be accomplished by placing a statement to execute the modem client driver just prior to the Windows invocation, Alternately, the user must can explicitly run the modem client driver from the Windows through the File, Run sequence. Once the TSR is loaded, then the Windows terminal emulator program, or other data/fax communication program, can be executed.

Client Device Drivers

By far, most PC Card client drivers are written as device drivers. Like any other device driver, a PC Card client driver must conform to the structure and architecture model of the operating system in which it is designed to operate. That is, if a client driver is implemented as a DOS device driver, it must then conform to the DOS device driver model. Similarly, if a client driver is written as a DOS TSR, then it must conform to the terminate-stay-resident model. For example, an OS/2 client driver must be written as a an OS/2 physical device driver. Therefore, it must conform to the OS/2 device driver model.

In general, client device drivers share four key sections: a header, an initialization routine, a callback handler, and an *interrupt service routine* (ISR). First, there is a header which contains critical data such as the device driver name and the overall size of the device driver. Under DOS, the device driver header must appear at address zero.

Next, there is an initialization routine. The initialization routine executes one time; when the device driver is initially loaded into memory. As the name implies, the initialization routine performs all the functions necessary to enter a ready state. For a client driver, this would include registering itself and its callback handler entry point with card services. Typically, the source code to a device driver is structured so that the initialization routine appears last. The reason for this is, once the initialization, the driver returns back to the operating system its overall size. Because device drivers usually initialize only once; when they are loaded, the size returned back to the operating system does not include the initialization routine. In other words, because this code is no longer needed it is essentially discarded. This reduces the size of the driver and is done to conserve memory.

The next element is a callback handler. The callback handler is the routine that is called by card services when a registered event has occurred. The handler interrogates the event and initiates the appropriate action. Finally, the callback handler is responsible for returning control back to card services and for passing any required data or result codes back to card services.

Finally, most, but not all, device drivers have an interrupt service routine. For example, a modem client driver does not have an ISR while a Token-Ring device driver does. In DOS, the communication application programs actually manage sending and receiving data to and from the COM port that was assigned to the PC Card. Under OS/2, the COM.SYS device driver performs this function. As a result, the modem client driver does not actually manage the physical device. Instead, it is concerned only with performing the steps required to make the modem PC Card appear as a COM port. In contrast, the LAN device driver is responsible for managing the device, such as sending and receiving data. As a result, it has an interrupt service routine.

A client device driver shares some of the same advantages of a TSR. Like a TSR, a client device driver lies dormant in system memory, waiting for an event to occur. While the client is waiting for another event to occur, other activity can take place on the system.

Unfortunately, client device drivers have a few disadvantages of their own. Unlike a TSR, a device driver can only be loaded via the CONFIG.SYS file at system *initial program load (IPL)* time. This means that the client ties up system memory even if the PC Card that it supports is never inserted into the system. Client drivers also have dependencies on the order of execution. They must be loaded into memory after card and socket services. Sometimes they must also be loaded after other drivers. For example, in OS/2, a PC Card modem client driver must appear after the COM.SYS (the serial port driver) because it interacts with that driver.

How Client Drivers Work

Client drivers are event driven. When an event occurs, a client driver is triggered into action. The client driver then makes requests to card services based on the event or set of events that occurred. While the actual program details vary by operating system environment and the type of implementation (application, TSR, or device driver) the interaction between a client driver and card services remains the same. In other words, all requests to and from card services is done via an industry standard API and events.

Card Services API

The card services API consists of a set of functions that are organized into five categories: advanced client services, bulk memory, client services, client utilities, and resource. The following syntax is used for all card services function calls:

result = CardServices(Function, Handle, fPointer, ArgumentLength, fArgumentPointer);

Where:

CardServices = A user written C routine that calls the CS API.
Result = 0 indicates success, otherwise *result* = error code
Function = card services function number
Handle = client handle
fPointer = far pointer to code/data (usually NULL)
ArgumentLength = size of buffer pointed to by ArgumentPointer
fArgumentPointer = far pointer to a argument buffer

As previously stated, because the PC Card environment is dynamic (cards can be inserted or removed at any time), it is important to check the result code returned from each request. If the result is non-zero, then the card services request failed and the non-zero value indicates the reason for the failure. Figure 3-1 is a C-language definition file of the possible return codes from card services.

```
//   Return Codes

#define  SUCCESS                      0x00
#define  BAD_ADAPTER                  0x01
#define  BAD_ATTRIBUTE                0x02
#define  BAD_BASE                     0x03
#define  BAD_EDC                      0x04
#define  BAD_IRQ                      0x06
#define  BAD_OFFSET                   0x07
#define  BAD_PAGE                     0x08
#define  READ_FAILURE                 0x09
#define  BAD_SIZE                     0x0A
#define  BAD_SOCKET                   0x0B
#define  BAD_TYPE                     0x0D
#define  BAD_VCC                      0x0E
#define  BAD_VPP                      0x0F
#define  BAD_WINDOW                   0x11
#define  WRITE_FAILURE                0x12
#define  NO_CARD                      0x14
#define  UNSUPPORTED_FUNCTION         0x15
#define  UNSUPPORTED_SERVICE          0x15
#define  UNSUPPORTED_MODE             0x16
#define  BAD_SPEED                    0x17
#define  BUSY                         0x18
#define  GENERAL_FAILURE              0x19
#define  WRITE_PROTECTED              0x1A
#define  BAD_ARG_LENGTH               0x1B
#define  BAD_ARGS                     0x1C
#define  CONFIGURATION_LOCKED         0x1D
#define  IN_USE                       0x1E
#define  NO_MORE_ITEMS                0x1F
#define  OUT_OF_RESOURCE              0x20
#define  BAD_HANDLE                   0x21
#define  BAD_VERSION                  0x22
```

Figure 3-1: Card Services Return Codes

Card Services Function Categories

Advanced Client Services

Advanced client service functions (***MapLogSocket, MapPhySocket***, etc.) are used to obtain low-level information from card services, such as mapping logical and physical sockets. These functions are used only by clients with unique needs.

Bulk Memory Services

Bulk memory service functions (***OpenMemory, ReadMemory***, etc.) are used to read, write, copy and erase memory. These services abstract the memory technology hardware details from the client. These functions are commonly used by file systems, memory client drivers, or install utilities.

Client Services

Client services functions (***GetCardServicesInfo***, ***RegisterClient***, etc.) are used during the initialization to see if card services is installed and to register a driver as a client.

Client Utility

Client utility functions (***GetFirstTuple***, ***GetNextTuple***, ***GetTupleData***, ***GetFirstPartition***, etc.) are used to process tuples and to access locate memory partitions on a PC Card. By using these services, clients do not have to duplicate this logic inside their code.

Resource Management

Resource management functions (***RequestIO***, ***ReleaseIO***, ***RequestIRQ***, ***ReleaseIRQ***, ***RequestWindow***, ***ReleaseWindow***, ***ModifyWindow***, etc.) are perhaps the most important set of card services duties. These functions provide the fundamental access to the available resources on a system (such as IRQs, I/O address space, and windows to access these resources). As previously stated, card services maintains a resource map to track available resources. It is through these functions that card services grants, frees, and rejects requests for system resources.

Using the Card Services API

Card services clients use various categories of functions for different purposes. For example, a MTD is highly dependent on the bulk memory services whereas a modem client driver would not use these services at all. Figure 3-2 illustrates how various client drivers utilize these set of services.

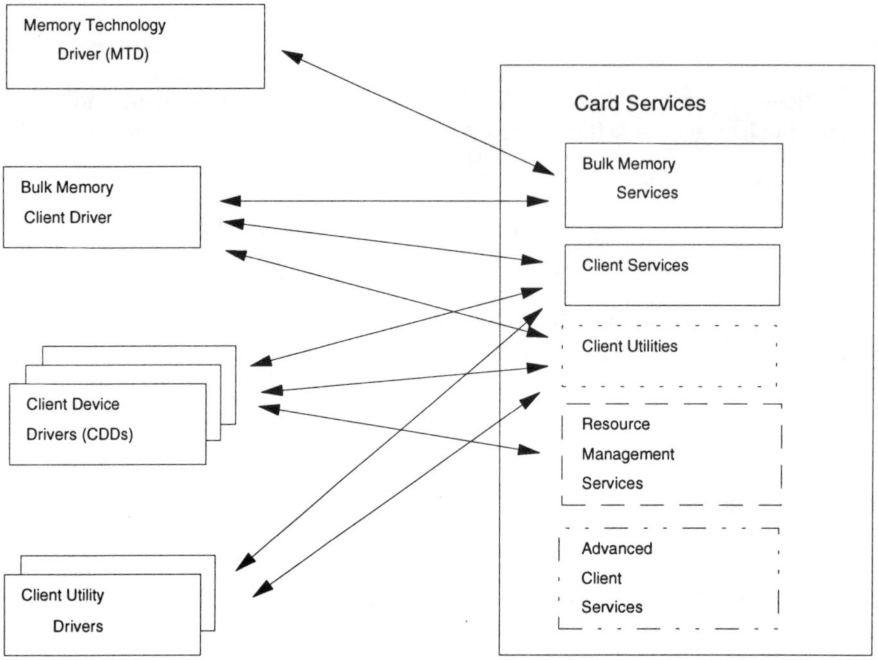

Figure 3-2: Client Driver Usage of Card Services Functions

Detecting Card Insertion: A Sample Client Driver

The best way to understand how a client driver works is to study a simple example. The following program listing excerpts are from a DOS client driver that detects that a PC Card has been inserted into the system. The client driver is written as an application program. Figure 3-3 illustrates the general flow of this program.

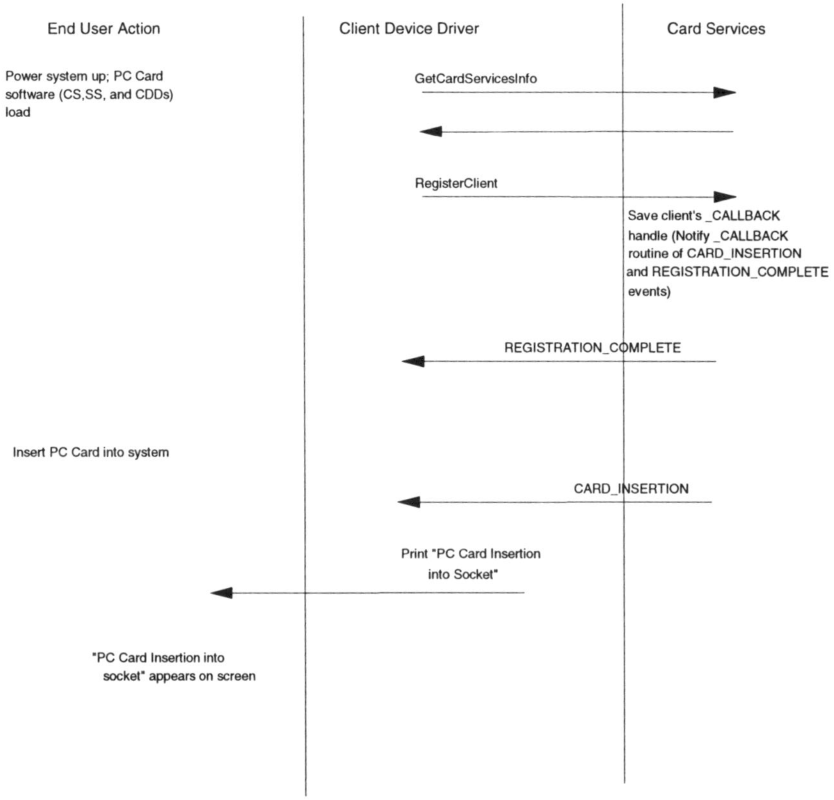

Figure 3-3: Flow of a Client Driver Detecting an Insertion Event

Card Services Function Codes

The first parameter in any card services call is the function code. This denotes to card services the command that is being requested. Figure 3-4 shows a set of C programming language definitions for the card services functions.

```
//   Client Services Function Codes

#define  GET_CARDSERVICES_INFO    0x0B
#define  REGISTER_CLIENT          0x10
#define  DEREGISTER_CLIENT        0x02
#define  GET_STATUS               0x0C
#define  RESET_CARD               0x11
#define  RESET_FUNCTION           0x11
#define  SET_EVENT_MASK           0x31
#define  GET_EVENT_MASK           0x2E

//   Resource Management Functions

#define  REQUEST_IO               0x1F
#define  RELEASE_IO               0x1B
#define  REQUEST_IRQ              0x20
#define  RELEASE_IRQ              0x1C
#define  REQUEST_WINDOW           0x21
#define  RELEASE_WINDOW           0x1D
#define  REQUEST_DMA              0x3A
#define  RELEASE_DMA              0x3B
#define  MODIFY_WINDOW            0x17
#define  GET_MEM_PAGE             0x39
#define  MAP_MEM_PAGE             0x14
#define  REQUEST_SOCKET_MASK      0x22
#define  RELEASE_SOCKET_MASK      0x2F
#define  REQUEST_CONFIGURATION    0x30
#define  RELEASE_CONFIGURATION    0x1E
#define  GET_CONFIGURATION_INFO   0x04
#define  MODIFY_CONFIGURATION     0x27
#define  GET_FIRST_WINDOW         0x37
#define  GET_NEXT_WINDOW          0x39


//   Advanced Client Services Functions

#define  RETURN_SS_ENTRY          0x23
#define  MAP_LOG_SOCKET           0x12
#define  MAP_PHY_SOCKET           0x15
#define  MAP_LOG_WINDOW           0x13
#define  MAP_PHY_WINDOW           0x16
#define  REGISTER_MTD             0x1A
#define  REGISTER_TIMER           0x28
#define  SET_REGION               0x29
#define  VALIDATE_CIS             0x2B
#define  REQUEST_EXCLUSIVE        0x2C
#define  RELEASE_EXCLUSIVE        0x2D
#define  GET_FIRST_CLIENT         0x0E
#define  GET_NEXT_CLIENT          0x2A
#define  GET_CLIENT_INFO          0x03
#define  ADD_SOCKET_SERVICES      0x32
#define  REPLACE_SOCKET_SERVICES  0x33
#define  VENDOR_SPECIFIC          0x34
#define  ADJUST_RESOURCE_INFO     0x35
#define  ACCESS_CONFIG_REGISTER   0x36

//   Client Utilities Functions

#define  GET_FIRST_TUPLE          0x07
#define  GET_NEXT_TUPLE           0x0A
#define  GET_TUPLE_DATA           0x0D
```

```
#define   GET_FIRST_REGION          0x06
#define   GET_NEXT_REGION           0x09
#define   GET_FIRST_PARTITION       0x05
#define   GET_NEXT_PARTITION        0x08

//    Bulk Memory Services Functions

#define   OPEN_MEMORY               0x18
#define   READ_MEMORY               0x19
#define   WRITE_MEMORY              0x24
#define   COPY_MEMORY               0x01
#define   REGISTER_ERASE_QUEUE      0x0F
#define   CHECK_ERASE_QUEUE         0x26
#define   DEREGISTER_ERASE_QUEUE    0x25
#define   CLOSE_MEMORY              0x00
```

Figure 3-4: Card Services Function Code Definitions

Determining Card Services Presence

The first step every client driver should perform is the **GetCardServicesInfo** call. It has the format:

result = CardServices(GetCardServicesInfo, null, null, *ArgumentLength, fArgumentPointer);*

This function is used to not only determine if card services is loaded, but it is also used to determine the number of sockets on the system. The PC Card Standard requires that the Signature field be cleared prior to invoking this function to prevent false sensing of card services.

Upon return from the call, note that both the result and the Signature field of this function are interrogated to determine if card services is loaded. If the result is set to zero (SUCCESS) and the Signature field contains an ASCII 'CS' (for card services), then card services is loaded. Once again, note on an Intel platform, this is actually stored as ‘SC’.

```
#define SIGNATURE 'SC'          // Ascii "CS" in memory on Intel System
typedef  struct _GETCARDSERVICESINFO
  {
       USHORT InfoLen;
       USHORT Signature;
       USHORT Count;
       USHORT Revision;
       USHORT CSLevel;                    // BCD compliance level of CS
       USHORT VStrOff;
       USHORT VStrLen,
       UCHAR  VendorString[1];
  } GETCARDSERVICESINFO;
typedef GETCARDSERVICESINFO near *NPGETCARDSERVICESINFO;
typedef GETCARDSERVICESINFO far  *FPGETCARDSERVICESINFO;

FPGETCARDSERVICESINFO    fpgci;
char CSBuffer[128];
WORD result, wCSVersion wSystemSlots, wSocket, wClientHandle = 0;
USHORT fRegistered = FALSE;          // Set for REGISTRATION_COMPLETE
USHORT fCardInserted = FALSE; // Set for CARD_INSERTION

// Set-up ptr to control block buffer
fpgci = (FPGETCARDSERVICESINFO)CSBuffer;
// Must clear this field before calling CS
fpgci->Signature = 0;
result = CardServices(GET_CARDSERVICES_INFO, 0, 0L, sizeof(CSBuffer),
        fpgci);
if ( (result != SUCCESS) || (fpgci->Signature != SIGNATURE))
               return (result); // Check retcode & Signature field
wCSVersion = fpgci->CSLevel; // Save Card Services Version
wSystemSlots = fpgci->Count; // Save # of PC Card slots on system
```

Figure 3-5: Detecting Card Services

The card services level (CSLevel field in the GETCARDSERVICESINFO structure) should be used by a client to determine if the required level of function is supported by the version of card services that is present. For example, if the CSLevel returned is 0x0200 then the logical socket numbering base is one. This means if there are two sockets present on this system, they are logically referred to as socket one and socket two. However, if the CSLevel returned is 0x0210 or higher, then the logical socket numbering is zero based. This means if there are two sockets present on the system, they are logically referred to as socket zero and socket one. This subtle difference is important if the logical socket number is used to index an array within the client driver program.

Registering as a Card Services Client

Next, the client registers itself with card services using the **RegisterClient** call, in the format:

result = CardServices(RegisterClient, null, *ClientEntry, ArgumentLength, fArgumentPointer);*

This function provides several key pieces of information to card services. First it becomes aware of an additional client. The function also serves to notify card services of the type of client that is registering: a memory client driver, a memory technology driver, or an I/O client driver. This is done via the bit-mapped attribute field shown in Figure 3-6.

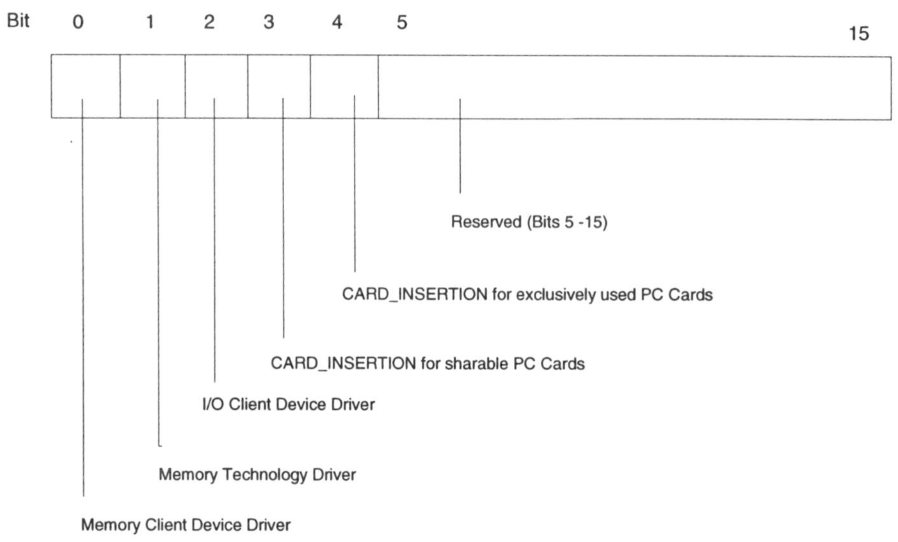

Figure 3-6: RegisterClient Attribute Field

Additionally, the client indicates via the EventMask field the events for which its desires notification. The lower eight bits of this field denote events that socket services generate, while the upper eight bits of this field are events that originate from card services. Figure 3-7 shows the definition of this bit-mapped field.

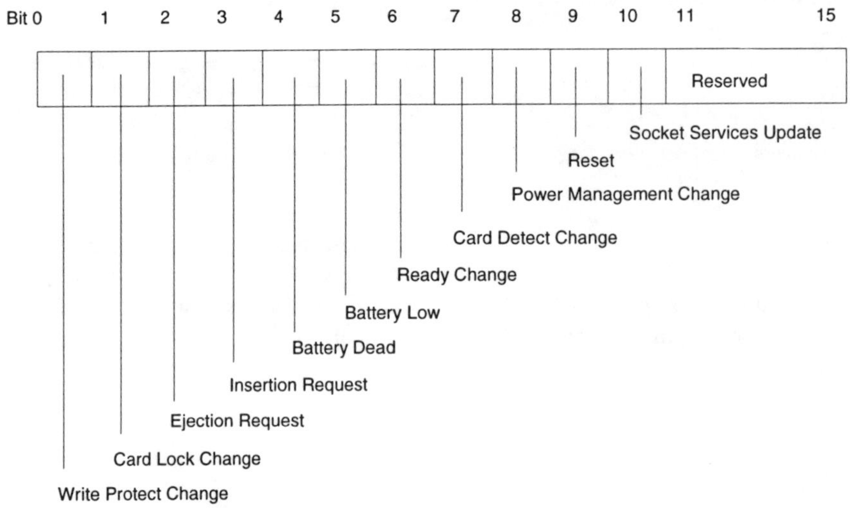

Figure 3-7: Event Mask field of the RegisterClient Function

Finally, the client supplies a *callback handler*. This is the address of the routine that will gain control when a requested event has occurred. If the CARD_INSERTION bit in the attributes field has been set correctly by the client, its callback routine will receive a REGISTRATION_COMPLETE event from card services indicating it has completed the registration process. A client should wait for this notification before proceeding because this signals card services is ready to process subsequent requests from the client.

Furthermore, all CARD_INSERTION events that are received by the client prior to the REGISTRATION_COMPLETE notification are considered *artificial insertion* events. An artificial insertion event are generated by card services as a means of notifying the client driver of PC Cards that were present in the system prior to the client registering.

```
// Register Client Attribute field masks

#define RC_ATTR_IO_CLIENT               0x0004 //Bit 2 I/O Client type
#define RC_ATTR_CARD_INSERT_SHARED      0x0008 //Bit 3 Card Insertion,

                // shared cards
#define RC_ATTR_CARD_INSERT_EXCL        0x0010 //Bit 4 Card Insertion,
                                               // exclusive use

//Register Client Event Field Masks
#define RC_EVENT_INSERTION_REQ          0x0008 // Bit 3 Card Insertion
#define RC_EVENT_CD_CHANGE              0x0080 // Bit 7 Card Detect Change

typedef struct _CLIENTDATA
  {
       USHORT    ClientVal;
       USHORT   ClientDS;
       USHORT   ClientOff;
       USHORT    Reserved;
  } CLIENTDATA;
typedef CLIENDATA  near   *NPCLIENTDATA;
typedef CLIENTDATA far    *FPCLIENTDATA;
typedef  struct _REGISTERCLIENT
  {
       USHORT Attributes;
       // Client driver attributes
       USHORT EventMask;
       // Event notification field
       CLIENTDATA  cd;
       USHORT Version;
       // CS Versions client supports
  } REGISTERCLIENT;
typedef REGISTERCLIENT   near  *NPREGISTERCLIENT;
typedef REGISTERCLIENT   far   *FPREGISTERCLIENT;
extern void  CALLBACKHANDLER();        // Assembly language routine
REGISTERCLIENT regclient

regclient.Attributes = RC_ATTR_IO_CLIENT | RC_ATTR_CARD_INSERT_SHARED |
                       RC_ATTR_CARD_INSERT_EXCL;
regclient.EventMask = RC_EVENT_CD_CHANGE | RC_EVENT_INSERTION_REQ;
regclient.Version = wCSVersion;
result = CardServices(REGISTER_CLIENT,0,CALLBACKHANDLER,
                       sizeof(regclient),&regclient,&wClientHandle);
```

Figure 3-8: Registering as a Client of Card Services

Generally, once these two functions complete successfully, a client driver remains idle until a given event occurs.

Fielding a Callback Event

When card services notifies a client of an event occurrence, it passes information to the client based on the event type. The syntax of a card services callback notification is:

result = Callback_handle(Event, Socket, Info, MTDRequest, Buffer, Misc, ClientData);

Where:

Callback_handle = the address passed to CS on the **RegisterClient** call:
Result = 0 indicates success, otherwise result = error code
Event = a value identifying the event that occurred
Socket = the socket/slot where the event occurred
Info = other information relative to the event being reported
MTDRequest = Used by MTD clients to support read, write, copy, and erase
Buffer = used to pass a buffer for the **GetClientInfo** request
Misc = used for miscellaneous information
ClientData = passes back information from the **RegisterClient** function

Keep in mind some fields are pertinent to specific card services calls. Figure 3-9 shows a C language definition file for the possible Event callback field.

```
//  Callback Event Codes
// Insertion Callback Events
#define  CARD_INSERTION            0x40

// Registration Complete Callback Events
#define  REGISTRATION_COMPLETE  0x82

// Status Change Callback Events
#define  BATTERY_DEAD              0x01
#define  BATTERY_LOW               0x02
#define  CARD_LOCK                 0x03
#define  CARD_READY                0x04
#define  CARD_REMOVAL              0x05
#define  CARD_UNLOCK               0x06
#define  REQUEST_ATTENTION         0x18
#define  WRITE_PROTECT             0x17

// Ejection/Insertion Callback Events
#define  EJECTION_COMPLETE         0x07
#define  EJECTION_REQUEST          0x08
#define  INSERTION_COMPLETE        0x09
#define  INSERTION_RQUEST          0x0A

// Client Information Callback Events
#define  CLIENT_INFO               0x14
```

```
// Erase Completion Callback Events
#define  ERASE_COMPLETE           0x81

// MTD Request Callback Event
#define  MTD_REQUEST              0x12

// Timer Callback Events
#define  TIMER_EXPIRED            0x15

// New Socket Services Callback Events
#define  SS_UPDATED               0x16

// Power Management Callback Events
#define  PM_RESUME                0x0B
#define  PM_SUSPEND               0x0C

// Exclusive Callback Events
#define  EXCLUSIVE_COMPLETE       0x0D
#define  EXCLUSIVE_REQUEST        0x0E


// Reset Callback Events
#define  RESET_PHYSICAL           0x0F
#define  RESET_COMPLETE           0x80
#define  CARD_RESET               0x11
#define  RESET_REQUEST            0x10
```

Figure 3-9: Callback Handler Event Definitions

The client callback handler must maintain all entry arguments unless otherwise indicated. The reason for this is that card services may need to pass this event to another client. Card services keeps a chain of clients based on the type of client and the order of registration. I/O-type clients are notified of card insertion events first in a LIFO fashion. That is, the last I/O client that registered will be the first to be notified of a card insertion event.

MTD type clients are then notified next, again in a LIFO fashion. Notifying I/O clients prior to MTD clients allows the I/O client time to configure the interface to the PC Card prior to an MTD attempting to access a memory region on that PC Card.

Memory type clients are notified last. This is to permit memory clients to avail themselves of the PC Card in a suitable configuration. It also facilitates the use of MTDs, already loaded, to access memory areas.

For the purpose of this example, the callback handler will only be invoked with a card insertion event. When the callback handler receives control, card services will set the Function (card insertion), the Socket number where the event occurred, and ClientData fields. As stated earlier, these fields all must be preserved because subsequent clients in the chain may receive notification of this same event.

For example, suppose two clients are registered with card services. The first is a modem client driver. It registers as an I/O type client interested in both card insertion and card ejection events. Next, a second client, designed to simply detect the insertion of a PC Card, registers as an I/O type client interested only in card insertion events.

When a card insertion event occurs, the client designed to detect a card insertion is notified first because card services notifies clients in a last-registered-first-called fashion. Once that client finishes with its task, it returns to card services. Card services then notifies the next client in line (the modem client driver) that a card has been inserted. If the first client that was notified of the card insertion event modified parameters that were passed into it, depending on the robustness of the card services implementation, the modem client driver could potentially receive faulty data.

Card Insertion Event

When the insertion of a PC Card is detected by CS, the client is notified that a registered event has occurred by invoking the client callback handle provided during the **RegisterClient** call. Because this client is written as a DOS application program, it is designed to poll a flag. As shown in Figure 3-10, the callback handler sets the flag and copies the two key pieces of information card services provided upon entry to the callback routine. It copies the type of event and the socket in which this event occurred. The registers in which card services stores this information is processor dependent, as is the method of requesting a card services function. The example that follows is designed for an Intel-based system.

```
int NP _loadds Callback (USHORT Event, USHORT Socket, USHORT
        Info,USHORT ClientData1,USHORT ClientData2, USHORT ClientData3,
        FARPOINTER MTDRequest,FARPOINTER Buffer)
  {
   switch(Event) {
        case REGISTRATION_COMPLETE:
               wRegistered = TRUE;
               return SUCCESS;           // Return SUCCESS to CS
        case CARD_INSERTION:
               fCardInserted = TRUE;  // Clear main program polling flag
               wSocket = Socket;      // Socket in which event occurred
               return SUCCESS;
        default:
               return SUCCESS;
     }
  }
```

Figure 3-10: Client Callback Handler C Routine

```
                EXTRN CALLBACK:near
                PUBLIC _CALLBACKHANDLER
                PUBLIC _acrtused
_DATA   segment word    public 'DATA'
_DATA   ends
CONST   segment word    public 'CONST'
CONST   ends
_BSS    segment word    public 'BSS'
_BSS    ends
DGROUP  group   CONST,_BSS,_DATA
_TEXT   segment word    public 'CODE'
        assume  cs:_TEXT,ds:DGROUP,es:NOTHING,ss:NOTHING
        .286P
 _CALLBACKHANDLER proc far

; ENTRY: AL = Event, CX = Socket, DX = Info, DI = 1st word of
; RegisterClient argument packet ClientData field, DS = 2nd word,
; and SI = 3rd word, SS:BP = MTD Request, ES:BX = Buffer,BX = Misc field
; when no buffer is specified
; EXIT: All registers preserved

        push    ds
        push    es
        xor     ah,ah
        push    ax
        push    cx
        push    dx
        push    di
        push    ds
        push    si
        push    ss
        push    bp
        push    es
        push    bx
        call    CALLBACK
        pop     es
        pop     ds
        ret
_CALLBACKHANDLER        endp
```

Figure 3-11: Client Callback Handler ASM Routine

Deregistering a Card Services Client

Once the flag the main program has been waiting on is set, the program displays a message indicating that a PC Card has been inserted. At this point, the program can either await the insertion of another PC Card or it can simply terminate. Should the program continue to wait, other DOS programs cannot execute. Either way, the program must eventually terminate. Prior to doing so, it is imperative that the client deregister itself with card services. This is done by passing in the Handle argument that was received back from the **RegisterClient** function as shown in Figure 3-12. The **DeregisterClient** function then removes this client from the list of clients registered with card services.

```
if (result == SUCCESS) {
        while (!fRegistered) { }    // Wait for REGISTRATION_COMPLETE
        while (!fCardInserted) { } // Wait for a card to be inserted
        printf("PC Card inserted into socket %d\n",wSocket);
                                  // De-register after 1 card is inserted
        if (CardServices(DEREGISTER_CLIENT, wClientHandle, 0L, 0, 0L))
             printf("Error De-registering Client\n");
}
```

Figure 3-12: Client Deregistration

Power Management for PC Cards

The original PCMCIA 2.0 specifications included the power management events PM_RESUME and PM_SUSPEND but did not define how these events are generated. The PC Card Standard 1995 then added definitions for how these events should be handled. Finally, the PC Card Standard 1997 includes a new tuple and a new register that PC Card makers can place in their CIS that describes how it handles suspend and resume events.

When Card Services vendors wrote to the PCMCIA 2.0 standard, they had to devise their own methods of power management. In the original IBM suite for DOS the device driver $ICPMDOS.EXE would convert Power Management events to Card Services events. If a user wanted to suspend a notebook computer, a key combination such as Fn-F4 would be pressed. The Card Services client driver would then receive an EJECTION_REQUEST. If it were possible to suspend, the driver would release resources, release the configuration, and return SUCCESS. Later, when the notebook computer was awakened, the client driver would receive a CARD_INSERTION and would request resources, request configuration, and return SUCCESS. The same was true of IBM's original PCMCIA suite for OS/2; the power management driver was named $ICPMOS2.SYS.

The PC Card Standard for 1995 finally added definitions for the PM_SUSPEND and PM_RESUME events. These events can seem complicated since a PC Card can be inserted or removed when a system is suspended, or a host system power manager can force the system into a low power state. These two events must take care of all cases.

A Card Services client driver registers for power management events by setting bit 8 in the *Event Mask* field in the structure used for **RegisterClient**.

When Card Services has received a suspend notification from the host power management software, it sends a PM_SUSPEND to each client that has registered for power management events. There are four types of PM_SUSPEND events: QUERY_REQUEST, SNAPSHOT_REQUEST, CONSERVE_POWER, and NO_POWER. The type of suspend event is passed in the *Info* argument of the callback handler.

Card Services can send these events based on two different algorithms. Which algorithm is used is based on how the host system power management software operates.

Algorithm 1:

1. The power management software on the host system receives a request to suspend the system.
2. Power Management sends the suspend request to Card Services.
3. Card Services sends a PM_SUSPEND event, type SNAPSHOT_REQUEST to all clients registered to receive power management events.
4. Each client saves any state data that would be lost if the system did suspend. The client either returns SUSPEND_OK or SUSPEND_NOT_OK.
5. Card Services returns to the power management software that the system can suspend if all clients returned SUSPEND_OK. If any client returned SUSPEND_NOT_OK, then Card Services returns to the power management software that the system cannot suspend.

Algorithm 2:

1. The power management software on the host system receives a request to suspend the system.
2. Power Management sends a query to suspend to Card Services.
3. Card Services sends a PM_SUSPEND event, type QUERY_REQUEST to all clients registered to receive power management events.
4. Each client returns either SUSPEND_OK or SUSPEND_NOT_OK, without saving any card state data.
5. Card Services returns to the power management software that the system can suspend if all clients returned SUSPEND_OK. If any client returned SUSPEND_NOT_OK, then Card Services returns to the power management software that the system cannot suspend.
6. Later, the host power management software decides to suspend, so it sends a request to Card Services.
7. Card Services sends a PM_SUSPEND event of type either CONSERVE_POWER or NO_POWER to all clients registered to receive power management events. If CONSERVE_POWER is received, the *Buffer* argument points to a bit-map of logical sockets; a client should set the bit representing the socket to a 1 if the PC Card must remain powered on. If NO_POWER is received, the client should save any state data and assume power is going to be removed.
8. Power is then removed from the socket and the PC Card for NO_POWER events or for CONSERVE_POWER events that returned a 0 in the logical socket position in the *Buffer* bit-map.

When Card Services has received a resume notification from the host power management software, it sends a PM_RESUME to each client that has registered for power management events. There are two types of PM_RESUME events: NORMAL_RESUME and CRITICAL_RESUME. The type of resume event is passed in the *Info* argument of the callback handler. If the system suspended without sending a PM_SUSPEND, it will send a CRITICAL_RESUME to resume the system. If the system send PM_SUSPEND to all clients before suspending, then it will send a NORMAL_RESUME to resume the system.

Card Services actually sends two PM_RESUME events to each client registered for power management events. The first is a BEGIN_RESUME and the second is END_RESUME. The *Misc* argument in the callback handler has the mode of the resume, begin or end. In between the two, there could be several CARD_INSERTION or CARD_REMOVAL events, if cards were inserted or removed while the system was suspended. The algorithm Card Services uses to send resume events follows:

1. Host power management software receives a request to resume from a low power state.
2. Host power management software sends the request to Card Services.
3. Card Services sends a PM_RESUME event of either type NORMAL_RESUME or CRITICAL_RESUME with the *Misc* argument set to BEGIN_RESUME. It is only sent to clients that registered for power management events.
4. If a PC Card was removed from a socket while the system was suspended, or if power was removed from the socket, Card Services sends a CARD_REMOVAL event to each client interested in this event for the socket.
5. If a PC Card was inserted into a socket while the system was suspended, or if power was applied to a socket, Card Services sends a CARD_INSERTION event to each client interested in this event for the socket.
6. Card Services send a PM_RESUME event with the *Misc* argument set to END_RESUME to each client registered for power management events.
7. Card Services returns to the host power management software.

The PC Card Standard from March of 1997 also defines a new tuple, CISTPL_PWR_MGMNT, and a new Function Configuration Register, *Power Management Support Register*, to describe a function's state save/restore method. They work together to describe how a function on a PC Card saves/restores state data for power changes. Notice that the register is part of the Function Configuration Registers. For a Multi-Function PC Card there would be one CISTPL_PWR_MGMNT tuple and one Power Management Support Register per function. The tuple would not be found in the global CIS; it would only be found in each function's CIS.

There are five fields in the CISTPL_PWR_MGMNT tuple. They are,

- PWR_METHOD
  This field describes how the PC Card saves/restores card state.
  00h PC Card state is saved/restored in Attribute Memory.
  01h PC Card state is saved/restored in Common Memory.
  80h PC Card state is save/restored in non-volatile storage on the PC Card.
- PWR_TIME
  The time required to save/restore the function state data. This field is specified in 4ms. increments.
- PWR_REG_ADDR
  The address of the PC Card function's Power Management Support Register in Attribute Memory. It should be at offset 20h in the Function Configuration Registers.
- PWR_OFFSET
  The address of the buffer to save/restore state data. It can be in Attribute Memory (PWR_METHOD = 00h) or in Common Memory (PWR_METHOD = 01H).
- PWR_BUFFSIZE
  The size of the above buffer in bytes.

The Power Management Support Register has fields that the host system and the PC Card would set/reset when state data has been saved/restored. First, the host system sets the *Save/Restore State* field and the *Begin/Done State* field to one. Next, the host allows the PC Card function the time defined in the CISTPL_PWR_MGMNT tuple, PWR_TIME field to save state data before removing power from the socket. Finally, the PC Card resets the *Begin/Done State* field to zero, indicating that state data has been saved. Later, when power is re-applied, the host sets the *Begin/Done State* to one, the host resets the *Save/Restore State* to zero, the PC Card restores the function state, and finally the PC Card resets the *Begin/Done State* to zero.

There are other fields that are set and reset by the host and the PC Card based on the method of saving state. If the CISTPL_PWR_MGMNT tuple PWR_METHOD field is 00h or 01h, the PC Card saves/restores state data in Attribute or Common Memory and then indicates to the host system that the buffer must be saved/restored. If the CISTPL_PWR_MGMNT tuple PWR_METHOD is 80h, the PC Card saves/restores state data in non-volatile memory; the host's only responsibility is to indicate when to save or restore state data.

Summary

Client Drivers and Point Enablers

Client drivers, together with card and socket services, play a very important role in solving some of the early ease-of-use problems with the PC Card technology. Not only does this software architecture facilitate a means to retrofit today's PC Card systems for use with future PC Card devices, but it also eliminates the need for cold insertion and removal. It also provides a way to preserve order within the system: card services manages the available system resources among all the registered clients. This is a vast improvement over the point enabler approach where there was no coordination among other enablers for system resources.

Card Services API

The card services API provides a set of functions and the interface through which clients may request resources. Not only do these functions insulate the clients from the hardware specific PC Card technology, but it also shields the hardware from the client.

Callback Handler

Card services notifies clients of registered event occurrences through the callback handler. Card services notifies clients of events in a priority order. I/O clients are notified first, in a last-registered-first-notified fashion, followed by MTD clients. Memory clients have the lowest priority. Because subsequent clients in the chain may be interested in the same event, unless otherwise noted, the data provided to a client's callback handler must not be modified.

Implementing Client Drivers

Finally, DOS client drivers may be written as an application program, a TSR, or as a device driver, while Windows 95, Windows NT, OS/2, and Linux clients must be written as device drivers.

PC Card Power Management

The PC Card Standard has evolved over the years from defining power management as a feature to be described in the future. The future is now here and the PC Card Standard of 1997 thoroughly defines events, tuples, and registers for power management of PC Cards.

Chapter 4: PC Cards and Host System Resources

While card and socket services help to abstract many of the PC Card details from client driver developers, it is important for programmers to understand certain aspects of the PC Card anatomy. One of the most important features to understand is its address spaces.

With 16-bit PC Cards, memory and I/O registers of the PC Card are individually mapped into the address range of the host computer system. As a result, the addresses on the card do not have to match those on the host. Instead, one or more *windows* are used by the host to directly access PC Card memory or register resources.

CardBus PC Cards map memory and I/O into the host system in a uniform manner and share the same address There is no address shifting capability with a CardBus PC Card. The address space of the CardBus PC Card is mapped into the host address space by the *Base Address Registers* (*BAR*'s) in the PC Card.

16-bit PC Cards

Memory and I/O Windows

There are two types of PC Card windows: memory and I/O. All 16-bit PC Card adapters support a minimum of four autonomous memory windows and two I/O windows per socket. Memory windows map PC Card memory into a host system's memory. A memory window can be set to map into either type of PC Card attribute or common memory.

To define a memory window, three parameters are required: a base address in the host system's address space, a base address in the PC Card's address space, and a window size. Memory windows must adhere to the alignment policy set forth by the PC Card adapter. However, all PC Card adapters support a minimum window size of 4k. Typically it should conform to a power of two and be aligned on a boundary that is a multiple of the window size for both the host system and PC Card address spaces I/O windows, on the other hand, have no alignment or size constraints.

16-bit PC Card Address Spaces

The 16-bit PC Card Standard defines three 64 megabyte address spaces on a PC Card: I/O, common, and attribute. The PC Card socket interface can address up to 16MB of any of these memory types. In either memory or I/O mode, the PC Card socket interface allows a PC Card to address up to 64K of I/O ports. Separate control signals, such as card detect and read/busy, indicate to the host system the status of the PC Card.

I/O Address Space

The I/O address space is a separate 64 megabytes of memory. This single region is then shared among all the cards present in the system. Note that system architectures, such as the AT bus systems (personal computers with an 80x86 architecture), support only a 64-kilobyte I/O address space.

Common Memory

Common memory is the primary memory address space on the PC Card. This memory space is generally used to store application data. Flash, SRAM, ROM, or EPROM can be used for common memory. The PC Card Standard defines common memory to be accessible in both 8-bit and 16-bit modes, however, some memory cards support an 8-bit only mode. Common memory supports both read-only and read/write operations, including direct-memory access (DMA). When directly mapped into the address space of a DMA controller, DMA access of common memory is possible. While common memory space is typically used for application data, attribute memory can physically reside here as well.

Attribute Memory and Attribute Memory Space

In the PC Card 2.X specifications, attribute memory refers to the physical composition of the memory: RAM, ROM, or EEPROM. Attribute memory space is the actual memory address range accessed during the memory reads or writes. While in the 2.X versions of the specifications all PC Cards have attribute memory space, not all have attribute memory. To save cost, some PC Cards implement attribute memory space in common memory. This is sometimes referred to as *aliased* memory.

Aliased memory is generally discouraged because PC Card data stored in common memory can be misinterpreted as tuple data by PC Card host software. If aliasing is employed, either mark the attribute memory space as NULL or use ROM-based attribute memory. A null attribute memory space tells the host PC Card software that attribute memory is part of common memory, while ROM based attribute memory prevents accidental erasure or corruption.

To insure compatibility with a variety of hosts, attribute memory can only be accessed in byte widths. As a result, unlike common memory, attribute memory cannot be used for DMA operations. Attribute memory is generally read-only and is divided into three areas: configuration registers, the card information structure (CIS), and a reserved area. In order to ensure addressability of the CIS across even the most primitive of hosts, the CIS must begin at address zero of attribute memory. In the case of null attribute memory, when the host PC Card software encounters this null marker, it will look to address zero of common memory for the CIS.

16-Bit Function Configuration Registers

In the PC Card Standard 2.X levels of the specification, each PC Card that is configurable contains a set of *function configuration registers.* These registers are used by PC Card software to control the electrical interface, I/O address space, interrupt request signal, and power requirement settings of a PC Card. The definition of these read/write, 8-bit registers is controlled by the PCMCIA committee and is detailed in the standard. Depending on the function of the card, some of the registers are mandatory but most are optional. For instance the *configuration option register* is required by all I/O PC cards while the *configuration and status register* is required by PC Cards that share interrupts or generate audio. These registers are found in attribute memory typically.

For 16-bit Multi-function PC Cards, there are additional registers that must be implemented. These are the I/O base and limit registers. For each function implemented on the PC Card, there is a corresponding set of Function Configuration registers.

To support power management, the PC Card Standard issued in 1997 also included a Power Manage Support Register.

Offset	Register	Optional/Required
0	Configuration Option	Required
2	Configuration and Status	Optional
4	Pin Replacement	Optional
6	Socket and Copy	Optional
8	Extended Status	Optional
10	I/O Base 0	Optional
12	I/O Base 1	Optional
14	I/O Base 2	Optional
16	I/O Base 3	Optional
18	I/O Limit	Optional
20	Power Management Support	Optional

Function Configuration Registers

- The Configuration Option register is used to configure the PC Card and issue a soft reset to the card.
- The Configuration and Status register allows for additional control over a function's configuration and reports status related to the function's configuration. This register is used by multi-function PC Cards to signal and acknowledge interrupts for the function.
- The Pin Replacement register is used to provide the card status information which was provided by pins 16, 33, 62, and 63 in Memory Only PC Cards.
- The Socket and Copy register is used by the system to differentiate between similar cards in a system.
- The Extended Status register contains information about changes in the card's status.
- The I/O Base registers determine the base address of the I/O range used to access function specific registers on the PC Card. (Required for Multi-function PC Cards).
- The I/O Limit register specifies the number of I/O ports that are available beginning at the I/O address specified in the I/O Base registers. For example, if the I/O base registers had a value of 0x3F8 and the I/O Limit register contained 7, the I/O address range from 0x3F8 to 0x3FF would be available.
- The Power Management Support register is used by the host system and the PC Card to preserve function state data for a function when power is removed or re-applied.

CardBus PC Cards

CardBus PC Card Address Spaces

Prior to the February 1995 PC Card Standard all PC Cards had a 16-bit interface. The CardBus PC Cards differ from these 16-bit PC Cards in a variety of ways. The most obvious difference is that CardBus PC Cards are 32-bit. They also have a different address space. As a result, they do not have attribute memory space. Instead CardBus PC Cards have a special 256-byte configuration space that their 16-bit cousins do not have. This space is patterned after the configuration space found in *Peripheral Component Interconnect (PCI)* devices. See Figure 4-1: CardBus PC Card Function Configuration Space. The 256 byte Configuration space is divided into two sections: A pre-defined header that is 64 (40h) bytes long. The remaining 192 bytes is referred to as the Device Dependent Space. This space can contain the CIS or any device specific registers. A pointer to the start of the CIS is stored inside the pre-defined header.. The CIS itself may reside in any address space on the CardBus card except in its I/O space.

Also absent are the configuration registers. In their place is a set of six *base address registers (BARs).* Each BAR is capable of responding to either an I/O or memory access in the host system address space.

In addition, CardBus PC cards may support up to eight separate functions on a single card. Each of these functions is treated almost as if it were a separate card. Each function has its own configuration space, CIS, and BARs.

Finally, the system adapter no longer maps memory or I/O. Instead, the CardBus PC card directly decodes host system access. The downside is that this requires additional logic on the card to handle the decoding. However, the card now controls the number of address spaces available for both memory and I/O.

The CardBus specification encompasses several key features, including a 32-bit multiplexed address and data bus, higher operational speeds, lower power consumption, multi-function support, and bus mastering capabilities.

Bits

31 16 15 0

Device ID (Allocated)		Vendor ID (Allocated)		00h
Status		Command		04h
Allocated			Allocated	08h
BIST	Header Type	Latency Timer	Cache Line Size	0Ch
Base Address Register				10h
Base Address Register				14h
Base Address Register				18h
Base Address Register				1Ch
Base Address Register				20h
Base Address Register				24h
CIS Pointer				28h
Reserved				2Ch
Expansion ROM Base Address				30h
Reserved				34h
Reserved				38h
Allocated	Allocated	Interrupt Pin	Allocated	3Ch
Beginning of Device Dependent Space				40h
				44h
Tuple Space				
Tuple Space				
End of Device Dependent Space				FFh

Figure 4-1: CardBus PC Card Function Configuration Space

In the Configuration Space definition, there are fields that are marked "allocated" and "reserved". Fields marked as "allocated" are not defined for CardBus and must not be redefined as other environments may use the register. Fields marked "reserved" are reserved for future use.

- The Command register specifies a function's ability to generate and respond to the different access cycles possible for CardBus PC Cards.
- The Status register holds run-time status for bus-related events.

- The Cache Line Size register specifies the system cahe line size in units of 32-bit words.
- The Latency Timer register specifies in units of bus clocks, the latency timer for this bus master.
- The Header Type register identifies the byte layout of bytes 10h to 3Fh in the configuration space and also whether the PC Card has multiple functions.
- The BIST (Built-in Self Test) register is used for control and status of Built-in Self Tests.
- The Base Address Registers provide the beginning Host System address for mapping CardBus PC Card memory and I/O spaces into the Host System.
- The CIS Pointer points to the beginning of the CIS in either the configuration space, memory space, or expansion ROM space.
- The Expansion ROM Base Address is defined to contain the base address and size for an expansion ROM.
- The Interrupt Pin register tells whether or not the function uses the interrupt pin.

CardBus Software Repercussions

Repercussions from CardBus are also felt in the PC Card software elements. While CardBus PC cards still rely on client drivers working in conjunction with card and socket services, modifications have been made to the metaformat and to card and socket services, while maintaining compatibility with the 16-bit client drivers. Most notably, in order to support the multi-function capability of these cards, both card and socket services have been modified.

Socket services has been extended to provide an **AccessConfigurationSpace** function that provides a means for accessing the CardBus configuration spaces. Extensions have also been made to other existing functions in order to manage and report on the capabilities and status of CardBus PC cards.

Likewise, several of the card services functions are impacted. The logical socket field on many of the functions has been modified. The field is now divided into two bytes, with the lower byte signifying the logical socket, while the upper byte now identifies the function on the card.

Similarly, in order to configure these various spaces on the CardBus PC card, the **AccessConfigurationRegister** service of card services has been modified to accept an argument denoting which configuration space is being accessed. Additionally, because CardBus PC cards use BARs instead of configuration registers, the **RequestWindow** function has been updated to accept a BAR number. Through this function, the BARs are programmed to respond to host system I/O access, thus replacing the **RequestIO** function for CardBus PC cards (however, its 16-bit PC Card cousins still employ this function).

The **RequestIO** function also has been revamped. This function may now be used to request I/O as well as memory windows. This means that 16-bit PC Card client drivers may use either the **RequestWindow** or the **RequestIO** calls to obtain an I/O window. For client drivers supporting only 16-bit Cards, the **RequestIO** function is the preferred method for I/O window creation because it is more flexible: multiple I/O ranges are allowed on a single call, I/O address space may be specified anywhere within a 4Gbyte address, and CardBus PC Card BARs may be specified as well.

Finally, the **GetConfigurationInfo** function has been enhanced to return more information to the client driver. It is important to note that these changes do not impact existing 16-bit client drivers. Rather, a CardBus PC Card client driver exploits these enhanced functions. Extreme care was taken to minimize the impact to the client interface of card services. The significant impact of these changes is contained within card services. However, a client that wishes to take advantage of these new features must verify that the card services level is 5.0 or higher by using the **GetCardServicesInfo** call.

Card Information Structure (CIS)

In order for a PC Card to comply with the PC Card Standard, it must contain at least a rudimentary CIS that resides in non-volatile memory. For a 16-bit PC Card, it must start at address zero of the attribute memory space on the card. A Cardbus PC Card has a pointer in its configuration header that points to its CIS. There is a separate CIS for each function on a Cardbus PC Card. Conceptually, the CIS is separate from the data that is actually stored on the PC Card. The CIS is a data structure that describes the capabilities of the PC Card, such as the type of device it is. The CIS, or *metaformat* as it is sometimes called, appears at the beginning of the card in 16-bit PC Cards, so that devices that can only address one megabyte of RAM can access it. This also helps to serve as a common reference point for PC Card host software to begin interrogating the card to determine its functions and capabilities.

The PC Card standard specifies the format and content of the CIS, which varies by device type. That is, the CIS of a modem card will greatly differ from a CIS of a LAN or Flash card. As a result, the attribute memory size required to house a CIS varies from card to card. In fact, the CIS can actually extend into common memory.

The CIS is divided into four layers: *basic compatibility, data recording format, data organization,* and *system-specific standards*. Of these layers, only the basic compatibility layer is required according to the Release 2.X specifications. Each of the layers is further organized into tuples. Tuples are blocks of data in a format set forth by the standard. All tuples contain a tuple code, a tuple link, and data specific to the tuple.

At the beginning of the CIS, the tuple code identifies the type of tuple, such as a configuration tuple, a device tuple, or an end-of-chain marker. Next, at byte one, the tuple link is stored. The tuple link is a pointer to the next tuple in the chain. Finally, data specific to the tuple type appears. The length of the data stored varies, which is why a tuple link field is required. However, not all tuples are pertinent for all PC Card types.

For example, a UART identification field tuple (TPLFE_UA) is appropriate for a modem card but not for a memory card.

Despite the fact that the CIS architecture is detailed in the PC Card Standard, some manufacturers improperly implement the CIS on their PC cards. If the CIS cannot be parsed correctly, this can result in inconsistent operation across system platforms and sometimes failure of the host system software to recognize the PC Card. Figure 4-2 illustrates the CIS and tuple concept.

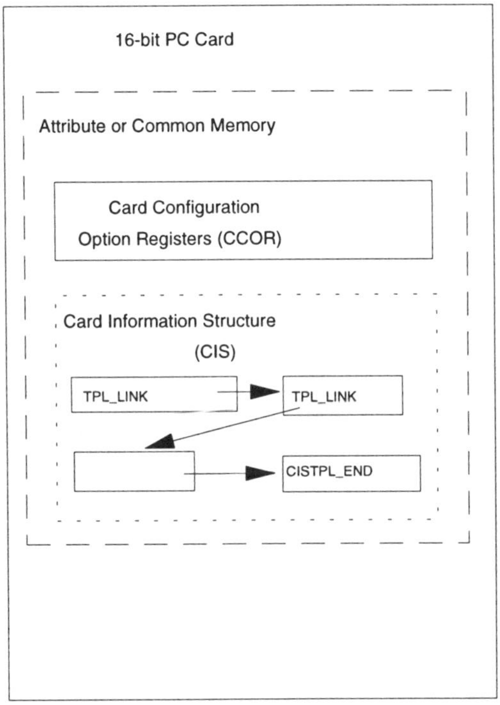

Figure 4-2: CIS and Tuple Concept

Basic Compatibility Layer

The basic compatibility layer is used to denote essential information about the PC Card such as the type of device, its size, speed and power requirements. This fundamental information is used by the PC Card host software to determine whether or not the card can be supported. For instance, a small handheld system may have a Type II st, but because it operates on small penlight batteries, it may be unable to power a Type II modem card. By reading the PC Card power requirements from the basic compatibility layer, the PC Card host software could reject the card.

While the basic compatibility layer detailed in the PC Card Standard is currently mandatory for all PC Cards, many working groups have come up with recommendations for minimum CIS content based on the function of the card, such as a modem.

Data Recording Layer

The data recording layer is used to denote the manner in which the data on the card is formatted: disk or memory. If the data is stored similar to a disk, then the card is made up of a number of data blocks, each of which has a fixed number of bytes. Likewise, if the card is formatted like memory, then it is accessed as a sequence of individually addressable data bytes.

Data Organization Layer

The data organization layer is used to denote how the data in a memory card partition is organized: DOS file system, Microsoft Flash file system, vendor specific, or application specific. In other words, the data organization layer specifies the file structure used on the card, while the data recording layer distinguishes the card as being either like a disk (block addressable) or like memory (byte addressable).

System Specific Layer

The system specific layer is used to contain operating environment-specific information. For example, the *eXecute In Place* (XIP) metaformat is stored in this system specific layer. The XIP portion of the standard provides a means for a host system to execute a program directly from common memory on a PC Card.

CIS Development

In the companion source code available via the World Wide Web, is code for a sample 5 volt 14.4 FAX/Modem Card Information Structure. This program can be built using an Intel Assembly language Assembler such as the Borland Turbo Assembler. The program shows the basic elements of any CIS and can be used as a basis for any future CIS. The CIS for a multi-function card, memory card, or other PC Card will have different requirements, but the basic structure is the same. "The PC Card Standard for the Metaformat" section of the standard outlines these differences and should be consulted when developing a CIS. The sample CIS that follows is written in Intel 80X86 Assembly Language. The source code is assembled to produce a binary image that can be placed into the PC Card either in Flash memory, *One Time Programmable* (OTP) memory, or other hardware on the PC Card. Source code excerpts are used to illustrate various tuple examples that follow.

On a 16-bit PC Card, the CIS resides at offset zero in attribute memory space. The electrical standard for 16-bit PC Cards requires that information be placed only in even-byte addresses of the attribute memory space. For compatibility purposes across various computer platforms, the odd-byte addresses of attribute memory are not defined. If the CIS is continued in common memory, each byte of the CIS is in consecutive bytes.

Developing a CIS can be very a tedious operation. There are different tuples for different types of PC Cards. Some tuples are mandatory, while others are optional. Some only apply to certain types of PC Cards, while others are common to all PC Cards. While a minimal CIS may meet the minimum requirements of PC Card, it is often inadequate for supporting software like Windows 95, super client drivers or other enablers. Therefore, it is best to place as much information as possible about the PC Card in the CIS so that present and future software can fully utilize the PC Card and understand its requirements and capabilities as well.

To develop a thorough CIS, the hardware, software, and functional characteristics of the PC Card must be known. In the metaformat section of the PC Card Standard, Table 2-4 indicates which tuples are mandatory, which tuples are recommended, and which tuples are not applicable to a particular PC Card. For a 5-volt 16-bit PC Card, the mandatory tuples are:

```
1.  CISTPL_VERS_1 (15H) Level 1 version/ product information tuple
2.  CISTPL_MANFID (20H)  Manufacturer Identification tuple
3.  CISTPL_CFTABLE_ENTRY (1BH)  Configuration Table Entry tuple
4.  CISTPL_CONFIG (1AH) Configuration tuple
```

CIS Sample Source Code for a 16-bit PC Card

According to the PC Card metaformat section of the standard, the first tuple in the primary chain of a 16-bit PC Card with a 5-volt key must either be a "device information tuple" (tuple code 01H), a "null control tuple" (tuple code 00H) or an "end of chain tuple" (tuple code FFH). This template starts with the device information tuple. This particular tuple only describes the common memory space. Another tuple, called the device information tuple for attribute memory (CISTPL_DEVICE_A), describes attribute memory space. The beginning of the CIS template is shown in Figure 4-3.

```
; This CIS begins in attribute memory at offset 0.
DATA            SEGMENT
                ORG     0H
CIS_BEGIN       LABEL   BYTE
;
; Device Information Tuple (Common Memory Space)
;
DEVICE_BEGIN    LABEL   BYTE
; TPL_CODE    Device Information Tuple
                DB      CISTPL_DEVICE
; TPL_LINK    Link to next tuple
                DB      DEVICE_END - $

;               BITS     76543210
;                        ++++---------> Device Type DTYPE_FUNCSPEC
;                        ||||
;                        ||||+--------> WPS = 0
;                        |||||+++-----> 250 ns device speed
;                        ||||||||
                DB       11010001b     ;
                DB       00H           ; .5K device size
DEVICE_END      DB       END_MARK
```

Figure 4-3: Sample CIS Tuple Source Code

Device Information Tuple (CISTPL_DEVICE_A)

This device information tuple indicates that there are 512 bytes of common memory on the card and that this memory is not to be used by the system as standard memory. In this example, no WPS (write protect switch) is present and the memory speed is 250ns. This tuple also indicates that 2K of 250ns static RAM is used for attribute memory.

```
;
; Device Information Tuple (attribute memory Space)
;
DEVICEA_BEGIN   LABEL   BYTE
; TPL_CODE     Device Information Tuple
                DB      CISTPL_DEVICE_A
; TPL_LINK     Link to next tuple
                DB      DEVICEA_END - $

;               BITS     76543210
;                        ++++----------> DTYPE_SRAM (Static RAM)
;                        ||||
;                        ||||+--------> WPS = 0
;                        |||||+++-----> 250 ns device speed
;                        ||||||||
                DB       01100001b      ;

;               BITS     76543210
;                        +++++--------> # 0f address units -1 (3)
;                        |||||          4 address units (4*.5K = 2K)
;                        |||||          2K total attribute memory
;                        |||||+++-----> size code (0.5K)
;                        ||||||||
                DB       00011000b      ;
DEVICEA_END     DB      END_MARK
```

Figure 4-4: Common Memory Device Information Tuple

Level 1 Version/Product Information Tuple (CISTPL_VERS_1)

The Level 1 version/product information tuple provides information about the manufacturer, the product, and its version.

```
;
; Level 1 Version/Product Information Tuple
;
VERS_BEGIN      LABEL   BYTE
; TPL_CODE     Product Information Tuple
                DB      CISTPL_VERS_1
; TPL_LINK     Link to next tuple
                DB      VERS_END - $
                DB      TPLLV1_MAJOR     ; Major Version
                DB      TPLLV1_MINOR     ; Minor Version
'
; Each line must be ended by a 0, e.g.
;                                 3
;                                 v
                DB      'SAMPLE',0       ; Manufacturer
                DB      'MODEM',0        ; Product

                DB      '12345678',0     ; Part number
;
```

```
                DB      'NONE',0          ; Sub Part number
VERS_END        DB      END_MARK
```

Figure 4-5: Version/Product Information Tuple

Manufacturer ID Tuple (TPLMID_MANF)

The manufacturer ID tuple is next. It contains information about the manufacturer of the PC Card. The TPLMID_MANF field is identifies the manufacturer and is assigned by the PCMCIA association and JEIDA to manufacturers of PC Cards. The TPLMID_CARD field is reserved for use by the PC Card's manufacturer. This field should contain unique identifier codes from the manufacturer.

```
;
; Manufacturer ID Tuple
;
MANFID_BEGIN    LABEL   BYTE
                DB      CISTPL_MANFID    ; TPL_CODE    Manufacturer ID
                DB      MANFID_END - $   ; TPL_LINK    Link to next tuple
                DW      TPLMID_MANF      ; PCMCIA PC Card Manufacturer code
                DW      TPLMID_CARD      ; Manufacturer info
MANFID_END      DB      END_MARK
```

Figure 4-6: Manufacturer ID Tuple

Function ID Tuple (CISTPL_FUNCID)

The function identification tuple describes the function of the PC Card. In this case, the function is a serial port or modem. This function code is defined in the PC Card Standards. At present, there are twelve defined function codes, including multi-function, memory, serial port, parallel port, fixed disk, video adapter, network adapter, AIMS (auto-incrementing mass storage), SCSI, Security, Instrument, and vendor specific. The TPLFID_SYSINIT byte is a bit-mapped field that has two bit defined. The POST bit indicates that power-on self-test routines may attempt to configure the card during system initialization. The ROM bit is used to indicate that expansion ROM is resident on this card and may be installed during system initialization.

```
;
; Function Identification Tuple
;
FUNCID_BEGIN    LABEL   BYTE
                DB      CISTPL_FUNCID    ; TPL_CODE  Card Function tuple
                DB      FUNCID_END - $   ; TPL_LINK  Link to next tuple
                DB      FUNCTION_SERIAL  ; code for Serial Port (modem)
;               BITS     76543210
```

```
;                              ++++++-------> Reserved for future use
;                              ||||||+------> ROM
;                              |||||||+-----> POST - configure card at POST
;                              ||||||||
                DB             00000001b       ; TPLFID_SYSINIT
FUNCID_END      DB             END_MARK
```

Figure 4-7: Function Identification Tuple

Function Extension Tuples

After the function identification tuple, each function code has a set of function extension tuples. The modem/serial PC card has a vast set of function extensions. These function extensions can be very complex and can require knowledge of the hardware integrated circuits on the PC Card. For more information on these extension tuples, refer to the complete listing of the CIS template included on the diskette that accompanies this book. After the function extension tuples in this template are the configuration tuples.

Configuration Tuples (CISTPL_CONFIG)

The configuration and configuration entry tuples describe the characteristics of the PC Card that are programmable. Including the type of interface (memory or memory and I/O), power requirements, timing information, and resource requirements (I/O ports, IRQ, and memory). The location of the configuration registers is provided as well. Figure 4-8 shows the configuration tuple.

```
; Configuration Tuple
;
CONFIG_BEGIN    LABEL   BYTE
                DB      CISTPL_CONFIG       ; TPL_CODE Configurable card tuple
                DB      CONFIG_END - $      ; TPL_LINK Link to next tuple
;
;               BITS     76543210
;                        ++-----------> Reserved for future use
;                        ||++++-------> TPCC_RMSZ (size of TPCC_RMSK
;                        ||||||              field - 1)
;                        ||||||++-----> TPCC_RASZ (size of TPCC_RADR)
;                        ||||||||
                DB       00000001b          ; TPCC_SZ 2 byte _RADR,
;                                             1 byte TPCC_RMSK
;
;               BITS     76543210
;                        ++-----------> Reserved for future use
;                        ||++++++-----> Last Index of final entry in
;                        ||||||||       card configuration table
;                        ||||||||
                DB       00100011b          ; TPCC_LAST index # of last entry
;
```

```
                DW      CONFIG_BASE     ; TPCC_RADR    cfg base address
                DB      CONF_REGS_MASK  ; TPCC_RMSK    cfg byte mask
CONFIG_END      DB      END_MARK
```

Figure 4-8: Configuration Tuple

The TPCC_RMSZ and TPCC_RASZ fields of this tuple give the size, in bytes, of the TPCC_RMSK and the TPCC_RASZ fields of the tuple. These are option base zero fields in that the actual size in bytes of the TPCC_RMSK and TPCC_RASZ fields is one more than the value in the bit fields.

In this case, the TPCC_RADR field is two bytes long. The TPCC_RMSK field is one byte long. The TPCC_RADR field gives the offset in attribute memory space where the configuration registers for the PC Card begin. The TPCC_RMSK field indicates what configuration registers are actually implemented in the PC Card. The TPCC_LAST field gives the index number of the last configuration table entry tuple. In this case, the first configuration table entry tuple has an index of 20H and the last has an index of 23H. As a result, any software that is scanning the tuples will now know when it has examined the last configuration table entry tuple.

Configuration Table Entry Tuple (CISTPL_CFTABLE_ENTRY)

The configuration entry table tuple follow the configuration tuple. These tuples are used to specify each possible configuration of a PC Card and to distinguish among the permitted configurations. Figure 4-9 the first configuration table entry tuple.

```
CFIG1_BEGIN     LABEL   BYTE
                DB      CISTPL_CFTABLE_ENTRY ; TPL_CODE Cfg entry table
                DB      CFIG1_END - $    ; TPL_LINK Link to next tuple
;
;               BITS     76543210
;                        +------------> Interface Cfg Byte Follows
;                        |+-----------> Default Table Indicator
;                        ||++++++-----> Configuration Entry Number
;                        ||||||||
                DB       11100000b      ; TPCE_INDX
;                                         Default Table 1
;                                         Interface byte follows
;               BITS     76543210
;                        +------------> Wait Signal support for
;                        |              Memory Cycles
;                        |+-----------> Ready/Busy is Active
;                        ||+----------> Write Protect not Active
;                        |||+---------> Battery Voltage Status not
;                        |||+           Active
;                        ||||++++-----> Interface Type (0001 = I/O)
;                        ||||||||
                DB       11000001b      ; TPCE_IF
```

```
;                                          I/O device type
;                                          Memory WAIT signal
;                                          support
;               BITS      76543210
;                         +-------------> Misc Fields Structure Follows
;                         |++-----------> no configuration dependent, memory
;                         |++             addr space used
;                         |||+----------> IRQ Structure Follows
;                         ||||+---------> I/O Space Structure Follows
;                         |||||+--------> Timing Structure Follows
;                         ||||||++------> Power Structure Follows
;                         ||||||++        (10 = VCC and VPP)
;                         ||||||||
                DB        10011110b       ; TPCE_FS
;                                          I/O Space Structure
;                                          Follows
;                                          IRQ Structure Follows
;                                          Memory Structure Follows
;                                          Vcc Power Description
;                                          Structure Follows
;
;  Power Description Structure
;
;
;  Vcc parameter selection byte
;
;
;               BITS      76543210
;                         +-------------> Reserved for future use
;                         |+------------> Power Down supply current
;                         ||+-----------> Maximum current over 10msec
;                         |||+----------> Maximum current over 1 sec
;                         ||||+---------> Continuous supply current req'd
;                         |||||+--------> Maximum operating voltage
;                         ||||||+-------> Minimum operating voltage
;                         |||||||+------> Nominal operating voltage
;                         ||||||||
                DB        01111111b       ; TPCE_PD
;                                          Nominal voltage tables
;                                          Cont. & Max (1 sec) tables
;
;               BITS      76543210
;                         +-------------> Extension
;                         |++++---------> Mantissa
;                         |||||+++------> Exponent
;                         ||||||||
                DB        01010101b       ; Nominal 5.0v

;
;               BITS      76543210
;                         +-------------> Extension
;                         |++++---------> Mantissa
;                         |||||+++------> Exponent
;                         ||||||||
                DB        11000101b       ; 4 * 1.0 = 4 Volts
;
                DB        01001011b       ; extension  0.75
;                                          4.75 Volts minimum
;
```

```
;               BITS    76543210
;                       +------------> Extension
;                       |++++--------> Mantissa
;                       |||||+++-----> Exponent
;                       ||||||||
                DB      11010101b      ; 5 * 1.0  = 5 volts

;
                DB      00011001b      ; extension  0.25
                                       ; 5.25 volts maximum


;
;               BITS    76543210
;                       +------------> Extension
;                       |++++--------> Mantissa
;                       |||||+++-----> Exponent
;                       ||||||||
                DB      10000110b      ; 1 * 100ma = 100ma.
;
                DB      01010000b      ; extension  80
                                       ; 100.8 ma static current
;
;               BITS    76543210
;                       +------------> Extension
;                       |++++--------> Mantissa
;                       |||||+++-----> Exponent
;                       ||||||||
                DB      10000110b      ; 1 * 100ma = 100ma.
;
                DB      01010000b      ; extension  80
                                       ; 100.8 ma average current
;
;               BITS    76543210
;                       +------------> Extension
;                       |++++--------> Mantissa
;                       |||||+++-----> Exponent
;                       ||||||||
                DB      00100110b      ; peak current= 200ma
;
;               BITS    76543210
;                       +------------> Extension
;                       |++++--------> Mantissa
;                       |||||+++-----> Exponent
;                       ||||||||
                DB      00110100b      ; Power down current=3 ma.

;
; Vpp parameter selection byte
;               BITS    76543210
;                       +------------> Reserved for future use
;                       |+-----------> Power Down supply current
;                       ||+----------> Maximum current over 10msec
;                       |||+---------> Maximum current over 1 sec
;                       ||||+--------> Continuous supply current req'd
;                       |||||+-------> Maximum operating voltage
;                       ||||||+------> Minimum operating voltage
;                       |||||||+-----> Nominal operating voltage
;                       ||||||||
                DB      00110111b      ; TPCE_PD
;                                      ; Nominal voltage tables
;                                      ; Cont & Max (1 sec) tables
```

```
;
;            BITS     76543210
;                     +------------> Extension
;                     |++++--------> Mantissa
;                     |||||+++-----> Exponent
;                     ||||||||
;            DB       10001110b     ; Nominal
;                                     1.2 * 10 volts = 12 volts
;
;            DB       01111101b     ; extension
;
;            BITS     76543210
;                     +------------> Extension
;                     |++++--------> Mantissa
;                     |||||+++-----> Exponent
;                     ||||||||
;            DB       10000110b     ; minimum  1 * 10 volts
;
;            DB       00001110b     ; extension  10.14 volts
;
;            BITS     76543210
;                     +------------> Extension
;                     |++++--------> Mantissa
;                     |||||+++-----> Exponent
;                     ||||||||
;            DB       10010110b     ; maximum
;                                     1.3* 10 volts = 13volts
;
;            DB       00011010b     ; extension  13.26 volts
;
;
;            BITS     76543210
;                     +------------> Extension
;                     |++++--------> Mantissa
;                     |||||+++-----> Exponent
;                     ||||||||
;            DB       00110101b     ; Average  10ma * 3 = 30ma.
;
;
;            BITS     76543210
;                     +------------> Extension
;                     |++++--------> Mantissa
;                     |||||+++-----> Exponent
;                     ||||||||
;            DB       00110101b     ; Peak  10ma * 3 = 30ma.
;
;  Configuration Timing Information
;
;
;                     +++----------> Reserved scale 7
;                     |||+++-------> Ready/Busy Scale
;                     ||||||++-----> Wait Scale
;                     ||||||||
;            DB       11101000b     ; TPCE_TD  wait scale
;            DB       00010100b     ; 12 us Wait
;            DB       01011111b     ; 5000 ms MAX time
```

```
;
;  I/O Space Addresses required for this configuration
;

;             BITS     76543210
;                      +-----------> Range
;                      |+----------> Bus16: Supports both
;                      |+              8 & 16 bit I/O
;                      ||+---------> Bus8: Supports only
;                      ||+              8 bit only I/O
;                      |||+++++----> 3 I/O Address lines
;                      ||||||||
              DB       10100011b       ; TPCE_IO

; range descriptor byte

;             BITS     76543210
;                      ++----------> Size of Length
;                      ||++--------> Size of Address
;                      ||||++++----> (# of I/O address ranges -1)
;                      ||||||||
              DB       01100000b
;
              DB       11111000b       ; Start of I/O Addr block

              DB       00000011b       ;
;
              DB       00000111b       ; Length of I/O Addr block

;             BITS     76543210
;                      +-----------> Share
;                      |+----------> Pulse
;                      ||+---------> Level
;                      |||+--------> Mask 0
;                      ||||++++----> IRQ Number
;                      ||||||||
              DB       00110000b       ; TPCE_IR

;             BITS     76543210
;                      +-----------> IRQ7
;                      |+----------> IRQ6
;                      ||+---------> IRQ5
;                      |||+--------> IRQ4
;                      ||||+-------> IRQ3
;                      |||||+------> IRQ2
;                      ||||||+-----> IRQ1
;                      |||||||+----> IRQ0
;                      ||||||||
              DB       10111100b       ;

;             BITS     76543210
;                      +-----------> IRQ15
;                      |+----------> IRQ14
;                      ||+---------> IRQ13
;                      |||+--------> IRQ12
;                      ||||+-------> IRQ11
;                      |||||+------> IRQ10
;                      ||||||+-----> IRQ9
;                      |||||||+----> IRQ8
;                      ||||||||
              DB       10000110b       ;
```

```
; Miscellaneous Features Field

;               BITS     76543210
;                        +------------> Extension
;                        |+-----------> Reserved
;                        ||+----------> Power down mode
;                        |||+---------> Read Only
;                        ||||+--------> Audio
;                        |||||+++-----> Max Twins Cards
;                        ||||||||
                DB       00101000b      ;    TPCE_MI


CFIG1_END       DB       END_MARK
```

Figure 4-9: Configuration Entry Tuple

This particular tuple can be quite lengthy. When the default bit for the TPCE_INDX field is set, this tuple supplies the default values for the other configuration table entry tuples that follow. The configuration table entry tuples that follow do not need to repeat most of this data and can be much shorter. This tuple indicates what kind of interface this card requires. It also indicates whether the card supports Ready/Busy and Wait signals. This information is provided in the TPCE_IF (Table Entry Interface) field. The following field TPCE_FS (Feature Selection Byte) indicates what features will be described in subsequent fields. These fields can describe the power requirements, the timing characteristics, I/O port types and range, IRQs that can be used, memory space needs and miscellaneous features of the PC card. As shown, this tuple can be quite complex.

The complexity of the tuple depends upon how much information is desired in the CIS. The following configuration table entry tuple does not need to repeat all of this common data. The next configuration table entry tuple only contains information on its index and the fact that only I/O port information is given in this tuple. Between configurations, only the index value and the address of the I/O ports needed for that configuration are supplied.

```
CFIG2_BEGIN     LABEL   BYTE
                DB      CISTPL_CFTABLE_ENTRY ; TPL_CODE
;                                          Configuration table entry
                DB      CFIG2_END - $      ; TPL_LINK Link to next tuple
;
;               BITS     76543210
;                        +-------------> Interface Cfg byte follows
;                        |+------------> Default Table Indicator
;                        ||++++++-----> Configuration Entry Number
;                        ||||||||
                DB       00100001b         ; TPCE_INDX Default table 1
;                                            Interface byte follows
;               BITS     76543210
;                        +-------------> Misc Fields Structure
;                        |               Follows
;                        |++-----------> Memory Space Structure
;                        |++             Follows
;                        |||+----------> IRQ Structure Follows
;                        ||||+---------> I/O Space Structure Follows
;                        |||||+--------> Timing Structure Follows
;                        ||||||++-----> Power Structure Follows
;                        ||||||||
                DB       00001000b         ; TPCE_FS
;                                            I/O Space Structure
;                                            Follows
;
;   I/O Space Addresses required for this configuration
;
;               BITS     76543210
;                        +-------------> Range
;                        |+------------> Bus16 - Supports
;                        |+                 8 & 16 bit I/O
;                        ||+-----------> Bus8 - Supports only
;                        ||+-----------> Bus8: Supports only
;                        ||+                8 bit only I/O
;                        |||+++++-----> 3 I/O Address lines
;                        ||||||||
                DB       10100011b         ; TPCE_IO range descriptor byte
;               BITS     76543210
;                        ++------------> Size of Length
;                        ||++----------> Size of Address
;                        ||||++++-----> (# of I/O addr ranges -1)
;                        ||||||||
                DB       01100000b         ;
;
;
;
                DB       11111000b         ; Start of I/O Addr block
                DB       00000010b         ;
;
                DB       00000111b         ; Length of I/O Addr block

CFIG2_END       DB       END_MARK
```

Figure 4-10: Second Configuration Entry Tuple

Multi-Function PC Card CIS differences

Multi-Function PC Cards must contain multiple Card Information Structures. There is a common or global CIS and then there is an individual CIS for each function

The global CIS must contain certain mandatory tuples. These are:

```
1. CISTPL_DEVICE       (01H) 5 volt Device Information Tuple
2. CISTPL_VERS_1       (15H) Level 1 Version / Product Information Tuple
3. CISTPL_MANFID       (20H) Manufacturers Identification tuple
4. CISTPL_LONGLINK_MFC (06H) Multiple Function 16-bit PC Card link tuple
5. CISTPL_END          (FFH) End-of-chain tuple
```

The global CIS starting at offset 0 in attribute memory space must identify the PC Card as a multi-function PC Card. This is done by including a CISTPL_LONGLINK_MFC (06H) tuple. This tuple specifies the number of sets of Function Configuration registers on the PC Card. It also describes the location of each function–specific CIS. These function specific CIS's can be in attribute or common memory. This tuple should never be used by a CardBus PC Card.

Here is an example CISTPL_LONGLINK_MFC tuple.

```
;
; Multiple Function 16-bit PC Card Link tuple
;
MFC_LONG_BEGIN  LABEL   BYTE
                DB      CISTPL_LONGLINK_MFC   ;TPL_CODE
                                              ; Multi-function Long Link
                DB      MFC_LONG_END - $ - 1  ;TPL_LINK  link to next tuple
                DB      NUM_FUNCTIONS         ;TPLMFC_NUM
                                              ; Number of cardfunctions
                DB      ATTR_TARGET           ;TPLMFC_TAS1
                                              ; Target is Attribute Memory
                DD      OFFSET LAN_TARGET     ; pointer to LAN CIS
                DB      ATTR_TARGET           ;TPLMFC_TAS2
                                              ; Target is Attribute Memory
                DD      OFFSET MODEM_TARGET   ; pointer to MODEM CIS
MFC_LONG_END    LABEL   BYTE

END_COMMON      LABEL   BYTE                  ; End of Common CIS
                DB      CISTPL_END
```

In this tuple, you can see the declaration for the number of functions (NUM_FUNCTIONS) declared in this CIS. In this case, the number of functions is 2. This could be an equate earlier in the file. After the number of functions is declared, the next field shows the target address for the CIS for the following function. In this case, the CIS for the LAN function is in attribute memory. The address pointers are stored as unsigned long values (four bytes) with the low order byte first.

Each function-specific CIS must contain the following tuples:

```
1.  CISTPL_LINKTARGET     (13H)  Link target tuple
2.  CISTPL_CONFIG         (1AH)  16-bit PC Card Configuration tuple
3.  CISTPL_CFTABLE_ENTRY  (1BH)  16-bit PC Card Configuration table
    entry    tuple
4.  CISTPL_END            (FFH)  End-of-chain tuple
```

At the beginning of each of the function-specific CIS sections, you must place the Link Target tuple (13H). Here is an example of a Link target tuple:

```
LAN_TARGET       LABEL   BYTE
                 DB      CISTPL_LINKTARGET       ; TPL_CODE Link Target
                 DB      LAN_TARGET_END - $ - 1  ; TPL_LINK
                                                 ; Link to next tuple
                 DB      'CIS'                   ; TPLTG_TAG
                                                 ; Target identifier
LAN_TARGET_END   LABEL  BYTE
```

This tuple is easy to recognize due to the characters "CIS" in the data. After this tuple, the function-specific CIS is written as a single-function CIS.

An example Multi-Function CIS is included with the sample code.

CardBus CIS differences

In CardBus PC Cards, the CIS is pointed to by the **CIS Pointer** in the function's configuration space header. There is a separate configuration space and CIS for each function on a CardBus PC Card. Each CIS must start with a Link Target tuple (13H) aligned on a 4-word boundary. This tuple is shown in the previous section on Multi-Function PC Cards. The CIS may reside in the following card spaces:

1. Configuration space
2. Memory space
3. Expansion ROM

There are CardBus specific tuples that should only be found in a CardBus PC Card. An example CardBus CIS for a LAN PC Card is included with the sample code.

Parsing the CIS: A Sample Client Driver

A client parses the CIS of a PC Card using card services client utility **GetFirstTuple, GetNextTuple** and **GetTupleData** functions. The two functions are used in conjunction with each other to find and retrieve the contents of a particular tuple.

The **GetFirstTuple** function returns the first tuple of a specified type from the CIS of the card in the specified socket. The function call has the following format:

*result = CardServices(***GetFirstTuple**, *NULL, NULL, ArgLength, ArgPointer);*

The *ArgPointer* is set to point to an argument buffer of this format:

```
#define  GFT_LINK_TUPLES    0x01
typedef struct _GETTUPLE
{
   USHORT      Socket;           // Socket # of PC Card CIS to parse
   USHORT      Attributes;       // Bit Mapped; when Bit 0 is set,
                                 // return link tuples
   UCHAR       DesiredTuple;     // Value of Tuple to match while
                                 // parsing the CIS
   UCHAR       TupleOffset;
   USHORT      Flags;            // CS Tuple Flags data (USED BY CS)
   ULONG       LinkOffset;       // CS Link State Info (USED BY CS)
   ULONG       CISOffset;        // CS CIS State Info (USED BY CS)
        union {
          struct {
        UCHAR TupleCode;         // Tuple that was found (RETURNED BY CS)
        UCHAR TupleLink;         // Link Value for Tuple Found (RETURNED
                                 // BY CS)
        } GetFirstNextTuple;
          struct {
        USHORT      TupleDataMax;
        USHORT      TupleDataLen;
        UCHAR       TupleData[1];
        } GetTupleData;
    } s;
}  GETTUPLE;
typedef GETTUPLE near   *NPGETTUPLE;
typedef GETTUPLE far    *FPGETTUPLE;
```

Figure 4-11: Argument Control Block for GetFirstTuple

The **GetTupleData** function returns the content of the last tuple returned by either the **GetFirstTuple** or the **GetNextTuple** functions. The function call has the following format:

result = CardServices(**GetTupleData**, NULL, NULL, ArgLength, ArgPointer);

The ArgPointer is set to point to the argument buffer shown in Figure 4-11. To demonstrate how a client driver accesses the CIS using these two function, the following approach has been taken. The CARD_INSERTION case of the callback routine has been modified to call a routine to handle this event. The CardInsertion routine locates the first tuple by issuing the **GetFirstTuple** call. If a tuple is found, the data from that tuple is retrieved via the **GetTupleData** call. Finally, the data retrieved from that tuple is compared to the string of the PC Card that this client driver is designed to support.

```
int NP _loadds Callback (USHORT Event,USHORT Socket,USHORT Info,
                         USHORT ClientData1, USHORT ClientData2,
                         USHORT ClientData3,
                         FARPOINTER MTDRequest, FARPOINTER Buffer)
{
switch(Event) {
        case REGISTRATION_COMPLETE:
                wRegistered = TRUE;
                return SUCCESS;         // Return SUCCESS to CS
        case CARD_INSERTION:
                CardInsertion(Socket); // Card insertion processing routine
                return SUCCESS;
        default:
                return SUCCESS;
    }
}

int CardInsertion(USHORT Socket)
{
        fpgt = (FPGETTUPLE) CSBuffer; // fpgt declared in main
        fpgt->Socket = Socket;
        fpgt-> Attributes = 0x0000;
        fpgt->DesiredTuple = 0x15;     // Find first tuple
        fpgt->TupleOffset = 0;
        if (CardServices(GET_FIRST_TUPLE,0,0,18,fpgt,0))
        {

        if(CardServices(GET_TUPLE_DATA,0,0,sizeof(CSBuffer),fpgt,0))
                if (correct_card_id(UCHAR far *) fpgt->TupleData))
                                        // See if card is supported
                        return(TRUE);
        }
        return(FALSE);
}

#define CARD_ID_LEN 11
static UCHAR pcCard_id[CARD_ID_LEN] = {0x49, 0x42, 0x4d, 0x00, 0x50, 0x43,
0x00, 0x43, 0x41, 0x52, 0x44};
BOOL correct_card_id(UCHAR far *dataP)
{
        USHORT i;
        for (i = 0; i <= CARD_ID_LEN; i++) {
                if (*(dataP + i) != pcCard_id[i])
                break;
     }
        if (i == CARD_ID_LEN)  return(TRUE);
        return(FALSE);
}
```

Figure 4-12: Callback Handler invoking a subroutine to parse the CIS

Accessing PC Card Address Space

The PC Card adapter plays an important role in accessing these three (I/O, common, and attribute) regions by providing memory or I/O windows through which these address spaces can be mapped into host system memory. To access any of the three address spaces, the PC card must be configured to either memory or I/O mode. When the PC Card is set to I/O mode any three of the regions can be simultaneously mapped into host system memory. However, when the PC Card is configured for memory mode, only attribute and common memory may be accessed.

Mapping PC Card Memory to System Memory

A client accesses PC Card memory through the card services resource management functions **RequestWindow** and **MapMemPage**. The **RequestWindow** function obtains a window of system memory and the **MapMemPage** maps the card memory to the system memory. The **RequestWindow** call has the following format:

result = CardServices(**RequestWindow**, ClientHandle, NULL, ArgLength, ArgPointer);

The ArgPointer is set to point to an argument control block whose format is shown in Figure 4-13.

```
typedef         struct _REQUESTWINDOW
{
        USHORT Socket;          // Socket # where card is present
        USHORT Attributes;      // Bit-Mapped: PC Card memory attributes
        USHORT Base;            // Physical location in system address space
                                // to map card memory. If set to zero CS
                                // uses available space and returns address
        USHORT Size;            // Memory Window Size in Bytes
        UCHAR  AccessSpeed;     // Bit Mapped: Window Speed Field
} REQUESTWINDOW;
typedef REQUESTWINDOW near     *NPREQUESTWINDOW;
typedef REQUESTWINDOW far      *FPREQUESTWINDOW;
```

Figure 4-13: RequestWindow Argument Control Block

The Attributes and the AccessSpeed fields of this control block are bit mapped. Figure 4-14 shows a sample C-language declarations for these fields.

```
    // RequestWindow Attribute Field Mask
#define RW_ATTR_COMMON_MEMORY          0x0000
#define RW_ATTR_ATTRIB_MEMORY          0x0002
#define RW_ATTR_ENABLED                0x0004
#define RW_ATTR_8_BIT                  0x0000
#define RW_ATTR_16_BIT                 0x0008
#define RW_ATTR_PAGED                  0x0020
#define RW_ATTR_FIRST_SHARED           0x0040
#define RW_ATTR_WINDOW_SIZED           0x0100

    // RequestWindow Access Speed Field Mask
#define RW_SPEED_USE_WAIT              0x80
#define RW_SPEED_250NS                 0x01
#define RW_SPEED_200NS                 0x02
#define RW_SPEED_150NS                 0x03
#define RW_SPEED_100NS                 0x04
#define RW_SPEED_EXPONENT_MASK         0x07
#define RW_SPEED_MANTISSA_MASK         0x78
```

Figure 4-14: RequestWindow Attribute Bit and Access Speed Field Declarations

Once a PC card is inserted into a socket and a client driver parses the CIS and determines that the card is one it supports, it will issue the **RequestWindow** and **MapMemPage** functions to access card memory. The **MapMemPage** function call has the following format:

result = CardServices(**MapMemPage**, WindowHandle, NULL, ArgLength, ArgPointer);

The ArgPointer is set to point to an argument control block whose format is shown in Figure 4-15, while Figure 4-16 shows how these functions can be coded.

```
typedef struct _MAPMEMPAGE
{
  // Absolute offset from start of PC Card to map into system memory
  ULONG         CardOffset;

  // Window page # that will be mapped into system address space
  UCHAR         Page;
} MAPMEMPAGE;

typedef MAPMEMPAGE     near    *NPMAPMEMPAGE;
typedef MAPMEMPAGE     far     *FPMAPMEMPAGE;
```

Figure 4-15: MapMemPage Argument Control Block

When a client is finished with the window, it should return this resource back to the system. This is done through another card services resource management function, **ReleaseWindow**.

```
#define 16K_WINDOW_SIZE        0x4000
#define RW_WINDOW_ZERO         0x00
ULONG lWindowBase, lWindowHandle;
WORD memory_handle;
FPMAPMEMPAGE           fpmmp;
FPREQUESTWINDOW        fprw;

int CS_RequestWindow (USHORT Socket)
{
  fprw = (FPREQUESTWINDOW) CSBuffer;
  fprw->Socket = Socket;
  fprw-> Attributes  =  RW_ATTR_8_BIT;
  fprw->Base = &lWindowBase;
  fprw->Size =  16K_WINDOW_SIZE;
  fprw->AccessSpeed =  RW_SPEED_150NS;
  memory_handle = ClientHandle;   return(CardServices(REQUESTWINDOW,
  &memory_handle,0,   sizeof(CSBuffer), fprw));
}

int CS_MapMemPage ()
{
  fpmmp = (FPMAPMEMPAGE) CSBuffer;
  fpmmp->CardOffset = 0x0000;
  fpmmp->Page = RW_WINDOW_ZERO;
  return(CardServices(MAPMEMPAGE, &lWindowHandle, 0, sizeof(CSBuffer),
  fpmmp));
}
```

Figure 4-16: RequestWindow and MapMemPage

Decoding I/O Address Space

To facilitate memory and I/O address windowing, the adapter has mapping registers (A0 through A25) that allow for partial or complete address decoding. A PC Card that supports only partial or independent address decoding, relies on the adapter to decode a portion of the address lines. Conversely, a PC Card that performs complete or overlapped address decoding performs the entire mapping or decoding function itself. By decoding only the lower portions of the address, partial decoding provides for a more flexible address mapping technique, because the system can map the card into any available I/O address space. This helps to eliminate potential conflicts with other cards that require specific address regions.

For example, a PC card supporting partial decoding needs only four lines (A0 through A3) to distinguish between its sixteen registers. Similarly another card containing eight registers needs to decode only three address lines (A0 through A2) to distinguish between these eight registers. The remaining address lines must be programmed into the adapter to complete the twenty-six bit address.

As previously mentioned, PC Cards that support I/O functions contain a card configuration table within the CIS. Registers within this table are used to indicate the windowing method the card is capable of performing. To configure the card for a particular mode, the CCR is initialized with an index that corresponds to the desired windowing method.

Obtaining System IRQs

The last system resource a client may require is an interrupt request line, or IRQ. An IRQ is requested through the card services ***RequestIRQ*** resource management function. The **RequestIRQ** function call has the following format:

*result = CardServices(***RequestIRQ***, ClientHandle, ISRAddress/NULL, ArgLength, ArgPointer);*

The ArgPointer is set to point to an argument control block whose format is shown in Figure 4-17.

```
typedef struct _REQUESTIRQ
{
   USHORT       Socket;         // Logical socket # where card is present
   USHORT       Attributes;     // Bit-Mapped: details about the type of
                                // IRQ desired
   UCHAR        AssignedIRQ;    // OUTPUT: IRQ Number assigned by CS
   UCHAR        IRQInfo1;       // Bit-Mapped: First PCMCIA IRQ Byte
   USHORT       IRQInfo2;       // Bit-Mapped: Optional PCMCIA IRQ bytes
}  REQUESTIRQ;
typedef REQUESTIRQ near   *NPREQUESTIRQ;
typedef REQUESTIRQ far    *FPREQUESTIRQ;
```

Figure 4-17: RequestIRQ Argument Control Block

The Attributes field is a bit-mapped field which details specifics about the type of IRQ the client desires.

```
//    RequestIRQ
#define  RIRQ_ATTR_EXCLUSIVE       0x0000
#define  RIRQ_ATTR_MULTI_SHARE     0x0001
#define  RIRQ_ATTR_DYNAMIC_SHARE   0x0002
#define  RIRQ_ATTR_FORCE_PULSE     0x0004
#define  RIRQ_ATTR_FIRST_SHARED    0x0008
#define  RIRQ_ATTR_ISRADDR_PROV    0x0010
#define  RIRQ_ATTR_PULSE_ALLOC     0x0100
```

Figure 4-18: RequestIRQ Attributes field Bit Map Declaration

The IRQInfo1 field is bit-mapped field that details the capabilities of the PC Card in the socket.

```
#define  RIRQ_INFO1_NMI            0x0001
#define  RIRQ_INFO1_IO_CHECK       0x0002
#define  RIRQ_INFO1_BUS_ERROR      0x0004
#define  RIRQ_INFO1_VENDOR_SPEC    0x0008
#define  RIRQ_INFO1_VALID_MASK     0x0010
#define  RIRQ_INFO1_LEVEL          0x0020
#define  RIRQ_INFO1_PULSE          0x0040
#define  RIRQ_INFO1_SHARE          0x0080
```

Figure 4-19: RequestIRQInfo1 Bit Mapped C Declarations

The following routine shows how an IRQ is acquired from CS.

```
FPREQUESTIRQ   fpirq;

int CS_RequstIRQ (USHORT irq_num)
{
    fprirq = (FPREQUESTIRQ) CSBuffer;
    fprirq->Socket =  Socket;
    fpirq->Attributes =  RIRQ_ATTR_DYNAMIC_SHARE;
    fpirq->IRQInfol = RIRQ_INFO1_LEVEL;
    fpirq->IRQInfo2 <<= irq_num ;
    return(CardServices(REQUESTIRQ, wClientHandle, 0,
        sizeof(CSBuffer), fprirq));
}
```

Figure 4-20: Client IRQ Request

Oftentimes a client requires a specific combination of I/O address space and IRQ such as a modem client driver that needs the PC modem card to appear as a standard COM device. It may first try to acquire both the address range of x'02F8' and the IRQ3 so that it would appear as a COM2 device. If it is unable to obtain both of these required elements, it may try the **RequestIRQ** and the **RequestIO** combination again to obtain the resources to appear as a COM3 device. However, it is important to note that if such a combination is required, the client driver must take care to release any resources it previously acquired.

For instance, if the modem client driver successfully obtained IRQ3 from the RequestIRQ call but failed to obtain the address range of x'02F8' during the **RequestIO** call, it should free IRQ3 via the **ReleaseIRQ** function before attempting to procure the resources for COM3.

Assigning System Resources to a PC Card

Once system resources, such as I/O address space and IRQs, have been successfully obtained from CS (via the **RequestIO** and **RequestIRQ** functions) the PC Card and the socket in which it resides must be configured. This is done via the CS resource management function **RequestConfiguration.** The function should be thought of as a "request to set the configuration" because its purpose is to configure the PC Card and the socket. Additionally, if power is not active to the socket, this function will apply it. The **RequestConfiguration** function call has the following format:

*result = CardServices(***RequestConfiguration***, ClientHandle, NULL, ArgLength, ArgPointer);*

The ArgPointer is set to point to an argument control block whose format is shown in Figure 4-21.

```
typedef struct _REQUESTCONFIGURATION
{
   USHORT  Socket;      // Logical Socket # where PC Card resides
   USHORT  Attributes; // Bit-Mapped: Only setting is to Enable IRQ
                        // Steering
                        // Power settings, in tenths of volts
   UCHAR   Vcc;         // Vcc Setting
   UCHAR   Vpp1;        // Vpp1 Setting
   UCHAR   Vpp2;        // Vpp2 Setting
   UCHAR   IntType;     // Memory or Memory and I/O interface
   ULONG   ConfigBase; // Card Base Address of Config Registers
                        // Register initialization settings,
                        // (if present)
   UCHAR   Status;      // Card Status Register
   UCHAR   Pin;         // Card Pin Register
   UCHAR   Copy;        // Card Socket/Copy Reg
   UCHAR   Option;      // Card Option Reg(COR)
   UCHAR   Present;     // Card Cfg Option Reg(CCOR)
}  REQUESTCONFIGURATION;
typedef REQUESTCONFIGURATION near   *NPREQUESTCONFIGURATION;
typedef REQUESTCONFIGURATION far    *FPREQUESTCONFIGURATION;
```

Figure 4-21: RequestConfiguration Argument Control Block Structure

```
//  Miscellaneous RequestConfiguration Declarations
#define  RC_ENABLE_IRQ_STEERING 0x02  // Attributes field
       // Masks to determine if specific registers are present
#define  RC_OPTION_REG          0x01  // option reg
#define  RC_STATUS_REG          0x02  // status reg
#define  RC_PIN_REG             0x04  // Pin reg present
#define  RC_COPY_REG            0x08  // Copy reg present
       // Socket interface setting; either memory or memory/IO
#define  RC_INTERFACE_MEMORY    0x01  // memory only
#define  RC_INTERFACE_MEMORY_IO 0x02  // memory and I/O
#define  RC_FIVE_VOLTS            50  // 5.0 volts x  0.1 = 50
#define  RC_NO_VOLTS              0
#define  RC_ZERO_REG            0x00  // Clear out register
```

Figure 4-22: RequestConfiguration Field Declarations

Figure 4-23 is an example of how the **RequestConfiguration** function could be coded for a modem client driver.

```
        // Base addr of Cfg regs in attribute memory
#define RC_CONFIG_BASE          0x100
        // Enable Ring indicate & Audio on Modem
#define RC_ENABLE_AUDIO_AND_RING_IND 0x18
        // Tuple - Configuration Index Default
#define RC_TPCE_INDX            0x21

FPREQUESTCONFIGURATION fprc;
int CS_RequstConfiguration ( )
{
  fprc = (FPREQUESTCONFIGURATION) CSBuffer;
  fprc->Socket =  Socket;
  fprc->Attributes =  RC_ENABLE_IRQ_STEERING;
  fprc->Vcc = RC_FIVE_VOLTS;
  fprc->Vpp1 =  RC_NO_VOLTS;
  fprc->Vpp2 =  RC_NO_VOLTS;
  fprc-> IntType = RC_INTERFACE_MEMORY_IO;
  fprc->ConfigBase = (ULONG) RC_CONFIG_BASE;
  fprc->Status = RC_ENABLE_AUDIO_AND_RING_IND;
  fprc->Pin = RC_ZERO_REG;
  fprc->Copy = RC_ZERO_REG;
  fprc->Option =  RC_TPCE_INDX;         // COM2 setting
                                        // Both option & status reg present
  fprc->Present = RC_OPTION_REG | RC_STATUS_REG;

  // If the first call fails with a BAD_VPP result, set Vpp1 and
  // Vpp2 to 5 volts. The standard requires 5 volt support

  result = CardServices(REQUESTCONFIGURATION, wClientHandle,
                        0,sizeof(CSBuffer), fprc);
  if (result == BAD_VPP)
  {
     fprc->Vpp1 =  RC_FIVE_VOLTS;
     fprc->Vpp2 =  RC_FIVE_VOLTS;
     result = CardServices(REQUESTCONFIGURATION, wClientHandle,
                           0,sizeof(CSBuffer), fprc);
  }
  return(result);
 }
```

Figure 4-23: Modem Client RequestConfiguration

As always, the calling routine would be responsible for checking the return code. If the **RequestConfiguration** failed, the IRQ and I/O address resources that were acquired should be freed. If the request was successful, when the client is finished with the socket (for instance, the card was ejected) the socket configuration should be released. The **ReleaseConfiguration** call returns the socket to the default configuration.

Management of System Resources: The Chain Reaction

The management of system resources begins when power is applied to the system and a map of available system IRQs, I/O, and emory address space is created. Once the map is created, card services is responsible for maintaining it. It does this through the set of resource management functions: **RequestIO, ReleaseIO, RequestIQ, ReleaseIRQ, RequestWindow, ReleaseWindow, ModifyWindow, MapMemPage, RequestSocketMask, ReleaseSocketMask, RequestConfiguration, ReleaseConfiguration**, **GetConfigurationInfo, ModifyConfiguration**, and **ReleaseConfiguration**.

When a client driver issues a request for a resource, using one of the resource management functions, card services consults the map to determine if the resource is available. If it is, the request is granted and the map is updated.

For instance, when a modem card is inserted into socket one of the system, the client driver begins its quest to obtain the resources necessary to support the modem: an IRQ and I/O address space. Most modem client drivers today attempt to acquire resources generally associated with a standard COM port. The reason for acquiring these specific resources is to maintain compatibility with existing communication applications.

For example, to configure a modem as COM2 the client driver needs to acquire both IRQ3 and the I/O address range of x'02F8'. As a result, it may first request exclusive of IRQ3 using the RequestIRQ function. Card Services examines the request and refers to the resource map. There it discovers that IRQ3 is already in use. As a result, the request is rejected and card services returns IN_USE as the reason for rejecting the request.

The modem client driver evaluates the result and determines IRQ3 is unavailable, so it may try to acquire the resources associated with COM3. It reissues the **RequestIRQ**, this time attempting to obtain IRQ4. Card services receives the request, refers to the resource map and determines that IRQ4 is available. It marks the IRQ4 in use and returns SUCCESS as a result.

Having acquired a suitable IRQ, the modem client driver then issues a **RequestIO** command to obtain an I/O address space of x'03E8' corresponding to COM2. Card services receives the request, refers to the resource map, and determines that x'03E8' is available. It marks the space in use and returns SUCCESS as a result. Having successfully obtained an IRQ and an I/O address for the modem, the client driver issues a **RequestConfiguration** to initialize socket one.

Similarly, when a client driver issues a request to release a resource it previously was granted, card services updates the map to reflect the return of the resource to the pool. For instance, when the modem card is ejected from the system, the modem client driver should issue a **ReleaseIRQ**, a **ReleaseIO**, and a **ReleaseConfiguration** command. Once these commands have completed successfully, the resource map appears as it did at system IPL time.

Summary

Card and socket services isolate a client driver from many of the low-level details of how things are actually carried out on a PC Card system. However, it cannot be shielded from everything. The very nature of a PC Card device is a new idea for many programs. The notion that the PC Card may not be present at power-up time or, if it is currently present, that it may suddenly disappear at any time, has impacts to the core of most program designs. Additionally, PC Cards may be assigned any available system resource — not just architected settings that complicate other system expansion designs. As a result of this flexibility, it is important to understand the interaction between PC Card devices and system resources.

Chapter 5: DOS/ Windows 3.1

DOS

Beginning with IBM PC DOS 6.1, PC Card support in the form of CS, SS, and a SCD is included in the base package. Phoenix Technologies supplies the Card and Socket services as well as other PC Card support software for PC DOS. This includes software for the support of RAM cards, Flash cards, and ATA disk drives. Microsoft did not provide this software with MS-DOS. OEM vendors of computers added Card and Socket services and other PC Card support software with their products when shipping MS-DOS. Phoenix Technologies and SystemSoft are two of the largest vendors of this software. As other PC Cards have been developed, e.g. Multi-function and CardBus PC Cards, the software has been upgraded to support them.

Microsoft Windows

Under Windows 3.1, DOS card and socket services and client drivers that load during CONFIG.SYS still communicate through the INT 1Ah interface, while callback handlers still communicate through the far call/return interface. Unfortunately Windows 3.1 native application programs cannot communicate with card services this way. Card services runs in the Virtual 86 (V86) mode, while Windows 3.1 application programs run in protected mode. Any card services calls requiring addresses need them to be in the SEGMENT:OFFSET format, while a Windows 3.1 application can only pass address in the SELECTOR:OFFSET format. To solve this, Windows 3.1 programs must use the *DOS Protect Mode Interface (DPMI)* to communicate between protected mode and V86 mode.

Certain rules must be followed for Windows 3.1 programs to properly request services from card services. They are:

1. Card services request packets must reside below the 1M address. To ensure this, a Windows client should allocate a memory region big enough to satisfy all its card services requests with the Windows function GlobalDosAlloc. As a guideline, examine all the CS requests the Windows client driver will issue and allocate a memory region large enough to contain the biggest request The PC Card Standard Card Services Specification documents the required size for the requests. Typically, the tuple processing requests require the largest amount of

space because they can describe varying degrees of information about a PC Card. The GlobalDosAlloc function allocates global memory within the first megabyte and returns a selector value that can be used in protected mode and a segment value that can be used in real mode. The Windows program would use the protected mode SELECTOR:OFFSET to fill in the request packet and would use the real mode SEGMENT:OFFSET in the call to card services.

2.Windows client programs must use the DPMI function *Simulate Real Mode Interrupt* (INT 31h, Function=0300h) to call card services through INT 1Ah. DPMI will transfer control to the address specified by the real mode interrupt vector. This is the only way to call card services from a Windows 3.1 program.

3.The callback handler must reside below the 1M address. The callback handler address sent to card services in the **RegisterClient** request must be a real mode address, so the DPMI function *Allocate Real Mode Callback Address* (INT 31h, Function=0303h) is used to acquire a real mode SEGMENT:OFFSET for the callback handler. This address is passed to card services so that the real mode card services can call procedures within the protected mode program.

If these three rules are followed, a Windows 3.1 protected mode program can be a card services client. Typically the callback handler would simply post a user defined message to the Windows 3.1 event queue. The Windows 3.1 main loop then processes the event in any manner it wishes.

DOS Client driver template

The DOS client driver template that is supplied with this book illustrates the basic principles of how to communicate with card services in an IBM PC DOS or MS-DOS environment. The template provided here illustrates the steps required to support a typical Ethernet I/O PC Card. This client uses card services to acquire the resources necessary for the card. It illustrates how to acquire I/O ports, memory resources, and an IRQ (Interrupt) level. It does not contain the code specific to transferring data or handling interrupts that a full-fledged Ethernet client driver requires.

With some minor modification, this client driver can easily be adapted to other PC Cards. Once the client driver is loaded and an IBM Ethernet PC Card is inserted into a Type II PC Card socket, the code will configure the card for operation. The client driver verifies the card and requests the necessary I/O ports, Interrupt Level, and Memory that this card needs to operate. It will also release the resources to card services when the card is removed from the socket. To use this template without purchasing an IBM PCMCIA Ethernet card simply comment out the card verification section and any PC Card will trigger the process.

Normally this code would be included as part of a full client driver for a device. This is a stand-alone program that illustrates how to detect card services, register with card services, and handle events from card services. It is written in C and in Intel 80X86 assembly language. This template was developed using the Borland C++ version 3.1 compiler and the Turbo Assembler version 3.0.

As an added feature, this template can be executed either as a device driver or a terminate-stay-resident (TSR) program. The assembly-language portion of the enabler provides the two interfaces to DOS. The C-language portion of the client makes the client easier to understand and update as needed. A device driver is typically loaded at CONFIG.SYS processing time. A TSR program is loaded during or after AUTOEXEC.BAT processing.

Device Driver Entry Point

A DOS device driver has a device header that begins at offset zero in the driver. This device header is used by DOS to link all device drivers into a singly linked list of device drivers. This singly linked list can be traversed to determine what drivers are in the system. The device header is illustrated in Figure 5-1.

```
;------ Device Header -----------------------------------------------------
header  dd      -1                      ; device link pointer
        dw      8000h                   ; device attribute, character
device
        dw      strategy                ; strategy entry pointer
        dw      intentry                ; interrupt entry pointer
        db      'CSCLIENT'              ; device name
;--------------------------------------------------------------------------
```

Figure 5-1: DOS Device Header Data Structure

The device header consists of five parts: the device link pointer, attribute word, a near pointer to the strategy routine, a near pointer to the interrupt routine, and the device name/unit field.

The device link pointer is a field that contains a far pointer address to the device header of the next device driver. The far pointer address is set by DOS at the time the device driver is loaded. This field should be initially set to a negative one (-1).

The attribute word identifies the device to DOS. It is a bit-mapped field that describes the characteristics of the driver. For this client, it is indicated that this driver is for a character device.

The near pointer to the strategy routine contains the address of the device driver's strategy routine. This is the routine that DOS calls first during initialization. The strategy routine does not process the request from DOS; rather it saves a pointer to the request packet. This address is passed in the ES:BX register pair. The strategy routine is shown in Figure 5-2.

```
;*---------------------------------------------------------------------*
;*   strategy    : proc                                                  *
;*                                                                       *
;*       Device driver's device strategy request process routine.      *
;*       DOS passes address of device request header in ES:BX. We store *
;*       its address here.                                               *
;*---------------------------------------------------------------------*
strategy  proc   far
        push    ds
        push    ax
        mov     ax,DGROUP
        mov     DS,ax
        mov     word ptr ds:ptrsave,bx          ; save segment and offset
        mov     word ptr ds:ptrsave+2,es        ; of request header
        pop     ax
        pop     ds
        ret
strategy  endp
;*------ end of proc ---------------------------------------------------*
```

Figure 5-2: DOS Device Driver Strategy Source Code

The near pointer to the interrupt routine contains the address of the device driver's interrupt routine. The interrupt routine's function is to perform the operation described by the request packet from DOS. The request packet that is processed by this client device driver is the initialization request packet. This request packet is received by device drivers when DOS is processing the CONFIG.SYS file.

The interrupt routine must save all of the registers on entry and restore all of the registers on exit. This client requires more stack space for the C code, so it changes from using the DOS stack to its own. This interrupt routine checks to be sure the request from DOS is an initialization request and if so, pushes a pointer to the command line parameters before calling the client initialization code (_client_init). The client initialization code is written in C. This is the point where the C-based routine gains control. The interrupt routine is shown in Figure 5-3.

```
;*---------------------------------------------------------------------*
; *   intentry    : proc - the entry point of the device interrupt      *
;*                                                                       *
;*  When DOS processes config.sys,DOS alls here with the initialize     *
;*  command following the strategy call. The functions performed here:  *
;*    - verify it is an initialization request. If not, return an error *
;*    - call client's main process routine                               *
;*    - set return code and parameters to exit and return to DOS         *
;*---------------------------------------------------------------------*
intentry  proc   far
        ;save all flags and registers
        pushf
        irp     reg,<ax,bx,cx,dx,si,di,bp,ds,es>
        push    reg
        endm
```

```
        mov     ax,DGROUP               ; set up DS
        mov     DS,ax
        ASSUME  DS: DGROUP
        cli
        mov     dd_spsave,sp            ; replace DOS stack with our
        mov     dd_sssave,ss            ; stack and save DOS stack
        mov     ax,STACK                ;
        mov     SS,ax
        ASSUME  SS: STACK
        mov     sp,offset stackend
        mov     spsave, sp              ; save our stack
        mov     sssave, ss
        sti
        les     bx,ptrsave              ; es:bx points req header struct
        xor     ax,ax                   ; verify request is init request
        mov     al,es:[bx]._cmd         ; get command code
        cmp     al,init_request         ; init request ?
        je      intentry1               ; yes, jump
        mov     al,3                    ; error = invalid command received
        jmp     short errexit

intentry1:
        push    es:[bx]._cmd_seg        ; segment of input parameters
        push    es:[bx]._cmd_off        ; offset of input parameters
        call    _client_init            ; CALL client's main
initialization
        add     sp,4                    ; adjust stack pointer

        ; set request header to be returned to DOS -- If any error code
        ; is returned from initial proc this dd need not stay resident
        ; so specify the starting addr of this driver as the terminate
        ; point the last address of TSR) here.

        les     bx,ptrsave                ; es:bx points req header struct
        and     ax,ax                     ; check return code from
_client_init
        jnz     dont_stay                 ; if error, jmp
        mov     word ptr es:[bx._address],offset ds:[_end_data] ;terminate
        mov     word ptr es:[bx._address+2],ds
        jmp     exitentry
dont_stay:
        mov     word ptr es:[bx._address],0             ; terminate point
        mov     word ptr es:[bx._address+2],cs
exitentry:
        mov     byte ptr es:[bx._unit],0                ; no drive
        xor     al,al
        mov     ah,01h                  ; set done bit
        jmp     short exit1
errexit:
        mov     ah,81h                  ; set error bit and done bit
exit1:  mov     es:[bx]._status,ax      ; set RC in request header
                                        ; restore all flags and registers
        cli
        mov     ax,dd_sssave
        mov     ss,ax
        mov     sp,dd_spsave
        irp     reg,<es,ds,bp,di,si,dx,cx,bx,ax>
        pop     reg
        endm
        popf
        ret
intentry  endp
```

```
;*------ end of proc --------------------------------------------------*
```

Figure 5-3: DOS Device Driver Interrupt Service Routine Entry Point

For a character mode device driver, the device name/unit field contains the name of the driver. This client uses the name CSCLIENT. If this device driver was for a block mode device like a disk drive, an integer value would reside in this field.

After returning from the C-based routines, the device driver is terminated. Whether the device driver remains in memory after initialization depends upon the return code from the client initialization C-based code. The return code is stored in the AX register from the call to _client_init. If the AX register contains zero, the client has initialized correctly and the device driver should remain in memory. If a nonzero return code is returned in the AX register, an error has occurred and there is no need for the driver to remain in memory.

The initialization request packet has fields that must be filled in when control is returned to DOS. These fields are used by DOS to determine how much, if any, of the device driver should remain in memory. If the client driver initialized correctly, the client should remain in memory. The address of the end of the device driver is placed in the request packet, which is denoted by the address of the _end_data variable. In the event that a nonzero return code has occurred, the initialization request packet is set to notify the system that it does not need to stay in memory. The ending address of the resident program code is set to [CS:0] and the number-of-units field is set to zero. Upon exiting the interrupt routine, DOS reuses the memory previously allocated to this driver.

Terminate-Stay-Resident (TSR) Entry Point

Unlike a device driver, a TSR program terminate stay resident (TSR) is executed from the DOS command (or via the AUTOEXEC.BAT file) instead of through the CONFIG.SYS file. However, like a device driver a TSR remains in memory after its execution. When this client driver is executed, it remains in memory to handle card services events providing card services exists in the system and the client could register with card services successfully. Its entry point (_entry) is specified after the END directive in the ENTRY.ASM file. This is the location that DOS passes control to when the program is executed. The DS register is set to the DGROUP segment of the client. This provides addressability to variables in the program. The current stack pointer [SS:SP] is saved for later reference.

When DOS loads the program into memory, it determines the lowest available address and assigns it to the program. This area of memory is referred to as the *program segment*. At offset zero within the program segment, DOS builds a *program segment prefix* control block. This control block contains various information concerning the program and its environment. At offset 81H in the program segment prefix, the command line parameters for the client are placed. A pointer to these parameters is placed in the ES:BX register pair and is pushed onto the stack. The client initialization code (_client_init) is now called. This is the entry point into the C-based code.

```
;*-------------------------------------------------------------------*
;*  _entry      : proc                                               *
;*                                                                   *
;*      Here is a entry point when called from the DOS command prompt.  *
;*      In this proc, performed functions are                        *
;*      - set up DS                                                  *
;*      - call client's main process routine                        *
;*      - exit program                                               *
;*-------------------------------------------------------------------*
_entry  proc far
        mov     dx,DGROUP                   ; set up DS
        mov     DS,dx
        ASSUME  DS: DGROUP
        mov     sssave,ss                   ; save our SS
        mov     spsave,sp                   ; save our SP

        ;
        mov     psp,es                      ; save psp addr
        mov     bx,psp_parms                ; command parms offset of psp
        push    es                          ; es = psp addr
        push    bx                          ; command parameters offset
        call    _client_init                ; call client's main
initialization
        add     sp,4                        ; adjust stack pointer
        ;
        and     ax,ax                       ; check return code
        jnz     do_not_stay                 ; if error, jmp
        ;
        lea     ax,ds:[_end_data]           ; terminate point address
        add     ax,0fh
        mov     cl,4
        shr     ax,cl                       ; get stack size in paragraph
        mov     dx,ds
        add     dx,ax                       ; terminate address in para
        sub     dx,psp                      ; get program size in paragraph
        mov     ax,3100h                    ; keep program resident
        jmp     exitprog
do_not_stay:
        mov     ah,4ch
        mov     al,0                        ; return code
exitprog:
        int     21h
_entry  endp
;*------ end of proc ------------------------------------------------*
```

Figure 5-4: DOS Device Driver Entry Point

The return code from the client initialization is placed in the AX register. If the return code is zero (SUCCESS), the program should remain in memory. To remain in memory, the client must use DOS function 31H (Terminate Process and Remain Resident). With this function, the number of paragraphs (16-byte pieces) of memory that should remain in memory is loaded into the DX register. The function code (3100h) is loaded into the AX register and the call to DOS is made. If a nonzero return code is returned in AX, an error has occurred and there is no need to set aside memory for the client. In this case, the AH register is set to 4CH. The INT 21H call is made to DOS and the program is exited without any memory set aside.

The primary difference between a card services client driver and a standard device driver is the fact that the client driver must have callback processing code and this code must remain in memory after the driver has undergone initialization.

To maintain maximum flexibility in a DOS PC Card client driver, it is a good idea to allow two different code paths for the driver during initialization. One path utilizes card and socket services to configure the PC Card. The other path is used in the event that a point enabler or super client driver is used to configure the card. Using a point enabler is not the most desirable method of configuring a card, but in the DOS environment, memory resources are always at a premium. If the user does not plan to remove or swap cards while using his machine, it is sometimes a necessary option.

With the advent of super client drivers, a PC Card may already be enabled by a super client driver before the driver has even executed. There are several options that can be taken to handle this situation. The super client driver may enable the card and the driver executes with the assumption that the card is already enabled. In this case, the client driver should not register with card services.

If it is desired that the client driver should enable the card, support in the super client driver can be disabled for the card. Most super client drivers have configuration tables that indicate what PC Cards they support. Simply remove references to the target PC Card from a table and the card should not be recognized and enabled by the super client driver.

Alternately, the client driver can be designed to use **RequestExclusive** processing. RequestExclusive support in a client driver is a more complicated way of insuring that the client driver will configure the card even with the presence of a super client driver. For the purposes of this template, assume that a super client driver or point enabler have not been executed and it is desired that card services is to configure the PC Card. **RequestExclusive** processing will discussed in later in this chapter.

Communication with card services is via parameters in the registers of the microprocessor and in an argument or request packet. The register definition and other host specific environment programming issues are called the *processor bindings*. The host environment is defined by the operating system and the architecture (example: Intel 80386) of the host platform. The bindings tell a programmer how to detect the presence of card services, issue requests and pass arguments to card services, how the binding-specific arguments and services are defined (example: Intel register usage under DOS), and how arguments are passed to and from the callback handler. The PC Card Standard Card Services Specification defines the processor bindings; for a DOS real-mode application the bindings are defined as follows:

[AL] = Function
[DX] = Handle
[DI]:[SI] = Pointer, [DI] is 16 bit segment, [SI] is 16 bit offset
[CX] = ArgLength
[ES]:[BX] = ArgPointer, [ES] is 16 bit segment, [BX] is 16 bit offset
[AX] = Status
[CF] = reset to zero when request was successful, set to one when request fails

When a callback event occurs, the register definitions on entry to the callback handler are:

[AL] = Function (Event code)
[CX] = Socket
[DX] = Info
DI] = first word of **RegisterClient** argument packet ClientData field
DS] = second word of **RegisterClient** argument packet ClientData field
[SI] = third word of **RegisterClient** argument packet ClientData field
[SS]:[BP] = MTDRequest
[ES]:[BX] = Buffer
[BX] = Miscellaneous (when no buffer is specified)
[AX] = Status on return to card services
[CF] = reset to zero if the callback completes successfully, set to one if Status is not SUCCESS

The call to card services follows this syntax:

result = CardServices(Function, Handle, Pointer, ArgLength, ArgPointer);

In this template, functional notation is used to communicate with card services. The functional parameters are transferred to a special structure that represents the registers of the microprocessor. The contents of this structure are then transferred to the microprocessor registers and the card services call is made. This special structure is based upon the REGS union structure that is common in C programming for the PC, as shown in Figure 5-5.

```
typedef struct          /* word registers */
        {
          WORD ax;
          WORD bx;
          WORD cx;
          WORD dx;
          WORD si;
          WORD di;
          WORD es;
          WORD ds;
          WORD cflag;
        } WORDREGS;

typedef struct
        {
          WORD ax;
          WORD bx;
          WORD cx;
          WORD dx;
          WORD si;
          WORD di;
          WORD es;
          WORD ds;
          WORD flag;
        } CALLBACKREGS;

typedef struct                  /* byte registers */
        {
          BYTE al, ah;
          BYTE bl, bh;
          BYTE cl, ch;
          BYTE dl, dh;
        } BYTEREGS;

typedef union
        {
          WORDREGS x;
          CALLBACKREGS cb_x;
          BYTEREGS h;
        } REGS;
```

Figure 5-5: DOS Intel Register Data Structures

The primary difference between this REGS union structure and the standard one that comes defined in DOS.H is the addition of the DS and ES registers. These two registers are added to complete the register definitions necessary for a complete binding implementation. The DS and ES registers are necessary for far pointer definitions.

The functional notation parameters are transferred to the REGS union structure in the function call to card services, as shown in Figure 5-6.

```
/***************************************************************************
*  Function: CardServices
*
*
***************************************************************************/
int CardServices(WORD function,          /* function code              */
                 WORD handle,            /* handle argument            */
                 void far *pointer,      /* pointer to extra argument */
                 WORD arglength,         /* length of packet           */
                 void far *argpointer,   /* pointer to packet          */
                 WORD far *returnhandle) /* handle returned from CS    */

{
  /* This function does the actual call to CS       */
  /* The desired function number is placed in AH.  */
  /* For CS the function number is AFH.             */
  /*                                                */
  /* This is how the real mode DOS interface        */
  /* is coded.                                      */
  /*                                                */

  regs.h.ah = 0xAF;                    /* Card services function call  */
  regs.h.al = (BYTE) function;         /* function to be used          */
  regs.x.cx = arglength;               /* argument length              */
  regs.x.es = GET_SEG(argpointer);     /* segment of pointer           */
  regs.x.bx = GET_OFF(argpointer);     /* offset of pointer            */
  regs.x.dx = handle;                  /*                              */
  regs.x.di = GET_SEG(pointer);        /*                              */
  regs.x.si = GET_OFF(pointer);        /*                              */

  int1a(&regs);                        /* make the call                */

  if (regs.x.cflag)                    /* if carry flag is set, error  */
     regs.h.ah = function;             /* failed fnc code to high byte */
                                       /* low byte contains return code*/
  *returnhandle = regs.x.dx;           /* returned handle              */
  return(regs.x.ax);                   /* this is the status word      */
}
```

Figure 5-6: DOS Source Code to Interface to Card Services

After the REGS union structure is initialized, a call to function INT1A is performed. The INT1A is a function written in assembly language. This code transfers the contents of the REGS union structure to the microprocessor registers, makes the INT1A call to card services, and then returns the microprocessor registers to the REGS union structure. This function resides in the ENTRY.ASM file on the program diskette included with this book.

```
;*----------------------------------------------------------------------*
;* _int1a      : proc                                                     *
;*                                                                        *
;* This proc makes the actual card services call (INT 1AH).              *
;* Set the registers from the REGS                                        *
;* structure, and issues INT 1AH call. After INT 1AH call, store         *
;* returned registers values to the structure and pass it back           *
;* to the caller.                                                         *
;*                                                                        *
;*----------------------------------------------------------------------*
_int1a  proc    near
        mov     si,sp
        mov     bx,ss:[si+2]        ; get offset of regs
        mov     reg_addr,bx         ; save it
        ;
        mov     ax,ds:[bx].x_ax     ; set registers
        push    ds:[bx].x_bx        ; save regs.h.bx value
        mov     cx,ds:[bx].x_cx     ;
        mov     dx,ds:[bx].x_dx     ;
        mov     si,ds:[bx].x_si     ;
        mov     di,ds:[bx].x_di     ;
        mov     es,ds:[bx].x_es     ;
        pop     bx                  ; finally, set bx
        ;
        int     1ah                 ; Services Call
        ;
        push    ds                  ; Save returned DS
        push    bx                  ; Save returned BX
        mov     bx,DGROUP           ;
        mov     ds,bx               ; get our DS
        mov     bx,reg_addr         ; restore offset of regs
        mov     ds:[bx].x_ax,ax     ; get returned AX
        pop     ds:[bx].x_bx        ; get returned BX
        mov     ds:[bx].x_cx,cx     ; get returned CX
        mov     ds:[bx].x_dx,dx     ; get returned DX
        mov     ds:[bx].x_si,si     ; get returned SI
        mov     ds:[bx].x_di,di     ; get returned DI
        mov     ds:[bx].x_es,es     ; get returned ES
        pop     ds:[bx].x_ds        ; get returned DS
        pushf
        pop     ds:[bx].x_cf        ; get flag register
        and     ds:[bx].x_cf,0001h  ; mask other than CF

        ret
_int1a  endp
```

Figure 5-7: DOS INT 1Ah Interface Source Code

Now that the linkage between the C-based REGS union structure and the assembly language module that calls card services exists, the calls to card services from the C-language code can occur.

The **GetCardServicesInfo** is the first call to card services made in a client driver. To make this call, a pointer to the argument packet is established. In this client, the argument packet is a global array of 128 bytes. The declaration of the argument packet for **GetCardServicesInfo** is shown Figure 5-8. All of the argument packets for the different card services functions are defined in the PCMCIA.H file contained on the diskette included with this book.

```
typedef struct _GETCARDSERVICESINFO
{
   unsigned short      InfoLen;
   unsigned short      Signature;
   unsigned short      Count;
   unsigned short      Revision;
   unsigned short      CSLevel;
   unsigned short      VStrOff;
   unsigned short      VStrLen;
   unsigned char       VendorString[1];
}  GETCARDSERVICESINFO;
```

Figure 5-8: DOS GetCardServicesInfo Data Structure

In this particular argument packet, all of the fields except Signature are output fields. This means that card services fills them in during the call to card services. If a field is defined as an input field, the client driver is required to initialize the field before the call to card services. Here, the Signature field of this argument packet should be set to zero. The Signature field is the only field in this argument packet that is considered an input/output (I/O) field. All of the other fields are set by card services. Figure 5-9 shows how to make the **GetCardServicesInfo** request.

```
/*-----------------------------------------------------------*
 * GetCardServicesInfo Request                                *
 *   Query CardServices exist. If CardServices has not been   *
 *   installed, display the warning message and exit program. *
 *-----------------------------------------------------------*/
 fpgcsi = (FPGETCARDSERVICESINFO)ArgPacket;
 fpgcsi->Signature = 0;

 if (CardServices(GET_CARDSERVICES_INFO, 0, 0, sizeof(ArgPacket),
                  fpgcsi, &d_handle))
    {
      flCSPresent = FALSE;
      post_msg("card services is not loaded.\n\r$");
      alarm();
      return(ERROR);
    }
```

Figure 5-9: DOS GetCardServicesInfo Source Code

Card services is present if the carry flag is reset (zero) after the call to INT 1A and the Signature field of the argument packet has the ASCII letters CS. The code below shows how this can be done. The "C" and the "S" are transposed due to the definition of the Signature field. The Signature field in this client driver is defined as an unsigned short, which is two bytes (which are reversed in the Intel architecture). Figure 5-10 shows how to this field is interrogated.

```
if (fpgcsi->Signature != 'S'*256 + 'C')
    {
      flCSPresent = FALSE;
      post_msg("card services Signature is incorrect.\n\r$");
      alarm();
      return(ERROR);
    }
```

Figure 5-10: DOS Card Services Presence Detection Source Code

If card services is present, the version of card services that is being used should be checked as shown in Figure 5-11. There are different levels of card services and some are incompatible with each other. This client driver checks for version 2.00 or higher, the first version commercially available in the United States.

```
/* Check card services Level. It should be 2.00 or higher */

 if (fpgcsi->CSLevel < SUPPORTED_CSVERSION){
    post_msg("Invalid card services Version.\n\r$");
    return(ERROR);
 }
```

Figure 5-11:DOS Card Services Version Source Code

If all is in order, the next step for the client driver is to register with card services. It is through this card services call that the client indicates to card services the type (memory, MTD, or I/O) of client it is, which events it desires notification of, and the routine card services is to call in order to post these events (callback handler).

The first part of setting up this function is to obtain the value of the DS register for the callback handler. It is vital that the DS register value returned by card services in the callback handler arguments matches the DS register of the client driver, or the addressing of variables will be incorrect. This is accomplished by getting the address of a global variable, as shown Figure 5-12.

```
far_p = &flags;                /* get SEG:OFF address    */
```

Figure 5-12: DOS Source Code to Save the Location of the Data Segment

Next, a pointer to the argument packet data area is created.

```
fprc = (FPREGISTERCLIENT)ArgPacket;
```

Figure 5-13: DOS Source Code to Create an Argument Packet Pointer

Finally the remaining data required for the **RegisterClient** argument packet is initialized.

```
typedef         struct _CLIENTDATA
{
   unsigned short     ClientVal;
   unsigned short     ClientDS;
   unsigned short     ClientOff;
   unsigned short     Reserved;
}  CLIENTDATA;

typedef struct _REGISTERCLIENT
{
   unsigned short       Attributes;
   unsigned short       EventMask;
   CLIENTDATA           cd;
   unsigned short       Version;
} REGISTERCLIENT;
```

Figure 5-14: DOS RegisterClient Data Structure

The Attributes field of the argument packet is used to denote the client type. A client supports either a memory card, a memory technology driver, or an I/O card. Since the Ethernet card is an I/O card, the Attributes field is set accordingly. The client also indicates that it wants to be notified of card insertion events. Finally it denotes whether or note the card is shared or exclusively used.

```
fprc->Attributes = RC_ATTR_IO_CLIENT |
           RC_ATTR_CARD_INSERT_SHARED |
           RC_ATTR_CARD_INSERT_EXCL;
```

Figure 5-15: DOS Source Code to Set Client Attributes

The EventMask field of the argument packet is used to indicate that card services should notify the client regarding the occurrence of certain events. In this example the client indicates that it desires to be notified about three different events: changes in card detection (whether a card is inserted or ejected), ejection or insertion requests, as well as any changes in power management. Figure 5-16 shows how to initialize the EventMask field for notification of these events.

```
fprc->EventMask =  RC_EVENT_CD_CHANGE |
                   RC_EVENT_EJECTION_REQ |
                   RC_EVENT_INSERTION_REQ |
                   RC_EVENT_PM_CHANGE;
```

Figure 5-16: Dos Source Code to Set the Client EventMask

In many client drivers, the card detect changes event may be the only event monitored. In a more sophisticated client driver, the driver may actually need to know about additional events, such as a battery being low on an SRAM PC Card.

A change in a card detection event occurs only if the computer has a motorized socket that controls how the I/O card is inserted and ejected from the socket. The ejection request and insertion request events are not the same as card insertion and card removal events. By knowing about an insertion or ejection request, the client driver could prepare for the actual CARD_INSERTION or CARD_REMOVAL events that would follow an INSERTION_REQUEST or EJECTION_REQUEST. Power management events occur on systems that automatically turn off subsystems that are unused, such as the hard disk. This frequently occurs in battery operated portable computers. Typically on power-managed systems, PC Cards receive a CARD_REMOVAL event before the system shuts down, and a CARD_INSERTION event when power is restored. This notifies client drivers or applications of an impending loss of power, so that they may take any action required to support this.

The **RegisterClient** card services call allows for binding specific client data to be included in the argument packet. In this example, the value of the DS register is passed in the second field of the CD data structure, as shown Figure 5-17. This ensures that the DS register is correctly set for the client callback handler. This is important for the correct addressing of data of the client.

```
fprc->cd.ClientDS = GET_SEG(far_p);
fprc->cd.ClientOff = 0;
```

Figure 5-17: DOS Source Code to Retrieve the Data Segment

Once all these fields are set, the call to card services to register the client can occur, as shown in Figure 5-18. The address of the callback handler (cb_entry) is passed to card services. If the card services call returns successfully, a client handle is passed back to the client. This is the value the client driver passes to card services so card services knows which client is generating the request.

```
if (CardServices(REGISTER_CLIENT, 0, (void far *)cb_entry,
        sizeof(REGISTERCLIENT), fprc, &rcHandle)) {
return ERROR;
}

flCSPresent = TRUE;
```

Figure 5-18: DOS RegisterClient Call

As a result of this call, card services registers the client in its database of clients. When card services has completed the registration process, it calls the callback handler (cb_entry) with a REGISTRATION_COMPLETE event.

To keep track of the state of the driver, a bit-mapped variable called flags is used. The client driver uses this variable to keep track of whether it is registered, present, or configured. These are not mutually exclusive states. In the callback handler, the client driver uses the states to serialize specific events. Primarily, this is necessary for CARD_INSERTION events and a REGISTRATION_COMPLETE events because it is desirable for the REGISTRATION_COMPLETE event to be processed before CARD_INSERTION events are processed. This is because a CARD_INSERTION event can occur before a REGISTRATION_COMPLETE event. As a result, ti is possible for the callback handler to start requesting resources from card services before a REGISTRATION_COMPLETE event has occurred. This can cause errors because the client may not have received its client handle from card services before requesting resources. In such instances, this will cause the resource requesting calls to card services to fail with a BAD_HANDLE return code.

This sample client driver waits for a REGISTRATION_COMPLETE event to occur before leaving the initialization code. Placing a watchdog timer in this section of code would be a good idea in case the REGISTRATION_COMPLETE callback event did not occur correctly. The while loop below could be expanded to test for the REGISTERED flag bit and check a counter that is decremented every 100 milliseconds for up to 10 seconds. If the REGISTERED flag bit was never set and the counter reached zero, the client could exit initialization with an error. The current while loop would hang in an infinite loop if the REGISTRATION_COMPLETE event did not occur.

```
while (!(flags & REGISTERED));  /* wait here for event */
  return (SUCCESS);
```

Figure 5-19: Loop to Wait for REGISTRATION_COMPLETE Event

The callback handler code resides in the files CALLBACK.C and ENTRY.ASM files. These files are included on the diskette that accompanies this book. There are two parts to the callback handler in this client. The portion card services invokes is contained in the ENTRY.ASM file. It is called cb_entry and is written in Intel 80X86 assembly language. When called by card services, this code takes the registers of the microprocessor and places them in a REGS structure whose address is then passed to the C-language callback_handler code. This is shown in the code excerpt in Figure 5-20.

```
; save received registers
        pushf
        irp     reg,<bx,cx,dx,si,di,bp,ds,es>
        push    reg
        endm
        ; put registers' value into the struct
```

```
        mov     si,offset _cbxs         ;this is the overlay for regs;
        mov     ds:[si].cbx_ax,ax
        mov     ds:[si].cbx_bx,bx
        mov     ds:[si].cbx_cx,cx
        mov     ds:[si].cbx_dx,dx
        mov     ds:[si].cbx_di,di
        mov     ds:[si].cbx_es,es
        pushf
        pop     ds:[si].cbx_fl
        push    ds                      ; pointer to the data
        push    si                      ; structure to be passed

        call    _callback_handler       ; call back handler

        pop     si                      ; get addressability to cbxs
struct
        pop     ds                      ; take values back off of the
stack

        mov     ax, ds:[si].cbx_ax      ; get proper return value

        irp     reg,<es,ds,bp,di,si,dx,cx,bx>
        pop     reg
        endm
        popf
```

Figure 5-20: DOS ASM Callback Handler Interface to "C" Routine

The _cbxs structure is defined in the ENTRY.ASM file. After this structure has been filled with the microprocessor register values, the C-language callback_handler is called and the address of the _cbxs structure is passed to it. The microprocessor registers are saved on the stack so they can be returned to card services unchanged. The AX register is returned to card services with a status code that indicates the success or failure of the card services call.

Following is the C-language callback_handler code. The critical portion of it is a simple switch statement that processes the event code value passed in the AL register, as shown below. As previously indicated, this client driver monitors these events: CARD_INSERTION, CARD_REMOVAL, REGISTRATION_COMPLETE, and CLIENT_INFO. For this example, monitoring these four events is sufficient. However, depending upon the application, a client driver may need to support more events. For the events that this client driver is notified of but does not support, an UNSUPPORTED_FUNCTION return code is returned to card services. The functions that are supported set the return code from the card services calls.

```
/***********************************************************************
*  Function: callback_handler (Call Back Handler)                      *
***********************************************************************/
void callback_handler(REGS *regs)
{
  switch (regs->h.al) {
    case PM_RESUME:
            break;
```

```
    case CARD_INSERTION:
            logical_socket = regs->cb_x.cx;         // current socket
            CardInsertion();
            regs->cb_x.ax = Status;
            break;
    case PM_SUSPEND:
    case BATTERY_DEAD:
    case BATTERY_LOW:
    case CARD_LOCK:
    case CARD_READY:
            regs->cb_x.ax = UNSUPPORTED_FUNCTION;
            break;
    case CARD_REMOVAL:
            logical_socket = regs->cb_x.cx;         // current socket
            if (logical_socket == my_socket)CardRemoval();
            regs->cb_x.ax = Status;
            break;
    case CARD_RESET:
    case CARD_UNLOCK:
    case EJECTION_COMPLETE:
    case EJECTION_REQUEST:
    case ERASE_COMPLETE:
    case EXCLUSIVE_COMPLETE:
    case EXCLUSIVE_REQUEST:
    case INSERTION_COMPLETE:
    case INSERTION_RQUEST:
            regs->cb_x.ax = UNSUPPORTED_FUNCTION;
            break;
    case REGISTRATION_COMPLETE:
            flags |= REGISTERED;
            regs->cb_x.ax = SUCCESS;
            if (flags & CCAPRESENT){
               logical_socket = regs->cb_x.cx;  // current socket
               CardInsertion();
               regs->cb_x.ax = Status;
            }
            break;
    case RESET_COMPLETE:
    case RESET_PHYSICAL:
    case RESET_REQUEST:
    case MTD_REQUEST:
            regs->cb_x.ax = UNSUPPORTED_FUNCTION;
            break;
    case CLIENT_INFO:
            CopyClientInfo(MK_FP(regs->cb_x.es, regs->cb_x.bx));
            regs->cb_x.ax = SUCCESS;
            break;
    case TIMER_EXPIRED:
    case SS_UPDATED:
            regs->cb_x.ax = UNSUPPORTED_FUNCTION;
         break;
  } // end switch
}
```

Figure 5-21: DOS Callback Handler Source Code

Registration Complete

During the **RegisterClient** call, the REGISTRATION_COMPLETE event was briefly discussed. The REGISTRATION_COMPLETE event occurs as a result of card services completing the registration of the client. In this example, when the client driver receives a REGISTRATION_COMPLETE event, the callback handler merely toggles the REGISTERED bit in the flags variable. Once this bit is set and control is returned to the main code, the initialization portion of the client driver is exited.

Card Insertion

The client driver receives a CARD_INSERTION event whenever any PC Card is inserted into a socket after the client driver is loaded. It also receives a artificial CARD_INSERTION event if a card is already present in a socket when the driver is loaded. A client driver need not differentiate between these two insertion events. Once the client driver has received a CARD_INSERTION event, it knows that a PC Card is present and the client driver changes the state variable flags to denote this.

Next the client driver checks to see if this client is registered with card services. This is part of the serialization of REGISTRATION_COMPLETE and CARD_INSERTION events. If the flags variable indicates that registration is incomplete, the callback handler is exited at this point. If the client is registered, the client remembers which socket generated the CARD_INSERTION event. This value is passed in the CX register. The C-language CardInsertion function is then called, as shown in Figure 5-22.

```
case CARD_INSERTION:
     logical_socket = regs->cb_x.cx;          // current socket
     CardInsertion();
     regs->cb_x.ax = Status;
     break;
```

Figure 5-22: CARD_INSERTION Event Detection

The CardInsertion function has several tasks to perform. First it must verify that the CARD_INSERTION event received is for the PC Card this client supports before attempting to configure it. Card services calls a client for every CARD_INSERTION event that occurs. Because this client is registered for CARD_INSERTION events every time a card is inserted into any socket on the system, the CardInsertion routine is invoked. It is the responsibility of the client to positively identify the PC Card as one it supports. Otherwise, the client could end up gathering resources for the wrong card.

To positively identify a PC Card, information from the card must be verified. This data is stored in the tuples of the card information structure (CIS) of the card. While there are many different tuples in a PC Card, the Level 1 Version/ Product Information Tuple is often used for identification purposes. This tuple usually contains character strings that are useful in identifying the card. These strings include the name of the manufacturer, the name of the product, and any additional product information that the manufacturer elects to include. For example, the IBM Ethernet PC Card contains a string in this tuple that says "IBM Corp. Ethernet" which can be used to identify the card.

Another tuple that can be used for identification purposes is the manufacturer identification tuple. This tuple contains information about the manufacturer of a PC Card. The manufacturer information portion of the tuple should be unique to a particular card.

The Level 1 Version/Product Information Tuple is often changed to suit OEM customers of PC Cards. For example, an OEM customer of an IBM Ethernet card may not want "IBM Corp. Ethernet" present in the CIS of their card. Instead, the OEM customer may want their own identifying tuple so the end user would think the PC Card was produced by the OEM.

Often, an OEM also buys the device drivers (including the client) for the card. If the driver developer used the original product identifier string to identify the card and the OEM wanted a different product identifier string, the device driver would not recognize the card and the driver would not function. Therefore, the choice of how to uniquely identify a particular card can be an important decision. In this template, the manufacturer identification tuple is used for positive identification.

To get the tuple information, it is necessary to make two calls to card services. These two calls are **GetFirstTuple** and **GetTupleData**. The **GetFirstTuple** card services call is used to find the particular tuple the client is interested in. In this case, it is the manufacturer identification Tuple (CISTPL_MANFID) (20H).

Figure 5-23 illustrates the first part of the CardInsertion function. It begins by building the argument packet for the **GetFirstTuple** call. The *logical socket* for the CARD_INSERTION event is placed in the argument packet, as well as the particular tuple card services is to find. Then the call to card services is made. The logical socket is the value that card services returned in the CX register during a callback event.

In turn, card services opens an attribute memory window and begins parsing the CIS structure. If card services finds the desired tuple, card services returns a SUCCESS return code and the function continues. If a problem occurs with card services, an alarm is sounded. This particular alarm is two alternating tones that indicate a problem. For development purposes, the code also displays a message to the screen that indicates the cause of the alarm. In a DOS environment, this is not normally done because DOS is not a reentrant operating system. As a result, displaying messages in an interrupt context like this can cause unexpected side effects. If a PC Card is plugged in while another program is printing to the screen and the client driver encounters a problem with card services, the error message will overwrite the other program's output. This may be undesirable. After the client code is functioning properly with card services, it is recommended that the message posting code be removed.

Assuming that the **GetFirstTuple** call returns successfully, the client must retrieve the data from the desired tuple. This is achieved with the **GetTupleData** card services call. If the call to card services returns successfully, the data from the desired tuple is placed in the argument packet as shown in Figure 5-23.

```
        void CardInsertion(void)
        {
         FPGETTUPLE fpgt;

  // This function is called when a card insertion event occurs. It first
  // verifies the card inserted to see if it is interested in it. If not
  // return, otherwise, begin the enabling process.
  // First get the Manufacturer's ID tuple and verify the card.

          fpgt = (FPGETTUPLE)ArgPacket;
          fpgt->Socket = logical_socket;
          fpgt->Attributes = 0;
          fpgt->DesiredTuple = CISTPL_MANFID;
          fpgt->TupleOffset = 0;

          if ((Status = CardServices(GET_FIRST_TUPLE, 0, 0, 18,
                   fpgt)) != SUCCESS)

             {
               alarm();
               post_msg("Get First Tuple Call failed.\n\r$");
               return;
             }

        // Now go and get the data

          fpgt->TupleOffset = 0;

          if ((Status = CardServices(GET_TUPLE_DATA, 0, 0,
                sizeof(ArgPacket),fpgt)) != SUCCESS){
                alarm();
               post_msg("Get Tuple Data Call failed.\n\r$");
               return Status;
          }
```

Figure 5-23: CARD INSERTION and Tuple Processing

Assuming that the GET_TUPLE_DATA card services call returns successfully, the client driver can compare the manufacturer identification data with the client driver's identification data. In this case, the client knows that the PCMCIA PC Card manufacturer code is (0xA4, 0) and the manufacturer information for the IBM Ethernet PC Card is (2,0). These four bytes make up the TPLMID_MANF and TPLMID_CARD fields of this tuple. If the data returned from card services matches what the client driver is testing for, the target card has been positively identified. If the data returned does not match what the client is expecting, the CARD_INSERTION event is aborted.

```
// Now verify the card.
if ((fpgt->s.GetTupleData.TupleData[0] != 0xA4) ||
     (fpgt->s.GetTupleData.TupleData[1] != 0)   ||
     (fpgt->s.GetTupleData.TupleData[2] != 2)   ||
     (fpgt->s.GetTupleData.TupleData[3] != 0))
      return SUCCESS;
```

Figure 5-24: DOS Source Code to Verify Tuple Data

Once the PC Card has been positively identified, resources for this card can be acquired from card services. Since the client is dealing with the correct card, the client must save the socket number that card services passed to the client. From now on, the client must use this socket number when acquiring resources for this card.

```
// Card is verified. Now begin acquiring resources.

  my_socket = logical_socket;          // save our socket number
```

Figure 5-25: Saving the Logical Socket Number

The IBM Ethernet PC Card requires three different resources to function. It requires I/O ports for data transfer and control, an interrupt level for the interrupt handler of the client driver, and 16K of shared RAM for operation. It is important to note that different PC Cards require different resources. Naturally, the resources for other PC Cards must be acquired properly to ensure their proper operation. Details on the resources a PC Card required should be contained in its CIS. The client driver can use the configuration table and configuration table entry tuples to determine what resources to acquire. This process can take a considerable amount of software. In DOS, the card services callback software should be as small as possible. If the client driver developer is aware of the resources required by the target PC Card, it is quicker to directly request them rather than parsing the tuples to determine the requirements of the card. This may, however, bind the client driver to this particular PC Card.

If the objective is to develop an all-purpose client or super client driver that recognizes many different cards and enables them, then it is desirable to create the routines to parse the CIS thoroughly. It is important to note though that there are often errors in the CIS of some PC Cards, which results in parsing problems. One possible downside of not obtaining the resource requirements from the CIS is the possibility that the card the client driver is designed for may have a hardware change in the future which is reflected in the CIS resource data. In this example, the required resources are known.

The first resources needed are the I/O ports. This card requires 32 consecutive I/O ports. A default I/O base address of 300h is desired. However, the base I/O port address may be changed in case of a conflict with another device in the system. To acquire the I/O ports, the I/O port base address and the socket number must be known. The &eth_parms parameter is the address of a global data structure

(ETHERNET_PARMS) that contains the resource settings for this card. Figure 5-26 illustrates how to acquire I/O port resources.

```
/***********************************************************************
*  Function: GetIOPorts
*
*  This function makes the request to card services for the I/O ports we
*  need for this card.
*
***********************************************************************/
int GetIOPorts(WORD socket, ETHERNET_PARMS *eth_parms)
{
FPREQUESTRELEASEIO fprio;

  fprio = (FPREQUESTRELEASEIO)ArgPacket;
  fprio->Socket=socket;
  fprio->BasePort1 = eth_parms->port_address;
  fprio->NumPorts1 = 32;
  fprio->Attributes1 = 0;
  fprio->BasePort2 = 0;
  fprio->NumPorts2 = 0;
  fprio->Attributes2 = 0;
  fprio->IOAddrLines = 5;

  if ((Status = CardServices(REQUEST_IO, rcHandle, 0,
        sizeof(REQUESTRELEASEIO), fprio, &d_handle)) != SUCCESS){
        post_msg("Request IO Call failed.\n\r$");
        return Status;
  }
  return Status;

}
```
Figure 5-26: DOS RequestIO Source Code

The first part of the function is to create a pointer to the argument packet memory. Once this is done, it is simply a matter of completing the argument packet for the **RequestIO** card services call. The I/O port base address is determined from the ETHERNET_PARMS data structure. This address is placed in the BasePort1 field. It is already known that the target card needs thirty-two I/O ports. This value is placed in the NumPorts1 field. In this particular case, the Attribute byte is zero. The Attributes1 and Attributes2 fields are used to set the width of the I/O port (8 or 16 bits) and whether the I/O ports are shared with anything else. The IBM Ethernet PC Card has a combination of 8-bit and 16-bit I/O ports. This client driver is requesting 8-bit I/O ports. On the PC Card interface, it is possible for the PC Card to signal that a 16-bit I/O operation is occurring. This is supported on most PC Card adapters. It is up to the particular implementation of card and socket services and the particular adapter being used as to how this is supported. It may be necessary to request two different I/O port windows for the I/O port requirements for a particular card.

The IBM Ethernet PC Card only decodes five address lines for I/O port operations. This is reflected in the number placed in the IOAddrLines field. Now the call to card services is performed. If the call is successful, thirty-two 8-bit I/O ports at eth_parms->port_address are acquired. If any or all of these I/O ports are already being used, the call is not successful and the routine is exited with the Status code of the failure. The message posted during a failure is just for development purposes and should be removed after debugging of the client is complete. card services can select the I/O ports available. Simply place an zero in the field and card services will return any available I/O port base address on a 32-byte boundary that it has in its resource map.

The next request for resources to card services is for an IRQ or interrupt level. In a standard Intel 80x86 based personal computer, PC Card supports hardware interrupts three through fifteen. Many of these interrupts are used by the system and are usually not available to I/O cards. However, interrupts 3,5,9,10,11, and 15 are usually available. This client driver defaults to using IRQ 5.

```
if ((Status = GetInterruptLevel(my_socket, &eth_parms))
        != SUCCESS){
      alarm();
      return Status;
  }
```

Figure 5-27: IRQ Level Inquiry

Figure 5-28 issues the **RequestIRQ** call to card services in order to acquire a desired interrupt level. This routine begins by setting a pointer to the argument packet. The argument packet is then filled in with information specific to the **RequestIRQ** card services call. This client is requesting an exclusive IRQ so that it is dedicated to this card and not shared with others. This is indicated by the RIRQ_ATTR_EXCLUSIVE bit setting in the bit-mapped Attributes field. The IRQInfo1 field is another bit-mapped field. The client uses this field to tell CS if the PC Card handles pulse or level mode interrupts. It also indicates that the IRQInfo2 field is valid for this call. IRQInfo2 is another bit-mapped field that is used to tell card services what interrupt the client is interested in. This particular client only tells card services about the one interrupt that it is requesting. It is possible to fill in more than one bit in the IRQInfo2 field and let card services provide a matching IRQ that is available. This is actually the preferred method of obtaining an interrupt. When a driver is a true card services client, setting the interrupt to a desired value is not absolutely essential. However, since resource conflicts often arise in systems (sometimes as the result of a point enabler), card services may have an incorrect resource map of the system and can return an improper value. Therefore, it is recommended that the design of the client should include the ability to request specific resources.

```
/*************************************************************************
*  Function: GetInterruptLevel
*
* This function makes the request to card services for Interrupt Level we
*  need for this card.
*
```

```
*************************************************************************/
int GetInterruptLevel(WORD socket, ETHERNET_PARMS *eth_parms)
{

  FPREQUESTIRQ fpirq;

  fpirq = (FPREQUESTIRQ)ArgPacket;
  fpirq->Socket=socket;
  fpirq->Attributes = RIRQ_ATTR_EXCLUSIVE;
  fpirq->IRQInfo1 = RIRQ_INFO1_VALID_MASK |
                    RIRQ_INFO1_LEVEL |
                    RIRQ_INFO1_PULSE;

  fpirq->IRQInfo2 = 0x0001;
  fpirq->IRQInfo2 = fpirq->IRQInfo2 << eth_parms->interrupt_level;

  if ((Status = CardServices(REQUEST_IRQ, rcHandle, 0, sizeof(REQUESTIRQ),
       fpirq, &d_handle)) != SUCCESS){
       post_msg("Request IRQ Call failed.\n\r$");
       return Status;
  }

// remember the IRQ that has been assigned to the card

  IRQ_assigned = fpirq->AssignedIRQ;
  return Status;
}
```

Figure 5-28: DOS RequestIRQ Source Code

After the call to card services is returned successfully, the value of the IRQ that card services provides is returned in the argument packet. This should be remembered for future use. The next step is to acquire the memory required by the card. This particular card uses 16K of RAM.

```
        if ((Status = GetMemoryWindow(my_socket, &eth_parms)) != SUCCESS){
              alarm();
              return Status;
          }
```

Figure 5-29: DOS RequestIRQ Source Code

The IBM Ethernet PC Card utilizes a 16K shared memory (RAM) window for the transmission and reception of data on an Ethernet segment. This memory is standard RAM or common memory. This card also has its *universal address* in Attribute memory at offset 0FF0h. The universal address is obtained from attribute memory and placed in the lowest six bytes of the shared RAM. When a separate LAN driver for this card is executed, it reads the universal address from the lowest six bytes of common memory. To access this universal address data, it is necessary to open an Attribute memory window. This is achieved with the **RequestWindow** card services call. As with other card services calls, a pointer to the argument packet is established and the necessary fields for the call are filled in. The call is socket specific, so the socket field is filled in with the proper socket number. The Attributes field is a bit-mapped field that informs card services of the type of memory window that is desired. The universal address for this card is in attribute memory, so a window that is eight bits wide is needed. The memory window is to appear at the RAM_address in the ETHERNET_PARMS structure.

There are typically two different address spaces in a PC Card system. One address space is the address space of the system. The other address space is the PC Card address space. With an adapter that bridges these two address spaces, it is possible to shift the address space of the PC Card bus relative to the system address space. The client driver always uses and sees the system address space. The address the client passes to card services is a physical address. The RAM_address parameter in the ETHERNET_PARMS structure is the segment value of this address. The segment value is converted to a physical address before being passed to card services. The size of this memory window is 16K, so the Size field of the argument packet is set to this value.

The AccessSpeed field for this card is set to a memory speed of 100ns, and it is instructed to use Wait if it is available. The memory speed for the PC Card is usually defined in the CISTPL_DEVICE tuple in the CIS of the PC Card. The wait signal can be used by a PC Card when an I/O cycle needs to be extended. The adapter typically supports different access speeds. These speed settings are passed from card services to socket services, and the access speed setting for the adapter is set accordingly. If the speed settings are incorrectly set, unreliable device operations may occur. This is sometimes detected through a debugger by looking at the memory. If the memory contents change when the screen is refreshed for the debugger, then the speed setting is most likely incorrect.

Finally, the call to card services is made. If card services can supply the requested memory window, a zero return code is received along with a handle to the RAM window in the DX register. The handle must be saved for any future card services operation with this RAM window. In this particular case, the driver will return this window to card services after the universal address is retrieved from attribute memory. When the **RequestWindow** is called, the memory window starts at zero in the PC Card address space. The universal address is acquired from the attribute memory, and the memory window is no longer needed. The driver makes a **ReleaseWindow** call to card services using the handle it received from card services when the memory window was opened. Card services now adds this memory window back to its database of available resources.

Last, the final memory window is requested. This window is for the shared RAM of the card. This window is for common memory that is sixteen bits wide and 16K in size. The argument packet for **RequestWindow** is filled in just like before and the call to card services is made. The handle for this memory window is returned upon a successful completion of this card services call. This memory window must be shifted in PC Card address space from zero to 0x4000 for this PC Card. This is performed by making a card services **MapMemPage** function call. This card services function shifts the PC Card address space relative to the workstation's address space. In this case, for example, the workstation sees the memory window starting at 0xD4000 in workstation address space, but the PC Card sees this memory start at 0x4000 in PC Card address space. This is the same physical memory but different addresses appear on the two different buses.

The card services function **MapMemPage** uses an argument packet to communicate to card services that the offset within the PC Card address space to memory window should be shifted. When the **RequestWindow** was called earlier, the Paged bit in the Attribute field was not set, so there is only one memory page for this memory window. The Page field in the **MapMemPage** argument packet should be set to zero in this case. When this call is successfully returned, the universal address acquired earlier is written to the first six bytes of the memory window. Figure 5-30 shows how these calls are combined to satisfy the memory window requirement for this card.

```
/*******************************************************************
*  Function: GetMemoryWindow
*
* This function makes the request to card services for the memory
* window we need for this card. It also gleans the network
* address out of the attribute memory.
*
*******************************************************************/
int GetMemoryWindow(WORD socket, ETHERNET_PARMS *eth_parms)

  FPREQUESTWINDOW fprwin;
  FPMAPMEMPAGE fprmmp;
  unsigned long address;
  BYTE network_address[6];               // obtained network address
  BYTE far *fpnet;                       // pointer to BYTE
  BYTE i;                                // index variable

  fprwin = (FPREQUESTWINDOW)ArgPacket;
  fprwin->Socket=socket;
  fprwin->Attributes = RW_ATTR_ATTRIB_MEMORY | RW_ATTR_ENABLED |
                       RW_ATTR_8_BIT;
  address = (unsigned long) (eth_parms->RAM_address);
  fprwin->Base = address << 4;
  fprwin->Size = 0x4000;                  // 16K of RAM
  fprwin->AccessSpeed = RW_SPEED_USE_WAIT | RW_SPEED_100NS;
  if ((Status = CardServices(REQUEST_WINDOW, rcHandle, 0,
        sizeof(REQUESTWINDOW),fprwin, &RAM_handle)) != SUCCESS){
       post_msg("Request Memory Window Call failed.\n\r$");
       return Status;
  }
// Get the network address. It is stored at offset 0x0FF0 in
// attribute memory on this Ethernet card. First get a pointer to
// this data area; since it is in Attribute memory, get every other
// byte.

   fpnet = MK_FP(eth_parms->RAM_address, 0x0FF0);
   for (i=0; i<6 ; i++)
     network_address[i] = fpnet[i*2];

// This network address will be written into the lowest 6 bytes of
// the final common memory window. Now release this memory window
// and request a 16 bit common memory window.

  if ((Status = CardServices(RELEASE_WINDOW, RAM_handle, 0, 0,
       0)) != SUCCESS){
       post_msg("Request Memory Call failed.\n\r$");
```

```
        return Status;
    }

// Request the final 16-bit Common memory window

    fprwin = (FPREQUESTWINDOW)ArgPacket;
    fprwin->Socket=socket;
    fprwin->Attributes = RW_ATTR_COMMON_MEMORY |
                         RW_ATTR_ENABLED |
                         RW_ATTR_16_BIT;
    fprwin->Base = address << 4;                    //
    fprwin->Size = 0x4000;                          // 16K of RAM
    fprwin->AccessSpeed = RW_SPEED_USE_WAIT |
                          RW_SPEED_100NS;

    if ((Status = CardServices(REQUEST_WINDOW, rcHandle, 0,
         sizeof(REQUESTWINDOW),fprwin, &RAM_handle)) != SUCCESS){
      post_msg("Request Memory Window Call failed.\n\r$");
      return Status;
    }


// Shift the memory window in PC Card space to offset 0x4000;

    fprmmp = (FPMAPMEMPAGE)ArgPacket;
    fprmmp->CardOffset = 0x4000;
    fprmmp->Page = 0;

    if ((Status = CardServices(MAP_MEM_PAGE, RAM_handle, 0,
         sizeof(MAPMEMPAGE),fprwin, &d_handle)) != SUCCESS){
        post_msg("Map Mem Page Call failed.\n\r$");
        return Status;
    }

// Copy the network address into the lowest 6 bytes of the
// memory window.

     fpnet = MK_FP(eth_parms->RAM_address, 0x0000);

     for (i=0; i<6 ; i++)
       fpnet[i] = network_address[i];

    return Status;

}
```

Figure 5-30: DOS RequestWindow and MapMemPage Source Code

If all of the card services calls have returned successfully, all of the necessary resources for the IBM Ethernet card have been acquired. The next step is to configure the card for operation. This is done using the card services **RequestConfiguration** function call. This is the function where the socket voltage settings are indicated, where the type of card interface (I/O or memory) is declared, and where the initial configuration register settings are indicated the PC Card. This is the final step in configuring a PC Card. If this request is successful, the PC Card should be functional.

```
if ((Status = RequestConfig(my_socket)) != SUCCESS){
      alarm();
return Status;
  }
```

Figure 5-31: Setting the PC Card Configuration

The argument packet for this call has many fields. Here is the structure definition:

```
typedef struct _REQUESTCONFIGURATION
{
   unsigned short        Socket;
   unsigned short        Attributes;
   unsigned char         Vcc;
   unsigned char         Vpp1;
   unsigned char         Vpp2;
   unsigned char         IntType;
   unsigned long         ConfigBase;
   unsigned char         Status;
   unsigned char         Pin;
   unsigned char         Copy;
   unsigned char         Option;
   unsigned char         Present;
}  REQUESTCONFIGURATION;
```

Figure 5-32: DOS RequestConfiguration Data Structure

As always, a pointer is set to the argument packet memory. This is a socket-specific function, interrupt line comes from a PC Card, IRQ steering is necessary and is performed by the adapter. An adapter has interrupt lines for any number of interrupts. The adapter redirects or steers the interrupt from the PC Card to a particular interrupt line that goes from the adapter to the programmable interrupt controller of the computer. When the PC Card asserts an IRQ, the redirected interrupt line is asserted and a system interrupt occurs.

The next three fields, Vcc, Vpp1, and Vpp2, all represent voltages expressed in tenths of a volt. They are set to 5.0 volts, as this card uses five-volt technologies.

The IntType field tells card services that this card is either a memory card or an I/O card. The IBM Ethernet PC Card is an I/O card with memory, so card services is informed of this.

The next field is the ConfigBase field. This field contains the offset from zero (base address) of the configuration registers. This particular card has its configuration registers starting at 0x20000 in attribute memory. The CIS of the card should have the address of the configuration registers in the configuration tuple (CISTPL_CONFIG).

The next three fields are values that should be written to these registers if they are present on the PC Card. The status register is implemented on this particular card, but the pin and copy registers are not.

The Option field is the value that is written to the configuration option register. This is the register that is used for resetting a card, setting the interrupt type that is supported (pulse or level mode), and an index that is used by the PC Card for configuration internally. The value 0x41 tells the system to use Level mode interrupts with this card and to use a configuration index of 0x01. Any nonzero value for the configuration index enables the I/O capabilities of the card. Otherwise the system would treat the card as a memory-only card. The configuration index can be obtained from the configuration table entry tuple (CISTPL_CFTABLE_ENTRY) for the card. The final field is the Present field. This bit-mapped field tells card services which configuration registers are present on this card. In this case, the configuration option, configuration, status, socket, and copy registers are implemented. Once all of the fields are defined, the call to card services can occur. If this call is successful, the PC Card should be operational.

```
/*******************************************************************
*   Function: RequestConfig
*
*   This function makes the request to card services to configure
*   the card.
*
*******************************************************************/
int RequestConfig(WORD socket)
{
  FPREQUESTCONFIGURATION fprcon;

  fprcon = (FPREQUESTCONFIGURATION)ArgPacket;
  fprcon->Socket = socket;                      // logical socket
  fprcon->Attributes = RC_ENABLE_IRQ_STEERING;// Enable IRQ
  fprcon->Vcc =  50;                            // 5 volts
  fprcon->Vpp1 = 50;                            // 5 volts
  fprcon->Vpp2 = 50;                            // 5 volts
  fprcon->IntType = RC_INTERFACE_MEMORY_IO;     // Memory and I/O
  fprcon->ConfigBase = 0x20000;  // offset 20000 in attribute mem
  fprcon->Status = 0;
  fprcon->Pin = 0;                              // not implemented
  fprcon->Copy = 0;
  fprcon->Option = 0x41;
  fprcon->Present = 0x0B;

  if ((Status = CardServices(REQUEST_CONFIGURATION, rcHandle, 0,
        sizeof(REQUESTCONFIGURATION),fprcon, &d_handle)) !=
SUCCESS)
        {post_msg("Request Configuration failed.\n\r$");
        return Status;
  }
  return Status;
}
```

Figure 5-33: DOS RequestConfiguration Source Code

To signify that the program has successfully configured the card, a happy beep can be implemented. This is just an audible acknowledgment to the user that all is fine.

Control is then returned to the program that was operating when the card was inserted. The CARD_INSERTION event has been examined. The next logical event to examine is the CARD_REMOVAL event.

Card Removal

The client driver receives a CARD_REMOVAL event whenever a PC Card is removed from its socket. Similar to the CARD_INSERTION event, the client receives this notification whether it's the PC Card the client is controlling or not. During a CARD_REMOVAL event, the socket number is passed in the CX register.

During the CARD_INSERTION event, after the PC Card is positively identified, the driver saved the socket number in a global variable called my_socket. Since CARD_REMOVAL events occur for any card being removed, it is essential that the driver determines if the CARD_REMOVAL event is for the card the client driver owns. The comparison of the logical socket and my_socket performs this determination. If the CARD_REMOVAL event is not for the client's card, the event is returned to card services without the releasing of any resources.

```
case CARD_REMOVAL:
    logical_socket = regs->cb_x.cx;        // current socket
    if (logical_socket != my_socket){
      regs->cb_x.ax = SUCCESS;
      break;
    }
    CardRemoval();
    regs->cb_x.ax = Status;
    break;
```

Figure 5-34: CARD_REMOVAL Event Detection

If the CARD_REMOVAL event is for the client's card, resources acquired during a previous CARD_INSERTION event are returned to card services. The first operation is to release the socket configuration. This is accomplished via the **ReleaseConfiguration** card services call, as shown in Figure 5-35 This will return the socket to its default state.

```
if ((Status = ReleaseConfig(my_socket)) != SUCCESS)
{
   alarm();
   return Status;
}
```

Figure 5-35: Freeing Socket Resources Assigned to a PC Card

The **ReleaseConfiguration** call requires only the proper socket number in its argument packet The client handle is passed to card services for this call as well.

```
fprcon = (FPRELEASECONFIGURATION)ArgPacket;
fprcon->Socket = socket;
if ((Status = CardServices(RELEASE_CONFIGURATION,rcHandle,0,
      sizeof(RELEASECONFIGURATION),fprcon,&d_handle)) != SUCCESS)
{
     post_msg("Release Configuration Call failed.\n\r$");
     return Status;
}
```

Figure 5-36: DOS ReleaseConfiguration Source Code

Upon completion, the system resources obtained and assigned to this PC Card are released back to card services. The first resource returned is the memory via the **ReleaseWindow** call. This requires only the handle for the memory window (RAM_handle) that the client obtain when the memory window was acquired earlier with the **RequestWindow** function.

```
if ((Status = CardServices(RELEASE_WINDOW, RAM_handle, 0, 0,
    0, &d_handle)) != SUCCESS)
{
  post_msg("Release Memory Call failed.\n\r$");
   return Status;
}
```

Figure 5-37: DOS ReleaseWindow Source Code

Next, the IRQ resource is returned to card services via the **ReleaseIRQ** call. The card services call is socket specific so the logical socket must be in the argument packet for this call. The Attributes field uses the same setting as when the IRQ was acquired. The IRQ resource returned to card services must be the same IRQ that was assigned to the client during **RequestIRQ** call.

```
FPRELEASEIRQ fpirq;

fpirq = (FPRELEASEIRQ)ArgPacket;
fpirq->Socket=socket;
fpirq->Attributes = RIRQ_ATTR_EXCLUSIVE;
fpirq->AssignedIRQ = IRQ_assigned;

if ((Status = CardServices(RELEASE_IRQ, rcHandle, 0,
        sizeof(RELEASEIRQ),fpirq, &d_handle)) != SUCCESS){
   post_msg("Release IRQ Call failed.\n\r$");
   return Status;
}
```

Figure 5-38: DOS ReleaseIRQ Source Code

Next, the I/O port resource is returned using the **ReleaseIO** call. The argument packet for this card services call must match the argument packet that was used to acquire the I/O ports. This call is socket specific so the current socket number is used.

```
FPREQUESTRELEASEIO fprio;

fprio = (FPREQUESTRELEASEIO)ArgPacket;
fprio->Socket=socket;
fprio->BasePort1 = eth_parms->port_address;
fprio->NumPorts1 = 32;
fprio->Attributes1 = 0;
fprio->BasePort2 = 0;
fprio->NumPorts2 = 0;
fprio->Attributes2 = 0;
fprio->IOAddrLines = 5;

if ((Status = CardServices(RELEASE_IO, rcHandle, 0,
        sizeof(REQUESTRELEASEIO),fprio, &d_handle)) != SUCCESS){
  post_msg("Release IO Call failed.\n\r$");
  return Status;
}
```

Figure 5-39: DOS ReleaseIO Source Code

If all of the card services calls are successful, all of the resources that were gathered during the CARD_INSERTION event for this client are returned to card services. These resources are now available for any other client that may need them. If the Ethernet PC Card is plugged back into any socket and no other client has gathered any of the resources needed, the card will be enabled in that particular socket.

Client Info

Another event that should be handled is the CLIENT_INFO event. This event is generated when another program executes a **GetClientInfo** card services call. A client or browsing utility could use this call to find out information about other clients already in the system.

Each client should have a client data area that describes itself. The data area contains information concerning the current revision number of the client, its level of card services compliance, the date of the revision, the name of the client, and any vendor string the client wants. Figure 5-40 is an example of a data structure for this information. This data is stored in a global data structure that remains resident in memory after the client has been initialized.

```
typedef struct _MY_CLIENT_DATA
{
  unsigned short  Revision;
  unsigned short  CSLevel;
  unsigned short  RevDate;
  unsigned short  NameOff;
  unsigned short  NameLen;
  unsigned short  VStringOff;
  unsigned short  VStringLen;
  unsigned char   NameString[9];
  unsigned char   VendorString[1];
} MY_CLIENT_DATA;
```

Figure 5-40: Data Structure Defining the Client

When the CLIENT_INFO event occurs, an argument packet address is passed to the client in the [ES]:[BX] registers. The software that made a **GetClientInfo** card services call supplies this argument packet memory space. The client that receives the event is supposed to copy its particular client data into this argument packet memory space. The format of the argument packet is illustrated in Figure 5-41.

```
typedef struct _GETCLIENTINFO
{
   unsigned short     MaxLen;
   unsigned short     InfoLen;
   unsigned short     Attributes;
  union
   {
     struct
       {
         unsigned short  Revision;
         unsigned short  CSLevel;
         unsigned short  RevDate;
         unsigned short  NameOff;
         unsigned short  NameLen;
         unsigned short  VStringOff;
         unsigned short  VStringLen;
         unsigned char   NameAndVendorString[1];
     } s;
  unsigned char      uc[1];
} ClientInfo;
    }  GETCLIENTINFO;
```

Figure 5-41: DOS GetClientInfo Data Structure

The data in the MY_CLIENT_DATA data structure of the client driver is a subset of the **GetClientInfo** argument packet structure whose address is passed to the client during the event. The client must determine from the **GetClientInfo** argument packet field, MaxLen, if the argument packet is large enough for the client's data. If the packet has enough space for the client data, the client copies the data to the argument packet memory. If the argument packet does not supply enough space for all of the client data, the client fills in as much client data as the argument packet allows. The program that generated the **GetClientInfo** card services call fills in the MaxLen field with the size of the argument packet memory space that it has set aside for this function. The client being queried fills in the length of the information returned by the client in the InfoLen field. The client fills in the Attributes field with the same data that it used in the Attributes field of the **RegisterClient** call when it registered. The upper byte of the Attributes field (info subservice) may contain a nonzero value. This permits a vendor to request vendor specific data. However, this programming example assumes the info subservice field is zero.

Now the replying client fills in the **GetClientInfo** structure with its own data. The MY_CLIENT_DATA structure below shows the data that this client uses. The CopyClientInfo routine shown in Figure 5-42 performs the transfer of this data.

```
MY_CLIENT_DATA client_data  =     // client specific data
  {
    0x100,                        // client revision number
    0x200,                        // card services compliance level
    0x1D72,                       // card services Revision date
    20,                           // Offset to Client name string
    9,                            // Length of ASCIIZ client name
    28,                           // Offset to Vendor string
    0,                            // Length of ASCIIZ vendor string
    "CSENABLE"                    // Client name string
                                  // Vendor name string
  };
```

Figure 5-42: Initialization of the Client Data Structure

After the replying client has copied its client data to the argument packet, the client returns a SUCCESS return code to card services and exits. The program that made the **GetClientInfo** call now has a copy of this client's data as shown in Figure 5-43.

```
/*******************************************************************
*  Function: CopyClientInfo
*  Copy our Client Info data into the buffer of the other client
*  requesting GetClientInfo CS function.
*******************************************************************/
void CopyClientInfo(GETCLIENTINFO far *gci)
{
  int count = sizeof(MY_CLIENT_DATA);  // our data length
  int i;
  BYTE *source;

  gci->InfoLen = count;          // set length of the
                                 // client's data
                                 // set in the client's
                                 // attributes
  gci->Attributes = RC_ATTR_IO_CLIENT |
                    RC_ATTR_CARD_INSERT_SHARED |
                    RC_ATTR_CARD_INSERT_EXCL;

  if (gci->MaxLen < count)       // Is there enough room to copy
```

```
            count = gci->MaxLen;        // client data?
        source = &client_data;          // point to the client's data

        for (i=0; i < count; i++){  // copy the client data to the
          gci->ClientInfo.uc[i] = source[i];    // CS buffer
        }
    }
```

Figure 5-43: DOS GetClientInfo Source Code

Request Exclusive

RequestExclusive processing is used in a client driver when the client wants to have exclusive control of the I/O card. A client driver can take control from another registered client(s) that may currently control the I/O card if the registered client(s) allow(s) it to. When a client makes a **RequestExclusive** call to card services, any clients driver that are registered for the card will receive an EXCLUSIVE_REQUEST event. This is a socket-specific operation. Only the registered clients who controls a card in a particular socket will get the EXCLUSIVE_REQUEST event.

If the existing registered client(s) return(s) SUCCESS, exclusive access is given to the client making the exclusive request. Any other registered client(s) of an I/O PC Card receive(s) CARD_REMOVAL events as if the PC Card had been removed from the socket. The client(s) receiving the CARD_REMOVAL events return(s) their resources to card services. The client requesting exclusive access receives the EXCLUSIVE_COMPLETE event and requests the resources from card services the way it desires. This all depends upon the other registered client(s) relinquishing control of the PC Card. If any client does not return SUCCESS on an EXCLUSIVE_REQUEST event, card services stops the **RequestExclusive** processing and the present client(s) retain(s) control.

RequestExclusive processing is useful when super client drivers are present in a system. The super client driver could enable a PC Card with resource settings (I/O ports, IRQ level, and memory) that are defined in the super client driver. These settings may not be the optimal settings for the PC Card. They could also be incorrect and the PC Card may not be functional with them. If a client driver is loaded after the super client driver has enabled the PC Card and the client supports request exclusive processing, the client can change the settings of the resources to match what it needs. In this way, the client driver does not care if the PC Card has already been enabled. The client driver's settings would override the super client driver's settings.

Without **RequestExclusive** processing, conflicts in resource settings are common. For example, an IBM PCMCIA Token-Ring PC Card requires 4 I/O ports, 1 IRQ level, and 2 memory windows. The setting values can vary depending upon the system and the software environment. There are standard defaults that are used by existing device drivers. If a super client driver is utilized and it configures the PC Card up in a nonstandard configuration, the I/O PC Card would not function properly. The settings that a super client driver configures a PC Card to may not agree with the defaults the device driver is assuming. For example, the standard IRQ level for the IBM PCMCIA Token-Ring PC Card is IRQ9. The super client driver from SystemSoft (CardID) configured this PC Card to IRQ 5 as the default. When the device driver for this PC Card executed, the IRQ levels did not agree and it would not function. This caused problems for users that did not understand the default values for the resources necessary for this PC Card. There are PC Cards that appear as modems to a system but are actually more sophisticated and require a more complicated configuration sequence. Wireless communication PC Cards are a good example. For these PC Cards, a super client driver may acquire the correct resources but do an inadequate job of configuring the PC Card. A client driver that utilizes **RequestExclusive** processing would be best for these devices.

This template utilizes **RequestExclusive** processing. It makes the callback processing a little more complicated than just handling simple CARD_INSERTION and CARD_REMOVAL events. There are two additional events that must be handled; these are the EXCLUSIVE_REQUEST event and the EXCLUSIVE_COMPLETE event. When a client makes a **RequestExclusive** card services call, card services calls each registered client with an EXCLUSIVE_REQUEST event. If a client receives exclusive access, it receives the EXCLUSIVE_COMPLETE event.

To perform **RequestExclusive** processing, it is a good idea to maintain the state of the driver in this process. The two states are: exclusive requested (EXCLUSIVE_REQUESTED) and exclusive completed (EXCLUSIVE_COMP). The client driver should not request resources from card services until the EXCLUSIVE_COMPLETE event has been received. The chronology for this client template utilizing **RequestExclusive** processing is as follows:

1. Invoke **RegisterClient** to register as a client driver with card services.
2. On a CARD_INSERTION event, verify the identity of the PC Card. If this is the PC Card the client is interested in, check to see if **RequestExclusive** has been requested. If request exclusive has not been requested, make the **RequestExclusive** call to card services and exit.
3. The **RequestExclusive** call to card services generates the EXCLUSIVE_REQUEST event from card services to registered client(s) for the PC Card in the socket.
4. If all of the registered clients for the PC Card in the socket return SUCCESS to the EXCLUSIVE_REQUEST event, these clients receive CARD_REMOVAL events. This includes the client that is requesting exclusive access.
5. The client requesting exclusive access receives another CARD_INSERTION event. If the EXCLUSIVE_COMPLETE event has not occurred yet, exit.

When the EXCLUSIVE_COMPLETE event finally occurs, process the card insertion completely by requesting resources from card services. This sequence of events should become clearer after looking at Figure 5-44.

```
void callback_handler(REGS *regs)
{
  switch (regs->h.al)
  {
    case PM_RESUME:
            break;
    case CARD_INSERTION:
            logical_socket = regs->cb_x.cx;    // current socket
            CardInsertion();
            regs->cb_x.ax = Status;
            break;
    case PM_SUSPEND:
    case BATTERY_DEAD:
    case BATTERY_LOW:
    case CARD_LOCK:
    case CARD_READY:
            regs->cb_x.ax = UNSUPPORTED_FUNCTION;
            break;
    case CARD_REMOVAL:
            logical_socket = regs->cb_x.cx;    // current socket
            if (logical_socket != my_socket){
              regs->cb_x.ax = SUCCESS;
              break;
            }
            if (flags & EXCLUSIVE_COMP){
              CardRemoval();
              regs->cb_x.ax = Status;
              break;
            }
            if (flags & EXCLUSIVE_REQUESTED)
              Status = SUCCESS;                // leave
            else
              CardRemoval();
            regs->cb_x.ax = Status;
            break;
    case CARD_RESET:
    case CARD_UNLOCK:
    case EJECTION_COMPLETE:
    case EJECTION_REQUEST:
    case ERASE_COMPLETE:
           regs->cb_x.ax = UNSUPPORTED_FUNCTION;
           break;
    case EXCLUSIVE_COMPLETE:
           flags |= EXCLUSIVE_COMP;
           logical_socket = regs->cb_x.cx;  // current socket
           CardInsertion();
           regs->cb_x.ax = Status;
           break;
    case EXCLUSIVE_REQUEST:    // If exclusiveness was granted,
                               // return an UNSUPPORTED return code
           if (flags & EXCLUSIVE_COMP)
             regs->cb_x.ax = UNSUPPORTED_FUNCTION;
           else
             regs->cb_x.ax = SUCCESS;
           break;
    case INSERTION_COMPLETE:
    case INSERTION_RQUEST:
            regs->cb_x.ax = UNSUPPORTED_FUNCTION;
            break;
    case REGISTRATION_COMPLETE:
            flags |= REGISTERED;
```

```
                regs->cb_x.ax = SUCCESS;
                if (flags & CCAPRESENT){
                   logical_socket = regs->cb_x.cx;  // current socket
                   CardInsertion();
                   regs->cb_x.ax = Status;
                }
                break;
        case RESET_COMPLETE:
        case RESET_PHYSICAL:
        case RESET_REQUEST:
        case MTD_REQUEST:
                regs->cb_x.ax = UNSUPPORTED_FUNCTION;
                break;
        case CLIENT_INFO:
                CopyClientInfo(MK_FP(regs->cb_x.es, regs->cb_x.bx));
                regs->cb_x.ax = SUCCESS;
                break;
        case TIMER_EXPIRED:
        case SS_UPDATED:
                regs->cb_x.ax = UNSUPPORTED_FUNCTION;
                break;
    }
}
```

Figure 5-44: DOS RequestExclusive Source Code

You may notice that the CardInsertion routine is called several times during this processing. It is used to verify the PC Card that has been inserted, make the **RequestExclusive** card services call, and to acquire the resources from card services after the EXCLUSIVE_COMPLETE event. The PC Card verification section and the resource acquisition sections of the CardInsertion routine are the same as those shown earlier. The only real difference is the addition of the **RequestExclusive** card services call and the checking of the state of the **RequestExclusive** processing that is occurring. Figure 5-45 shows the CardInsertion routine after the card verification section.

```
// Now request exclusive access...
  if (!(flags & EXCLUSIVE_REQUESTED)){
    if ((Status = RequestExclusive(my_socket)) != SUCCESS){
         alarm();
         return Status;
    }
    flags |= EXCLUSIVE_REQUESTED;
    return Status;
  }

 if (!(flags & EXCLUSIVE_COMP))return SUCCESS;

 if ((Status = GetIOPorts(my_socket, &eth_parms)) != SUCCESS){
      alarm();
      return Status;
  }
 if ((Status = GetInterruptLevel(my_socket, &eth_parms))
        != SUCCESS){
      alarm();
      return Status;
  }
```

```
    if ((Status = GetMemoryWindow(my_socket, &eth_parms)) != SUCCESS){
            alarm();
            return Status;
     }
    if ((Status = RequestConfig(my_socket)) != SUCCESS){
            alarm();
            return Status;
     }
    happy_beep();
    return Status;
   }
```

Figure 5-45: CARD_INSERTION RequestExclusive Processing

By using the request exclusive states (EXCLUSIVE_REQUESTED and EXCLUSIVE_COMP), the CARD_INSERTION and CARD_REMOVAL events can occur multiple times without resources being requested or returned to card services unnecessarily.

Debugging Tips and Techniques

With this template, it is possible to debug a client driver with a debugger such as Turbo Debugger or CodeView. The startup code can be single stepped and variables can be monitored. The big problem comes after the initialization has occurred and the driver has terminated. At this point in time, events occur from card services and it is more difficult to use a Turbo Debugger product.

Another type of debugger like Soft-ICE or Periscope is handy for debugging device driver code and callback processing code. This template also has limited printing capabilities for message generation. It is best not to print during callback processing. DOS is not a reentrant operating system, and printing in the callback processing (interrupt) context is not recommended as a general rule. For development purposes, this printing is acceptable.

Another method of providing feedback to the developer is via audible sounds. The sounds can be used to signal different things. This template signals when the client has successfully finished configuration. The sounds are two ascending audio tones. This is commonly known as a "happy beep". An "unhappy beep" could be utilized to indicate a card services call that finished unsuccessfully. This method of signaling a user is common with super client drivers as well.

This template includes a procedure called MyINT3 which implements an INT 3 breakpoint. This can be used as a breakpoint in the C source code. Simply place this procedure call wherever the user wants to get control of the processing with a debugger. An INT 3 instruction is used in the assembly language portion of this template when control is desired in this code.

Most errors that are encountered while interfacing to card services can be determined easily. A list of all the card services function codes, event codes, and error codes helps speed debugging. A copy of the PC Card Standard is valuable when particular parameters are in question. Oftentimes, debugging of card service's calls involves determining valid values of argument packet parameters. To determine card services errors, it is often helpful for the debugger to break on any INT 1Ah. This allows the developer to gain control right before a card services call. The developer can then verify the registers and the values in the argument packet for the card services call.

Once the card and socket services callback code is working as desired, problems may occur due to the way card and socket services actually configure the adapter hardware on the computer. At this time, it is important to utilize a tool that makes the registers of the adapter visible. PC Card adapters are made by many different manufacturers. Most manufacturers have utilities available that can be used to query or change the settings of a PC Card adapter. For example, Intel provided a utility called PCIC.EXE with their PCMCIA Modem evaluation kit several years ago that performed such a function. This utility is no longer available. A utility like PCIC.EXE is provided with this book. It is described in Chapter 10 and is called WinPCIC.EXE.

Using this utility, the speed of the memory and I/O ports can be changed to see the effect upon the system. Simply check the values of the registers of the PC Card adapter after card and socket services have set values in the PC Card adapter and vary them to see the results.

Chapter 6: OS/2

The first implementation of PC Card support for OS/2 showed up in in OS/2 2.1. After realizing some shortcomings, IBM enhanced PC Card support in OS/2 Warp. This chapter begins with explaining the history of the subtle differences between these two implementations.

IBM OS/2 2.1

IBM started shipping Card Services with OS/2 2.1 as the PCMCIA.SYS device driver. It was up to the hardware developer to provide OS/2 Socket Services for the computer. For the IBM ThinkPad 720, Socket Services is provided on a utility diskette that ships with the ThinkPad. It is called IBM2SS02.SYS. The same holds true for the IBM ThinkPad 750, except its Socket Services is called IBM2SS01.SYS.

This split is logical: Card Services is dependent only on the operating system it is running on, while Socket Services is hardware specific. OS/2 would provide the hardware-independent part, leaving the hardware dependent part to the computer maker. There was one major problem: computer makers would provide OS/2 Socket Services after DOS so OS/2 users had to wait for support. Some computer manufacturers still do not provide OS/2 Socket Services. In 1994 IBM started to provide OS/2 Socket Srvices for computers other than ThinkPads. These are available on their bulletin board systems (BBSs), their World Wide Web site (www.ibm.com), and on CompuServe.

In addition to Card and Socket services, a driver called the *Resource Map Utility (RMU)* was also provided. The RMU, like Socket Services is hardware specific (ICRMU02.SYS for the ThinkPad 720 and ICRMU01.SYS for the ThinkPad 750). During system IPL, this driver enumerates used resources (I/O ports, IRQs, memory windows) and reports them to Card Services so that it could maintain its internal database of system resources.

The remaining PC Card device drivers (including clients) must then load in the following order:

1. Card Services. During loading, Card Services initializes its default database of I/O ports, IRQs, and memory windows. These defaults do not reflect any resources already in use.
2. Socket Services. During loading, Socket Services sends its *interdevice driver communication* (IDC) entry point to card services. It also sends socket information to Card Services.

3. Resource Map Utility. During loading, the RMU determines which I/O ports, IRQs and memory windows are in use and sends **AdjustResouceInfo** requests to Card Services.

The big question now is, with all of these drivers talking to each other, where does the client driver load? Oddly enough, client drivers load either before Card Services or in between Card Services and Socket Services. At first it seems unusual that the client driver could load before Card Services, but the reason follows. Starting with OS/2 2.1, a new device driver strategy request, INIT_COMPLETE, was introduced. After all device drivers are loaded and initialized by their INIT request, any device drivers that support INIT_COMPLETE are called in the reverse order that they appear in CONFIG.SYS. Client drivers would then have to support INIT_COMPLETE to call Card Services correctly. The device drivers would then load as follows:

1. The client driver receives an INIT request and simply announces its presence with a message to the display.
2. Card Services receives an INIT request.
3. Socket Services receives an INIT request.
4. The Resource Map Utility receives an INIT request.
5. All other remaining device drivers load.
6. The Resource Map Utility receives an INIT_COMPLETE request. It proceeds to obtain the Card Services IDC entry point and sends **AdjustResourceInfo** requests to CS to reflect the current hardware in use.
7. Socket Services receives an INIT_COMPLETE request. It proceeds to obtain the Card Services IDC entry point and sends socket information to Card Services.
8. Card Services receives an INIT_COMPLETE request.
9. Finally the client driver receives an INIT_COMPLETE request. It too obtains the Card Services IDC entry point and starts making Card Services requests.

So the order of DEVICE statements is crucial for all of this to work properly. Any statement out of order can cause a client driver not to work at all.

These early Card Services and Socket Services had two annoying problems. First, the configuration ordering of device drivers was confusing and oftentimes complicated. Secondly, newly emerging devices such as PC Card SCSI cards were under development. This posed a new problem because SCSI drivers are BASEDEVs, which load prior to DEVICE drivers, creating the proverbial chicken and egg syndrome.

To solve both problems, IBM converted Card and Socket Services into BASEDEVs. As a result, every BASEDEV device driver loads before DEVICE drivers load. With Card and Socket Services loading as BASEDEVs, the client drivers that load as DEVICE drivers no longer need to follow the stringent ordering. Card Services is already loaded before the client driver, although the client driver still must wait until the

INIT_COMPLETE to call Card Services finishes (INIT occurs at Ring-3 while the INIT_COMPLETE occurs at Ring-0. According to the PC Card processor bindings, all Card Services calls must be done at Ring-0). Even though the device ordering has been removed, INIT_COMPLETE must still be used as a starting point for calling Card Services.

As for PC Card SCSI cards, BASEDEV device drivers have their own order of loading. All .SYS BASEDEVs will load before .ADD BASEDEVs. As long as the SCSI driver has the .ADD suffix it will load after Card Services and will function properly. The IBM PCMCIA SCSI card is a special case. It uses a "Card Services Enabler" to power-on the card. After the card is turned on the Future Domain driver, FD16-700.ADD drives the card. The "Card Services Enabler" code ends in .SYS so it must follow Socket Services in the CONFIG.SYS file. It ends in .SYS so it is guaranteed to load before the .ADD driver. By doing this, Card Services will load, then Socket Services, then the enabler, and finally the .ADD.

Besides a Ring-0 device driver interface, OS/2 also contains a Ring-3 programming interface into Card Services. An application program can use DosOpen on the PCMCIA$ device to obtain a file handle for access to Card Services. It can then issue DosDevIOCtl calls to perform most of the Card Services functions. In the DosDevIOCtl call, a program would use Category 13, Function 0x4F. Chapter 6 contains some utility programs that demonstrate usage of this interface.

The Ring-3 programming interface differs slightly from the Ring-0 interface. The differences are:

- At Ring-3 the interface is not register based. Since a programmer must use DosDevIOCtl, a data structure is passed as a parameter packet to Card Services. The structure resembles the register-based interface into Card Services. The structure is shown in Figure 6-1.

```
struct _PARMPACK
{
    USHORT     Function;
    USHORT     Handle;
    ULONG      EventSemHandle;
    USHORT     ArgLength;
    CHAR       ArgPacket[];
};
```

Figure 6-1: OS/2 DosDevIOCtl Parameter Packet Data Structure

- At Ring-3 a program cannot register a callback handler. Since Card Services resides at Ring-0 and all callback handlers must reside at Ring-0, the **RegisterClient** call has been modified to accept an event semaphore that will change values when a registered event occurs. The application program would spin a thread waiting for the event semaphore to change and then would make the Card Services call **VendorSpecific** to retrieve the events for the client.

The COM.SYS driver of OS/2 also has hooks to allow for hot insertion of modem cards. After a modem client driver attaches to PCMCIA$ to get the Card Services entry point, it can attach to the COM1 device to get the interdevice driver communications entry point for COM.SYS. When a modem client driver detects the insertion of a modem card, it would make the Card Services requests to get the required resources and then call the COM.SYS interdevice communications entry point to tell COM.SYS that a new COMx port has been added to the PC. When the modem client driver receives the CARD_REMOVAL event when a modem card is removed, it would call the COM.SYS entry point to tell it that a COMx port has been removed from the PC. The structure format is shown in Figure 6-2.

```
struct _COM_REQUEST
{
        USHORT  ComRequest_cmd;          // 0=remove, 1=install
        USHORT  ComRequest_num;          // 1-4 = COM1-COM4
        USHORT  ComRequest_addr;         // I/O address to use
        USHORT  ComRequest_irq;          // interrupt line to use
        USHORT  ComRequest_rc;           // return code
};
```

Figure 6-2: OS/2 COM.SYS IDC Data Structure

To call COM.SYS, the client driver would first fill in the structure and then move the segment and offset of this structure into ES:BX, and finally call the entry point received earlier from attaching to the COM1 device.

OS/2 WARP

OS/2 Warp eliminated the resource map utility. Warp has a built in resource manager that keeps track of which drivers own which I/O ports, IRQs, and memory regions. Now, Card Services communicates with the resource manager to determine whether any of these system resources can be given to a client driver.

Complete OS/2 CONFIG.SYS sample files can be found for OS/2 2.1 and OS/2 Warp in the .ZIP file for this book at the publisher's web site, ***ftp.peer-to-peer.com***. Both DEVICE and BASEDEV examples, including Card and Socket Services, are shown. Configurations with popular cards, such as the IBM PCMCIA Token-Ring, Ethernet, and SCSI cards, can be found as well as configurations with various modems.

Client Driver Template and Sample

This section describes the OS/2 client driver template supplied with this book. There are actually two parts to this section; the first part introduces a template that does nothing; it simply illustrates the concepts of calling Card Services and how a callback handler works. The second part uses this template to create a client driver that enables an IBM Token-Ring PC Card. This Token-Ring device driver is not specific to any protocol. Its purpose is to show the steps necessary to implement a PC Card client driver. The template can be used as a basis for other LAN PC Card client drivers.

Two stand-alone programs are also provided to show that the driver works. One reads frames from the driver and one writes frames to the driver. Since these programs are used to debug the driver, there will be no technical discussion of the programs. It is left as an exercise to the reader to understand them.

The Template

The template is mostly written in C. Two small parts, the entry into the device driver from the OS/2 kernel and the entry to the callback handler from card services, are written in Intel 80x86 assembler. Since the interface from the OS/2 kernel to a device driver is register based, the best way to enter a device driver is from assembler language. This code can be found in the CSSTART.ASM file on the program diskette that accompanies this book. Table 6-1 shows the assemblers, compilers, and toolkits required to build the code.

Sample Program	Assembler	Compiler	Toolkit
TRING.SYS	Microsoft Macro Assembler 5.10	Microsoft C 6.0	N/A
TEMPLATE.SYS	Microsoft Macro Assembler 5.10	Microsoft C 6.0	N/A

Table 6-1: Required OS/2 Program Template Software Tools

The first subroutine, _STRAT, simply pushes ES:BX onto the stack and calls the C-routine to process the request packet. The second subroutine in the file, _CALLBACKHANDLER, pushes the register based parameters on the stack and calls the C language routine to process the event. By performing most functions in the C language code, it is easier to maintain than assembler and is more portable to other operating environments.

The callback handler is the main difference between a card services client driver and a standard device driver. During the initialization request of a standard device driver, the driver would normally search for the hardware it services and return an error if it is not found. In a card services client driver the hardware it services may or may not be present during initialization. Therefore, the client driver will search for card services and return an error if it is not found. If card services is found, the client driver registers a callback handler that responds to events such as a card being inserted or removed. It is during the card insertion event that the client driver will search for the hardware it services.

There is one small problem with all of this. the OS/2 CS API is implemented via an interdevice driver communications (IDC) entry point. All IDC calls must occur at Ring-0 and should only be issued at task time in the kernel context. Initialization of an OS/2 driver occurs at Ring-3. To solve this, OS/2 2.1 introduced a new device driver strategy command, INIT_COMPLETE, which transfers control to a device driver as soon as it is moved from a Ring-3 to a Ring-0 level. When a client device driver receives the INIT_COMPLETE command, it may proceed to issue commands to CS.

For a device driver to get this request it must be at device driver level 3 and have a capabilities bit strip following the device name in the device driver header. Setting the driver level to 3 tells the OS/2 kernel that the driver supports the capabilities bit strip. Setting bit 4 in the capabilities bit strip tells the OS/2 kernel that the driver supports the INIT_COMPLETE command. The device header for the template is shown in Figure 6-3.

```
DEVICEHDR devhdr = {
    (void far *) 0xFFFFFFFF,
    (DAW_CHR | DAW_OPN | DAW_LEVEL3),
    (OFF) STRAT,
    (OFF) 0,
    "CSSHELL$",
    "\0\0\0\0\0\0\0\0",
    CBS_INIT,
};
```

Figure 6-3: OS/2 Device Driver Header

Notice the strategy routine entry point is STRAT. Since it follows the C calling convention it is really _STRAT and is the assembler routine discussed above. The _STRAT calls _main which, is the C-routine to process request packets.

So now, during the INIT command, the device driver simply gets the Device Helper entry point and announces its presence. No searching for any devices or card services just yet. The real work is done during INIT_COMPLETE and later in the callback handler. Figure 6-4 shows the INIT command strategy routine. Notice that the subroutine Init is at the end of the code segment. Since this code is no longer needed after initialization, so it is discarded to make the code segment smaller.

```
int main(PREQPACKET rp)
{
    switch(rp->RPcommand)
```

```
    {
    case RPINIT:             /* 0x00                         */

        /* init called by kernel in protected mode */

        return Init(rp);
               .
               .
               .
int Init(PREQPACKET rp)
{

    /* store DevHlp entry point */

    DevHlp = rp->s.Init.DevHlp;    /* save DevHlp entry point */


    if (SegLimit(HIUSHORT((void far *) Init),
        &rp->s.InitExit.finalCS) ||
        SegLimit(HIUSHORT((void far *) BannerMsg),
        &rp->s.InitExit.finalDS))  ;
        Abort();

    DosPutMessage(1, strlen(BannerMsg), BannerMsg);

    return (RPDONE);
}
```

Figure 6-4: OS/2 Device Driver Initialization

After the INIT command is processed, the next time the driver is called is during INIT_COMPLETE. The OS/2 kernel processes INIT commands in the order the device statements are found in the CONFIG.SYS file. The kernel processes the INIT_COMPLETE commands in the reverse order, after all drivers have been loaded. So, for example, if the following device drivers are found in the CONFIG.SYS file and are card services client drivers, the commands would be processed in the order shown:

INIT	DEVICE DRIVER	INIT_COMPLETE
1	D:\IBMCOM\MACS\PCMNICCS.OS2	3
2	D:\IBMCOM\MACS\IBMTOKCS.OS2	2
3	D:\IBMCOM\MACS\CSTD.OS2	1

The device ordering is important for any interdevice driver communications that must take place. A driver that needs to communicate with another driver must make sure that that driver is loaded and operational.

The main steps in the INIT_COMPLETE command are to get the card services entry point address, make sure it is present, and register the callback handler that handles the card services events. In OS/2, card services is implemented as a device driver (PCMCIA.SYS). All communications with card services are through its IDC entry point. To get this entry point a driver uses the device helper routine DevHlp_AttachDD. DevHlp_AttachDD returns the real-mode and protect-mode IDC entry points. Only the protect-mode entry point is needed. The code in Figure 6-5 shows the DevHlp_AttachDD call.

```
int main(PREQPACKET rp)
{
    switch(rp->RPcommand)
    {
                .
                .
                .
       case RPINIT_DONE:        /* 0x1f */

        /* init done                    */

        if (AttachDD(PCMCIA, &aaCSAddr))
        {
           flCSPresent = FALSE;
           return(RPDONE | RPERR | ERROR_GEN_FAILURE);
        }

    }
}
```

Figure 6-5: OS/2 Device Driver Initialization

If the DevHlp_AttachDD call succeeds, then the card services device named PCMCIA$ exists. If the call fails, then a device named PCMCIA$ does not exist; meaning the PCMCIA.SYS file was not loaded as part of the CONFIG.SYS file. The client driver only knows of the existence of the device; it still does not know if card services really is present. Another device driver, which is not card services, may have chosen PCMCIA$ as its name. The client driver must then call the IDC entry point with a card services request to ensure it is actually present and that the level of card services can support the client driver. This is done via the **GetCardServicesInfo** request.

GetCardServicesInfo returns the number of logical sockets installed and information about card services presence, such as a revision value, level, and a vendor string. The complete argument packet is shown in Figure 6-6.

```
//   GetCardServicesInfo
typedef struct _GETCARDSERVICESINFO
{
   USHORT      InfoLen;
   USHORT      Signature;
   USHORT      Count;
   USHORT      Revision;
   USHORT      CSLevel;
   USHORT      VStrOff;
   USHORT      VStrLen;
   UCHAR       VendorString[1];
} GETCARDSERVICESINFO;
```

Figure 6-6: OS/2 GetCardSevicesInfo Data Structure

The next step in the client driver is to interrogate the data returned by **GetCardServicesInfo**. To ensure card services is present, the Signature field must be CS. If it is not, then card services is not present and the client driver returns with an error. After the client driver knows that card services is present it then checks the CSLevel to ensure that it can work with the level of card services installed. If the client driver determines that it can work with the level of card services, it then registers a callback handler to be notified of interested events. The template client driver checks whether the level of card services is between 2.0 and 2.1. If it is, the client then registers its callback handler and is finished with its INIT_COMPLETE processing.

When a client driver registers a callback handler, it must tell card services the type of client it is and what type of artificial CARD_INSERTION events card services should generate. This information is the bit-mapped Attributes field of the **RegisterClient** argument packet. The client driver template is for an I/O client that needs to receive artificial CARD_INSERTION events for both sharable and exclusively used PC cards. Artificial CARD_INSERTION events are generated either during IPL time or if a card is already inserted in a socket when the **RegisterClient** request is issued. By receiving these artificial events, the client driver can establish its initial internal state without polling sockets to determine whether PC Cards are already inserted.

The EventMask field of the **RegisterClient** argument packet is a bit-map that specifies the events that card services should generate for the client. Notification for events such as EJECTION_REQUEST, EJECTION_COMPLETE, INSERTION_REQUEST, INSERTION_COMPLETE, PM_SUSPEND, PM_RESUME can be registered. The template driver in this book only requires card detect change notification. This equates to only receiving CARD_INSERTION and the CARD_REMOVAL events. A complete driver may want to register for the REQUEST/COMPLETE events to support sockets with locking mechanisms. Or a driver may want to register for the power management events PM_SUSPEND and PM_RESUME. Unfortunately, card services specification (version 2.1) does not specify how the power management events are handled but the PM_SUSPEND and PM_RESUME events are specified.

The third field in the argument packet for **RegisterClient** is ClientData. This data is usually set to pointers to internal data areas which is returned to the callback handler on entry. The callback handler then has addressability into the client driver data areas without having to load any registers. However, this template driver does not need any client data so the ClientData field is left NULL.

The fourth and final field in the argument packet is the Version of card services the client expects to use. This value is used by card services to provide better backward compatibility (the template assumes card services version 2.1).

After all the fields are set, the template driver then makes the card services **RegisterClient** request. The call returns immediately to the client while card services performs the registration in the background. When card services has completed the processing, it notifies the client driver callback handler with a REGISTRATION_COMPLETE event. After the **RegisterClient** is made, the template client driver performs a DevHlp_Block to suspend foreground processing to prevent the driver from making any further card services requests before the registration is complete. In the callback handler, the driver performs a DevHlp_Run during REGISTRATION_COMPLETE so that INIT_COMPLETE can continue. Performing the block/run ensures that the registration process starts and finishes before any further card services requests are made. This will be better explained in the Token-Ring driver example later.

Once the block has been run, INIT_COMPLETE is done. All of the logic from the **GetCardServicesInfo** call to the end of INIT_COMPLETE is shown in Figure 6-7.

```
fpgci = (FPGETCARDSERVICESINFO)CSBuffer;
fpgci->Signature = 0;
if (CardServices(GET_CARDSERVICES_INFO, 0, 0, sizeof(CSBuffer),
                 fpgci, 0)){
   flCSPresent = FALSE;
   return(RPDONE | RPERR | ERROR_GEN_FAILURE);
}

if (fpgci->Signature != 'S'*256 + 'C')
{
   flCSPresent = FALSE;
   return(RPDONE | RPERR | ERROR_GEN_FAILURE);
}

//  Check card services Level.  It must be 2.0 - 2.1 for the
//  code to continue.
if ((fpgci->CSLevel < 0x0200) || (fpgci->CSLevel > 0x0210))
{
   flCSPresent = FALSE;
   return(RPDONE | RPERR | ERROR_GEN_FAILURE);
}
rc.Attributes = RC_ATTR_IO_CLIENT |
                    RC_ATTR_CARD_INSERT_SHARED |
                    RC_ATTR_CARD_INSERT_EXCL;
rc.EventMask = RC_EVENT_CD_CHANGE;

BlockID = (ULONG)rp + 1;
CardServices(REGISTER_CLIENT, 0, CALLBACKHANDLER,
                  sizeof(rc), &rc, &rcHandle);
Block(BlockID, 10000, 1, &errcode);

flCSPresent = TRUE;
return(RPDONE);
```

Figure 6-7: OS/2 GetCardServicesInfo and RegisterClient Example

All that remains to discuss in the template driver is the callback handler. The callback handler is simply a switch/case statement for interesting events. The only events this template client driver is interested in are REGISTRATION_COMPLETE, CARD_INSERTION, CARD_REMOVAL.

The REGISTRATION_COMPLETE event in this template is only used to run the blocked INIT_COMPLETE thread, thus signaling that the initialization of the driver is finally complete and card services requests can be made.

Card services sends a CARD_INSERTION event to every registered client whenever a PC Card is inserted in a socket. A client must be able to determine whether the PC Card is a card it can support. One method to do this is to read a string out of the card's CIS that uniquely identifies the card and compare it to a string that the client driver knows. The Level 1 Version/Product Information Tuple contains just such a string. The string has the name of the manufacturer followed by the name of the product. These two strings together uniquely identify the PC Card inserted in the socket. Therefore, at the top of the CARD_INSERTION event, the template client driver makes the card services requests **GetFirstTuple** and **GetTupleData** to read the card's Level 1 Version/Product Information Tuple and determine what card has been inserted in the socket. Since this is just a template, there really is no string for comparison. The comments below the card services requests describe the standard processing. Basically, if the strings match, request any required resources from card services. If the strings do not match, then the PC Card inserted into the socket is not supported by the client, so the program just returns.

For CARD_REMOVAL events, card services works the same as it does for CARD_INSERTION events. All registered clients receive a CARD_REMOVAL event when a PC Card is removed from a socket. Since this is just a template and does not support a specific card, the usual processing is stated in comments. Basically, if the socket the card was removed from matches the socket the driver saved from a previous CARD_INSERTION event, release the resources that were requested during the CARD_INSERTION event.

The template is now completely explained. The entire callback handler is shown in Figure 6-8.

```
int NP _loadds  CallBack(USHORT Function, USHORT Socket,
                         USHORT Info,
                         USHORT ClientData1, USHORT ClientData2,
                         USHORT ClientData3,
                         FARPOINTER MTDRequest,
                         FARPOINTER Buffer)
{
switch (Function)
    {
    case REGISTRATION_COMPLETE:
        Run(BlockID);
        return 0;

    case CARD_INSERTION:
        CardInsertion(Socket);
        return 0;

    case CARD_REMOVAL:
        CardRemoval(Socket);
        return 0;

    default:
        return 0;
    }
}


int CardInsertion(USHORT  Socket)
{
    fpgt = (FPGETTUPLE)CSBuffer;
    fpgt->Socket = Socket;
    fpgt->Attributes = 0;
    fpgt->DesiredTuple = 0x15;
    fpgt->TupleOffset = 0;
    CardServices(GET_FIRST_TUPLE, 0, 0, 18, fpgt, 0);
    CardServices(GET_TUPLE_DATA,  0, 0, sizeof(CSBuffer),
                 fpgt, 0);
    return 0;
}



int CardRemoval(USHORT  Socket)
{
// if Socket = socket card removed from
//     release resources assigned to card
}
```

Figure 6-8: OS/2 Callback Handler

The Sample Token-Ring Client Device Driver

This part of the chapter will start with the template described above and add code to support the IBM PCMCIA Token-Ring adapter. The client driver is capable of transmitting and receiving data frames on a Token-Ring LAN. It does not conform to any driver specification (ODI, NDIS, or Packet Driver), but it can be used as a basis for one.

Starting at the top of the Token-Ring client driver, notice that not much has really changed from the template. Since the driver now supports an actual device, the device name (TRING$) has been changed to better reflect the device it supports. The device header is shown in Figure 6-9.

```
DEVICEHDR devhdr = {
    (void far *) 0xFFFFFFFF,
    (DAW_CHR | DAW_LEVEL3),
    (OFF) STRAT,
    (OFF) 0,
    "TRING$   ",
    "\0\0\0\0\0\0\0\0",
    CBS_INIT,
};
```

Figure 6-9: OS/2 Token-Ring Device Driver Header

New to the data segment is a queue to hold artificial insertion events. The queue is represented by the array ArtificialInsertSocket that holds eight elements and the counter NumArtificialInsert that holds the number of elements in the array. Some drivers register for artificial insertion events in order to establish their initial state, but cannot act on the event as they arrive because the client registration process has not completed; as is the case with this driver. As a result, the TRING$ driver blocks and waits for the REGISTRATION_COMPLETE event to occur.

During the CARD_INSERTION event the Token-Ring card is opened, which requires a block and wait for the card to reset. A driver cannot block the same thread twice. To overcome this, the TRING$ driver performs the block after **RegisterClient** and waits for the run to be issued from the routine handling the REGISTRATION_COMPLETE event. Any artificial insertion events that occur during this period are held in the queue. After the driver returns from the block it processes any artificial insertion events that occurred.

The initialization code is still the same as the template in regard to PC Card. Now that the driver actually supports a device that requires resources, code has been added to acquire these resources. The first resource acquired is a pointer to the global information segment. This segment contains information such as time in seconds, milliseconds, hours, minutes, seconds, major revision number, minor revision number, and other system values. The Token-Ring driver is only interested in the time fields for critical timing and delay. The global information segment pointer is not used now, but is kept around for later. The next two resources the driver acquires from the system are GDT selectors for its memory mapped I/O (MMIO) area and its shared RAM (SRAM) area. The driver can only acquire the selectors for now; since it is not known whether or not the Token-Ring card is in the socket, the selectors cannot be mapped to physical memory just yet. Finally the driver announces its presence with DosPutMessage and sets some default values for MMIO, SRAM, and the IRQ level it will later use. The complete initialization sequence is shown in Figure 6-10.

```
int Init(PREQPACKET rp)
{
    DevHlp = rp->s.Init.DevHlp;    /* save DevHlp entry point     */
    GetDOSVar(1, &pginfo);     /* Get ptr to global info segment */

    AllocGDTSelector(1, &MMIOSel); /* Get GDT selectors            */
    AllocGDTSelector(1, &SRAMSel);


    if (SegLimit(HIUSHORT((void far *) Init),
        &rp->s.InitExit.finalCS) ||
         SegLimit(HIUSHORT((void far *) BannerMsg),
         &rp->s.InitExit.finalDS))   ;
    Abort();

    DosPutMessage(1, strlen(BannerMsg), BannerMsg);

    //  Assume MMIO at CC000, SRAM at D8000, and IRQ 9.
    MMIOAddress = 0xCC000;
    SRAMAddress = 0xD8000;
    IRQLine     = 9;
    return (RPDONE);
}
```

Figure 6-10: OS/2 Token-Ring Device Driver Sample Initialization Source Code

The INIT_COMPLETE strategy command for the Token-Ring driver has only three lines of code added to the template: the call to DevHlp_AllocCtxHook and the processing of the artificial insertion event queue. A context hook is a thread that the OS/2 kernel will dispatch after the device driver returns to the OS/2 kernel. The context hook runs in a kernel context. In early versions of the IBM OS/2 card services, the callback handler was entered in an interrupt context. In the more recent versions this was modified so that the callback handler is entered in the kernel context. This sampe driver is written so that it can be used both versions of card services. Hence, the context hook, is important since some functions require a kernel context. AllocCtxHook tells OS/2 the address of the thread; OS/2 returns a handle to the context hook so that it can be armed later. The processing of the context hook will be described in detail during the CARD_INSERTION event.

If the driver received any CARD_INSERTION events before the REGISTRATION_COMPLETE event, the socket numbers for the insertions are saved in the ArtificialInsertSocket array and the number of insertions is saved in the

NumArtificialInsert variable. After the return from the block after the **RegisterClient** request, the driver loops over the artificial insertions and calls the CardInsertion subroutine to process the artificial insertions. It does this so that the initial state of the cards in the sockets is set at the end of initialization of the driver. The dequeuing process is shown in Figure 6-11.

```
CardServices(REGISTER_CLIENT, 0, CALLBACKHANDLER,
                sizeof(rc), &rc, &rcHandle);
Block(BlockID, 10000, 1, &errcode);

//  Flag registration as complete
flRegComplete = TRUE;

//  Process queued Artifical Insertions.
for (i=0; i<NumArtificalInsert; i++)
{
   CardInsertion(ArtificialInsertSocket[i]);
}
```

Figure 6-11: OS/2 Artificial Insertion Dequeuing Sample Source Code

The next two case statements are the READ and WRITE entries. These two entries are not specific to any card services client driver or to any networking specification. They are provided here to test the driver by returning data to a calling program or writing data on a LAN from a calling program. The READ entry looks for any data in a buffer. If there is data, it moves it into the calling program's data buffer and the driver returns. If there is no data available, the driver blocks the calling thread for either 60 seconds, until data is available, or until the thread is interrupted (possibly by the BREAK key being pressed). If data is received during the block, it is moved into the calling program's data buffer and the driver returns. The WRITE entry moves data into a transmit buffer, issues a transmit command, and returns. The READ and WRITE entries are shown in Figure 6-12.These two entries complete the main processing of the Token-Ring driver.

```
case RPREAD:
    if (BufLen != 0)
    {
       MoveData(Buffer, (FARPOINTER)rp->s.ReadWrite.buffer,
                BufLen,MOVE_VIRTTOPHYS);
       rp->s.ReadWrite.count = BufLen;
       BufLen = 0;
       return(RPDONE);
    }
    else
    {
       ReadBlockID = (ULONG) rp;
       Block(ReadBlockID, 60000, 0, &errcode);
       switch (errcode)
       {
       case 0:
           MoveData(Buffer, (FARPOINTER)rp->s.ReadWrite.buffer,
                    BufLen,MOVE_VIRTTOPHYS);
           rp->s.ReadWrite.count = BufLen;
           BufLen = 0;
           ReadBlockID = 0;
           return(RPDONE);
       case 1:
           ReadBlockID = 0;
           return(RPDONE | RPERR | ERROR_NOT_READY);
       case 2:
           ReadBlockID = 0;
           return(RPDONE | RPERR | ERROR_CHAR_CALL_INTERRUPTED);
       }
    }


case RPWRITE:
    MoveData((FARPOINTER)rp->s.ReadWrite.buffer, XmitBuffer,
                   rp->s.ReadWrite.count, MOVE_PHYSTOVIRT);
    XmitBufLen = rp->s.ReadWrite.count;
    XmitFrame();
    return(RPDONE);


/* all other commands are flagged */
default:
    return(RPDONE | RPERR | ERROR_BAD_COMMAND);
```

Figure 6-12: OS/2 Sample Token-Ring Source Code to Handle READ and WRITE Request Packets

The callback handler for the Token-Ring driver starts out the same as the template; the REGISTER_CLIENT event simply runs the blocked INIT_COMPLETE thread. The differences start with the CARD_INSERTION event processing. Since artificial insertions are being queued the driver first checks if registration is complete. If it is, the driver actually performs the insertion event processing. If registration is not complete, the driver queues the event by saving the socket number in the array ArtificialInsertSocket and updates the number of queued events in the counter NumArtificialInsert. A more robust driver might want to save all of the data from the CARD_INSERTION event (e.g. the Client data and the information data). Since this simple driver does not have any other data, only the socket number is saved. The REGISTRATION_COMPLETE and CARD_INSERTION event processing is shown in Figure 6-13.

```
case REGISTRATION_COMPLETE:
    Run(BlockID);
    return 0;

case CARD_INSERTION:
    if (flRegComplete)
       CardInsertion(Socket);
    else
       ArtificialInsertSocket[NumArtificalInsert++] = Socket;
    return 0;
```

Figure 6-13: OS/2 Event Handling Source Code

Whether the CARD_INSERTION event was artificial or not, the processing of the event is the same. Every registered card services client that asked to receive CARD_INSERTION events will receive the event when a card is inserted in a socket. The client driver must determine whether or not it works with the card that was inserted. To do this, the client driver reads the Level 1 Version/Product Information Tuple and uses the name of the manufacturer and/or the name of the product to verify that the card is indeed the card it works with. The sample Token-Ring driver only works with the IBM PCMCIA Token-Ring card has the Level 1 Version/Product Information Tuple information as shown in Figure 6-14.

```
Tuple Code:  15
Tuple Link:  1F
Tuple Major: 04
Tuple Minor: 01
Name of Manufacturer: IBM
Name of Product:      TOKEN RING
Additional Product Info:  0933929
Additional Product Info:  NONE
```

Figure 6-14: IBM PCMCIA Token-Ring Card Level 1 Version/Product Information Tuple

Since the driver works only with this card, the driver checks only for the letters TO in the exact place where the Name of Product is found. A more robust driver should check for the IBM and the TOKEN RING names. If the card that caused this event is not an IBM PCMCIA Token-Ring card, the driver simply returns to card services. If the card is the correct card, the driver saves the socket number and starts to request the resources it needs from card services. The code that gets and compares the tuple data is shown in Figure 6-15.

```
/*  Read tuple 0x15 to make sure this is a Token-Ring card  */
/*  in the socket.                                          */
fpgt = (FPGETTUPLE)CSBuffer;
fpgt->Socket = Socket;
fpgt->Attributes = 0;
fpgt->DesiredTuple = 0x15;
fpgt->TupleOffset = 0;
CardServices(GET_FIRST_TUPLE, 0, 0, 18, fpgt, 0);
CardServices(GET_TUPLE_DATA,  0, 0, sizeof(CSBuffer), fpgt, 0);

/*  Look for 'TO' in the buffer or write a string
    routine to check for the entire 'TOKEN RING'
    product name in the tuple data                  */

if ((fpgt->s.GetTupleData.TupleData[8] == 'T') &&
    (fpgt->s.GetTupleData.TupleData[9] == 'O')){
   MySocket = Socket;
         .
         .
}
```

Figure 6-15: OS/2 Tuple Processing Source Code

The resources a PC Card requires are defined in the card configuration table entry tuples in the CIS. A robust driver would read the tuples to find out what I/O, IRQ, and memory windows are needed for the card to operate, and then go and request them. This simple driver does not read the tuples; instead, since it works specifically with the one PC Card, it uses default values. The resources the IBM PCMCIA Token-Ring card uses can be found in the complete CIS listing in the Local Area Network, Credit Card Adapters Technical Reference (part number 33G9243). The card configuration table entry for this card is shown in Figure 6-16. It is seen from the entry that the card requires the following resources:

- One I/O range, 16 address bits wide
- A level mode interrupt in the range 0 through 15
- A memory window 8K in length
- A memory window 64K in length

Address	Byte Value	Name	Description
5C	1B	CISTPL_CE	Card entry tuple
5E	1E	TPL_LINK	Link to next tuple
60	E1	TPCE_INDEX	Default, Index=X'21'
62	81	TPCE_IF	Interface Description
64	7D	TPCE_FS	Feature Selection Byte
66	11	TPCE_PD	Power Description
68	55		
6A	46		
6C	FC	TPCE_TD	Wait scale only
6E	09		Max Wait=1 microsecond
70	B0	TPCE_IO	8-bit I/O, 16 address bits
72	60		1 range, I/O addr=2 bytes
74	20		Start I/O address (LSB)
76	0A		Start I/O address (MSB)
78	07		Length of range=8 bytes
7A	30	TPCE_IR	Level mode, mask for intrrupt
7C	FF		All level enable
7E	FF		
80	11	TPCE_MEN	Length size=2, window=2
82	20		1st window = 8K (LSB)
84	00		1st window = 8K (MSB)
86	00		2nd window = 64K (LSB)
88	10		2nd window = 64K (MSB)
8A	FF		End of list

Figure 6-16: Card Configuration Table Entry

The first resource the driver requests is the I/O ports. To request the I/O ports from card services, the REQUESTRELEASEIO structure is filled in with the values the driver needs to configure the card. The Socket field contains the logical socket that contains the desired PC Card. The **RequestIO** card services request can request two I/O ranges. This particular card only requires one I/O range so the BasePorts1 field contains the first port address requested, 0xA20; the BasePorts2 field contains 0x000. The NumPorts1 field contains 4 since only ports 0xA20-0xA23 are really needed for the card to operate. The Attributes1 field is a bit-map with the following bit definitions:

• Bit 0	Shared (set=true)
• Bit 1	First Shared (set=true)
• Bit 2	Force Alias Accessibility
• Bit 3	Data Path Width for I/O Range (0=8 bit, 1=16bit)
• Bits 4-7	Reserved

For this particular card the Attributes1 field is set to zero since the I/O is not sharable and its data path is 8 bit. Since a second I/O port range is not required, the NumPorts2 and Attributes2 fields are set to zero. The last field set is the IOAddrLines field and is the number of I/O address lines decoded by the PC Card, and for this driver, the value is sixteen. After the structure is filled in, the driver calls card services with the **RequestIO** request. The code that performs all of this is shown in Figure 6-17.

```
// Assume PRIMARY Adapter.  Get 4 I/O ports starting at A20.
ri.Socket = Socket;
ri.BasePort1 = 0xA20;
ri.NumPorts1 = 4;
ri.Attributes1 = 0;
ri.BasePort2 = 0;
ri.NumPorts2 = 0;
ri.Attributes2 = 0;
ri.IOAddrLines = 16;
CardServices(REQUEST_IO, rcHandle, 0, sizeof(ri), &ri, 0);
```

Figure 6-17: OS/2 RequestIO Source Code

After getting the I/O ports, the driver then requests an interrupt request line from card services. Just like the **RequestIO** request, a structure must be filled in before calling card services. The structure used here is called REQUESTIRQ. The first field is again the logical socket containing the PC Card. The next is the Attributes field. This field is another bit-mapped field that specifies details about the type of interrupt desired by the client. The bit definitions are:

- Bits 0,1 — IRQ Type
  00 = Exclusive
  01 = Time-Mulitplexed Sharing
  10 = Dynamic Sharing
  11 = RESERVED
- Bit 2 — Force Pulse (set=true)
- Bit 3 — First Shared (set=true)
- Bits 4-7 — Reserved (reset to zero)
- Bit 8 — Pulse IRQ Allocated (set=true on return)
- Bits 9-15 — Reserved (reset to zero)

The Token-Ring card only requires the IRQ type to be exclusive. The next field set is *IRQInfo1*. It is another bit-mapped field. The bits are:

• Bits 0-3	IRQ requested if Bit 4 is reset to zero or
• Bit 0	NMI
• Bit 1	IOCK
• Bit 2	BERR
• Bit 3	VEND
• Bit 4	Mask, if set to one, the IRQInfo2 bytes are valid
• Bit 5	Level
• Bit 6	Pulse
• Bit 7	Share

The Token-Ring card only sets bit four (the IRQInfo2 field contains a mask) and it sets bit five (the IRQ is a level interrupt). Finally, the IRQInfo2 field is a bit-map of the IRQs the card can use Bit 0=IRQ0, Bit 1=IRQ1, Bit 2=IRQ2, up to Bit 15=IRQ15. Multiple bits can be set, telling card services to pick an available IRQ out of the map. This driver defaults to the value in IRQLine, but can be changed to 0xFFFF to let card services select an interrupt between IRQ 0 and IRQ 15.

Once the structure is completed, the card services **RequestIRQ** call is performed. Card services returns the IRQ that was assigned in the AssignedIRQ field. The code that requests the IRQ is shown in Figure 6-18.

```
//  Get the IRQ.
rirq.Socket = Socket;
rirq.Attributes = RIRQ_ATTR_EXCLUSIVE;
rirq.IRQInfo1 = RIRQ_INFO1_VALID_MASK | RIRQ_INFO1_LEVEL;
rirq.IRQInfo2 = 1 << IRQLine;
CardServices(REQUEST_IRQ, rcHandle, 0, sizeof(rirq), &rirq, 0);
```

Figure 6-18: OS/2 RequestIRQ Source Code

After card services grants access to the IRQ, the driver sets up the interrupt mask register port and the interrupt disable/enable bytes. These values are used later in the interrupt handler to disable and enable the interrupt line.

The next resource the driver requests from card services is one of the memory windows. The Token-Ring card requires two memory windows: one for its memory mapped I/O (MMIO) and BIOS, the other for its shared RAM (SRAM). This first card services request is for the MMIO/BIOS area. This area is characterized by being in common memory, having a 16-bit data path, and being 8K in length, having an access speed of 250ns, and using the wait line if available. All of these values are configurable via various bit-mapped fields in the **RequestWindow** structure. The first field is, of course, the *Socket* field, which contains the logical socket to map into the system memory address space. The next field is the Attributes field. It is bit-mapped and describes the attributes of the memory window. The bit definitions are:

- Bit 0 Reserved
- Bit 1 Memory Type (set=attribute)
- Bit 2 Enabled (set=true, reset=disabled)
- Bit 3 Data path width (reset=8-bit, set=16-bit)
- Bit 4 Paged (set=true)
- Bit 5 Shared (set=true)
- Bit 6 First Shared (set=true)
- Bit 7 Binding Specific
- Bit 8 Card offsets are window sized (set=true)
- Bits 9-15 Reserved

For the Token-Ring card, only bits two and three are set to denote that the memory window is enabled and 16-bits in width. The next field, Base, contains the four-byte value of the physical location in the PC memory space to map to PC Card memory. The Size field contains the size of the window, in bytes; in this case it is 8K. Finally, the AccessSpeed field is set to the memory window speed. It is bit-mapped and is defined as follows:

- Bits 0-2 Device speed code, if speed mantissa is zero
- Bits 0-2 Speed exponent , if speed mantissa is not zero
- Bits 3-6 Speed mantissa
- Bit 7 Wait (set=use wait, if available)

If the speed mantissa is zero, the speed codes are

Code	**Speed**
• 0	Reserved
• 1	250ns
• 2	200ns
• 3	150ns
• 4	100ns
• 5-7	Reserved

The Token-Ring card uses 250ns and Wait, if available. After the structure is initialized, the card services **RequestWindow** function is issued. Card services returns with a handle to the memory window. This handle is used in the **MapMemPage** card services request to map the area of PC Card memory to the system memory window obtained with the **RequestWindow** call. The MAPMEMPAGE structure only has two fields: the PC card offset and the Page number. For the Token-Ring card, simply map the

PC Card memory to the same address as the system memory. Since the *Paged* bit was not set for this window, set the Page field here to zero.

The next resource the driver requests is the SRAM memory window. The processing here is the same as for the MMIO/BIOS area, except a different address and segment size are required. The code for requesting and mapping the MMIO/BIOS and SRAM areas is shown in Figure 6-19.

```
//  MMIO Window.
rw.Socket = Socket;
rw.Attributes = RW_ATTR_COMMON_MEMORY | RW_ATTR_ENABLED |
                       RW_ATTR_16_BIT;
rw.Base = MMIOAddress;
rw.Size = 0x02000L;
rw.AccessSpeed = RW_SPEED_USE_WAIT | RW_SPEED_250NS;
CardServices(REQUEST_WINDOW, rcHandle, 0, sizeof(rw), &rw,
                       &MMIOWindow);

//  Map the memory.
mmp.CardOffset = MMIOAddress;
mmp.Page = 0;
CardServices(MAP_MEM_PAGE, MMIOWindow, 0, sizeof(mmp), &mmp, 0);

//  SRAM Window.
rw.Socket = Socket;
rw.Attributes = RW_ATTR_COMMON_MEMORY | RW_ATTR_ENABLED |
                       RW_ATTR_16_BIT;
rw.Base = SRAMAddress;
rw.Size = 0x04000L;
rw.AccessSpeed = RW_SPEED_USE_WAIT | RW_SPEED_250NS;
CardServices(REQUEST_WINDOW, rcHandle, 0, sizeof(rw), &rw,
                       &SRAMWindow);

//  Map the memory.
mmp.CardOffset = SRAMAddress;
mmp.Page = 0;
CardServices(MAP_MEM_PAGE, SRAMWindow, 0, sizeof(mmp), &mmp, 0);
```

Figure 6-19: OS/2 RequestWindow and MapMemPage Source Code

After all of the card services requests have been granted, the driver finally calls card services to configure the card. Upon receiving the **RequestConfiguration**, card services will apply power to the socket, only if the socket was not already powered on, and establish the configuration in the socket adapter and the PC Card. The **RequestConfiguration** structure is filled with the following values:

Field	Description	Token-Ring Value
Socket	Logical socket to be configured	Logical Socket
Attributes	Bit-mapped	Enable IRQ Steering
Vcc	Vcc Setting in tenths of volts	50
Vpp1	Vpp1 Setting in tenths of volts	50
Vpp2	Vpp2 Setting in tenths of volts	50
IntType	Interface Type Memory or Memory and I/O	Memory and I/O
ConfigBase	Card Base address of config registers	0x800
Status	Card Status register, if present	0x20
Pin	Card Pin register, if present	0
Copy	Card Socket/Copy register, if present	0
Option	Card Option register, if present Also known as ConfigIndex	0x61
Present	Card Configuration regs present	OPTION and STATUS

All of the values above can be read from configuration tuples on the PC Card. The ConfigBase, Present, and Option field values can be found in the configuration tuple. The rest of the fields can be found in the card configuration table entry tuple. A more robust driver could read these tuples and then fill in the **RequestConfiguration** structure; since this is a simple example driver, the values were simply taken from the technical reference for this card. The code that configures the card is shown in Figure 6-20.

```
// Configure the card.
rcf.Socket = Socket;
rcf.Attributes = RC_ENABLE_IRQ_STEERING;
rcf.Vcc = 50;
rcf.Vpp1 = 50;
rcf.Vpp2 = 50;
rcf.IntType = RC_INTERFACE_MEMORY_IO;
rcf.ConfigBase = 0x800L;
rcf.Status = 0x20;
rcf.Pin = 0;
rcf.Copy = 0;
rcf.Option = 0x61;
rcf.Present = RC_OPTION_REG | RC_STATUS_REG;
CardServices(REQUEST_CONFIGURATION, rcHandle, 0, sizeof(rcf),
             &rcf, 0);
```

Figure 6-20: OS/2 RequestConfiguration Source Code

Once the card has been configured by card services, the driver then arms the context hook to complete the CARD_INSERTION event. The context hook, as described earlier in the chapter, runs under a kernel mode context. Earlier, the **RequestIRQ** card services request was performed to ask card services for an IRQ to use. Now the driver must tell OS/2 it wants to use an IRQ. At the top of the context hook, the DevHlp_SetIRQ call is performed to tell OS/2 the subroutine to call for the IRQ requested. The reason this call is done in the context hook is because the DevHlp_SetIRQ can only be made in a kernel mode context, while the callback handler runs in an interrupt mode context. By splitting the CARD_INSERTION event into a card services request part and an OS/2 and hardware specific part, the driver is a well-behaved card services client and requests resources only when needed and releases the resources when not needed (CARD_REMOVAL). Without the context hook, the driver would have to call DevHlp_SetIRQ during initialization, call **RequestIRQ** during CARD_INSERTION, and never call **ReleaseIRQ** or DevHlp_UnSetIRQ when the card is removed and the IRQ is no longer needed.

After the DevHlp_SetIRQ call is made, the driver writes some I/O ports to configure and turn on the Token-Ring card. The I/O ports and values written are specific to the Token-Ring card and can be found in the technical reference for this adapter. After the card is turned on, it is reset and opened; opening the adapter inserts it into the ring, allowing data to be transmitted and received. This completes the entire CARD_INSERTION event. The context hook code is shown in Figure 6-21.

```
void far InsertHook()
{
    UCHAR          ConfigReg;

    SetIRQ(IRQLine, (PFUNCTION)IHandler, 0);

    /*  Turn on the TR CCA.  */
    /*  Write the 4 bytes of the Configuration Register.  */
    ConfigReg = MMIOAddress >> 16;
    outp(0xA20, ConfigReg);
    ConfigReg = 0x10 | ((MMIOAddress >> 12) & 0x0E);
    outp(0xA20, ConfigReg);
    outp(0xA20, 0x26);
    outp(0xA20, 0x36);     //  Assume 16k SRAM, 16Mbit, PRIMARY
    outp(0xA20, 0x40);

    /*  Reset the adapter to a known state.  */
    ResetAdapter();

    /*  Open the adapter.  */
    OpenAdapter();
}
```

Figure 6-21: OS/2 Context Hook Source Code

The last event the Token-Ring driver acts on is the CARD_REMOVAL event. This event is received by all card services client drivers. It is up to the client driver to determine if it should act on the event. At the top of the CARD_REMOVAL event, the driver checks whether the socket saved earlier from the CARD_INSERTION event matches the socket reported by this CARD_REMOVAL event. If they match, the driver starts to release all of the resources it acquired during the CARD_INSERTION event. If the sockets values do not match, the driver simply returns to card services.

The client driver must first tell OS/2 that it no longer needs the IRQ by invoking the DevHlp_UnSetIRQ function. After that, the PC Card configuration is released by the card services **ReleaseConfiguration** request. **ReleaseConfiguration** returns the PC Card and socket to a memory only interface and configuration of zero. If no other clients are using the PC Card, card services may remove power from the socket, but this is not required. After the card configuration is released, the memory windows are then released with the card services request **ReleaseWindow**. Finally, the IRQ and I/O addresses are released. With the **ReleaseIRQ** and **ReleaseIO** card services requests, no changes are made to the socket; only the card services internal map of resources is updated to reflect that the IRQ and I/O address can be requested by other clients. The complete CARD_REMOVAL processing is shown in Figure 6-22.

```
int CardRemoval(USHORT  Socket){
    if (Socket == MySocket)  {
       UnSetIRQ(9);
       rlcf.Socket = Socket;
       CardServices(RELEASE_CONFIGURATION, rcHandle, 0,
                    sizeof(rlcf), &rlcf, 0);

       CardServices(RELEASE_WINDOW, MMIOWindow, 0, 0, 0, 0);
       CardServices(RELEASE_WINDOW, SRAMWindow, 0, 0, 0, 0);

       rlirq.Socket = Socket;
       rlirq.Attributes = RIRQ_ATTR_EXCLUSIVE;
       rlirq.AssignedIRQ = IRQLine;
       CardServices(RELEASE_IRQ, rcHandle, 0, sizeof(rlirq),
                    &rlirq, 0);

       ri.Socket = Socket;
       ri.BasePort1 = 0xA20;
       ri.NumPorts1 = 4;
       ri.Attributes1 = 0;
       ri.BasePort2 = 0;
       ri.NumPorts2 = 0;
       ri.Attributes2 = 0;
       ri.IOAddrLines = 16;
       CardServices(RELEASE_IO, rcHandle, 0, sizeof(ri), &ri, 0);
    }

    return 0;
}
```

Figure 6-22: OS/2 CARD_REMOVAL Processing Source Code

Enhancements

The template and Token-Ring client drivers are simple examples of writing OS/2 card services client drivers. More robust drivers can be built on these as a basis. The enhancements that could be made for these, and other client drivers for other PC Cards, are as follows as follows:

1. Read the card configuration entry tuple to determine the PC Card's configuration base address and its configuration register presence mask. During a CARD_INSERTION event, once the driver knows it should work with the PC Card inserted in the socket, this tuple could be read from the CIS to determine these values and not have to rely on hard-coded values in the driver.
2. Read and parse the card configuration table entry tuples to determine the kinds of resources that are required and their respective sizes. These tuples contain information such as:
   - Configuration Table Index Byte
   - Interface Type (Memory or I/O or both)
   - Power Descriptions
   - Timing Descriptions
   - I/O Descriptions
   - Interrupt Request Descriptions
   - Memory Space Descriptions
3. Let card services select an I/O range rather than hard-code one. Some PC Cards only require a range of I/O somewhere between 0x300 and 0xFFF that is not specific; the IBM PCMCIA Ethernet card works like this. A driver would fill in the BasePort1 and/or BasePort2 fields with zero and the rest of the of the structure with the attributes, number of ports, and I/O address lines to decode as required. On return from the card services request **RequestIO**, the BasePort1 and/or BasePort2 fields will contain a valid starting address for the PC Card to use.
4. Let card services select an IRQ rather than hard-code one. Each bit in the bit-mapped word of IRQs can be set, if the PC Card can support the IRQ, before calling card services with **RequestIRQ**. On return from card services, the AssignedIRQ field will contain the IRQ card services selected for the card. For example, a modem card might support IRQs 2,3,4,10,11,12, and 15. The bit-mapped word would be 0x9C1C. Card services would then pick an available interrupt from this bit-map for the card to use. How card services picks the interrupt is implementation specific. Typically, a card configuration table entry tuple will have the mask value to use for the RequestIRQ card services call.

5. Let card services select the memory window rather than hard-code one. This is similar to requesting the I/O range. The driver would fill in the Base field with zero and the rest of the structure as it normally would. On return from the card services **RequestWindow** function, the Base field and the Size field will be filled with the system base address and memory window size card services chose to use.
6. More robust error handling. Since an OS/2 driver cannot display messages after initialization, any card services errors cannot be displayed. One method to denote an error in a call is to use the speaker. A driver can different types of unhappy beeps and happy beeps when card services fails or succeeds.
7. Support more events. The EJECTION_REQUEST, EJECTION_COMPLETE, INSERTION_REQUEST, and INSERTION_COMPLETE events can be used when the socket has a locking mechanism to lock a card in a socket. When a card is requested to be removed from a socket, the client driver would receive the EJECTION_REQUEST event. The drive could then stop all processing that uses the card and return SUCCESS. The driver would then receive the EJECTION_COMPLETE event where it could then release all resources assigned to the card. Similarly, the client driver would receive the INSERTION_REQUEST event when a card is about to be inserted into a socket. The client driver could request all resources and return. Later, when the card receives the INSERTION_COMPLETE event, it could start any processing needed for the card.

   Another event a driver could support is the CLIENT_INFO event. A user program could call card services with the **GetClientInfo** request to retrieve information describing a client. The information includes revision codes, client names, and vendor names. A more robust client driver would receive the CLIENT_INFO event in its callback handler and return this information to card services, which would return the information to the caller.

Debugging Tips and Techniques

Unfortunately, debugging an OS/2 device driver requires the debug kernel and a terminal connected via a null modem cable. No real symbolic debugging is available as in debugging application programs. The programmer can look at registers, return codes from card services calls, and set breakpoints to determine when an error occurred, which is very primitive. The I/O ports assigned to a PC Card adapter are at fixed addresses and are vendor specific. If the PC Card adapter is an Intel 82365sl or clone, the person doing the debugging can look at the PC Card adapter registers by using the IN and OUT instructions to ports 0x3E0 and 0x3E1. By looking at these registers, the programmer can ensure that the registers have the correct values (e.g. speeds, wait states, locations) and can tell whether or not the card was successfully configured.

Similarly, if the PC Card adapter is from DataBook, once the programmer knows the I/O port addresses assigned to the PC Card adapter, then IN and OUT instructions to those ports can be used to determine whether a card is configured correctly. Typically, the DataBook PC Card adapter resides at ports 0x240 to 0x24F. For other controllers, the programmer should contact the corresponding PC Card adapter manufacturer for documentation.

During initialization a driver can use DosPutMessage or DosWrite to display any debug messages on the screen. After initialization there is no method to display error conditions. So, for example, if during a CARD_INSERTION event a driver requests a block of I/O ports and cannot get them, there is no visible way for the driver to tell the user the error condition. However, there is an audible way. When a card services function fails, the driver could use the DevHlp_Beep function to give the user an audible warning that something failed. Most of the IBM PCMCIA LAN adapters work this way. When a card services request fails, the speaker emits an 800Hz tone followed by a 550Hz tone, and then repeats the two tones again.

The IBM PCMCIA Token-Ring card additionally logs errors into the LANTRAN.LOG file found in the \IBMCOM subdirectory. Any IBM product that includes "LAN Adapters and Protocol Support" (LAPS) contains device drivers and an executable program that allows LAN device drivers to log errors into the LANTRAN.LOG file and optionally display the errors. When a card services request fails, the Token-Ring driver logs the failing request and the error return code. This helps in locating the source of the failure. Without the log, the only notification is an audible beep indicating a failure occurred, which makes debugging more difficult.

Summary

This chapter introduced a template for writing OS/2 card services client drivers. A Token-Ring driver was then built off of this template to demonstrate the mechanics of well-behaved card services client drivers. From the Token-Ring driver, it was shown that some drivers must queue the artificial insertion events, since the event may require system actions that cannot be performed because the driver is waiting for the card services registration to complete. Some possible enhancements were described for building more robust drivers. Finally, some debugging tips and techniques were introduced.

Chapter 7: Windows 95/ 98

The Windows 95 operating system provides built-in support for PC Card devices. For this support, it may be necessary to execute the PCMCIA wizard program that comes with Windows 95. This is found in the Control Panel by selecting the PC Card (PCMCIA) Icon. The PCMCIA wizard program comments out the real-mode drivers in CONFIG.SYS and AUTOEXEC.BAT and loads the software to enable the PCMCIA sockets.

Windows 95 has many device drivers for many different PC Cards ranging from modems and LAN cards to SCSI and memory cards. The ability to "hot plug" devices is integrated into the system. PC Cards are identified and the corresponding device driver is loaded by the system when a PC Card is detected. This can happen when the system is booting up or after the system has been running for a while. To support multiple PC Cards, it is not necessary to load up all of the corresponding device drivers at boot time as with other operating systems, such as DOS. Windows 95 dynamically loads and unloads the corresponding device drivers when a system identified PC Card is added or removed from a system. This is a feature of a plug-and-play operating system. Plug-and-play is a technology that detects the presence of hardware and directs the automatic loading of software drivers for that hardware. It also detects changes in the hardware and directs drivers to unload if the hardware is removed.

A plug-and-play operating system has three critical features that are used to support PC Card technology:

1. Centralized, dynamic resource management,
2. Dynamic device driver loading and unloading,
3. Dynamic event messaging.

The centralized dynamic resource management aspect deals with one component of the operating system that keeps track of the resources (I/O ports, Interrupts, and Memory) that a system has. In Windows 95, this is the *configuration manager.* The configuration manager manages the resources for the entire system, allowing hot or warm insertion of PC Cards. Resources can be allocated and reclaimed dynamically at any time. The corresponding device driver for the PC Card is loaded on the successful identification of the PC Card and is unloaded if the PC Card is removed from the system. Dynamic event messaging allows for PC Card software to be executed when a particular PC Card is inserted into a system.

The PC Card adapter in a system is controlled by a PC Card *bus enumerator.* This software incorporates the card services functions as well as functions for the enumeration, identification, and configuration of PC Cards. Each bus architecture, whether it is PC Card, ISA, EISA, Micro Channel, or another bus has its own bus enumerator. Windows 95 also has card and socket services but a client driver callback handler is not required. In fact, the goal in these plug-and-play systems is to allow one device driver to handle PC Card devices as well as devices on ISA, EISA, Micro Channel, PCI, or any other bus architecture supported. This minimizes the number of device drivers that must be developed to support different implementations of a device.

Since the release of the original Windows 95, there have been additions to PC Card support in the operating system. Windows 95 did not support multi-function PC Cards, multiple voltage PC Cards (5/3.3 volts) , 32 bit PC Cards (CardBus) or any PC Cards that used DMA across the PCMCIA interface. With the release of OEM Service Release #2 (OSR2), support for these types of PC Cards has been added.

Figure 7-1 shows how PC Card support is integrated into the Windows 95 software architecture.

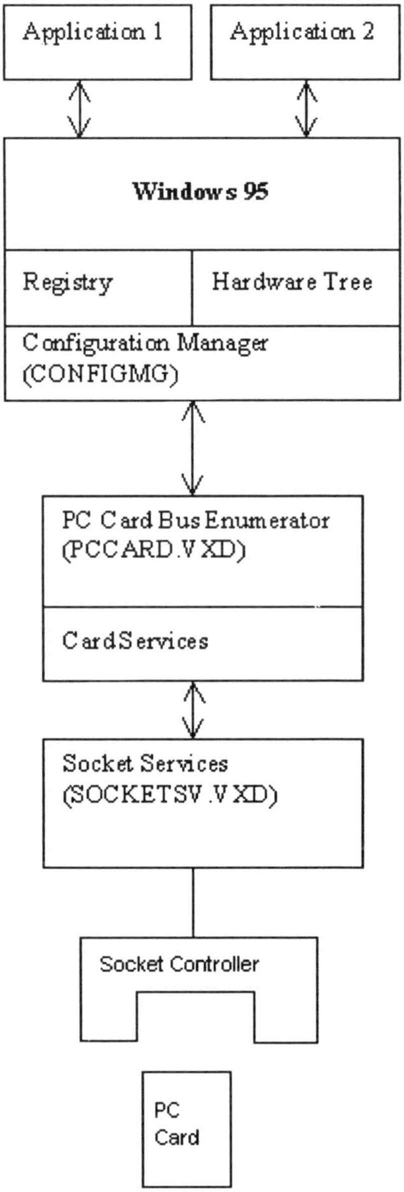

Figure 7-1 Windows 95/98 PC Card Architecture

Windows 95 PC Card Installation

The operating system must keep track of every device in the system. This requires that each device have a unique identification number or ID. Each device must also have an information file (.INF file) that associates the ID number with information in the .INF file that is required by the operating system to locate the proper device driver for the device. The .INF file contains other information necessary for class-specific and configuration functions for the device. The bus enumerator creates the ID for the device it enumerates. The *device installer* component of the bus enumerator is responsible for accessing the .INF file for the particular ID. This .INF file can come with the system or be provided by the PC Card's manufacturer. If the .INF file cannot be located for the ID created, Windows 95 puts up a dialog that allows the user to select a PC Card similar to the one being configured or allows a user to supply the .INF file to the system via a diskette. See Figure 7-2. Many manufacturers OEM their products to other companies. As such, it is likely that a given PC Card will already be supported by Microsoft under a similar name. For example, IBM markets its PC Cards to many other companies. These companies change the CIS on the card for identification. Even though these cards do not have their own entry in an .INF file, they can use the IBM entry and operate just fine.

Once the .INF file has been located, the information found in the file is stored in the *registry* of the operating system. This registry is a tree-structured database that contains vital system information. When this particular PC Card is inserted in the future, the device installer is not required because information for the card is retrieved from the registry. To examine the registry access REGEDIT which is shipped with Windows 95.

Figure 7-2 New Hardware Found Dialog

Windows 95 PC Card Identification

To generate a unique ID number for a PC Card, the PC Card bus enumerator utilizes the tuples in the CIS of the card. With the release of OSR2, an additional method of identifying I/O PC Cards has been added. This new method was developed in response to problems with the original method. The original method of generating a unique ID generated an overly-unique ID. This overly-unique ID affected the mapping of PC Cards to their device drivers. Any changes to the CIS were reflected in a new unique ID and this required changes in the .INF file associated with the PC Card. The .INF file had to change so that Windows 95 could automatically install the device. In many cases, bug fixes to the CIS or other changes did not affect the device driver loaded for the particular PC Card but they did affect the unique ID generated by the system.

The new method limits ID changes to those that actually require a new .INF file. Hardware vendors now have more control over when real .INF file changes are required for a piece of hardware. The two different methods for generating a unique ID are outlined below. Both are supported now. This ensures that existing PC Cards and .INF files will continue to work.

Below is the original formula for determining a unique device ID in Retail Windows 95:

"PCMCIA\Manufacturer-Product-CRC16"

Below is the actual Unique Device ID generated by Windows 95 for the Ericcson Mobile Phone Modem DC23:

PCMCIA\ERICSSON-MODEM__DC23-24F7

The Manufacturer-Product portion of the ID is determined from the first two strings of the Level 1 Version/Product Information tuple (15h). This tuple typically contains the name of the manufacturer and the name of the product. Characters that cannot be printed are removed from the strings and space characters are converted to underscores. The CRC16 portion of the ID is a unique number determined from the identification and configuration tuples. Table 7-1 shows the tuples that are used in determining the ID for an I/O card.

Tuple	Tuple Code	Tuple ID	Comments
Level 1 Version/ Product Information	CISTPL_VERS_1	15H	Only data in the tuple up through the first 2 strings is included in the CRC16 portion of the ID
Manufacturer Identification	CISTPL_MANFID	20H	Card manufacturer ID code
Device Information	CISTPL_DEVICE	01H	Device size and type are used to determine if the card should be treated as a storage device
16-bit PC Card Configuration	CISTPL_CONFIG	1AH	Indicates location of configuration registers
16-bit PC Card Configuration Table Entry	CISTPL_CFTABLE_ENTRY	1BH	Configuration requirements should be specified for I/O ports, interrupts, memory, etc.

Table 7-1: I/O Card Identification and Configuration Tuples

Tuple	Tuple Code	Tuple ID	Comments
Device Information	CISTPL_DEVICE	01H	The size of memory regions is used to determine the size of the storage device.
JEDEC-C Identifier	CISTPL_JEDEC_C	18H	Used to determine the programming algorithm to be used with a region of programmable memory.
Device Geometry	CISTPL_DEVICE_GEO	1EH	Used to configure the programming algorithm to be used with a region of programmable memory.
Format	CISTPL_FORMAT	41H	Describes partition size and boundaries
Organization	CISTPL_ORG	46H	Describes partition type

Table 7-2: Memory Card Identification and Configuration Tuples

Memory PC Cards are assigned an ID based on some other tuples. The PC Card bus enumerator uses this information to create the ID and to correctly set up the file system(s) and driver(s). Table 7-2 shows these tuples.

Microsoft provides a DOS utility program called DTPL.EXE that can be used to determine the ID of a PC Card. The DTPL.EXE program can be found on the Microsoft Web Site at www.Microsoft.com. This program also can be used to parse and verify the CIS of a PC Card to display the tuple values and contents. **Note:** To use this program, you must have a DOS system with Card and Socket Services installed and loaded..

The new additional method for determining a Unique ID introduced with OSR2 and used in Windows 98 is shown below

"PCMCIA\Manufacturer String-Product String –XXXX-YYYY"

The actual Unique Device ID generated by OSR2 for the Ericcson Mobile Phone Modem DC23 is shown below

PCMCIA\ERICSSON-MODEM__DC23-016B-0100

The fisrt two parts of this ID are determined from the CISTPL_VERS_1 tuple. The Manufacturer String is the Product Information String, name of the Manufacturer terminated by a Null (00H). The Product String is the product name and is the next string in the tuple terminated by a Null (00H). The XXXX is the PC Card Manufacturer code (TPLMID_MANF) section of the CISTPL_MANFID tuple. The YYYY is the manufacturer information (TPLMID_CARD) section of the CISTPL_MANFID tuple.

Windows 95 Client Device Drivers

PC Cards in Windows 95 typically utilize a standard plug-and-play device driver. These are implemented as virtual device drivers that can be dynamically loaded (VxD). All resource allocation for the driver is done by the configuration manager, based on the required resource information supplied by the tuples in the CIS. The configuration manager allocates the resources and the configuration of the card is done by the bus enumerator. This combination of bus enumerator and configuration manager actually enables the PC Card for operation. The PC Card adapter is set up for the IRQ, I/O ports, and memory windows needed for operation. Once the successful enabling has occurred, a "happy beep" of two ascending tones sounds. The device driver is then loaded into memory and control is passed to it. It is important to realize that PC Cards that do not have the required tuples or have incorrect tuples cannot be supported by plug-and-play drivers because the PC Card bus enumerator would be unable to identify and configure the card.

Windows 95 PC Card Removal

There are two different ways that a PC Card can be removed from a system. One is the "surprise style" method where the PC Card is ejected from the machine with no prior indication to the machine. The other is the "VCR style" of card removal where the user tells the system that they want to remove a PC Card. In Windows 95 it is best to use the "VCR style" of card removal. This allows for a graceful unloading of all drivers, buffers, and connections associated with the PC Card. On the status line at the bottom of the user screen, a PC Card icon is shown on the bottom right-hand corner. By clicking the mouse on this icon, the user can have the system prepare for card removal. After the system has finished preparing for this card removal, it posts a dialog box indicating that the user can remove the PC Card. This is the safest method of card removal. A surprise style card removal can in some cases cause a machine to hang. This can occur when the device driver for the affected PC Card is copying data from memory and the memory disappears, for example. Essential status information that the device driver is waiting upon may never come and the driver could be locked in an infinite loop.

Windows 95 Card Services (PCCARD.VXD)

Card services (PCCARD.VXD) in Windows 95 adheres to the flat 32-bit protect-mode model. Typically it is not necessary to develop a PC Card client driver since the PC Card bus enumerator and configuration manager already perform insertion recognition, resource acquisition and configuration, as well as ejection recognition and resource deallocation. However, when writing a PC Card client driver, there are limitations with the system to consider.

Card services is implemented to the standard bindings for 32-bit protect-mode Vxds. The register definitions for passing arguments to card services from the Vxd are:

[AH] CS ID = AFH
[AL] Service = function code
[DX] Handle = client handle
[ESI] Pointer = 32-bit flat offset
[CX] ArgLength = length of arguments
[EBX] ArgPointer= 32-bit flat offset

Card services returns the following registers:

[CF] Success/Fail = if [CF] is 0, the request succeeded, otherwise it failed
[AX] Status = return code from card services
[DX] Handle = client hamdle
[ESI] Pointer = 32-bit flat offset
[CX] ArgLength= (unchanged from input)
[EBX] ArgPointer= (unchanged from input)

Windows VxD clients make card services requests using the VxD services interface through the VxDcall macro. The first request must be

```
VxDCall        PCCARD_Get_Version
```

This call is used to make sure PCCARD.VXD is loaded and operational. It cannot be issued at Device_Init. It can only be issued after all devices have been loaded so a good time to call it is at Init_Complete or Sys_Dynamic_Device_Init.

After a driver knows that Card Services is present it can make requests by loading the required registers and using the following instruction:

```
VxDCall        PCCARD_Card_Services
```

For more information on host specific bindings, please refer to Appendix D of the PC Card Standard Card Services Specification.

The device driver CSDRVR described in Chapter 10 demonstrates the usage of these calls.

Note: To develop software for a Windows 95/98 system that utilizes Card Services calls, it is essential that you use the latest Win32 Platform SDK, Windows 95 DDK, Visual C++ 5.0 compiler, and MASM 6.11 Assembler.

Why develop software with Card Services calls?

Under normal circumstances, it is unnecessary to develop software that explicitly calls Card Services functions in Windows 95/98. A PC Card with a complete CIS with all the necessary tuples does not require a Card Services client driver ordinarily. The standard Plug and Play device driver architecture handles PC Card configuration for both card insertion and removal. If a PC Card has incorrect entries in the CIS but the necessary tuples are present, tuple overrides in the .INF file for the device can correct these deficiencies. If the PC Card has an incomplete CIS (missing tuples), it would be necessary to develop a Card Services client driver for the device. Other reasons to develop a client would be for software tools to examine PC Card resources. The CSINFW32 tool described in Chapter 10, utilizes Card Services calls to gather tuple data and status information from a PC Card and display this information. The software for this tool illustrates how an application can call a device driver to make Card Services requests. The device driver makes the actual Card Services calls and provides a DeviceIoControl interface to applications. Through this DeviceIoControl interface, applications can make Card Services requests.

Template for calling Card Services functions from a Device Driver

The software examples for this book are available for download at ***ftp.peer-to-peer.com/pubs/pc-card.*** The zip file contains a template for a Card Services client. There are two files in this template. One file CSTEMP.ASM, is in assembly language and provides the control dispatch table for a Windows 95 Vxd. It also provides the interface to Card Services. The other file (SYSCTRL.C) is written in C and makes the Card Services calls.

This template shows how to obtain Card Services information and register a callback handler with Card Services. The sample callback handler handles events such as card insertion, card removal, and registration complete. Additional events could easily be added. A kernel debug environment is required to display the messages built into the template. The user could modify the event handling software for his/her own purpose.

Windows 95/98 PC Card Configuration

Before describing how Windows 95/98 configures PC Card adapters and PC Cards some terminology must be defined.

- **Enumerator**
  A VxD that runs at boot time to determine what hardware devices are currently installed and the resources they require. There is a unique enumerator for each bus type on a system: PCMCIA, PCI, SCSI, USB, etc.
- **Device Loader**
  A VxD that loads other VxDs. The Windows 95/98 device driver architecture is somewhat layered because some drivers rely on other drivers to manage a device. Serial ports are one example of this layering. VCOMM is the device loader for the target driver SERIAL.VXD.
- **Arbitrator**
  A VxD that determines conflict-free assignment of a specific resource (IRQ, I/O, Memory Range, etc.) An arbitrator gets called from the Configuration Manager to assign a specific resource to a set of devices, taking into account whether or not the devices can share the resource or if they can actually be configured with the resource.
- **Target Device Driver**
  A VxD that manages a device. It uses the Configuration Manager to learn what resources were assigned to it.
- **Device Node**
  An entry in the hardware configuration tree. It contains information about logical configurations , current configuration, status, and driver information.
- **Hardware Tree**
  A tree structure of device nodes that represents the hardware in a system. See Figure 7-3.

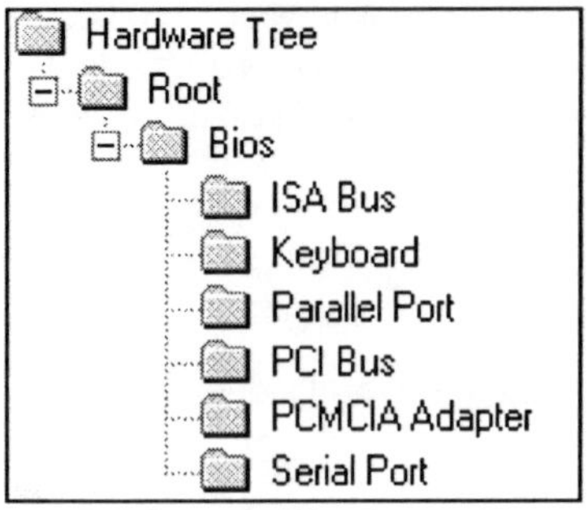

Figure 7-3 Sample Hardware Tree

During the boot process, the Configuration Manager examines the registry section HKEY_LOCAL_MACHINE\Enum for enumerators. There are enumerators for System BIOS (HKEY_LOCAL_MACHINE\Enum\BIOS), PCI Bus (HKEY_LOCAL_MACHINE\Enum\PCI), legacy devices (HKEY_LOCAL_MACHINE\Enum\Root), and other buses and devices. The Configuration Manager calls each enumerator to enumerate all devices on the bus. When the enumerator finds a device, it creates a new device node in the hardware tree and then loads the device loader for the device. The device loader then loads the device driver. The device driver then registers a configuration callback handler with the Configuration Manager. The Configuration Manager then uses arbitrators to assign resources so that they do not conflict with other devices. Finally, the Configuration Manager starts at the top of the hardware tree and calls every node's configuration callback handler to notify the driver of its resource assignments or to let it override certain configurations.

For PCMCIA, when Windows 95/98 starts, the bus enumerator will detect the PCMCIA adapter. For Intel 82365 style adapters, the enumerator will be found at HKEY_LOCAL_MACHINE\Enum\Root*PNP0E00\0000 since the adapter is on a root device. For TI-1130 CardBus Bridge adapters, the enumerator will be found at HKEY_LOCAL_MACHINE\Enum\PCI\VEN_104C&DEV_AC12 since the adapter is on the PCI bus. The "Driver" string points to a registry entry in HKEY_LOCAL_MACHINE\System\CurrentControlSet\Services\Class that actually has the name of the device loader and the driver. PCCARD.VXD is both the enumerator and device loader for PC Card devices. For Intel 82365 style adapters the driver is socketsv.vxd while for the TI-1130 CardBus bridge the driver is cbss.vxd. Configuration Manager then calls Socket Services to filter and configure its IRQ, I/O, and memory window. PC Card support is now configured.

Now that PC Card support has been installed, the next step during the boot process is for the PCMCIA bus enumerator to enumerate all cards in sockets. For each socket, the bus enumerator, PCCARD.VXD, will generate a unique hardware ID from the tuples on the card. It will then add a new device node to the hardware tree and build logical configurations based on the tuples on the card. PCCARD.VXD will then search the registry database of PC Cards and try to match the hardware ID with one in the database. The database is located at HKEY_LOCAL_MACHINE\Enum\PCMCIA\. Each entry in the database is a unique hardware ID followed by the instance of the hardware device. So, for example, the first Ericsson DC-23 Modem can be found at HKEY_LOCAL_MACHINE\Enum\PCMCIA\ERICSSON-MODEM__DC23-24F7\0. At this location is a "Class" string that describes the device class and a "Driver" string that points to where the device loader and target driver can be found. See Figure 7-4 for an example registry entry. Configuration Manager will then examine the registry at HKEY_LOCAL_MACHINE\System\CurrentControlSet\Services\Class\<device class>\<driver> and load the device loader that loads the driver. See Figure 7-5 for an example registry entry. After the driver is loaded it registers its configuration callback handler with Configuration Manager. Configuration Manager then calls the driver with CONFIG_FILTER events so that the driver can filter out any configurations that are not logical. Finally, after Configuration Manager has a valid configuration for the card, it calls the adapter driver's callback handler with CONFIG_START. Afterwards, the PCMCIA bus enumerator will call Card Services to map the PC Card's I/O, IRQ, and memory windows requested. Lastly, the driver's callback handler will be called with a CONFIG_START event after all resources have been allocated and mapped.

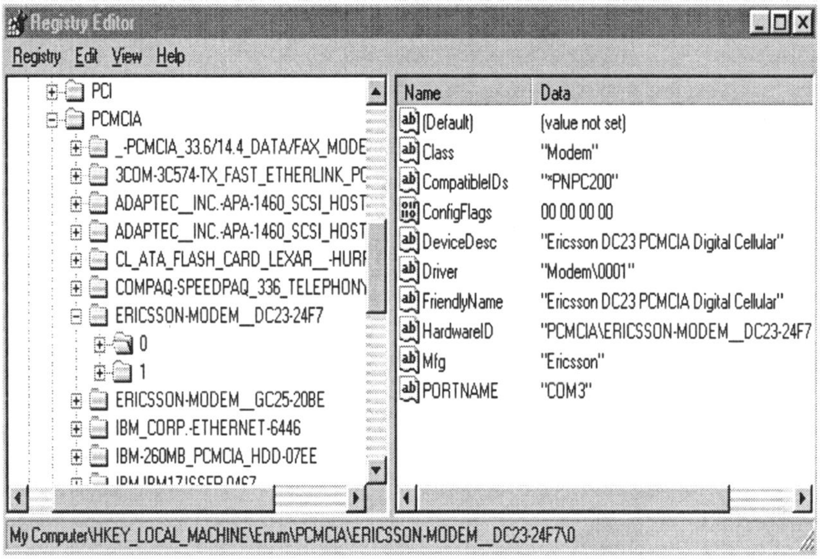

Figure 7-4 PCMCIA Hardware Database in the Registry

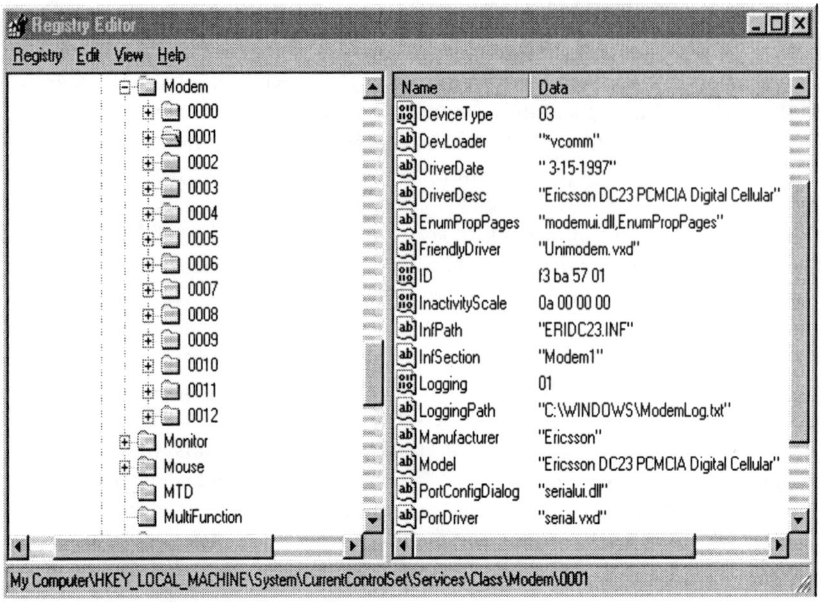

Figure 7-5 Registry Modem Class

Windows 95/98 Plug and Play architecture limits the capabilities of a Card Services client driver such as this. In DOS or OS/2, a Card Services client driver can allocate and free resources. Only during the CONFIG_FILTER stage can a driver call Card Services to allocate or free resources. Once the CONFIG_START event occurs, the resources have been allocated and mapped; the Card Services call RequestConfiguration has been made. At this time no more resources can be requested or released.

Windows 95 Socket Services

Socket services is implemented as a dynamically loaded Virtual Driver (VxD) in Windows 95. It is written to the socket services 2.1 level. Windows 95 socket services support exists for the Intel 82365SL and compatibles as well as the Databook PC Card adapter. OSR2 and Windows 98 also include CardBus socket services for the TI-1130, TI-1131, and TI-1250 CardBus to PCI brige chips.

Multi-Function PC Card Support

Retail Windows 95 did not have support for Multi-Function PC Cards, although it could be tweaked into working. A true Multi-Function CIS has a global CIS that contains at least three of the five tuples required to form the unique hardware ID; CISTPL_VERS_1, CISTPL_MANFID, and CISTPL_DEVICE. The last tuple in the global CIS is the long link to the next CIS chain, CISTPL_LONGLINK_MFC. This tuple has the number of functions the card performs and links to CIS chains that describe the functions. The CIS chain for each function contains the last two tuples required by Windows 95 to form the unique hardware ID; CISTPL_CONFIG and CISTPL_CFTABLE_ENTRY. Because these two tuples are not in the global CIS, PCCARD.VXD could not form a unique hardware ID for the PC Card and would fail to recognize the card. The CIS was considered incomplete.

To overcome this situation several multi-function PC Card manufacturers would add the two function specific tuples from one of the functions to the global CIS and still leave them in the function's CIS. By doing this, PCCARD.VXD would see a complete CIS and could form the unique hardware ID required for the PC Card. The drivers for the card would then be loaded and the functions enabled.

If the PC Card only has one set of function configuration registers, then there is only one CIS and it does not contain the CISTPL_LONGLINK_MFC tuple. The PC Card will have more than one CISTPL_FUNCID. The first CISTPL_FUNCID will have a function code of zero to indicate the card is a multi-function card with only one set of configuration registers. After that tuple, there will be one CISTPL_FUNCID for each function the card performs. Both retail Windows 95/98 and the OSR2 versions of Windows 95 can support this type of multi-function PC Card.

Multi-Function PC Cards also require more than one .INF file for installation. One for the parent to describe the resources needed for the card and one for each function on the card. The parent .INF file is for a "Multi-function" class device and contains the unique hardware ID for the PC Card. Later in the file are hardware Ids and resource allocations for each function. To see good examples of multi-function .INF files, look in the C:\WINDOWS\INF subdirectory. It is usually a hidden subdirectory. The files to look at are

- CEMMF.INF – The Xircom Ethernet+Modem parent file
- NETCEM.INF – The Xircom Ethernet+Modem network file
- MDMCPI.INF – The Xircom Ethernet+Modem modem file

The parent .INF file contains the unique hardware ID for the PC Card, PCMCIA\XIRCOM-CREDITCARD_ETHERNET+MODEM_II-3DFC. Later in the file is the hardware ID and resource allocations for each function on the card. For the example Xircom card,

```
HKR,Child0000,HardwareID,,MF\XIRCOMCEM_DEV0
HKR,Child0000,ResourceMap,1,00,02,05
HKR,Child0001,HardwareID,,MF\XIRCOMCEM_DEV1
HKR,Child0001,ResourceMap,1,00,01,02,03,04,05
```

Of the six resources the card requires, the first function only uses resources 00, 02, and 05 while the second function uses all six resources.

The .INF file for each function is a standard .INF file for the class of the device. The only difference is the unique hardware ID. For the first function on the Xircom card, the modem function, the hardware ID is MF\XIRCOMCEM_DEV0 while for the second function, the network function, the hardware ID is MF\XIRCOMCEM_DEV1. If you look in MDMCPI.INF and NETCEM.INF you can see this.

Once the card is inserted and the driver is installed, the registry has several entries in the HKEY_LOCAL_MACHINE\Enum section. First, in the PCMCIA database, the unique hardware ID entry for the card has sub-entries for each child. The child entries only contain a unique hardware ID and the resources required for the function. This is shown in Figure 7-6. The unique hardware ID actually points to another section in the registry that describes the class of the device and where the driver is located. These Ids start with MF\ and point to HKEY_LOCAL_MACHINE\Enum\MF\<id>. See Figure 7-7 for an example.

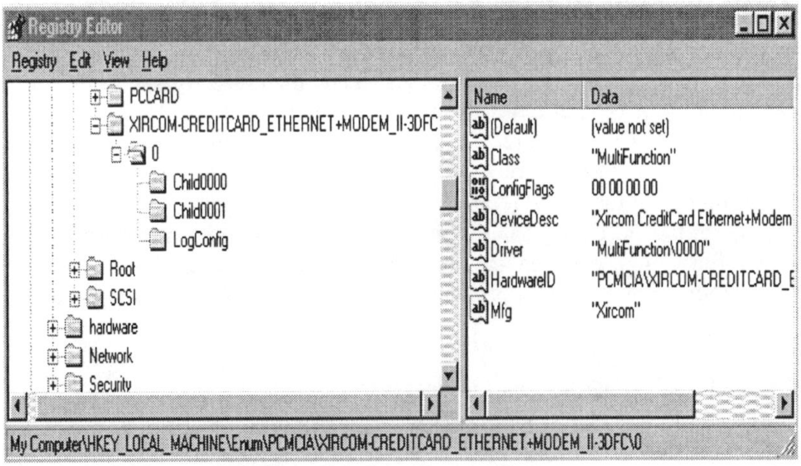

Figure 7-6 Xircom Ethernet+Modem Parent Entry

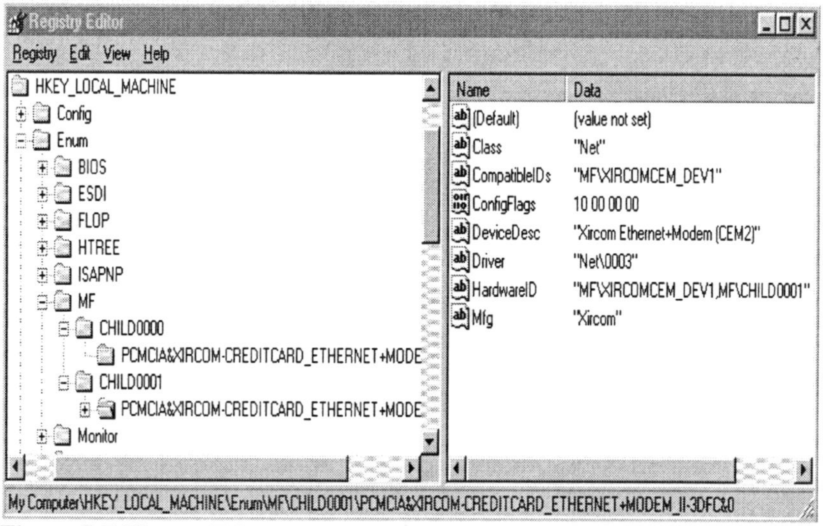

Figure 7-7 Xircom Ethernet+Modem Network Child Entry

The OSR2 version of Windows 95 introduced better support for multi-function PC Cards. By changing the algorithm that generates the unique hardware ID so that it uses the Level 1 Version/Product Information tuple and the Manufacturers Identification tuple, the configuration tuples are no longer required in the global CIS and should only be found in the CIS chain for each function. The PCMCIA enumerator now recognizes the Longlink to the next chain on a Multiple Function tuple (CISTPL_LONGLINK_MFC) so that an .INF file for the parent is no longer required; only an .INF file for each child function is needed. The hardware ID for each function contains the unique PC Card ID with the addition of DEV0, DEV1, etc. Below are the hardware Ids for the parent and children functions of an IBM Fax/Modem/Ethernet PC Card:

PCMCIA\IBM-HOME_AND_AWAY_28.8_PC_CARD_____-C84F
PCMCIA\IBM-HOME_AND_AWAY_28.8_PC_CARD_____-DEV0-C84F
PCMCIA\IBM-HOME_AND_AWAY_28.8_PC_CARD_____-DEV1-C84F

After the card is inserted and the drivers are installed, the registry entries are slightly different than retail Windows 95. The parent and both children entries are in the PCMCIA database. The parent entry no longer points to entries in the MF section. Figure 7-8 shows the parent and children entries for the IBM Fax/Modem/Ethernet PC Card.

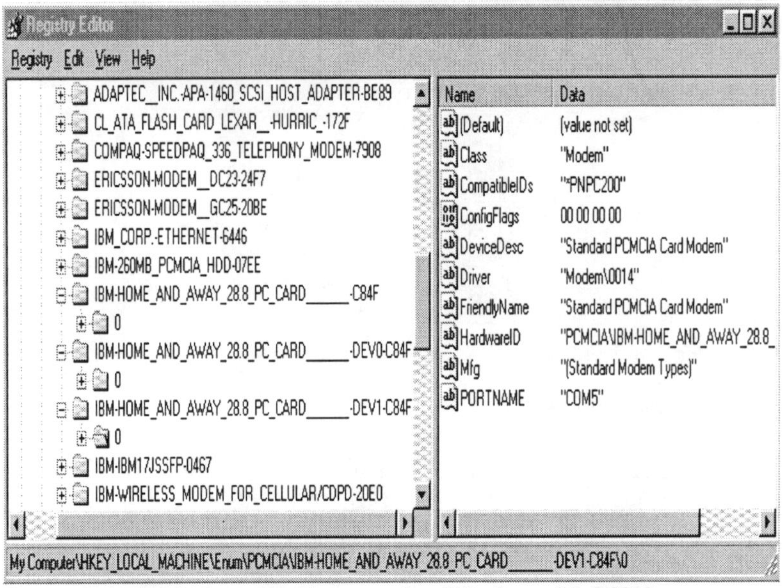

Figure 7-8 Multi-Function Entry under Windows 95 OSR2

At the time of this writing, Windows 98 handled Multi-Function PC Cards the same as Windows 95 OSR2.

CardBus PC Card Support

Retail Windows 95 did not have support for CardBus PC Cards. Most CardBus PC Card manufacturers would tell users to disable 32-bit PC Card Support via the Control Panel, then they would install a a driver that would configure the CardBus bridge and then the card. One such card is the 3Com Fast EtherLink XL CardBus PC Card. The User Guide has separate instructions for Windows 95 and Windows 95 OSR2.

Windows 95 OSR2 introduced support for CardBus bridges with a CardBus Bridge Socket Services. The CardBus bridge entry in the registry can be found in the PCI database, HKEY_LOCAL_MACHINE\Enum\PCI. A sample entry for the TI-1250 CardBus Bridge is shown in Figure 7-9. The entry name is based on the PCI Vendor ID and Device ID. Each socket is represented by sub-entries based on Bus Number, Device Number, and Function Number. In the example in Figure 7-9, socket 0 has an entry of PCI\VEN_104C&DEV_AC16\BUS_00&DEV_02&FUNC_00. This entry says that the device driver for socket 0 can be found at System\CurrenControlSet\Services\Class\PCMCIA\0000.

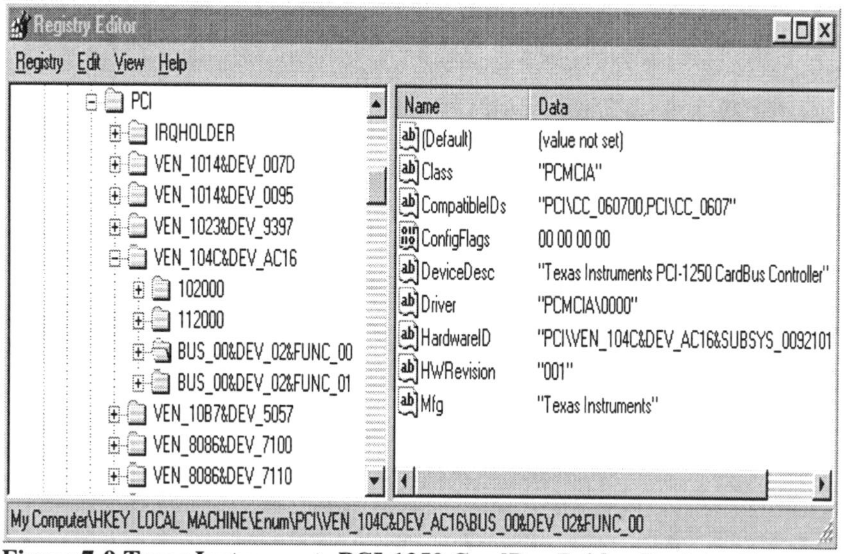

Figure 7-9 Texas Instruments PCI-1250 CardBus Bridge Registry Entry

Instead of adding entries to the PCMCIA database in the registry, Windows 95 OSR2 and Windows 98 add CardBus PC Card entries to the PCI database. The entry name is based on the card's Vendor ID and Device ID. The hardware ID is based on the card's Vendor ID, Device ID, Subsystem, and Revision. Figure 7-10 shows an entry for the 3Com Fast EtherLink XL CardBus PC Card inserted in socket 0. Notice that there is an entry when the card is inserted in socket 0 (VEN_10B7&DEV_5057\001000) and another when the card is inserted in socket 1 (VEN_10B7&DEV_5057\001100). This is inherent in the nature of PCI devices; each socket is defined as a different function and when a card is inserted in a socket, the card is considered to be on a different bus. When the card is inserted in socket 0, in PCI space it is on Bus 1. When the card is inserted in socket 1, in PCI space it is on Bus 2. Because of this, if you insert a CardBus PC Card in one socket and install the drivers, if you later remove the card and insert it in a different socket, Windows 95 OSR2 and Windows 98 will ask you to re-install the drivers.

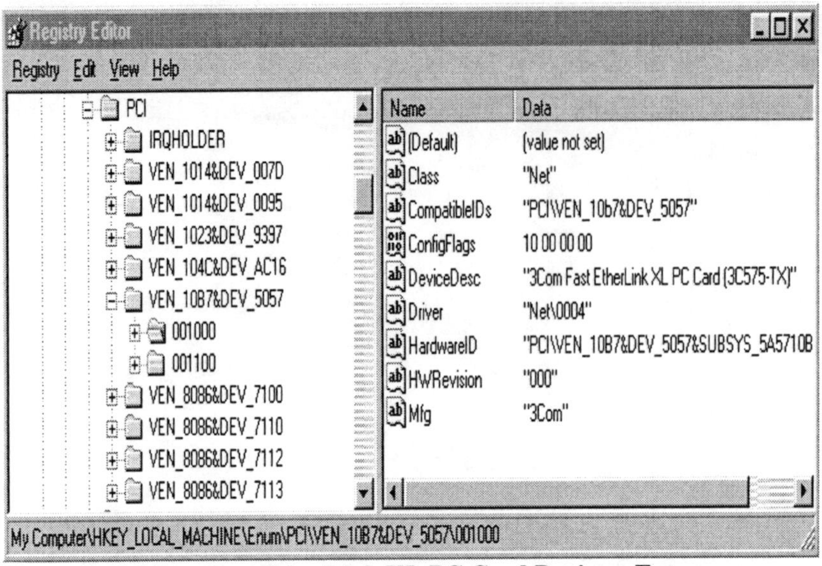

Figure 7-10 3Com Fast EtherLink XL PC Card Registry Entry

Application Notifications

In Windows 95, Windows 98, and Windows CE a message is broadcast to windowed applications whenever a device is added to or removed from the system. This message is WM_DEVICECHANGE. It is described in the Microsoft Visual C++ 5.0 include file DBT.H.

When a windowed application receives the WM_DEVICECHANGE message, the "wParam" contains the type of event while the "lParam" points to a structure with more information about the event. The types of events one would be interested in are

- DBT_DEVICEARRIVAL
- DBT_DEVICEQUERYREMOVE
- DBT_DEVICEQUERYREMOVEFAILED
- DBT_DEVICEREMOVEPENDING
- DBT_DEVICEREMOVECOMPLETE
- DBT_DEVICETYPESPECIFIC

The actual device type information is found in the structure pointed to by the "lParam." These values are

- DBT_DEVTYP_OEM
- DBT_DEVTYP_DEVNODE
- DBT_DEVTYP_VOLUME
- DBT_DEVTYP_PORT
- DBT_DEVTYP_NET

When a modem PC Card is inserted into a socket, the windowed application would first receive a WM_DEVICECHANGE message for the device node being added to the hardware tree (DBT_DEVICEARRIVAL, DBT_DEVTYP_DEVNODE). Then it would receive another WM_DEVICECHANGE for the port being added to the system (DBT_DEVICEARRIVAL, DBT_DEVTYP_PORT).

Later, when you want to remove the modem PC Card, you would click on the PC Card (PCMCIA) icon in the Control Panel to stop the card. The windowed application would receive a WM_DEVICECHANGE message to query if the device can be removed (DBT_DEVICEQUERYREMOVE, DBT_DEVTYP_DEVNODE). At this time, if any application returns FALSE to this message, the device cannot be removed and the DBT_DEVICEQUERYREMOVEFAILED message is broadcast. If all applications return TRUE, eventually the DBT_DEVICEREMOVECOMPLETE message is broadcast for the device node and for the port.

By catching the WM_DEVICECHANGE for device nodes, an application can interrogate the registry for the type of device added to or removed from the system. In the HKEY_DYN_DATA\Config Manager\Enum section is a list of device nodes. An application can filter out arrivals and removals of device nodes and display information about the devices. The sample application DEVCHG that is distributed with the companion software to this book performs this function. It can be compiled for Windows 95/98 or Windows CE. At the time of this writing, Windows NT 5.0 did not support this message, but according to the Microsoft Developer Network Library, it will.

Summary

This chapter described the plug-and-play features of the Windows 95 and Windows 98 operating systems. It contained sample registry entries for a variety of PC Cards. Finally, it described the programming interface into PCCARD.VXD and how to get application notifications for insertion and removal of PC Cards.

Chapter 8: Windows NT/CE

Windows NT

Windows NT 3.1 and 3.5 did not officially support PC Cards. Any PC cards that function in this environment use vendor-supplied point enablers to enable the PC Card. This enabler code can be embedded in the device driver or run separately before the hardware device driver. Windows NT 3.51 introduced built-in PC Card support in the form of a point enabler called PCMCIA.SYS. This same architecture is used in Windows NT 4.0. The current Beta version of Windows NT 5.0 is similar to Windows NT 4.0 but supports "hot-plugging". Windows NT 5.0 (code named "Cairo") is available if you are member of the Microsoft Developer's Network (MSDN).

PC Cards currently supported include modems, SCSI cards, disk drives, and LAN cards. For Windows NT 3.51 and 4.0, the PC card must be inserted into the machine when the machine is booted and must remain in the machine until it is turned off. Windows NT 5.0 introduces hot plugging of PC Cards. Although Windows NT 5.0 supports hot plugging, it does not have card and socket services. There is software available that supplies Card and Socket Services support for NT from third-party vendors, e.g. SystemSoft.

PCMCIA.SYS is executed very early in the boot process. (It is loaded right after the HAL or Hardware Abstraction Layer). This is necessary to allow for the usage of SCSI cards and disk drives. Currently, PCMCIA.SYS supports Intel 82365 or compatible PC Card adapters only. There is no support for the Databook controller at present.

PC Cards are enabled with information that is contained in the *registry*. The registry is a tree- structured database that contains information concerning the computer system. This includes hardware, software, and resource settings that are used by the computer. The registry is accessed with a utility program called Regedit.exe or Regedt32.exe. These programs come with your Window NT operating system.

The registry has an entry for Pcmcia in the section called KEY_LOCAL_MACHINE\SYSTEM\CurrentControlSet\Services. The Pcmcia section contains a database of the PC Cards that it knows about. Each PC Card has its own section in the database. The database is structured with entries using information from the Level 1 Version/Product Information tuple (tuple 15h). The Manufacturer string section of this tuple is the first entry under the DataBase tag in the Pcmcia Database. The Product string section of the tuple forms the second entry under the first entry in the Database. An optional third section under the Product String Section is the CRC.

Example:

An Accton Ethernet PC Card has been installed on your Windows NT machine. It has a Product ID tuple in the CIS that has the following information:

Manufacturer Information ----- Accton
Product Information------------- EN2216-PCMCIA-ETHERNET

(These fields are delimited by 0h in the tuple.)

The Registry tree entry would look like this:

HKEY_LOCAL_MACHINE\SYSTEM\CurrentControlSet\Services\Pcmcia\DataBase\Accton\EN2216-PCMCIA-ETHERNET

Figure 8-1is a sample output of the Registry Editor showing the database entry for this example.

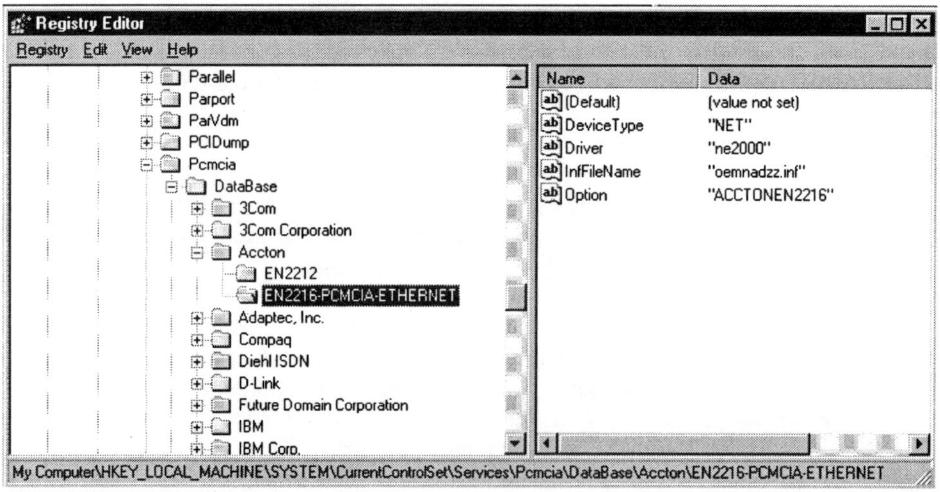

Figure 8-1: Sample Pcmcia Database entry

Registry Keywords

At this level in the registry, the database contains information concerning the PC Card. These keywords are used:

- **DeviceType** --- The type of PC Card. e.g. DeviceType:REG_SZ:NET for a LAN PC Card or DeviceType:REG_SZ:SCSI for a SCSI PC Card.
- **Driver** --- The section of the Registry that contains additional information that concerns the PC Card. e.g. Driver:REG_SZ:ne2000 for an Ethernet PC Card. This is not the name of the device driver that is executed when this card is detected.
- **InfFileName ---** The name of the .inf file that was used to install the PC Card. e.g. InfFileName:REG_SZ:oemnadzz.inf
- **Option** --- The name of the section in the .inf file where processing starts for the PC Card installation. e.g. Option:REG_SZ:ACCTONEN2216

(note: REG_SZ indicates the type of data for the field is a string terminated with zero.)

The Driver section in the database directs PCMCIA.SYS to other information that is crucial to setting up the hardware and software for a PC Card. The string in this section of the database is the name of the registry section for the PC Card. At this location in the registry is the software information for the PC Card. For the example above, the software section would be:

HKEY_LOCAL_MACHINE\SYSTEM\CurrentControlSet\Services\ne2000.

Windows NT typically can handle multiple adapters. There is usually one software section in the registry and following the software section would be one or more instances of hardware that use the same software. A hardware instance for the example above could be:

HKEY_LOCAL_MACHINE\SYSTEM\CurrentControlSet\Services\ ne20001.

A number is appended to the software registry entry to signify a hardware instance for the software.

Unfortunately, Windows NT can only enable a single instance of a particular PC Card. It can handle multiple PC Cards but they must be different from each other. For example, if two identical Ethernet PC Cards were installed (same CIS information), only one would be enabled by PCMCIA.SYS. The other PC Card would not get enabled. If two different Ethernet PC Cards (different CIS information) were installed, they both could function as long as they were different.

The hardware section contains hardware specific information for the PC Card. The information we are interested in at this time are the keywords that PCMCIA.SYS uses to configure the socket controller properly for the PC Card. Keywords are used to tailor the socket controller to the PC Card's requirements for I/O ports, interrupts, and memory .

Here are the keywords that can be used in the registry and their function:

- **PCMCIA** -- (REG_DWORD) This keyword must be set to 1.
- **Address_16** -- (REG_DWORD) This keyword, when set to 1, is used to set the memory window to 16 bit operation. Without this keyword, PCMCIA.SYS sets memory windows to 8 bit operation. Socket controllers like the Intel 82365 and compatibles have five memory address windows. To use this keyword for other memory windows, the keyword becomes **AddressX_16** with X being 1,2,3 or 4.
- **AttributeMemory_16** -- (REG_DWORD) This keyword , when set to 1, is used to set an attribute memory window to 16 bit operation. Without this keyword, the attribute memory window is accessed in 8 bit mode. To use this keyword for other attribute memory windows, the keyword becomes **AttributeMemoryX_16** with X being 1,2,3, or 4.
- **InterruptNumber** -- (REG_DWORD) This keyword sets the interrupt level that the socket controller asserts when the interrupt line on the PC Card is asserted.
- **IoBaseAddress** -- (REG_DWORD) This keyword sets the base address for I/O port access. Socket controllers like the Intel 82365 and compatibles have two I/O port windows. To use this keyword for a second I/O port window, the keyword becomes **IoBaseAddress_1**.
- **IoLength** -- (REG_DWORD) This keyword is used to indicate how many consecutive I/O ports are needed. It is actually the number of I/O ports needed - 1. To use this keyword for a second I/O port window, the becomes **IoLength_1**.
- **MemoryMappedBaseAddress** -- (REG_DWORD) This keyword is used to set the physical memory address that a device driver would use to access memory on the PC Card. This is the address where the workstation "sees" the PC Card's memory. Socket controllers like the Intel 82365 and compatibles have five memory address windows. To use this keyword for other memory windows, the keyword becomes **MemoryMappedBaseAddress_X** with X being 1,2,3 or 4.
- **MemoryMappedSize** -- (REG_DWORD) This keyword is used to set the size of the memory mapped window. To use this keyword for other memory windows, the keyword becomes **MemoryMappedSize_X** with X being 1,2,3, or 4.
- **PCCARDMemoryWindowOffset** -- (REG_DWORD) This keyword is used to set the address in PCMCIA address space that the PC Card will decode its memory. Socket controllers allow the workstation memory and the PC Card's memory addresses to be shifted from each other. To use this keyword for other memory windows, the keyword becomes **PCCARDMemoryWindowOffset_X** with X being 1,2,3, or 4.

(note: REG_DWORD indicates the type of data for the field is a double word integer value (32 bit).)

Figure 8-2 shows a sample registry entry for an IBM Token-Ring PC Card. This shows almost all the keywords in a valid configuration.

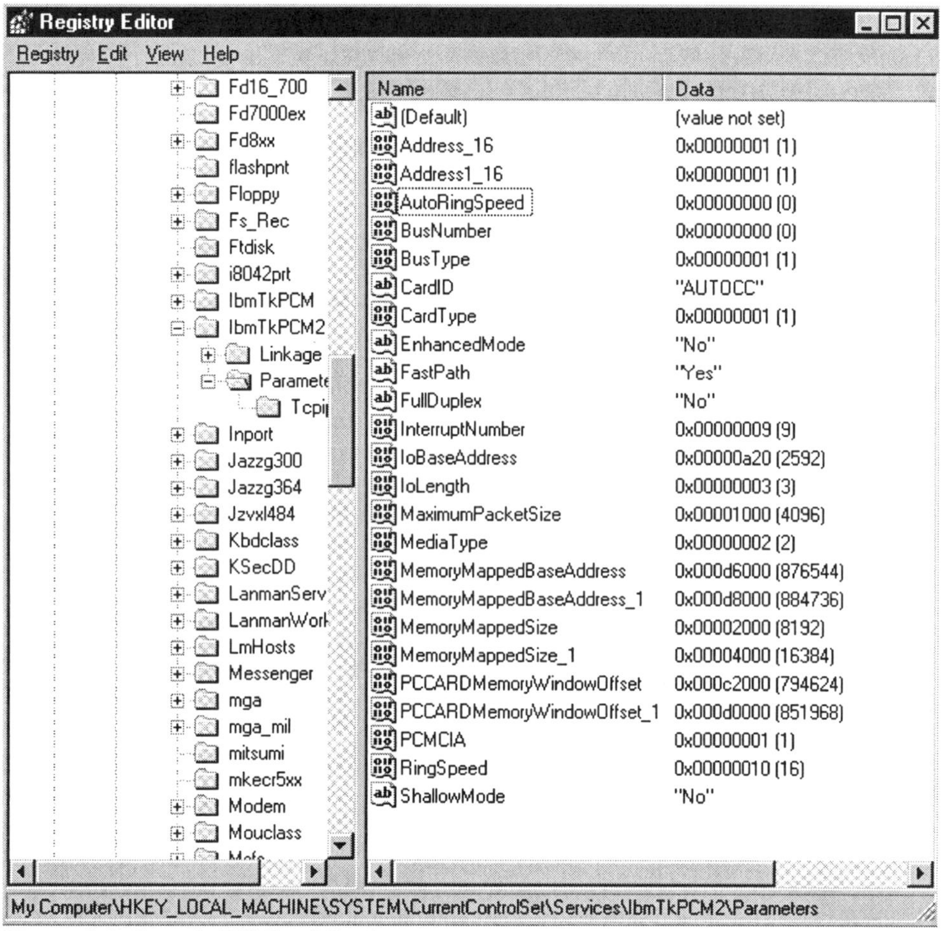

Figure 8-2: Sample PC Card Registry entry

Figure 8-2 shows a PC Card with one interrupt, four I/O ports, and two memory windows. The interrupt is set for IRQ 9. There are four I/O ports starting at 0xA20. There are two memory windows. One is 8K in size and has a workstation address of 0xD6000. The other is 16K in size and has a workstation address of 0xD8000. These two memory windows are shifted so that the PC Card "sees" them at 0xC2000 and 0xD0000 in PCMCIA address space. The memory windows are 16 bits in width.

With these keywords, it should be possible to configure any 16 bit PC Card with a valid CIS. When Windows NT starts its boot sequence, PCMCIA.SYS queries the CIS of any detected PC Cards. It uses the Manufacturer ID String, Device ID String, and CRC values that are read from the CIS tuples to locate card information in the registry. If information for this PC Card is found in the registry, the PC Card is configured with the settings found in the registry.

Modem PC Cards do not require entries in the Pcmcia Database to function. Modems require an interrupt and some I/O ports (COM1, COM2, etc.). The Function ID tuple (21H) identifies the PC Card as a modem or serial card. To determine the resources that NT has configured for a modem PC Card, go to the Control Panel and select PC Card (PCMCIA). A list of inserted PC Cards is displayed. Select the modem and click on Properties. The Cardinfo tab will show the com port used. Select the resources tab and the interrupt and I/O port values are displayed. Now that you know the resources used, go back to the Control Panel and click on Ports. You want to add your new Com port. Select Add and match the resource settings to the modem configuration settings determined earlier. Select OK and your new Com port is added to the system. Now you must add your modem to the system. This is done from the Control Panel again. Select modems and add your modem. The next window gives you the option of NT detecting your modem or you selecting your modem from a list of modems. If NT is used to detect the modem, NT will check all of the Com ports for a modem. NT sends AT commands to the ports to determine characteristics of the modem. With this information, NT can configure a modem as a standard modem or you can select your modem from a list or use a manufacturer provided .Inf file for configuration.

Multi-Function PC Cards

Since Windows NT 4.0 uses an enabler to enable PC Cards, the support for Multi-Function PC Cards is the same as for single function PC Cards. The only difference is that the driver for the card must enable it for both functions and the registry must have entries for both devices.

An example of a Multi-Function PC Card is the Xircom CreditCard Ethernet+Modem II. The registry entry in the PCMCIA database has the name of the driver, cm2ndis3 and describes the card as a network card. This is described in Figure 8-3.

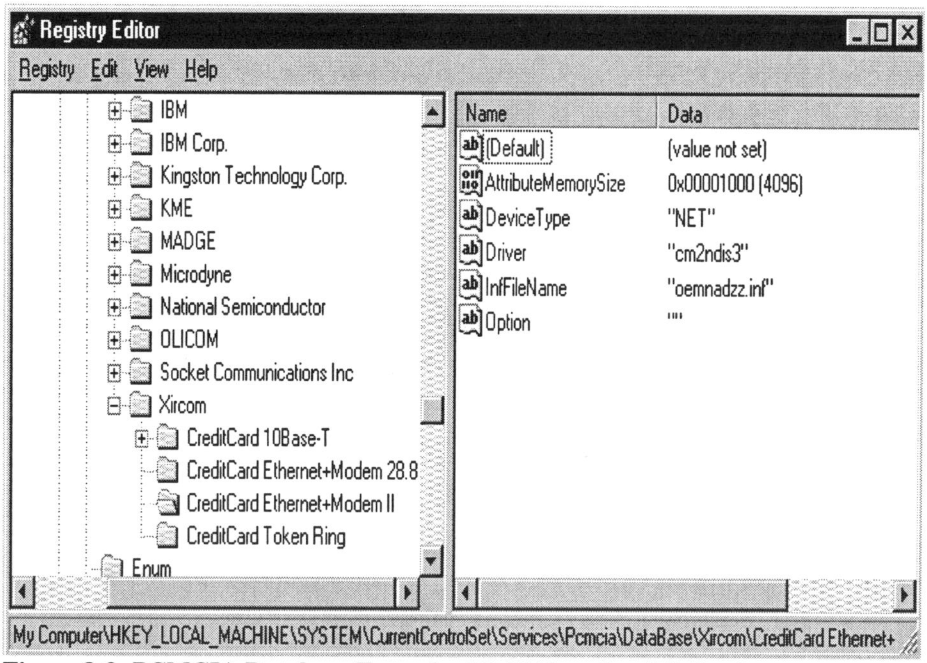

Figure 8-3: PCMCIA Database Entry for Multi-Function PC Card

The Services section of the registry then has an entry containing the hardware parameters required for the driver to configure the PC Card. For the Xircom card example, it was installed as COM4, the network I/O base address is at 300h, and the IRQ is at IRQ7. Figure 8-4 shows the sample registry entry.

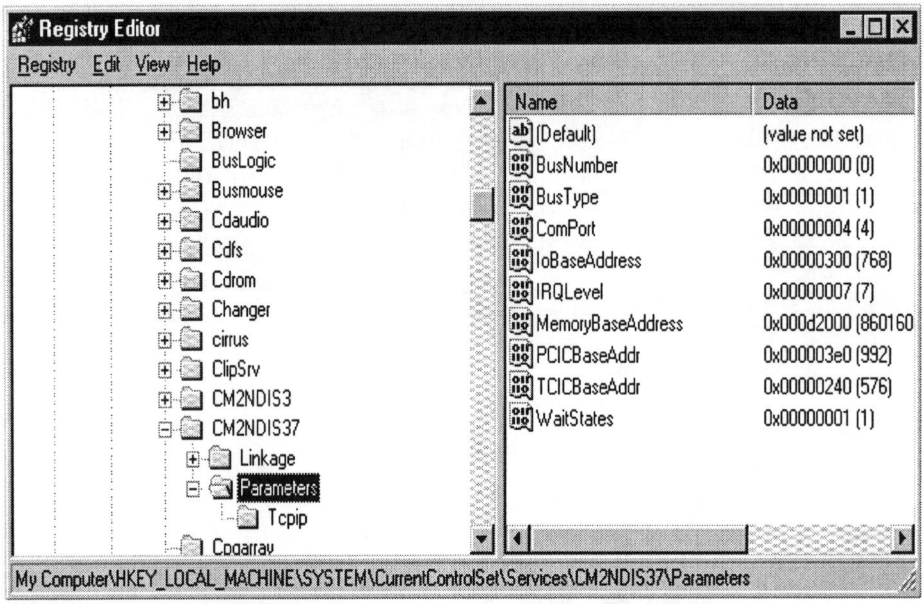

Figure 8-4: Network Driver Entry for a Multi-Function PC Card

In order for the Windows NT 4.0 to add a modem to the system, there must be entries in the registry for a serial port. There are two entries required: One that describes the COM port and one that describes the resources required. Figures 8-5 and 8-6 show then entries for the Xircom card.

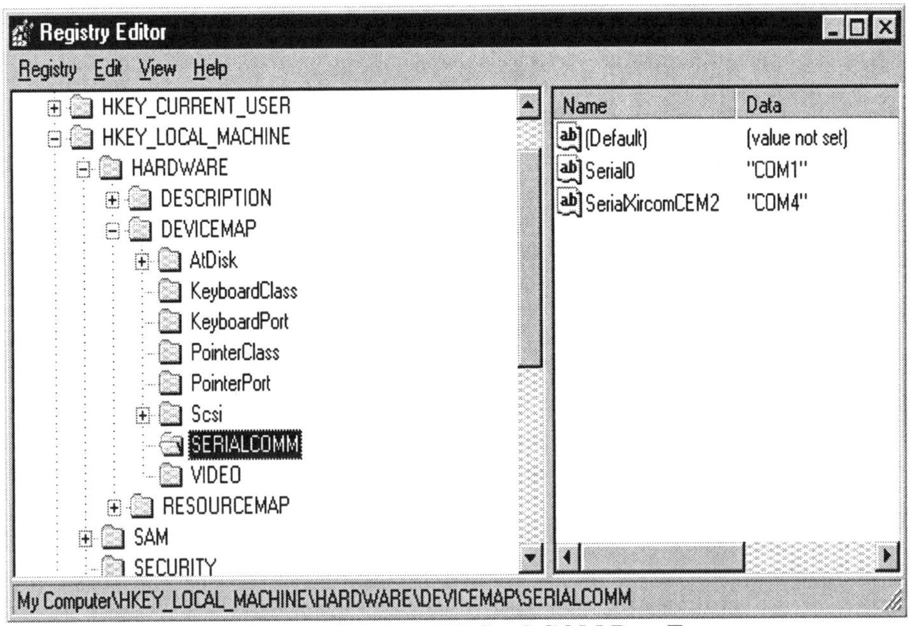

Figure 8-5: Xircom Ethernet+Modem PC Card COM Port Entry

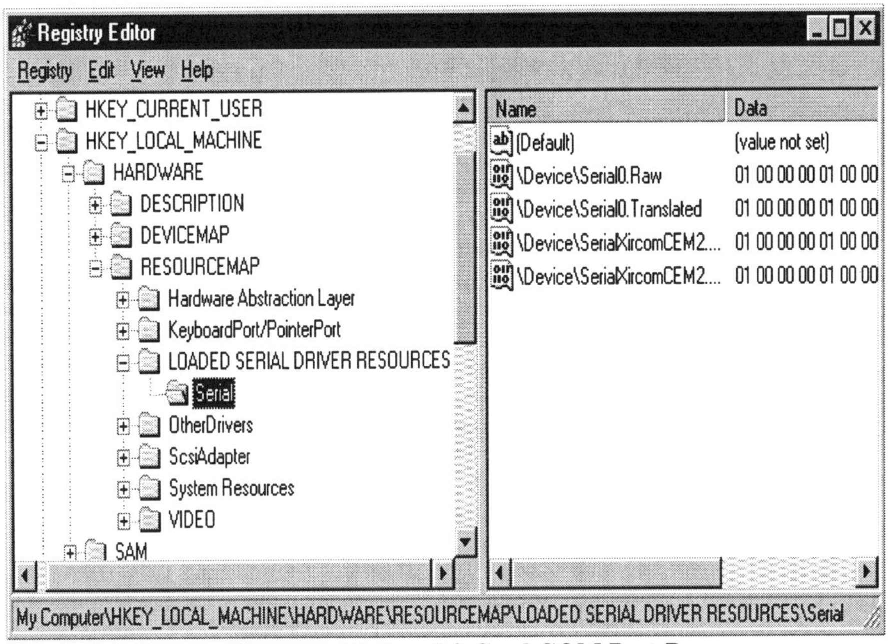

Figure 8-6: Xircom Ethernet+Modem PC Card COM Port Resources

At the time of this writing, Windows NT 5.0 Beta 1 handled Multi-Function PC Cards the same as Windows 4.0.

CardBus PC Cards

There is no CardBus support in PCMCIA.SYS for Windows NT 3.51, 4.0 and 5.0 Beta 1. Makers of CardBus PC Cards must provide point enablers for their products. These enablers configure the CardBus bridge to function properly after PCMCIA.SYS has been executed. These enablers are installed as services. The registry entry for the 3Com Fast EtherLink XL CardBus PC Card is shown in Figure 8-7.

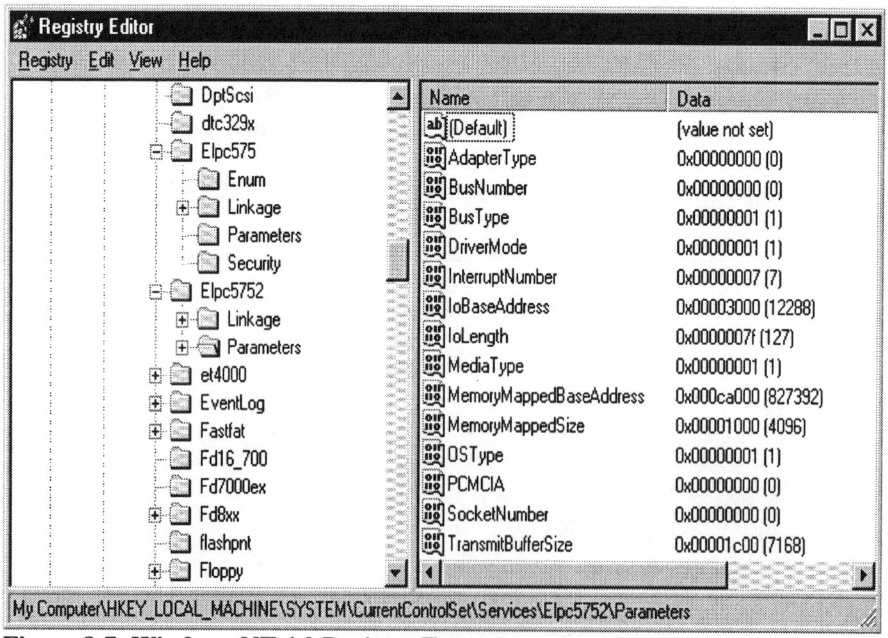

Figure 8-7: Windows NT 4.0 Registry Entry for a CardBus PC Card

All the required parameters for the PC Card are in this registry entry. The driver will read these entries and configure the CardBus bridge and the CardBus PC Card. Notice that the card has a MemoryMappedBaseAddress at CA000h for a length of 4k. This memory is used to map the CardBus Socket Registers and the ExCA Base Address into the PC memory. Chapter 10 contains information on a utility program that can display the CardBus bridge information. This utility program, WINPCIC, can be used to ensure that the CardBus bridge and PC Card are configured according to the registry settings.

Application Notifications

Windows NT 4.0 does not have any mechanism for reporting card insertion and removal since cards must be inserted at boot up for PCMCIA.SYS to enable the PC Card. At the time of this writing Windows NT 5.0 Beta 1 does not support application notifications, but the Win32 Software Developer's Kit describes the WM_DEVICECHANGE as being supported in Windows NT 5.0. For more information on this application notification, see Chapter 7.

Windows NT 5.0 introduces the Win32 Driver Model (WDM) which has Plug and Play capabilities. The new WDM expands on the Windows NT 4.0 driver model. WDM is also included in Windows 98 for new devices such as USB devices.

In the Windows NT 4.0 device driver model, as a bus is enumerated, the I/O Manager calls a device driver's *DriverEntry* routine. This routine is typically responsible for finding hardware the driver supports, calling **IoCreateDevice** to create a device object, making a symbolic Win32 link with **IoCreateSymbolicLink**, and connecting to any interrupt objects. It also fills in a table with other entry points into the driver such as Unload, CREATE, CLOSE, READ, WRITE, and DEVICE_CONTROL. For this to work, the device must be present at bus enumeration time. A fragment of a *DriverEntry* routine is shown below:

```
NTSTATUS DriverEntry(IN PDRIVER_OBJECT DriverObject,
                     IN PUNICODE_STRING RegistryPath)
{
    //
    //  Get Hardware info. From registry.

    //
    //  Report hardware usage.

    //
    //  Export driver entry points.
    DriverObject->DriveUnload = DriverUnload;
    DriverObject->MajorFunction[IRP_MJ_CREATE] = DriverCreate;
    DriverObject->MajorFunction[IRP_MJ_CLOSE] = DriverClose;
    DriverObject->MajorFunction[IRP_MJ_READ] = DriverRead;
    DriverObject->MajorFunction[IRP_MJ_WRITE] = DriverWrite;

    IoCreateDevice(…);
    IoCreateSymbolicLink(…);

}
```

The WDM in Windows NT 5.0 now expands on this by adding some features from Windows 95/98, namely a Configuration Manager and a Plug and Play Manager. It has also extended the DriverObject pointer to include two new I/O Request Packet Major Functions (IRP_MJ_PNP and IRP_MJ_POWER), several new minor functions (IRP_MN_START_DEVICE, IRP_MN_REMOVE_DEVICE, IRP_MN_STOP_DEVICE, etc), and a new driver extention (AddDevice). With these extensions, PCMCIA can take advantage of the new Plug and Play features.

In this new driver model, when a PC Card is inserted in a socket, the bus driver enumerates the device and the Configuration Manager loads the drivers for the device. The Plug and Play Manager then calls the driver's DriverEntry routine. DriverEntry simply fills in the DeviceObject structure with routines to add a device, unload a device, start a device, etc. After successful completion of the DriverEntry routine, the driver is initialized and must now initialize its devices. The Plug and Play Manager then calls the driver's AddDevice routine which now creates the device object with **IoCreateDevice** and creates the Win32 symbolic link with **IoCreateSymbolicLink**.

Once the device is added to the system, the Plug and Play Manager assigns resources to the device and calls the driver's Plug and Play routine to start, stop, remove, re-configure, query, etc. the driver. These are defined in the I/O Request Packet Minor functions IRP_MN_START_DEVICE, IRP_MN_STOP_DEVICE, etc. A small code fragment for this model is shown below:

```
NTSTATUS DriverEntry(IN PDRIVER_OBJECT DriverObject,
                     IN PUNICODE_STRING RegistryPath)
{
    //
    //  Export driver entry points.
    DriverObject->DriveUnload = DriverUnload;
    DriverObject->DriverExtension->AddDevice = AddDevice;
    DriverObject->MajorFunction[IRP_MJ_CREATE] = DriverCreate;
    DriverObject->MajorFunction[IRP_MJ_CLOSE] = DriverClose;
    DriverObject->MajorFunction[IRP_MJ_READ] = DriverRead;
    DriverObject->MajorFunction[IRP_MJ_WRITE] = DriverWrite;
    DriverObject->MajorFunction[IRP_MJ_PNP] = DriverPnP;
    DriverObject->MajorFunction[IRP_MJ_POWER] = DriverPower;
            .
            .
}


NTSTATUS AddDevice(IN PDRIVER_OBJECT DriverObject,
                   IN PDEVICE_OBJECT DeviceObject)
{
            .
            .
    IoCreateDevice(...);
    IoCreateSymbolicLink(...);
            .
```

```
}

NTSTATUS DriverPnP(IN PDEVICE_OBJECT DeviceObject,
                IN PIRP Irp)
{
            .
            .
    switch (minorfunction)
    {
       case IRP_MN_START_DEVICE:
            StartDevice(…);
            break;

       case IRP_MN_REMOVE_DEVICE:
            RemoveDevice(…);
            break;
                    .
                    .
    }
            .
            .
}

NTSTATUS DriverPower(IN PDEVICE_OBJECT DeviceObject,
                  IN PIRP Irp)
{
            .
            .
    switch (minorfunction)
    {
       case IRP_MN_QUERY_POWER:
            //
            //  Is it safe to change power states?
                    .
                    .
            break;

       case IRP_MN_SET_POWER:
            //
            //  Change power states.
                    .
                    .
            break;
                    .
                    .
           case IRP_MN_WAIT_WAKE:
            //
            //  Hardware will wake up system later.
                    .
                    .
            break;
```

```
            case IRP_MN_POWER_SEQUENCE:
                 //
                 //  How many times states have changed?
                          .
                          .
                 break;
                          .
                          .
        }
                 .
                 .
    }
```

When the Plug and Play Manager calls the driver with the minor request IRP_MN_START_DEVICE, it is asking the driver to start the device. Information about the resources allocated is passed in. The driver must connect any interrupts and initialize the device. When StartDevice completes, the device is ready to be opened and used.

Removing a PC Card is just the reverse of inserting it. Minor functions to stop the device and query if the device can be removed are called. Finally, the resources are released and the driver is removed.

In the case of power manage, the Power Manager will call the device driver at its DriverPower entry with various minor power functions. When a driver receives IRP_MN_QUERY_POWER, the system is asking the driver if it is possible to change power states. The driver must check with the hardware it services and return STATUS_SUCCESS if it is possible or STATUS_UNSUCCESSFUL if it is not possible to change power states. Sometime later a driver will receive an IRP_MN_SET_POWER to actually change power states. Occasionally a driver will not receive the IRP_MN_QUERY_POWER but will still receive the IRP_MN_SET_POWER. In this case, the driver is being told it will change power states.

Two other minor functions are IRP_MN_WAIT_WAKE and IRP_MN_POWER_SEQUENCE. These two minor functions are initiated by the driver. If a device can wake up a system, the driver will initiate an IRP_MN_WAIT_WAKE before entering a low power state. Later, when the hardware wakes the system, IRP_MN_WAIT_WAKE will be completed and power can be restored. The IRP_MN_POWER_SEQUENCE minor function is used to retrieve the number of power state sequence changes. This can be used by a driver to determine if it actually must perform any functions during a power state change.

At the time of this writing, the Windows NT DDK (for Windows NT Workstation 5.0 Beta 1) describes all of this functionality. This information is only available to Microsoft Developer Network members.

Windows CE

An increasing number of Handheld PCs (HPC) include a PC Card socket and run Windows CE. Windows CE is included briefly in this chapter because it more closely resembles Windows NT. Also, all development tools are hosted on Windows NT when developing for Windows CE. For more information on Windows CE development, see the Windows CE Platform SDK Documentation available from Microsoft.

Windows CE Device Driver Architecture

There are two types of drivers supported by Windows CE: built-in device drivers and installable device drivers. Built-in device drivers provide support for devices built in to the hardware platform. These would be LCD displays, touch screens, and infrared ports. Installable device drivers provide support for devices that can be added to the hardware platform. One good example is a PC Card. The device driver for the PC Card socket would be built-in while the drivers for the PC Cards that can be inserted would be installable. This section will cover installable device drivers.

An installable device driver under Windows CE is simply a dynamic link library (DLL). The DLL is structured and built just like any Windows 95/98/NT DLL. Its purpose is to expose the functions of a hardware device to Win32 applications. To do this, the driver makes the device appear as a file in the HPC file system and exports routines to initialize, open, close, read, write, etc. the device through Win32 functions.

If a driver is generic and can support a class of PC Cards, it also needs a "detect function" that will identify if the driver supports a card after it is inserted. Typically, the detect function will read tuples off of the card and determine if the driver can support the card. If so, it returns success. For more information on the detect function and how drivers are loaded, see the section *Windows CE Registry Structure*.

One more mandatory function in the driver is the DllMain function. The system calls this entry point when the driver gets attached to and detached from a process. The driver really only needs to allocate or de-allocate any per-process resources and then return TRUE.

Windows CE supports a subset of Card Services, but only at the device driver layer; application code cannot make Card Services calls. Most of the Card Services calls require a CARD_SOCKET_HANDLE which contains a socket and function pair. This handle acts just like the "Socket" field of most structures in the PC Card Standard 1995 and higher. It identifies both the socket and the function so that multi-function PC Cards can be used in a system.

Card Services calls on Windows CE are slightly different than the standard Card Services calls. All of the functions start with *Cardxxxxx*. So, for example, to get the first tuple on a card, you would call *CardGetFirstTuple* with the appropriate structure filled in. To get the next tuple, you would call *CardGetNextTuple*. To register a Card Services client you would call *CardRegisterClient*.

A Card Services client driver would register a client in its Init routine. Then the client would map any I/O, IRQ, or memory resources required for the PC Card and finally call *CardRequestConfiguration* to configure the card. The Read/Write/Open/Close entry points to the driver would perform any function specific to the device. Only the Init routine configures the card while the Deinit routine releases the card configuration and any resources used by the card.

Windows CE Registry Structure

Just like Windows 95/98 and Windows NT, Windows CE maintains a registry database of PC Cards and drivers. The unique plug and play device ID names are the same as the ones used in Windows 95/98, although the registry areas are slightly different. In Windows CE, the registry areas of interest are,

```
HKEY_LOCAL_MACHINE\Drivers\
        Active\
        Builtin\
        PCMCIA\
                Detect\
                Plug and Play ID\
                Driver Name\
```

Listed in the HKEY_LOCAL_MACHINE\Drivers\Active subkey are the subkeys of drivers that are loaded and running. Various information about the loaded drivers can be found in this subkey, such as the registry path to the device key in \Drivers\PCMCIA\, the unique plug and play ID, the socket handle, and the device name.

The HKEY_LOCAL_MACHINE\Drivers\Builtin subkey has the list of drivers for hardware that is built into the platform. This typically includes an *IrComm* entry for infrared devices, a *Serial* entry for COM ports, and a *WaveDev* entry for WAV playing devices.

Finally, the most interesting entries for our discussion, are the HKEY_LOCAL_MACHINE\Drivers\PCMCIA subkeys. The first subkey, Detect, has a list of numbered subkeys that the Device Manager uses to auto-detect a PC Card that does not have a plug and play ID or an entry in the database of plug and play Ids. The Device Manager searches this area in sequential order, from 00 to 99.

Each numbered entry under Detect has a Dll subkey and an Entry subkey. The Dll subkey has the name of a DLL that contains a detect function, named in the Entry subkey. After the Device Manager loads the DLL, it calls the detect function to determine if the driver supports the inserted card. If it does, it returns SUCCESS and the Device Manager stops checking further entries. If the driver does not return SUCCESS, the Device Manager goes to the next sequential entry, loads the DLL, and calls the detect function. A sample registry entry for a Modem Detect subkey is shown in Figure 8-8. In this example, the driver name is Serial.dll while the detect function is DetectModem

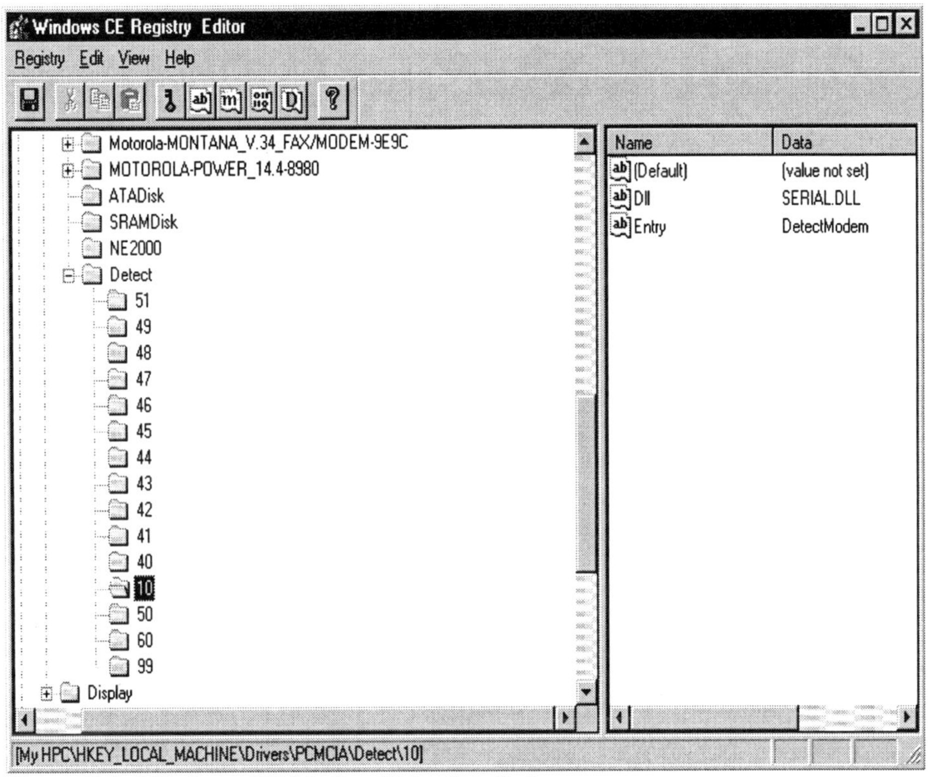

Figure 8-8: Windows CE Modem Detection Entry

The next subkey of interest in the PCMCIA area of the registry is the PCMCIA database of unique plug and play Ids, found at HKEY_LOCAL_MACHINE\Drivers\PCMCIA\<plug and play id>. The unique id is formed just like the one in Windows 95/98. See *Chapter 7 Windows 95/98* on how this unique id is formed. When a PC Card is inserted, the Device Manager reads the tuples off of the card and forms the unique plug and play id. It then searches the PCMCIA database for a match. If a match is found, the driver specified is loaded and registers the device in the system. A sample PCMCIA database entry is shown in Figure 8-9.

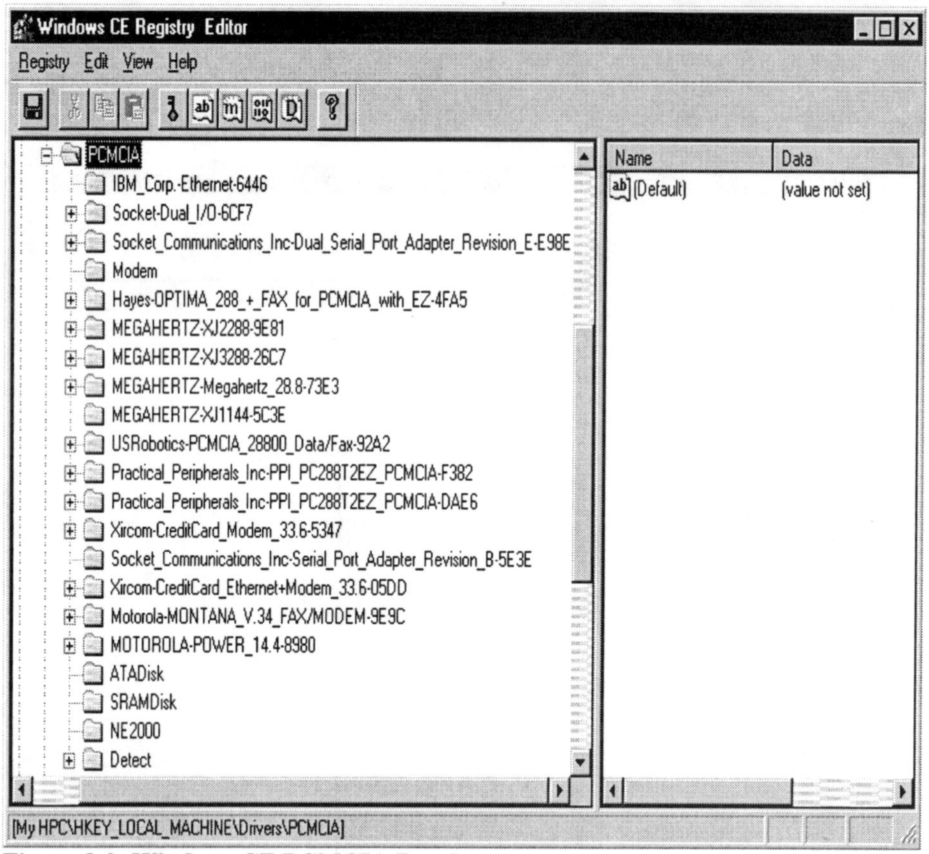

Figure 8-9: Windows CE PCMCIA Database

The subkeys under the unique plug and play id are the DLL name, a device prefix, and an index value that gets appended to the device name. If the index value is not present, the Device Manager assigns a number and appends it to the device name. Multiple devices can be supported by the driver in this case. If the index value is present, the index is appended to the device name and the driver can only support this one device. As an example, see Figure 8-10 for a plug and play modem entry. Since the Index value is not present, the Device Manager will assign COM1, COM2, COM3, etc. to each modem found.

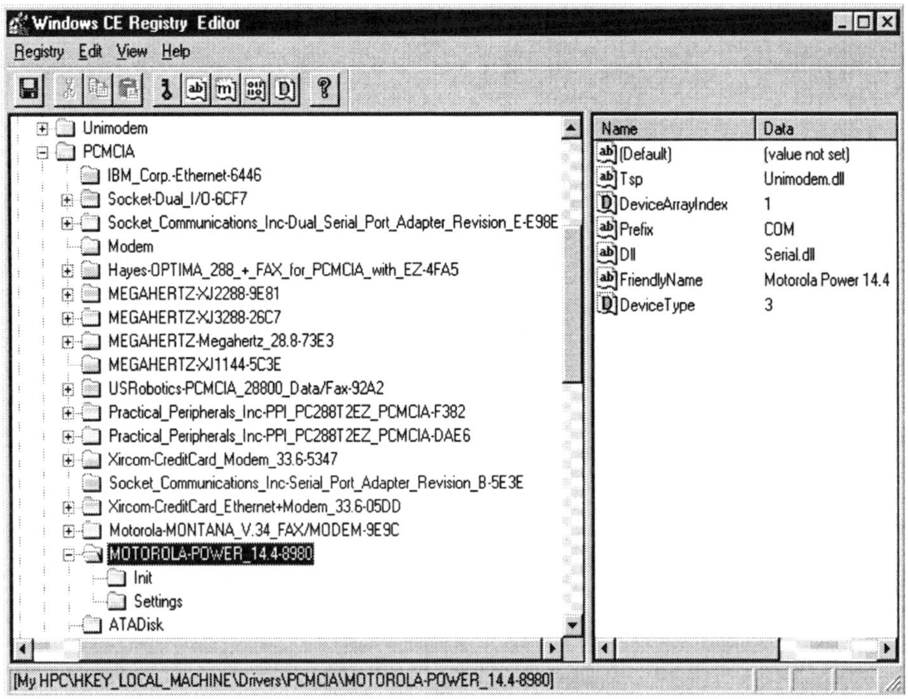

Figure 8-10: Windows CE Plug and Play ID Modem Entry

The last area of interest in the PCMCIA section of the registry is the HKEY_LOCAL_MACHINE\Drivers\PCMCIA\<driver name> subkey. The subkeys here are for generic drivers that work with the HKEY_LOCAL_MCHINE\Drivers\PCMCIA\Detect subkeys. If a PC Card is inserted that does not have a unique plug and play id, the Device Manager searches the Detect area for a detect function. When a driver is found that supports a PC Card (the detect function returns SUCCESS), the Device Manager searches the <driver name> subkeys for the DLL name, device name, and index number, just like the entries with unique plug and play ids. See Figure 8-11 for a sample generic modem subkey. Notice the DLL is Serial.dll and the device prefix is COM, just like the specific modem with the plug and play id.

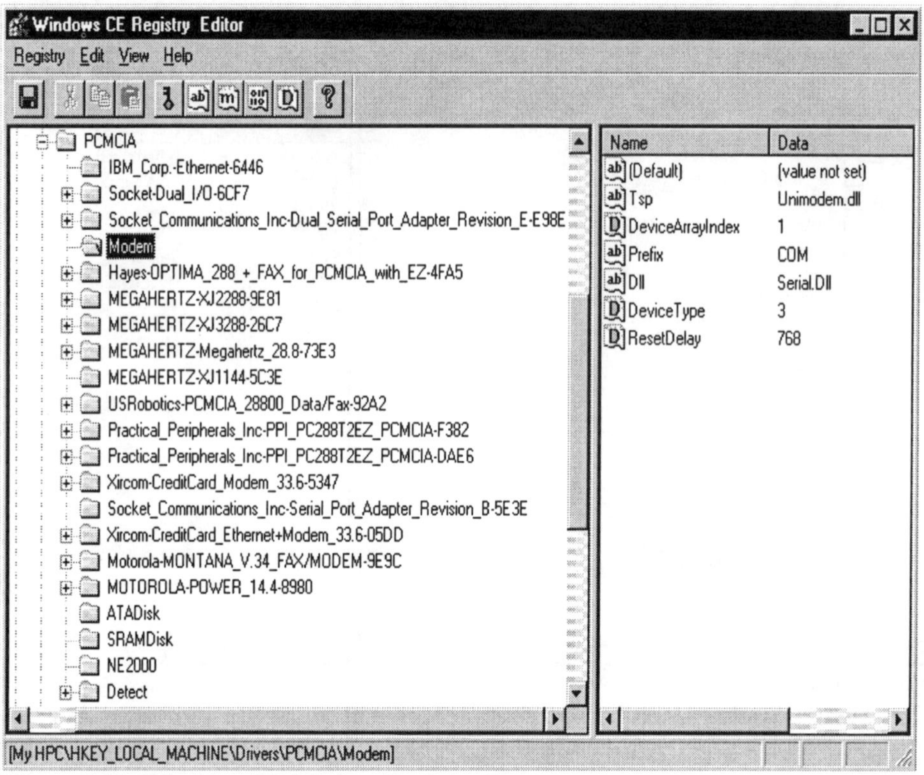

Figure 8-11: Windows CE Modem Registry Entry

Windows CE Application Notifications

Just like Windows 95/98, and in the future Windows NT 5.0, there are notifications broadcast to application programs through the WM_DEVICECHANGE message. Messages are broadcast when devices are added to or removed from the system. For a more thorough discussion of this, see *Chapter 7 Windows 95/98*. A sample application, DEVCHG, is included in the software that accompanies this book. This sample code works on Windows 95/98/CE.

Summary

This chapter started with an introduction of the difficulties of PC Card support under Windows NT 4.0. The biggest difficulty is that PC Cards must be enabled via the PCMCIA.SYS enabler and by entries in the registry describing how to enable the card. It then described the plug-and-play features of the forthcoming Windows NT 5.0. The chapter finally ended with describing how PC Cards are supported under Windows CE.

Chapter 9: Linux PCMCIA Programmer's Guide

Chapter 9 is included, by permission, courtesy of David Hinds. Minor modifications have been made to this guide to ensure consistent use of font style and terminology.

By David Hinds, dhinds@hyper.stanford.edu
V2.9, 1998/06/07 12:51:54

This document describes how to write kernel device drivers for the Linux PC Card services interface. It also describes how to write user-mode utilities for communicating with card services. The latest version of this document can always be found at ftp://hyper.stanford.edu/pub/pcmcia/doc.

An HTML version is at http://hyper.stanford.edu/HyperNews/get/pcmcia/home.html.

Introduction

The Linux kernel PC Card system has three main components. At the lowest level are the socket drivers. Next is the card services module. Drivers for specific cards are layered on top of card services. One special card services client, called driver services, provides a link between user level PC Card utility programs and the kernel PC Card facilities.

The socket driver layer is loosely based on the socket services API. There are two socket driver modules. The tcic module supports the Databook TCIC-2 family of PC Card adapters. The i82365 module supports the Intel i82365sl family and various Intel-compatible adapters, including Cirrus, VLSI, Ricoh, and Vadem chips. In addition, the i82365 module implements support for CardBus controllers that follow the ``Yenta'' register-level specification.

Card services is the largest single component of the PC Card package. It provides an API somewhat similar to DOS card services, adapted to a Unix environment.

The Linux implementation was based in part on the Solaris PCMCIA interface specification. It is implemented in the pcmcia_core module.

The driver services layer implements a user mode pseudo-device for accessing some card services functions from PC Card utility programs. It is responsible for keeping track of all PC Card client drivers, and for matching up drivers with physical sockets. It is implemented in the ds module.

This document describes the kernel interface to the card services and driver services modules, and the user interface to driver services. It is intended for use by PC Card device driver developers. The Linux PCMCIA-HOWTO describes how to install and use Linux PC Card support. It is available from hyper.stanford.edu in /pub/pcmcia.

Acknowledgments

I'd like to thank all the Linux users who have helped test and debug this PC Card software, and who have helped with driver development. I should also thank Linus Torvalds, Donald Becker, Alan Cox, and Bjorn Ekwall for Linux kernel development help. I'm especially grateful to Michael Bender for many helpful discussions about the Solaris PC Card implementation.

Basic PC Card Concepts

The PC Card Socket Interface

The PC Card bus has two basic operating modes: memory-only and memory and I/O. The first mode was defined by the original Version 1.0 specification and only supports simple memory cards. The second mode, defined in Version 2.0, redefines a few of the memory card control signals to support I/O port addressing and I/O interrupt signaling.

16-PC Cards have two memory spaces: attribute memory and common memory. The PC Card interface can address up to 16MB of each type of memory. Attribute memory is typically used for holding descriptive information and configuration registers. Common memory may include the bulk storage of a memory card, or device buffers in the case of I/O cards. All cards that are compliant with the version 2.0 PC Card specification should have a Card Information Structure (CIS) in attribute memory, which describes the card and how it should be configured.

Separate control signals allow cards to signal their operating status to the host. These signals include card detect, ready/busy, write protect, battery low, and battery dead.

The memory and I/O interface mode allow cards to address up to 64K of I/O ports. It also allows cards to signal I/O interrupts, and routes one card output to the host system's speaker. In this mode, several of the memory card control signals are unavailable because those pins are used to carry the extra I/O card signals. On some cards, these signals can instead be read from a special configuration register in attribute memory, the Pin Replacement Register.

The 16-bit PC Card Socket Adapter

The PC Card adapter serves as a bridge between PC Cards and the system bus. There are several varieties of adapters, but all share the same basic functionality. The Socket services software layer takes care of all the details of how to program the PC Card adapter.

The PC Card adapter has the job of mapping windows of addresses in the host memory and I/O spaces to windows of addresses in card space. All PC Card adapters support at least four independent memory windows and two I/O windows per socket.

Each memory window is defined by a base address in the host address space, a base address in the card address space, and a window size. Some adapters differ in their alignment rules for memory windows. However, all adapters support windows whose size is at least 4K and also a power of two, and where the base address is a multiple of the window size. Each window can be programmed to point to either attribute or common memory.

I/O windows differ from memory windows in that host addresses that fall within an I/O window are not modified before they are passed on to an I/O card. Effectively, the base addresses of the window in the host and card address spaces are always equal. I/O windows also have no alignment or size restrictions; an I/O window can start and end on any byte boundary in the 64K I/O address space.

The PC Card bus defines a single interrupt signal from the card to the adapter. The adapter then has the responsibility of steering this interrupt to an appropriate interrupt request (IRQ) line. All adapters support steering card I/O interrupts to essentially any free interrupt line. Because steering happens in the adapter, the card itself is unaware of which interrupt it uses.

All PC Card adapters can generate interrupts in response to card status changes. These interrupts are distinct from the I/O interrupts generated by an I/O card, and use a separate interrupt line. Signals that can generate interrupts include card detect, ready/busy, write protect, battery low, and battery dead.

Card Services Subfunction Descriptions

Card services calls have the general form:

```
#include "cs_types.h"
#include "cs.h"

int CardServices(int subfunc, void *arg1, void *arg2, ...);
```

Some card services functions require additional #include statements. The particular subfunction determines the number of expected arguments. A return code of CS_SUCCESS indicates that a call succeeded. Other return codes indicate errors.

Client Management Functions

Device drivers that use card services functions are called clients. A device driver should use the **RegisterClient** call to get a client handle before using other services. Most card services functions will take this client handle as an argument. Before unloading, drivers should also unregister with **DeregisterClient**.

RegisterClient

```
int CardServices(RegisterClient, client_handle_t *client, client_reg_t *reg);
```

The client_reg_t data structure is given by:

```
typedef struct client_reg_t {
```

```
        dev_info_t          *dev_info;
        u_int               Attributes;
        u_int               EventMask;
        int                 (*event_handler)(event_t event, int priority,
                             event_callback_args_t *args);
        event_callback_args_t     event_callback_args;
        u_long              Version;
} client_reg_t;
```

RegisterClient establishes a link between a client driver and card services, and connects the client with an appropriate socket. The dev_info parameter is used by card services to match the client with a socket; this correspondence is normally established by driver services via a call to **BindDevice**. If successful, a client handle will be returned in client.The following flags can be specified in Attributes:

INFO_MASTER_SERVICES
: For use only by the driver services client, among other things, specifies that this client should not be automatically unbound when a card is ejected from this socket.

INFO_IO_CLIENT
: Specifies that this client is an I/O card driver.

INFO_MTD_CLIENT
: Specifies that this client is a Memory Technology Driver.

INFO_MEM_CLIENT
: Specifies that this client is a memory card driver.

INFO_CARD_SHARE
: Included for compatibility, has no effect.

INFO_CARD_EXCL
: Included for compatibility, has no effect.

EventMask specifies what events this client should be notified of. The event_handler entry point will be called by card services when an event in EventMask is processed. The event_handler_args structure is a template for the structure that will be passed to the event handler. The Version parameter identifies the card services version level that this driver expects; it is currently ignored. A driver should be prepared to handle card services events before calling **RegisterClient**. This call will always generate a CS_REGISTRATION_COMPLETE event and may also generate an artificial CS_CARD_INSERTION event if the socket is currently occupied.

Return codes:

CS_OUT_OF_RESOURCE
: An appropriate socket could not be found for this driver.

DeregisterClient

```
int CardServices(DeregisterClient, client_handle_t client);
```

DeregisterClient severs the connection between a client and card services. It should be called after the client has freed any resources it has allocated. Once a connection is broken, it cannot be reestablished
until after another call to **BindDevice**.

Return codes:

CS_BAD_HANDLE
: The client handle is invalid.

CS_IN_USE
: The client still has allocated resources, such as I/O port windows or an interrupt, or the socket configuration is locked.

SetEventMask

```
int CardServices(SetEventMask, client_handle_t client, eventmask_t *mask);
```

The eventmask_t structure is given by:

```
typedef struct eventmask_t {
        u_int       Attributes;
        u_int       EventMask;
} eventmask_t;
```

SetEventMask updates the mask that determines which events this client will be notified of.

Return codes:

CS_BAD_HANDLE
: The client handle is invalid.

BindDevice

```
int CardServices(BindDevice, bind_req_t *req);
```

The bind_req structure is given by:

```
typedef struct bind_req_t {
        socket_t        Socket;
        u_char          Function;
        dev_info_t      *dev_info;
} bind_req_t;
```

BindDevice associates a device driver with a particular socket. It is normally called by driver services after a newly inserted card has been identified. Once a driver has been bound to a socket, it will be eligible to register as a client of that socket. Note that this call does not take a client handle as an argument. This is the only card services call that takes a socket number as an argument.

The **Function** field specifies which function(s) of a multi-function card are to be bound to this driver. Function numbers correspond to entries in the card's **CISTPL_LONGLINK_MFC** tuple. If Function is set to **BIND_FN_ALL**, the driver will be bound to all card functions. A driver will only be able to access CIS tuples corresponding to functions for which it is bound.

Return codes:

CS_BAD_SOCKET
: The specified socket number is invalid.

Socket State Control

These functions are more or less concerned with getting and setting the current operating state of a socket. GetStatus returns the current socket state. ResetCard is used to send a hard reset signal to a socket. SuspendCard and ResumeCard can be used to power down and power up a socket without releasing the drivers currently bound to that socket. EjectCard and InsertCard essentially mimic real card ejection and insertion events.

GetStatus

```
int CardServices(GetStatus, client_handle_t client, status_t *status);
```

The status_t data structure is given by:

```
typedef struct status_t {
        u_char      Function;
        u_int       CardState;
        u_int       SocketState;
} status_t;
```

GetStatus returns the current status of a client's socket. For cards that are configured in IO mode, GetStatus uses the Pin Replacement Register and Extended Status Register to determine the card status. For normal clients, the Function field is ignored, but for clients bound with BIND_FN_ALL, this field specifies the function whose configuration registers should be used to determine the socket state, if the socket is currently configured. The following flags are defined in CardState:

CS_EVENT_CARD_DETECT
: Specifies that the socket is occupied.

CS_EVENT_CB_DETECT
: Specifies that the socket is occupied by a CardBus Device.

CS_EVENT_WRITE_PROTECT
: Specifies that the card is currently write protected.

CS_EVENT_BATTERY_LOW
: Specifies that the card battery is low.

CS_EVENT_BATTERY_DEAD
: Specifies that the card battery is dead.

CS_EVENT_READY_CHANGE
: Specifies that the card is ready.

CS_EVENT_PM_SUSPEND
: Specifies that the socket is suspended.

CS_EVENT_REQUEST_ATTENTION
: Specifies that the request attention bit in the extended status register is set.

CS_EVENT_CARD_INSERTION
: Specifies that a card insertion event is in progress. An insertion event will be sent to the client when socket setup is complete.

CS_EVENT_3VCARD
: Indicates that the card supports 3.3V operation.

CS_EVENT_XVCARD
: Indicates that the card supports "X.X"V operation. The actual voltage is currently undefined in the specification.

SocketState is currently unused, but in theory, it should latch changes in the state of the fields in CardState.

Return codes:

CS_BAD_HANDLE
The client handle is invalid.

ResetCard

int CardServices(ResetCard, client_handle_t client);

ResetCard requests that a client's socket be reset. When this call is made, card services sends all clients a CS_EVENT_RESET_REQUEST event. If any client rejects the request, card services sends a CS_EVENT_RESET_COMPLETE event to the initiating client with event_callback_args.info set to the return code of the client that rejected the request. If all clients agree to the request, card services sends CS_EVENT_RESET_PHYSICAL event, then resets the socket. When the socket signals that it is ready, a CS_EVENT_CARD_RESET event is generated. Finally, a CS_EVENT_RESET_COMPLETE event is sent to the initiating client, with event_callback_args.info set to zero.

Return codes:

CS_BAD_HANDLE
The client handle is invalid.
CS_NO_CARD
The socket assigned to this client is currently vacant.
CS_IN_USE
This socket is currently being reset.

SuspendCard

int CardServices(SuspendCard, client_handle_t client);

Card services sends all clients CS_EVENT_PM_SUSPEND events, then shuts down and turns off power to the socket.

Return codes:

CS_BAD_HANDLE
The client handle is invalid.
CS_NO_CARD
The socket assigned to this client is currently vacant.
CS_IN_USE
This socket is already suspended.

ResumeCard

int CardServices(ResumeCard, client_handle_t client);

After restoring power to the socket, card services will notify all clients with CS_EVENT_PM_RESUME events.

Return codes:

CS_BAD_HANDLE
The client handle is invalid.
CS_NO_CARD
The socket assigned to this client is currently vacant.
CS_IN_USE
This socket is not currently suspended.

EjectCard

int CardServices(EjectCard, client_handle_t client);

Card services sends eject events to all clients, then shuts down and turns off power to the socket. All clients except for driver services will be unlinked from the socket.

Return codes:

CS_BAD_HANDLE
: The client handle is invalid.

CS_NO_CARD
: The socket assigned to this client is currently vacant.

InsertCard

int CardServices(InsertCard, client_handle_t client);

Card services sends insertion events to all clients of this socket (normally, only driver services).

Return codes:

CS_BAD_HANDLE
: The client handle is invalid.

CS_NO_CARD
: The socket assigned to this client is currently vacant.

CS_IN_USE
: The socket has already been configured.

I/O Card Configuration Calls

The normal order of events is for a driver to reserve I/O ports and an interrupt line with calls to RequestIO and RequestIRQ, then to call RequestConfiguration to actually configure the socket. If any of these calls fails, a driver should be sure to release any resources it successfully reserved.

Multi-function cards can have separate configurations for each card function. However, the configurations do need to be consistent with one another. While each card function has its own set of configuration registers, each socket has only a single interrupt line and can only map two contiguous ranges of I/O ports.

CardBus cards are configured somewhat differently. The RequestIO and RequestConfiguration calls have similar roles, however, Card Services takes responsibility for most of the configuration details, and the contents of the request structures are ignored.

RequestIO

int CardServices(RequestIO, client_handle_t client, io_req_t *req);

The io_req_t data structure is given by:

```
typedef struct io_req_t {
        ioaddr_t     BasePort1;
        ioaddr_t     NumPorts1;
        u_int        Attributes1;
        ioaddr_t     BasePort2;
        ioaddr_t     NumPorts2;
        u_int        Attributes2;
        u_int        IOAddrLines;
} io_req_t;
```

RequestIO reserves I/O port windows for a card. If BasePort1 is non-zero, it specifies the I/O port address of the window to be reserved; if it is zero, card services will find an available window and set BasePort1 to this address. If NumPorts2 is non-zero, a second I/O port window will also be reserved. IOAddrLines specifies the number of address lines that are actually decoded by the PC Card; this is not currently used.

With multi-function cards, this call will allocate IO ports for each card function in such a way that all a card's ports can be mapped by the two low-level IO port windows associated with each physical socket. For example, if the drivers for a hypothetical four-function card each attempt to allocate one IO window of 8 ports, Card Services will consolidate these into a single contiguous 32-port block.

When this function is invoked by a CardBus client, the IO request structure is ignored. Instead, Card Services examines the card and allocates any necessary system resources: this includes IO and memory space, as well as an interrupt, if needed. One call will reserve all resources needed for all card functions, not just the function of the client making the call.

This call does not actually configure a socket's I/O windows: this is done by a subsequent call to RequestConfiguration.

The following flags can be specified in Attributes1 and Attributes2:

IO_DATA_PATH_WIDTH
: This field may either be IO_DATA_PATH_WIDTH_16 for 16-bit access, or IO_DATA_PATH_WIDTH_8 for 8-bit access, or IO_DATA_PATH_WIDTH_AUTO

to dynamically size the bus based on the access size.

Return codes:

CS_BAD_HANDLE
: The client handle is invalid.

CS_NO_CARD
: The socket assigned to this client is currently vacant.

CS_IN_USE
: This socket's I/O windows have already been reserved.

CS_CONFIGURATION_LOCKED
: This socket's configuration has been locked by a call to RequestConfiguration.

CS_BAD_ATTRIBUTE
: An unsupported attribute flag was specified.

ReleaseIO

```
int CardServices(ReleaseIO, client_handle_t client, io_req_t *req);
```

ReleaseIO deallocates I/O port windows allocated by a previous call to RequestIO. The req parameter should be the same one passed to RequestIO. If several card functions are sharing a larger IO port window, ports released by one function may not become available for other uses until all card functions have released their IO ports.

For a CardBus client, this call releases all system resources allocated for this card.

Return codes:

CS_BAD_HANDLE
: The client handle is invalid.

CS_CONFIGURATION_LOCKED
: This socket's configuration has been locked by a call to **RequestConfiguration**. The configuration should be released before calling **ReleaseIO**.

CS_BAD_ARGS
: The parameters in req do not match the parameters passed to **RequestIO**.

RequestIRQ

```
int CardServices(RequestIRQ, client_handle_t client, irq_req_t *req);
```

The irq_req_t structure is given by:

```
typedef struct irq_req_t {
        u_int           Attributes;
        u_int           AssignedIRQ;
        u_int           IRQInfo1, IRQInfo2;
        void            *(Handler)(int, struct pt_regs *);
void            *Instance
} irq_req_t;
```

RequestIRQ reserves an interrupt line for use by a PC Card. The IRQInfo1 and IRQInfo2 fields correspond to the interrupt description bytes in a CFTABLE_ENTRY tuple. If IRQ_INFO2_VALID is set in IRQInfo1, then IRQInfo2 is a bit-mapped mask of allowed interrupt values. Each bit corresponds to one interrupt line: bit 0 = irq 0, bit 1 = irq 1, etc. So, a mask of 0x1100 would mean that interrupts 12 and 8 could be used. If IRQ_INFO2_VALID is not set, IRQInfo1 is just the desired interrupt number. If the call is successful, the reserved interrupt is returned in AssignedIRQ.

If the IRQ_HANDLER_PRESENT flag is set, then this call also specifies an interrupt handler to be installed when the interrupt is enabled. When RequestConfiguration is called, the handler given by Handler will be installed. For 2.0 and later kernels, the interrupt handler will be installed with the device ``instance" given in Instance. For pre-2.1.60 kernels, the kernel irq2dev_map table will also be updated. With multi-function cards, the interrupt will be allocated in shared mode, and the handler(s) have responsibility for determining which card function(s) require attention when an interrupt is received. If a client instead bypasses Card Services to install its own interrupt service routine, it should allocate the interrupt in shared mode if this client could be bound to a multi-function card.

The following flags can be specified in Attributes:

IRQ_FORCED_PULSE
: Specifies that the interrupt should be configured for pulsed mode, rather than the default level mode.

IRQ_TYPE_TIME
: Specifies that this interrupt can be time-shared with other card devices drivers. Only one driver should enable the interrupt at any time.

IRQ_FIRST_SHARED

In conjunction with IRQ_TYPE_TIME, this should be set by the first driver requesting a shared interrupt.

IRQ_HANDLER_PRESENT

Indicates that the Handler field points to an interrupt service routine that should be installed.

Return codes:

CS_BAD_HANDLE

The client handle is invalid.

CS_NO_CARD

The socket assigned to this client is currently vacant.

CS_IN_USE

An interrupt has already been reserved for this socket, or the requested interrupt is unavailable.

CS_CONFIGURATION_LOCKED

This socket's configuration has been locked by a call to **RequestConfiguration**.

CS_BAD_ATTRIBUTE

An unsupported attribute flag was specified.

ReleaseIRQ

```
int CardServices(ReleaseIRQ, client_handle_t client, irq_req_t *req);
```

ReleaseIRQ unreserves an interrupt assigned by an earlier call to **RequestIRQ**. The req structure should be the same structure that was passed to **RequestIRQ**.

Return codes:

CS_BAD_HANDLE

The client handle is invalid.

CS_CONFIGURATION_LOCKED

This socket's configuration has been locked by a call to **RequestConfiguration**. The configuration should be released before calling **ReleaseIRQ**.

CS_BAD_IRQ

The parameters in req do not match the parameters passed to **RequestIRQ**.

RequestConfiguration

```
int CardServices(RequestConfiguration, client_handle_t client, config_req_t
        *req);
```

The config_req_t structure is given by:

```
typedef struct config_req_t {
        u_int       Attributes;
        u_int       Vcc, Vpp1, Vpp2;
        u_int       IntType;
        caddr_t     ConfigBase;
        u_char      Status, Pin, Copy;
        u_char      ConfigIndex;
        u_int       Present;
} config_req_t;
```

RequestConfiguration is responsible for actually configuring a socket. This includes setting voltages, setting CIS configuration registers, setting up I/O port windows, and setting up interrupts.

IntType specifies the type of interface to use for this card. It may either be INT_MEMORY, INT_MEMORY_AND_IO, or INT_CARDBUS. Voltages are specified in units of 1/10 volt. Currently, Vpp1 must equal Vpp2.

With multi-function cards, each card function is configured separately. Each function has its own set of CIS configuration registers. However, all functions must be configured with the same power and interface settings.

When invoked by a CardBus client, the request structure is ignored, and all card functions will be configured based on data collected in a previous RequestIO call. This includes configuring the CardBus bridge, as well as initializing the Command, Base Address, and Interrupt Line registers in each card function's configuration space.

The following flags can be specified in Attributes. DMA and speaker control are not supported on all systems.

CONF_ENABLE_IRQ
Enable the I/O interrupt reserved by a previous call to **RequestIRQ**.

CONF_ENABLE_DMA
Enable DMA accesses for this socket.

CONF_ENABLE_SPKR
Enable speaker output from this socket. The Present parameter is a bit map specifying which CIS configuration registers are implemented by this card. ConfigBase gives the offset of the configuration registers in attribute memory. The following registers can be specified:

PRESENT_OPTION
Specifies that the Configuration Option Register is present. The COR register will be set using the ConfigIndex parameter.

PRESENT_STATUS
Specifies that the Card Configuration and Status Register is present. The CCSR will be initialized with the Status parameter.

PRESENT_PIN_REPLACE
Specifies that the Pin Replacement Register is present. The PRR will be initialized with the Pin parameter.

PRESENT_COPY
Specifies that the Socket and Copy Register is present. The SCR will be initialized with the Copy parameter.

PRESENT_EXT_STATUS
Specifies that the Extended Status Register is present. The ESR will be initialized with the ExtStatus parameter.

Return codes:

CS_BAD_HANDLE
The client handle is invalid.

CS_NO_CARD
The socket assigned to this client is currently vacant.

CS_OUT_OF_RESOURCE
Card services was unable to allocate a memory window to access the card's configuration registers.

CS_CONFIGURATION_LOCKED
This socket's configuration has already been locked by another call to **RequestConfiguration**.

CS_BAD_VCC
The requested Vcc voltage is not supported.

CS_BAD_VPP
The requested Vpp1/Vpp2 voltage is not supported.

ModifyConfiguration

```
int CardServices(ModifyConfiguration, client_handle_t client, *mod);
```

The modconf_t structure is given by:

```
typedef struct modconf_t {
        u_int       Attributes;
        u_int       Vcc, Vpp1, Vpp2;
} modconf_t;
```

ModifyConfiguration modifies some attributes of a socket that has been configured by a call to **RequestConfiguration**. The following flags can be specified in Attributes:

CONF_IRQ_CHANGE_VALID
: Indicates that the CONF_ENABLE_IRQ setting should be updated.

CONF_ENABLE_IRQ
: Specifies that I/O interrupts should be enabled for this socket.

CONF_VCC_CHANGE_VALID
: Indicates that Vcc should be updated.

CONF_VPP1_CHANGE_VALID
: Indicates that Vpp1 should be updated.

CONF_VPP2_CHANGE_VALID
: Indicates that Vpp2 should be updated.

Currently, Vpp1 and Vpp2 must always have the same value. So, the two values must always be changed at the same time.

Return codes:

CS_BAD_HANDLE
: The client handle is invalid.

CS_NO_CARD
: The socket assigned to this client is currently vacant.

CS_CONFIGURATION_LOCKED
  This actually means that this socket has not been locked.
CS_BAD_VCC
  The requested Vcc voltage is not supported.
CS_BAD_VPP
  The requested Vpp1/Vpp2 voltage is not supported.

ReleaseConfiguration

int CardServices(ReleaseConfiguration, client_handle_t client, config_req_t *req);

ReleaseConfiguration unconfigures a socket previously set up by a call to **RequestConfiguration**. The req parameter should be the same one used to configure the socket.

Return codes:

CS_BAD_HANDLE
  The window handle is invalid, or the socket is not configured.

GetConfigurationInfo

int CardServices(GetConfigurationInfo, client_handle_t client, config_t *config);

The config_t structure is given by:

```
typedef struct config_t {
        u_int       Attributes;
        u_int       Vcc, Vpp1, Vpp2;
        u_int       IntType;
        caddr_t     ConfigBase;
        u_char      Status, Pin, Copy, Option;
        u_int       Present;
        u_int       AssignedIRQ;
        u_int       IRQAttributes;
        ioaddr_t    BasePort1;
        ioaddr_t    NumPorts1;
        u_int       Attributes1;
        ioaddr_t    BasePort2;
        ioaddr_t    NumPorts2;
        u_int       Attributes2;
        u_int       IOAddrLines;
} config_t;
```

GetConfigurationInfo returns the current socket configuration as it was set up by **RequestIO**, **RequestIRQ**, and **RequestConfiguration**. It can only be applied to a fully configured socket. For normal clients bound to a single card function, the Function field is ignored, and data for that client's assigned function is returned. For clients bound toBIND_FN_ALL, this field specifies which function's configuration data should be returned.

Return codes:

CS_BAD_HANDLE
: The window handle is invalid, or the socket is not configured.

CS_NO_CARD
: The socket assigned to this client is currently vacant.

CS_CONFIGURATION_LOCKED
: This actually means that the configuration has not been locked.

Card Information Structure (CIS) calls

The definition of the card information structure (CIS) is the darkest chapter of the PC Card Standard. All version 2 PC Cards should have a CIS, which describes the card and how it should be configured. The CIS is a linked list of tuples in the card's attribute memory space (16-bit PC Cards). Each tuple consists of an identification code, a length byte, and a series of data bytes. The layout of the data bytes for some tuple types is absurdly complicated, in an apparent effort to use every last bit.

The **ValidateCIS** call checks to see if a card has a reasonable CIS. The **GetFirstTuple** and **GetNextTuple** calls are used to step through CIS tuple lists. **GetTupleData** extracts data bytes from a tuple. And **ParseTuple** unpacks most tuple types into more easily used forms. Finally, the **ReplaceCIS** call allows a client to provide Card Services with a substitute for the CIS found on the card.

GetFirstTuple, GetNextTuple

```
#include "cistpl.h"
int CardServices(GetFirstTuple, client_handle_t client, tuple_t *tuple);
int CardServices(GetNextTuple, client_handle_t client, tuple_t *tuple);
```

The tuple_t data structure is given by:

```
typedef struct tuple_t {
        u_int        Attributes;
        cis_data_t   DesiredTuple;
        u_int        Flags;
        cisdata_t    TupleCode;
        u_int        TupleLink;
        cisdata_t    TupleOffset;
        cisdata_t    TupleDataMax;
        cisdata_t    TupleDataLen;
        cisdata_t    *TupleData;
} tuple_t;
```

GetFirstTuple searches a card's CIS for the first tuple code matching DesiredTuple. The special code RETURN_FIRST_TUPLE will match the first tuple of any kind. If successful, TupleCode is set to the code of the first matching tuple found, and TupleLink is the address of this tuple in attribute memory.

GetNextTuple is like **GetFirstTuple**, except that given a tuple_t structure returned by a previous call to **GetFirstTuple** or **GetNextTuple**, it will return the next tuple matching DesiredTuple. These functions will automatically traverse any link tuples found in the CIS. For multi-function cards having a CISTPL_LONGLINK_MFC tuple, these functions will automatically follow just the CIS chain specific to a client driver's assigned function. If a client was bound to BIND_FN_ALL, then all tuples will be returned.

The following flags can be specified in Attributes:

TUPLE_RETURN_LINK
: indicates that link tuples (CISTPL_LONGLINK_A, CISTPL_LONGLINK_C, CISTPL_LONGLINK_MFC, CISTPL_NOLINK, CISTPL_LINKTARGET) should be returned. Normally these tuples are processed silently.

TUPLE_RETURN_COMMON
: indicates that tuples in the ``common'' CIS section of a multi-function CIS should be returned. In the absence of this flag, normally, Card Services will only return tuples specific to the function bound to the client.

Return codes:

CS_BAD_HANDLE
: The client handle is invalid.

CS_OUT_OF_RESOURCE
: Card services was unable to set up a memory window to map the card's CIS.

CS_NO_MORE_ITEMS
: There were no tuples matching DesiredTuple.

GetTupleData

```
#include "cistpl.h"
int CardServices(GetTupleData, client_handle_t client, tuple_t *tuple);
```

GetTupleData extracts a series of data bytes from the specified tuple, which must have been returned by a previous call to **GetFirstTuple** or **GetNextTuple**. A maximum of TupleDataMax bytes will be copied into the TupleData buffer, starting at an offset of TupleOffset bytes. The number of bytes copied is returned in TupleDataLen.

Return codes:

CS_BAD_HANDLE
: The client handle is invalid.

CS_OUT_OF_RESOURCE
: Card services was unable to set up a memory window to map the card's CIS.

CS_NO_MORE_ITEMS
: The tuple does not contain any more data. TupleOffset is greater than or equal to the length of the tuple.

ParseTuple

```
#include "cistpl.h"
int CardServices(ParseTuple, client_handle_t client, tuple_t *tuple, *parse);
```

The cisparse_t data structure is given by:

```
typedef union cisparse_t {
        cistpl_device_t          device;
        cistpl_checksum_t        checksum;
        cistpl_longlink_t        longlink;
        cistpl_longlink_mfc_t    longlink_mfc;
        cistpl_vers_1_t          version_1;
        cistpl_altstr_t          altstr;
        cistpl_jedec_t           jedec;
        cistpl_manfid_t          manfid;
        cistpl_funcid_t          funcid;
        cistpl_config_t          config;
        cistpl_cftable_entry_t   cftable_entry;
        cistpl_device_geo_t      device_geo;
        cistpl_vers_2_t          version_2;
        cistpl_org_t             org;
} cisparse_t;
```

ParseTuple interprets tuple data returned by a previous call to **GetTupleData**. The structure returned depends on the type of the parsed tuple. See the CISTPL.H file for these structure definitions; some of them are quite complex.

Return codes:

CS_BAD_TUPLE
An error was encountered during parsing of this tuple. The tuple may be incomplete, or may be formatted incorrectly.

CS_UNSUPPORTED_FUNCTION
ParseTuple cannot parse the specified tuple type.

ValidateCIS

```
int CardServices(ValidateCIS, client_handle_t client, cisinfo_t *cisinfo);
```

The cisinfo_t structure is given by:

```
typedef struct cisinfo_t {
        u_int           Chains;
} cisinfo_t;
```

ValidateCIS attempts to verify that a card has a reasonable card information structure. It returns the number of tuples found in Chains. If the CIS appears it cannot be interpreted, Chains will be set to zero.

Return codes:

CS_BAD_HANDLE
The client handle is invalid.

CS_OUT_OF_RESOURCE
Card services was unable to set up a memory window to map the card's CIS.

ReplaceCIS

```
int CardServices(ReplaceCIS, client_handle_t client, cisdump_t *cisinfo);
```

The cisdump_t structure is given by:

```
typedef struct cisdump_t {
        u_int               Length;
        cisdata_tData[CISTPL_MAX_CIS_SIZE];
```

} cisinfo_t;

ReplaceCIS allows a client to pass Card Services a replacement for the CIS found on a card. Its intended application is for cards with incomplete or inaccurate CIS information. If a correct CIS can be deduced from other information available for the card, this allows that information to be provided to clients in a clean fashion. The alternative is to pollute client source code with fixes targeted for each card with a CIS error. The replacement CIS remains in effect until the card is ejected, and all tuple-related services will use the replacement instead of the card's actual CIS.

The Length field gives the number of bytes of CIS data in the Data array. The Data array can be considered to be just the even bytes of a card's attribute memory. It should contain all required features of a normal CIS, including an initial CISTPL_DEVICE tuple and a final CISTPL_END tuple. Long links (including CISTPL_LONGLINK_MFC may be used: all target addresses are interpreted in the replacement CIS space. In general, a replacement CIS should also contain the same basic identification tuples (CISTPL_MANFID, CISTPL_VERS_1) as the original card.

Return codes:

CS_BAD_HANDLE
    The client handle is invalid.
CS_OUT_OF_RESOURCE
    Card Services was unable to allocate memory to hold the replacement CIS.

Memory Window Control

Each socket can have up to four active memory windows, mapping portions of PC Card memory into the host system address space. A 16-Bit PC Card device can address at most 16MB of both common and attribute memory. Windows should typically be sized to a power of two, and be aligned on a boundary that is a multiple of the window size in both the host and card address spaces.

A memory window is initialized by a call to **RequestWindow**. Some window attributes can be modified using **ModifyWindow**. The segment of card memory mapped to the window can be modified using **MapMemPage**. And windows are released with **ReleaseWindow**. Unlike almost all other card services subfunctions, the memory window functions normally act on window_handle_t handles, rather than client_handle_t handles.

RequestWindow

```
int CardServices(RequestWindow, client_handle_t *handle, win_req_t *req);
```

The win_req_t structure is given by:

```
typedef struct win_req_t {
        u_int       Attributes;
        u_long      Base;
        u_int       Size;
        u_int       AccessSpeed;
} win_req_t;
```

RequestWindow maps a window of card memory into system memory. On entry, the handle parameter should point to a valid client handle. On return, this will be replaced by a window_handle_t handle that should be used in subsequent calls to **ModifyWindow**, **MapMemPage**, and **ReleaseWindow**.

The following flags can be specified in Attributes:

WIN_MEMORY_TYPE
: This field can be either WIN_MEMORY_TYPE_CM for common memory, or WIN_MEMORY_TYPE_AM for attribute memory.

WIN_DATA_WIDTH.
: Either WIN_DATA_WIDTH_16 for 16-bit accesses, or WIN_DATA_WIDTH_8 for 8-bit access.

WIN_ENABLE
: If this is set, the window is turned on.

WIN_USE_WAIT
: Specifies that the adapter should observe the card's MWAIT signal.

Base specifies the base address of the window in system memory. If zero, card services will set Base to the first available window address. Size specifies the window size in bytes. If zero, Card Services will set Size to the smallest window size supported by the host controller. AccessSpeed specifies the memory access speed, in nanoseconds.

Return codes:

CS_BAD_HANDLE
: The client handle is invalid.

CS_NO_CARD
: The socket assigned to this client is currently vacant.

CS_BAD_ATTRIBUTE
: An unsupported window attribute was requested.

CS_OUT_OF_RESOURCE
: The maximum number of memory windows for this socket are already being used.

CS_IN_USE
: **RequestWindow** was unable to find a free window of system memory.

ModifyWindow

```
int CardServices(ModifyWindow, window_handle_t, modwin_t *);
```

The modwin_t structure is given by:

```
typedef struct modwin_t {
        u_int           Attributes;
        u_int           AccessSpeed;
} modwin_t;
```

ModifyWindow modifies the attributes of a window handle returned by a previous call to **RequestWindow**. The following Attributes can be changed:

WIN_MEMORY_TYPE
: This field can be either WIN_MEMORY_TYPE_CM for common memory, or WIN_MEMORY_TYPE_AM for attribute memory.

WIN_DATA_WIDTH
: Either WIN_DATA_WIDTH_16 for 16-bit accesses, or WIN_DATA_WIDTH_8 for 8-bit access.

WIN_ENABLE
: If this is set, the window is turned on. AccessSpeed gives the new memory access speed, in nanoseconds.

Return codes:

CS_BAD_HANDLE
: The window handle is invalid.

MapMemPage

```
int CardServices(MapMemPage, window_handle_t, memreq_t *);
```

The memreq_t structure is given by:

```
typedef struct memreq_t {
        u_int       CardOffset;
        page_t      Page;
} memreq_t;
```

MapMemPage sets the address of card memory that is mapped to the base of a memory window to CardOffset. The window should have been created by a call to **RequestWindow**. The Page parameter is not implemented in this version and should be set to zero.

Return codes:

CS_BAD_HANDLE
: The window handle is invalid.

CS_BAD_PAGE
: The Page value was non-zero.

ReleaseWindow

```
int CardServices(ReleaseWindow, window_handle_t handle);
```

ReleaseWindow releases a memory window previously allocated with **RequestWindow**.

Return codes:

CS_BAD_HANDLE
: The window handle is invalid.

Bulk Memory Services

Bulk memory services provide a higher level interface for accessing memory regions than that provided by the memory window services. A client using bulk memory calls does not need to know anything about the underlying memory organization or access methods. The device-specific code is packaged into a special card services client called a Memory Technology Driver.

RegisterMTD

```
int CardServices(RegisterMTD, client_handle_t handle, mtd_reg_t *reg);
```

The mtd_reg_t data structure is given by:

```
typedef union mtd_reg_t {
        u_int      Attributes;
        u_int      Offset;
        u_long     MediaID;
} mtd_reg_t;
```

RegisterMTD informs card services that this client MTD will handle requests for a specified memory region. The Offset field specifies the starting address of the memory region. The following fields are defined in Attributes:

REGION_TYPE
: Either REGION_TYPE_CM for common memory, or REGION_TYPE_AM for attribute memory.

The MediaID field is recorded by card services, and will be passed to the MTD as part of any request that references this memory region. Once an MTD is bound to a memory region by a call to **RegisterMTD**, it will remain bound until the MTD calls **DeregisterClient**.

Return codes:

CS_BAD_HANDLE
: The client handle is invalid.

CS_BAD_OFFSET
Either the Offset does not match a valid memory region for this card, or another MTD has already registered for this region.

GetFirstRegion, GetNextRegion

```
int CardServices(GetFirstRegion, client_handle_t handle, region_info_t
        *region);
int CardServices(GetNextRegion, client_handle_t handle, region_info_t
        *region);
```

The region_info_t data structure is given by:

```
typedef union region_info_t {
        u_int     Attributes;
        u_int     CardOffset;
        u_int     RegionSize;
        u_int     AccessSpeed;
        u_int     BlockSize;
        u_int     PartMultiple;
        u_char    JedecMfr, JedecInfo;
        memory_handle_t next;
} region_info_t;
```

GetFirstRegion and **GetNextRegion** summarize the information in a card's CISTPL_DEVICE, CISTPL_JEDEC, and CISTPL_DEVICE_GEO tuples. CardOffset gives the starting address of a region. RegionSize gives the length of the region in bytes. AccessSpeed gives the device's cycle time in nanoseconds. BlockSize gives the erase block size in bytes, and PartMultiple gives the minimum granularity of partitions on this device, in units of BlockSize. JedecMfr and JedecInfo give the JEDEC identification bytes for this region.

The following fields are defined in Attributes:

REGION_TYPE
Either REGION_TYPE_CM for common memory, or REGION_TYPE_AM for attribute memory.

When these calls are made by an MTD client, only regions that have been bound to this client through calls to **BindMTD** will be returned.

Return codes:

CS_BAD_HANDLE
: The client handle is invalid.

CS_NO_MORE_ITEMS
: No more memory regions are defined.

OpenMemory

```
int CardServices(OpenMemory, client_handle_t *handle, open_mem_t *req);
```

The open_mem_t structure is given by:

```
typedef struct open_mem_t {
        u_int       Attributes;
        u_int       Offset;
} open_mem_t;
```

OpenMemory is used to obtain a handle for accessing a memory region via the other bulk memory services. The Offset field specifies the base address of the region to be accessed. If successful, the client handle argument is replaced by the new memory handle.

The following fields are defined in Attributes:

MEMORY_TYPE
: Either MEMORY_TYPE_CM for common memory, or MEMORY_TYPE_AM for attribute memory.

MEMORY_EXCLUSIVE
: Specifies that this client should have exclusive access to this memory region.

Return codes:

CS_BAD_HANDLE
: The window handle is invalid.

CS_BAD_OFFSET
Either the Offset does not specify a valid region, or the region does not have an associated MTD to service bulk memory requests.

CloseMemory

```
int CardServices(CloseMemory, memory_handle_t handle);
```

CloseMemory releases a memory handle returned by a previous call to **OpenMemory**. A client should release all memory handles before calling **DeregisterClient**.

Return codes:

CS_BAD_HANDLE
The memory handle is invalid.

ReadMemory, WriteMemory

```
int CardServices(ReadMemory, memory_handle_t handle mem_op_t *req,
        caddr_t buf);
int CardServices(WriteMemory, memory_handle_t handle, mem_op_t *req,
        caddr_t buf);
```

The mem_io_t structure is given by:

```
typedef struct mem_op_t {
        u_int       Attributes;
        u_int       Offset;
        u_int       Count;
} mem_op_t;
```

ReadMemory and **WriteMemory** read from and write to a card memory area defined by the specified memory handle, returned by a previous call to **OpenMemory**. The Offset field gives the offset of the operation from the start of the card memory region. The Count field gives the number of bytes to be transferred. The buf field points to a host memory buffer to be the destination for a **ReadMemory** operation, or the source for a **WriteMemory** operation.

The following fields are defined in Attributes:

MEM_OP_BUFFER
Either MEM_OP_BUFFER_USER if the host buffer is in a user memory segment, or MEM_OP_BUFFER_KERNEL if the host buffer is in kernel memory.

MEM_OP_DISABLE_ERASE
Specifies that a card area should not be erased before it is written.

MEM_OP_VERIFY
Specifies verification of write operations.

Return codes:

CS_BAD_HANDLE
The window handle is invalid.

CS_BAD_OFFSET
The specified card Offset is beyond the end of the memory region.

CS_BAD_SIZE
The specified transfer Count extends past the end of the memory region.

RegisterEraseQueue

```
int CardServices(RegisterEraseQueue, client_handle_t *handle, eraseq_hdr_t
        *header);
```

The eraseq_hdr_t structure is given by:

```
typedef struct erase_queue_header_t {
        int             QueueEntryCount;
        eraseq_entry_t  *QueueEntryArray;
} eraseq_hdr_t;
```

This call registers a queue of erase requests with card services. An eraseq_handle_t handle will be returned in *handle. When this client calls **CheckEraseQueue**, card services will scan the queue and begin asynchronous processing of any new requests.

The eraseq_entry_t structure is given by:

```
typedef struct eraseq_entry_t {
        memory_handle_t Handle;
```

```
        u_char    State;
        u_int     Size;
        u_int     Offset;
        void      *Optional;
} eraseq_entry_t;
```

In an erase queue entry, the Header field should be a memory handle returned by a previous call to **OpenMemory**. The State field indicates the state of the erase request. The following values are defined:

ERASE_QUEUED
: Set by the client to indicate that this is a new request.

ERASE_IDLE
: Set by the client to indicate that this entry is not active.

ERASE_PASSED
: Set by the MTD to indicate successful completion.

ERASE_FAILED
: Set by the MTD to indicate that the erase failed.

ERASE_MEDIA_WRPROT
: Indicates that the region is write protected.

ERASE_NOT_ERASABLE
: Indicates that this region does not support erase operations.

ERASE_BAD_OFFSET
: Indicates that the erase does not start (Offset) on an erase block boundary.

ERASE_BAD_SIZE
: Indicates that the requested erase Size is not a multiple of the erase block size.

ERASE_BAD_SOCKET
: Set by the MTD to indicate that there is no card present.

Additionally, the macro ERASE_IN_PROGRESS() will return a true condition for values of State that indicate an erase is being processed. The Size field gives the size of the erase request in bytes. The Offset field gives the offset from the start of the region. The Size and Offset should be aligned to erase block boundaries. The Optional field is not used by card services and may be used by the client driver.

Return codes:

CS_BAD_HANDLE

The client handle is invalid.

DeregisterEraseQueue

int CardServices(DeregisterEraseQueue, eraseq_handle_t handle);

DeregisterEraseQueue frees a queue previously registered by a call to **RegisterEraseQueue**. If there are any pending requests in the specified queue, the call will fail.

Return codes:

CS_BAD_HANDLE
The erase queue handle is invalid.
CS_BUSY
The erase queue has erase requests pending.

CheckEraseQueue

int CardServices(CheckEraseQueue, eraseq_handle_t handle);

This call notifies card services that there are new erase requests in a queue previously registered with **RegisterEraseQueue**. Typically, a client will initially assign each erase queue entry the state value ERASE_IDLE. When new requests are added to the queue, the client will set their states to ERASE_QUEUED, and call **CheckEraseQueue**. When the client is notified of an erase completion event, it will check the state field to determine whether the request was successful.

Return codes:

CS_BAD_HANDLE
The erase queue handle is invalid.

Miscellaneous Calls

GetCardServicesInfo

```
int CardServices(GetCardServicesInfo, servinfo_t *info);
```

The servinfo_t structure is given by:

```
typedef struct servinfo_t {
        char      Signature[2];
        u_int     Count;
        u_int     Revision;
        u_int     CSLevel;
        char      *VendorString;
} servinfo_t;
```

GetCardServicesInfo returns revision information about this version of card services. Signature is set to 'CS'. Count is set to the number of sockets currently configured. Revision is set to the revision level of the card services package, and CSLevel is set to the level of compliance with the PC Card Standard. These are encoded as BCD numbers. VendorString is set to point to an RCS identification string. This call always succeeds.

AccessConfigurationRegister

```
#include "cisreg.h"
int CardServices(AccessConfigurationRegister, client_handle_t handle,
        conf_reg_t *reg);
```

The conf_reg_t structure is given by:

```
typedef struct conf_reg_t {
        u_char     Function;
        u_int      Action;
        off_t      Offset;
        u_int      Value;
} conf_reg_t;
```

The Action parameter can be one of the following:

CS_READ
: Read the specified configuration register and return Value.

CS_WRITE
: Write Value to the specified configuration register.

AccessConfigurationRegister either reads or writes the one-byte CIS configuration register at Offset from the start of the config register area. It can only be used for a socket that has been configured with **RequestConfiguration**.

The following values for Offset are defined in the CISTPL.H file:

CISREG_COR
: The Configuration Option Register.

CISREG_CCSR
: The Card Configuration and Status Register.

CISREG_PRR
: The Pin Replacement Register.

CISREG_SCR
: The Socket and Copy Register.

CISREG_ESR
: The Extended Status Register.

CISREG_IOBASE0..CISREG_IOBASE3
: The I/O Base Registers.

CISREG_IOSIZE
: The I/O Size Register.

Return codes:

CS_BAD_HANDLE
: The client handle is invalid.

CS_BAD_ARGS
: The specified Action is not supported.

CS_CONFIGURATION_LOCKED
: This actually means that the configuration has not been locked.

CS_OUT_OF_RESOURCE
: Card services was unable to allocate a memory window to access the card's configuration registers.

AdjustResourceInfo

```
int CardServices(AdjustResourceInfo, client_handle_t handle, adjust_t *adj);
```

The adjust_t structure is given by:

```
typedef struct adjust_t {
        u_int           Action;
        u_int           Resource;
        u_int           Attributes;
        union {
                struct memory {
                        caddr_t         Base;
                        u_long          Size;
                        } memory;
                struct io {
                        ioaddr_t        BasePort;
                        ioaddr_t        NumPorts;
                        u_int           IOAddrLines;
                        } io;
                        struct irq {
                                u_int           IRQ;
                        } irq;
                } resource;
} adjust_t;
```

AdjustResourceInfo is used to tell card services what resources may or may not be allocated by PC Card devices. The normal Linux resource management systems (the *_region calls for I/O ports, interrupt allocation) are respected by card services, but this call gives the user another level of control. The Action parameter can have the following values:

ADD_MANAGED_RESOURCE
: Place the specified resource under card services control, so that it may be allocated by PC Card devices.

REMOVE_MANAGED_RESOURCE
: Remove the specified resource from card services control.

At initialization time, card services assumes that it can use all available interrupts, but I/O ports and memory regions must be explicitly enabled with ADD_MANAGED_RESOURCE.

The Resource parameter can have the following values:

RES_MEMORY_RANGE
: Specifies a memory range resource, described by adj->resource.memory.

RES_IO_RANGE
: Specifies an I/O port resource, described by adj->resource.io.

RES_IRQ
: Specifies an interrupt resource, described by adj->resource.irq.

The following flags may be specified in Attributes:

RES_RESERVED
: Indicates that the resource should be reserved for PC Card devices that specifically request it. The resource will not be allocated for a device that asks card services for any available location. This is not implemented yet.

Return codes:

CS_UNSUPPORTED_FUNCTION
: The specified Action or Resource is not supported.

CS_BAD_BASE
: The specified I/O address is out of range.

CS_BAD_SIZE
: The specified memory or I/O window size is out of range.

CS_IN_USE
: The specified interrupt is currently allocated by a card services client.

ReportError

```
int CardServices(ReportError, char *prefix, int func, int ret);
```

The error_info_t structure is given by:

```
typedef struct error_info_t {
        int         func;
        int         retcode;
} error_info_t;
```

ReportError generates a kernel error message given a card services function code and its return code, with an optional prefix string. For example: CardServices(ReportError, "serial_cs", RequestIO, CS_BAD_HANDLE); would generate the following message: serial_cs: RequestIO: Bad handle

This call always succeeds.

Card Information Structure Definitions

CIS Tuple Definitions

The card services **ParseTuple** function interprets raw CIS tuple data from a call to **GetTupleData** and returns the tuple contents in a form dependent on the tuple type.

```
#include "cistpl.h"
```

CISTPL_CHECKSUM

The cistpl_checksum_t structure is given by:

```
typedef struct cistpl_checksum_t {
                    u_short     addr;
        u_short     len;
        u_char      sum;
} cistpl_checksum_t;
```

CISTPL_LINKTARGET, CISTPL_NOLINK CISTPL_LONGLINK_A, CISTPL_LONGLINK_C

The cistpl_longlink_t structure is given by:

```
typedef struct cistpl_longlink_t {
        u_int         addr;
} cistpl_longlink_t;
```

These tuples are pointers to additional chains of CIS tuples, either in attribute or common memory. Each CIS tuple chain can have at most one long link. CISTPL_LONGLINK_A tuples point to attribute memory, and CISTPL_LONGLINK_C tuples point to common memory. The standard CIS chain starting at address zero in attribute memory has an implied long link to address zero in common memory. A CISTPL_NOLINK tuple can be used to cancel this default link. The first tuple of a chain pointed to by a long link must be a CISTPL_LINKTARGET. The CS tuple handling code will automatically follow long links and verify link targets; these tuples are normally invisible unless the TUPLE_RETURN_LINK attribute is specified in **GetNextTuple**.

CISTPL_LONGLINK_MFC

The cistpl_longlink_mfc_t structure is given by:

```
typedef struct cistpl_longlink_mfc_t {
        int      nfn;
        struct {
                u_char  space;
                u_int   addr;
        } fn[CISTPL_MAX_FUNCTIONS;
} cistpl_longlink_mfc_t;
```

This tuple identifies a multi-function card, and specifies long link pointers to CIS chains specific for each function. The space field is either CISTPL_MFC_ATTR or CISTPL_MFC_COMMON for attribute or common memory space.

CISTPL_DEVICE, CISTPL_DEVICE_A

The cistpl_device_t structure is given by:

```
typedef struct cistpl_device_t {
        int             ndev;
        struct device_info {
                u_char          type;
                u_char          wp;
                u_int           speed;
                u_int           size;
        } dev[CISTPL_MAX_DEVICES];
} cistpl_device_t;
```

The CISTPL_DEVICE tuple describes address regions in a card's common memory. The CISTPL_DEVICE_A tuple describes regions in attribute memory. The type flag indicates the type of memory device for this region. The wp flag indicates if this region is write protected. The speed field is in nanoseconds, and size is in bytes. Address regions are assumed to be ordered consecutively starting with address zero. The following device types are defined:

CISTPL_DTYPE_NULL
: Specifies that there is no device, or a hole in the card address space.

CISTPL_DTYPE_ROM
: Masked ROM

CISTPL_DTYPE_OTPROM
: One-type programmable ROM.

CISTPL_DTYPE_EPROM
: UV erasable PROM.

CISTPL_DTYPE_EEPROM
: Electrically erasable PROM.

CISTPL_DTYPE_FLASH
: Flash EPROM.

CISTPL_DTYPE_SRAM
: Static or non-volatile RAM.

CISTPL_DTYPE_DRAM
: Dynamic or volatile RAM.

CISTPL_DTYPE_FUNCSPEC
: Specifies a function-specific device, such as a memory-mapped I/O device or buffer, as opposed to general purpose storage.

CISTPL_DTYPE_EXTEND

Specifies an extended device type. This type is reserved for future use.

CISTPL_VERS_1

The cistpl_vers_1_t structure is given by:

```
typedef struct cistpl_vers_1_t {
        u_char      major;
        u_char      minor;
        int         ns;
        int         ofs[CISTPL_VERS_1_MAX_PROD_STRINGS];
        char        str[254];
} cistpl_vers_1_t;
```

The ns field specifies the number of product information strings in the tuple. The string data is contained in the str array. Each string is null terminated, and ofs gives the offset to the start of each string.

CISTPL_ALTSTR

The cistpl_altstr_t structure is given by:

```
typedef struct cistpl_altstr_t {
        int         ns;
        int         ofs[CISTPL_ALTSTR_MAX_STRINGS];
        char        str[254];
} cistpl_altstr_t;
```

The ns field specifies the number of alternate language strings in the tuple. The string data is contained in the str array. Each string is null terminated, and ofs gives the offset to the start of each string.

CISTPL_JEDEC_C, CISTPL_JEDEC_A

The cistpl_jedec_t structure is given by:

```
typedef struct cistpl_jedec_t {
        int                 nid;
        struct jedec_id {
                u_char  mfr;
                u_char  info;
        } id[CISTPL_MAX_DEVICES];
} cistpl_jedec_t;
```

JEDEC identifiers describe the specific device type used to implement a region of PC Card memory. The nid field specifies the number of JEDEC identifiers in the tuple. There should be a one-to-one correspondence between JEDEC identifiers and device descriptions in the corresponding CISTPL_DEVICE tuple.

CISTPL_CONFIG, CISTPL_CONFIG_CB

The cistpl_config_t structure is given by:

```
typedef struct cistpl_config_t {
        u_char      last_idx;
        u_int       base;
        u_int       rmask[4];
        u_char      subtuples;
} cistpl_config_t;
```

The last_idx field gives the index of the highest numbered configuration table entry. The base field gives the offset of a card's configuration registers in attribute memory. The rmask array is a series of bit masks indicating which configuration registers are present. Bit 0 of rmask[0] is for the COR, bit 1 is for the CCSR, and so on. The subtuples field gives the number of bytes of subtuples following the normal tuple contents.

For CISTPL_CONFIG_CB, rmask is undefined, and base points to the CardBus status registers.

CISTPL_BAR

The cistpl_bar_t structure is given by:

```
typedef struct cistpl_bar_t {
        u_char          attr;
        u_int           size;
} cistpl_long_t;
```

A CISTPL_BAR tuple describes the characteristics of an address space region pointed to by a PCI base address register, for CardBus cards.

The following bit fields are defined in attr:

CISTPL_BAR_SPACE

Identifies the base address register, from 1 to 6. A value of 7 describes the card's Extension ROM space.

CISTPL_BAR_SPACE_IO

If set, this address register maps IO space (as opposed to memory space).

CISTPL_BAR_PREFETCH

If set, this region can be prefetched. controller.

CISTPL_BAR_CACHEABLE

If set, this region is cacheable as well as prefetchable.

CISTPL_BAR_1MEG_MAP

If set, this region should only be mapped into the first 1MB of the host's physical address space.

CISTPL_CFTABLE_ENTRY

The cistpl_cftable_entry_t structure is given by:

```
typedef struct cistpl_cftable_entry_t {
                u_char          index;
                u_char          flags;
                u_char          interface;
                cistpl_power_t  vcc, vpp1, vpp2;
                cistpl_timing_t timing;
                cistpl_io_t     io;
                cistpl_irq_t    irq;
                cistpl_mem_t    mem;
                u_char          subtuples;
        } cistpl_cftable_entry_t;
```

A CISTPL_CFTABLE_ENTRY structure describes a complete operating mode for a card. Many sections are optional. The index field gives the configuration index for this operating mode; writing this value to the card's Configuration Option Register selects this mode. The following fields are defined in flags:

CISTPL_CFTABLE_DEFAULT
: Specifies that this is the default configuration table entry.

CISTPL_CFTABLE_BVDS
: Specifies that this configuration implements the BVD1 and BVD2 signals in the Pin Replacement Register.

CISTPL_CFTABLE_WP
: Specifies that this configuration implements the write protect signal in the Pin Replacement Register.

CISTPL_CFTABLE_RDYBSY
: Specifies that this configuration implements the Ready/Busy signal in the Pin Replacement Register.

CISTPL_CFTABLE_MWAIT
: Specifies that the WAIT signal should be observed during memory access cycles.

CISTPL_CFTABLE_AUDIO
: Specifies that this configuration generates an audio signal that can be routed to the host system speaker.

CISTPL_CFTABLE_READONLY

Specifies that the card has a memory region that is read-only in this configuration.

CISTPL_CFTABLE_PWRDOWN
: Specifies that this configuration supports a power down mode, via the Card Configuration and Status Register.

The cistpl_power_t structure is given by:

```
typedef struct cistpl_power_t {
        u_char      present;
        u_char      flags;
        u_int       param[7];
} cistpl_power_t;
```

The present field is bit mapped and indicates which parameters are present for this power signal. The following indices are defined:

CISTPL_POWER_VNOM
: The nominal supply voltage.

CISTPL_POWER_VMIN
: The minimum supply voltage.

CISTPL_POWER_VMAX
: The maximum supply voltage.

CISTPL_POWER_ISTATIC
: The continuous supply current required.

CISTPL_POWER_IAVG
: The maximum current averaged over one second.

CISTPL_POWER_IPEAK
: The maximum current averaged over 10 ms.

CISTPL_POWER_IDOWN
: The current required in power down mode.

Voltages are given in units of 10 microvolts. Currents are given in units of 100 nanoamperes.

The cistpl_timing_t structure is given by:

```
typedef cistpl_timing_t {
        u_int       wait, waitscale;
        u_int       ready, rdyscale;
        u_int       reserved, rsvscale;
} cistpl_timing_t;
```

Each time consists of a base time in nanoseconds and a scale multiplier. Unspecified times have values of zero.

The cistpl_io_t structure is given by:

```
typedef struct cistpl_io_t {
        u_char      flags;
        int         nwin;
        struct {
                u_int       base;
                u_int       len;
        } win[CISTPL_IO_MAX_WIN;
} cistpl_io_t;
```

The number of I/O windows is given by nwin. Each window is described by a base address, base, and a length in bytes, len. The following bit fields are defined in flags:

CISTPL_IO_LINES_MASK
: The number of I/O lines decoded by this card.

CISTPL_IO_8BIT
: Indicates that the card supports split 8-bit accesses to 16-bit I/O registers.

CISTPL_IO_16BIT
: Indicates that the card supports full 16-bit accesses to I/O registers.

The cistpl_irq_t structure is given by:

```
typedef struct cistpl_irq_t {
        u_int       IRQInfo1;
        u_int       IRQInfo2;
} cistpl_irq_t;
```

The following bit fields are defined in IRQInfo1 :

IRQ_MASK
: A specific interrupt number that this card should use.

IRQ_NMI_ID, IRQ_IOCK_ID, IRQ_BERR_ID, IRQ_VEND_ID
: When IRQ_INFO2_VALID is set, these indicate if a corresponding special interrupt signal may be assigned to this card. The four flags are for non-maskable, I/O check, bus error and vendor specific interrupts.

IRQ_INFO2_VALID
: Indicates that IRQInfo2 contains a valid bit mask of allowed interrupt request numbers.

IRQ_LEVEL_ID
: Indicates that the card supports level mode interrupts.

IRQ_PULSE_ID
: Indicates that the card supports pulse mode interrupts

IRQ_SHARE _ID
: Indicates that the card supports sharing of interrupts

If IRQInfo1 is zero, then no interrupt information is available. IRQInfo2 is a bit mask of allowed interrupt request numbers. The cistpl_mem_t structure is given by:

```
typedef struct cistpl_mem_t {
        u_char          nwin;
        struct {
                u_int           len;
                u_int           card_addr;
                u_int           host_addr;
        } win[CISTPL_MEM_MAX_WIN;
} cistpl_mem_t;
```

The number of memory windows is given by nwin. Each window is described by an address in the card memory space, card_addr, an address in the host memory space, host_addr, and a length in bytes, len. If the host address is zero, the position of the window is arbitrary.

CISTPL_CFTABLE_ENTRY_CB

The cistpl_cftable_entry_cb_t structure is given by:

```
typedef struct cistpl_cftable_entry_cb_t {
        u_char          index;
        u_char          flags;
        cistpl_power_t  vcc, vpp1, vpp2;
        u_char          io;
        cistpl_irq_t    irq;
        u_char          mem;
        u_char          subtuples;
} cistpl_cftable_entry_cb_t;
```

A CISTPL_CFTABLE_ENTRY_CB structure describes a complete operating mode for a CardBus card. Many fields are identical to corresponding fields in CISTPL_CFTABLE_ENTRY.

The io and mem fields specify which base address registers need to be initialized for this configuration. Bits 1 through 6 correspond to the six base address registers, and bit 7 indicates the expansion ROM base register.

CISTPL_MANFID

The cistpl_manfid_t structure is given by:

```
typedef struct cistpl_manfid_t {
        u_short     manf;
        u_short     card;
} cistpl_manfid_t;
```

The manf field identifies the card manufacturer. The card field is chosen by the vendor and should identify the card type and model.

CISTPL_FUNCID

The cistpl_funcid_t structure is given by:

```
typedef struct cistpl_funcid_t {
        u_char      func;
        u_char      sysinit;
} cistpl_funcid_t;
```

The func field identifies the card function. The sysinit field contains several bit-mapped flags describing how the card should be configured at boot time. The following functions are defined:

CISTPL_FUNCID_MULTI
: A mutlifunction PC Card.

CISTPL_FUNCID_MEMORY
: A simple memory device.

CISTPL_FUNCID_SERIAL
: A serial port or modem device.

CISTPL_FUNCID_PARALLEL
: A parallel port device.

CISTPL_FUNCID_FIXED
: A fixed disk drive.

CISTPL_FUNCID_VIDEO
: A video interface.

CISTPL_FUNCID_NETWORK
: A network PC Card.

CISTPL_FUNCID_AIMS
: An auto-incrementing mass storage device.

The following flags are defined in the sysnit field.

CISTPL_SYSINIT_POST
: Indicates that the system should attempt to configure this PC Card during its power-on initialization.

CISTPL_SYSINIT_ROM
Indicates that the PC Card contains a system expansion ROM that should be configured at boot time.

CISTPL_DEVICE_GEO

The cistpl_device_geo_t structure is given by:

```
typedef struct cistpl_device_geo_t {
        int             ngeo;
        struct geo {
                u_char          buswidth;
                u_int           erase_block;
                u_int           read_block;
                u_int           write_block;
                u_int           partition;
                u_int           interleave;
        } geo[CISTPL_MAX_DEVICES];
} cistpl_device_geo_t;
```

The erase_block, read_block, and write_block sizes are in units of buswidth bytes times interleave. The partition size is in units of erase_block.

CISTPL_VERS_2

The cistpl_vers_2_t structure is given by:

```
typedef struct cistpl_vers_2_t {
        u_char          vers;
        u_char          comply;
        u_short         dindex;
        u_char          vspec8, vspec9;
        u_char          nhdr;
        int             vendor, info;
        char            str[244];
} cistpl_vers_2_t;
```

The vers field should always be zero. The comply field indicates the degree of standard compliance and should also be zero. The dindex field reserves the specified number of bytes at the start of common memory. The vspec8 and vspec9 fields may contain vendor-specific information. The nhdr field gives the number of copies of the CIS that are present on this PC Card. The str array contains two strings: a vendor name and an informational message describing the PC Card. The offset of the vendor string is given by vendor, and the offset of the product info string is in info.

CISTPL_ORG

The cistpl_org_t structure is given by:

```
typedef struct cistpl_org_t {
        u_char      data_org;
        char        desc[30];
}
```

This tuple describes the data organization of a memory partition. The follow values are defined for the data_org field :

CISTPL_ORG_FS
: The partition contains a file system.

CISTPL_ORG_APPSPEC
: The partition is in an application specific format.

CISTPL_ORG_XIP
: The partition follows the execute-in-place specification.

The desc[30] field gives a text description of the data organization.

CIS Configuration Registers

The PC Card Standard defines a few standard configuration registers located in a PC Card's attribute memory space. A PC Card's CONFIG tuple specifies which of these registers are implemented. Programs using these definitions should include:

```
#include "cisreg.h"
```

Configuration Option Register

This register should be present for virtually all I/O PC Cards. Writing to this register selects a configuration table entry and enables a PC Card's I/O functions.

The following bit fields are defined:

COR_CONFIG_MASK
: Specifies the configuration table index describing the PC Card's current operating mode.

COR_LEVEL_REQ
: Specifies that the PC Card should generate level mode (edge-triggered) interrupts, the default.

COR_SOFT_RESET
: Setting this bit performs a soft reset operation. Drivers should use the **ResetCard** call to reset a PC Card, rather than writing directly to this register.

Card Configuration and Status Register

The following bit fields are defined:

CCSR_INTR_ACK
: If this bit is set, then the CCSR_INTR_PENDING bit will remain set until it is explicitly cleared.

CCSR_INTR_PENDING

Signals that the PC Card is currently asserting an interrupt request. This signal can be used to support interrupt sharing.

CCSR_POWER_DOWN
: Setting this bit signals that the PC Card should enter a power down state.

CCSR_AUDIO_ENA
: Specifies that the PC Card's audio output should be enabled.

CCSR_IOIS8
: This is used by the host to indicate that it can only perform 8-bit I/O operations and that 16-bit accesses will be carried out as two 8-bit accesses.

CCSR_SIGCHG_ENA
: This indicates to the PC Card that it should use the SIGCHG signal to indicate changes in the WP, READY, BVD1, and BVD2 signals.

CCSR_CHANGED
: This bit signals to the host that one of the signals in the Pin Replacement Register has changed state.

Pin Replacement Register

Signals in this register replace signals that are not available when a socket is operating in memory and I/O mode. An I/O PC Card will normally assert the SIGCHG signal to indicate that one of these signals has changed state, then a driver can poll this register to find out specifically what happened.
This register can also be written. In this case, the STATUS bits act as a mask; if a STATUS bit is set, the corresponding EVENT bit is updated by the write. The following bit fields are defined:

PRR_WP_STATUS
: The current state of the write protect signal.

PRR_READY_STATUS
: The current state of the ready signal.

PRR_BVD2_STATUS
: The current state of the battery warn signal.

PRR_BVD1_STATUS
: The current state of the battery dead signal.

PRR_WP_EVENT
: Indicates that the write protect signal has changed state since the PRR register was last read.

PRR_READY_EVENT

Indicates that the ready signal has changed state since the PRR register was last read.

PRR_BVD2_EVENT

Indicates that the battery warn signal has changed state since the PRR register was last read.

PRR_BVD1_EVENT

Indicates that the battery dead signal has changed state since the PRR register was last read.

Socket and Copy Register

This register is used when several identical PC Cards may be set up to share the same range of I/O ports, to emulate an ISA bus card that would control several devices. For example, an ISA hard drive adapter might control several drives, selectable by writing a drive number to an I/O port. For several PC Card drives to emulate this adapter interface, each needs to know which drive it is, so that it can identify which I/O operations are intended for it. The following bit fields are defined:

SCR_SOCKET_NUM

This should indicate the socket number in which the PC Card is located.

SCR_COPY_NUM

If several identical PC Cards are installed in a system, this field should be set to a unique number identifying which of the identical PC Cards this is.

Extended Status Register

The following bit fields are defined:

ESR_REQ_ATTN_ENA

When set, the CCSR_CHANGED bit will be set when the ESR_REQ_ATTN bit is set, possibly generating a status change interrupt.

ESR_REQ_ATTN

Signals a card event, such as an incoming call for a modem.

I/O Base and Size Registers

For multi-function cards, these registers are used to tell the card how the host I/O windows have been configured for each card function. There are four I/O Base registers, from CISREG_IOBASE_0 to CISREG_IOBASE_3, for the low-order through high-order bytes of an I/O address up to 32 bits long. The CISREG_IOSIZE register is supposed to be written as the number of I/O ports allocated, minus one. For MFC-compliant cards, Card Services will automatically set all of these registers when RequestConfiguration is called.

Card Services Event Handling

Card services events have several sources:

Card status changes reported by the low-level socket drivers.
Artificial events generated by card services itself.
Advanced Power Management (APM) events.
Events generated by other card services clients.

Socket driver events may be either interrupt-driven or polled.

Event Handler Operations

When card services recognizes that an event has occurred, it checks the event mask of each client to determine which clients should receive an event notification. When a client registers with Card services, it specifies an event handler callback function. This handler should have the form:

```
int (*event_handler)(event_t event, int priority, event_callback_args_t *args);
```

The priority parameter is set to either CS_EVENT_PRI_LOW for ordinary events, or CS_EVENT_PRI_HIGH for events that require an immediate response. The only high priority event is CS_EVENT_CARD_REMOVAL. A client event handler should process this event as efficiently as possible so that card services can quickly notify other clients. The event_callback_args_t structure is given by:

```
typedef struct event_callback_args_t {
        client_handle_t        client_handle;
        void                   *info;
        void                   *mtdrequest;
        void                   *buffer;
        void                   *misc;
        void                   *client_data;
} event_callback_args_t;
```

The client_handle member is set to the handle of the client whose socket was responsible for the event. This is useful if a driver is bound to several sockets. The info field is currently only used to return an exit status from a call to ResetCard. The client_data field may be used by a driver to point to a local data structure associated with this device. The remaining fields are currently unused.

Event Descriptions

CS_EVENT_CARD_INSERTION
: This event signals that a PC Card has been inserted. If a driver is bound to an already occupied socket, card services will send the driver an artificial insertion event.

CS_EVENT_CARD_REMOVAL
: This event signals that a PC Card has been removed. This event should be handled with minimum delay so that card services can notify all clients as quickly as possible.

CS_EVENT_BATTERY_LOW
: This event signals a change of state of the battery low signal.

CS_EVENT_BATTERY_DEAD
: This event signals a change of state of the battery dead signal.

CS_EVENT_READY_CHANGE
: This event signals a change of state of the ready signal.

CS_EVENT_WRITE_PROTECT
: This event signals a change of state of the write protect signal.

CS_EVENT_REGISTRATION_COMPLETE
: This event is sent to a driver after a successful call to RegisterClient.

CS_EVENT_RESET_REQUEST
: This event is sent when a client calls ResetCard. An event handler can veto the reset operation by returning failure.

CS_EVENT_RESET_PHYSICAL
: This is sent to all clients just before a reset signal is sent to a PC Card.

CS_EVENT_CARD_RESET
: This event signals that a reset operation is finished. The success or failure of the reset should be determined using GetStatus.

CS_EVENT_RESET_COMPLETE
: This event is sent to a client that has called ResetCard to signal the end of reset processing.

CS_EVENT_PM_SUSPEND
: This event signals that card services has received either a user initiated or APM suspend request. An event handler can veto the suspend by returning failure.

CS_EVENT_PM_RESUME
: This signals that the system is back on line after a suspend/resume cycle.

CS_EVENT_MTD_REQUEST
: This is used to initiate an MTD memory operation. A description of the request is passed in the mtdrequest field of the callback arguments. A host buffer address may be passed in the buffer.

CS_EVENT_ERASE_COMPLETE
: This is used to signal a client that a queued erase operation has completed. A pointer to the erase queue entry is returned in the info field of the callback argument.

Client Driver Event Handling Responsibilities

A client driver should respond to CS_EVENT_CARD_INSERTION and CS_EVENT_CARD_REMOVAL events by configuring and un-configuring the socket. Because card removal is a high priority event, the driver should immediately block I/O to the socket, perhaps by setting a flag in a device structure, and schedule all other shutdown processing to happen later using a timer interrupt.

When a CS_EVENT_PM_RESET_REQUEST event is received, a driver should block I/O and release a locked socket configuration. When a CS_EVENT_CARD_RESET is received, a driver should restore the socket configuration and unblock I/O.

A CS_EVENT_PM_SUSPEND event should be handled somewhat like a CS_EVENT_PM_RESET_REQUEST event in that I/O should be blocked and the socket configuration should be released. When a CS_EVENT_PM_RESUME event is received, a driver can expect a PC Card to be ready to be reconfigured, similar to when a CS_EVENT_CARD_RESET event is received.

Memory Technology Drivers

A Memory Technology Driver (MTD) is used by card services to implement bulk memory services for a particular type of memory device. An MTD should register as a normal card services client with a call to RegisterClient. When it receives a card insertion event, it should use GetFirstRegion and GetNextRegion to identify memory regions that it will administer. Then, it should use RegisterMTD to take control of these regions. MTD read, write, copy, and erase requests are packaged into CS_EVENT_MTD_REQUEST events by card services, and passed to the MTD's event handler for processing.

MTD Request Handling

An MTD receives requests from card services in the form of CS_EVENT_MTD_REQUEST events. Card services passes a description of the request in the mtdrequest field of the event callback arguments. For requests that transfer data to or from the host, the host buffer address is passed in the buffer field. The mtd_request_t structure is given by:

```
typedef struct mtd_request_t {
        u_int       SrcCardOffset;
        u_int       DestCardOffset;
        u_int       TransferLength;
        u_int       Function;
        u_long      MediaID;
        u_int       Status;
        u_int       Timeout;
} mtd_request_t;
```

The Function field is bit mapped and describes the action to be performed by this request:

MTD_REQ_ACTION
: Either MTD_REQ_ERASE, MTD_REQ_READ, MTD_REQ_WRITE, or MTD_REQ_COPY.

MTD_REQ_NOERASE
: For a write command that is sized and aligned on erase block boundaries, this specifies that no erase should be performed.

MTD_REQ_VERIFY
: Specifies that writes should be verified.

MTD_REQ_READY
: Indicates that this request is a retry of a previously request that was delayed until the card asserted READY.

MTD_REQ_TIMEOUT
: Indicates that this request is a retry of a previously request that was delayed by a timeout.

MTD_REQ_FIRST
: Indicates that this request is the first in a series of requests.

MTD_REQ_LAST
: Indicates that this request is the last of a series of requests.

MTD_REQ_KERNEL
: Indicates that the host buffer for a read or write command is located in kernel memory, as opposed to user memory.

The MediaID field is the value specified in the RegisterMTD request for this region. The Status field is used by the MTD when it is unable to satisfy a request because a device is busy. MTD requests normally run without blocking. If an MTD request would block, it should return an error code of CS_BUSY, and set Status to one of the have the following values:

MTD_WAITREQ
: Specifies that the request should be retried after another MTD request currently in progress completes.

MTD_WAITTIMER
: Specifies that the request should be continued after the time specified in the Timeout field.

MTD_WAITRDY
: Specifies that the request should be continued when the PC Card signals READY, or when the time specified in Timeout elapses, whichever happens first.

MTD_WAITPOWER
: Specifies that the request should be retried after something happens that affects power availability to the socket.

For MTD_WAITTIMER and MTD_WAITRDY, the Timeout field will specify the timeout interval in milliseconds.

MTD Helper Functions

Since an MTD processes requests generated by card services, there may be some restrictions on the sorts of card services calls that can be safely made from the MTD event handler. The MTD helper functions provide a limited set of special services that may be needed by an MTD but would be tricky to implement using the normal card services calls. In the Linux PC Card implementation, most CS calls can be safely made from an MTD event handler, but the MTD helper interface is included for compatibility.

```
#include "cs_types.h"
#include "cs.h"
#include "bulkmem.h"
int MTDHelperEntry(int subfunc, void *arg1, void *arg2);
```

MTDRequestWindow, MTDReleaseWindow

```
int MTDHelperEntry(MTDRequestWindow, client_handle_t *handle, win_req_t *mod);

int MTDHelperEntry(MTDReleaseWindow, window_handle_t handle);
```

These services are identical to the standard Card Services RequestWindow and ReleaseWindow calls.

MTDModifyWindow

```
int MTDHelperEntry(MTDModifyWindow, memory_handle_t handle,
mtd_mod_req_t *mod);
```

The mtd_mod_req_t structure is given by:

```
typedef struct mtd_mod_req_t {
        u_int        Attributes;
        u_int        AccessSpeed;
        u_int        CardOffset;
} mtd_mod_req_t;
```

MTDModifyWindow is essentially equivalent to using the normal ModifyWindow and MapMemPage calls. The following flags can be specified in Attributes:

WIN_MEMORY_TYPE
: Either WIN_MEMORY_TYPE_CM for common memory, or WIN_MEMORY_TYPE_AM for attribute memory.

WIN_USE_WAIT
: Specifies that the adapter should observe the PC Card's MWAIT signal.

A window configured with MTDModifyWindow will always be enabled and have a 16 bit data width.

Return codes:

CS_BAD_HANDLE
: The memory handle is invalid.

MTDSetVpp

```
int MTDHelperEntry(MTDSetVpp, client_handle_t client, mtd_vpp_req_t
                   *req);
```

```
typedef struct mtd_vpp_req_t {
        u_char       Vpp1, Vpp2;
} mtd_vpp_req_t;
```

MTDSetVpp changes the programming voltage for a socket. Vpp1 and Vpp2 should be given in units of 1/10 volt. Currently, Vpp1 should always equal Vpp2. Return codes:

CS_BAD_HANDLE
The client handle is invalid.
CS_BAD_VPP
The specified Vpp is not available, or Vpp1 does not equal Vpp2.

MTDRDYMask

```
int MTDHelperEntry(MTDRDYMask, client_handle_t client, mtd_rdy_req_t
                                *req);

typedef struct mtd_rdy_req_t {
        u_int           Mask;
} mtd_rdy_req_t;
```

MTDRDYMask selects whether or not CS_EVENT_READY_CHANGE events will be enabled. The client should already have indicated to card services that it should receive ready change events, via a call to either RegisterClient or SetEventMask. Ready change events will be enabled if the CS_EVENT_READY_CHANGE bit is set in the Mask argument.

Return codes:

CS_BAD_HANDLE
The client handle is invalid.

Driver Services Interface

Driver services provides a link between card services client drivers and user mode utilities like the cardmgr daemon. It is a sort of card services super-client. Driver services uses the BindDevice function to link other client drivers with their corresponding PC Card. Unlike other clients, driver services remains permanently bound to all sockets as PC Cards are inserted and removed.

Interface to Other Client Drivers

Driver services keeps track of all client drivers that are installed and ready to attach to a socket. Client drivers need to have entry points for creating and deleting device instances, where one device instance is everything needed to manage one PC Card. Each client driver is identified by a unique 16-character tag that has the special type dev_info_t, defined in CS_TYPES.H file. Each device instance is described by a dev_link_t structure.

The dev_link_t Structure

The dev_node_t and dev_link_t data structures are given by:

```
#include "ds.h"

typedef struct dev_node_t {
        char                    dev_name[DEV_NAME_LEN];
        u_char                  major, minor;
        struct dev_node_t       *next;
}

        typedef struct dev_link_t {
                dev_node_t              *dev;
                u_int                   state, open;
                struct wait_queue       *pending
                struct timer_list       release
                client_handle_t         handle;
                io_req_t                io;
                irq_req_t               irq;
                config_req_t            conf;
                window_handle_t         win;
                void                    *priv;
                struct dev_link_t       *next;
        } dev_link_t;
```

The dev field of the dev_link_t structure points to a linked list of dev_node_t structures. In dev_node_t, the dev_name field should be filled in by the driver with a device file name for accessing this device, if appropriate.

For example, the serial_cs driver uses names like ``tty''. The major and minor fields give major and minor device numbers for accessing this device. Driver Services relays these fields to user mode programs via the DS_GET_DEVICE_INFO ioctl.
In dev_link_t, the state field should be used to keep track of the current device state.

The following flags are defined:

DEV_PRESENT
: Indicates that the PC Card is present. This bit should be set and cleared by the driver's event handler in response to PC Card insertion and removal events.

DEV_CONFIG
: Indicates that the PC Card is configured for use.

DEV_CONFIG_PENDING
: Indicates that configuration is in progress.

DEV_SUSPEND
: Indicates that the PC Card is suspended.

DEV_BUSY
: Indicates that an I/O operation is in progress. This bit may be used as an interlock to prevent access conflicts.

DEV_STALE_CONFIG
: For some drivers, when a running card is ejected, the socket should not be unconfigured until any devices corresponding to this PC Card are closed. This flag indicates that the socket should be unconfigured when the device is closed.

DEV_STALE_LINK
: A driver instance should not be deleted until all its PC Card resources are released. This flag indicates that this driver instance should be freed as soon as the socket is unconfigured.

The open field is a usage count for this device. The device should only be freed when the open count is zero. The pending field can be used to manage a queue of processes waiting to use the device.
The release field is used to schedule device shutdown processing when a PC Card is ejected. A card removal event needs to be handled at high priority, so a driver's event handler will typically deal with an eject by resetting the DEV_PRESENT bit in the device state, then scheduling the shutdown processing to run at a later time.

The handle, io, irq, conf, and win fields comprise all the normal PC Card data structures needed to configure an ordinary I/O PC Card. The priv field can be used for any sort of private data structure needed to manage the device. The next field can be used to build linked lists of dev_link_t structures, for drivers that can handle multiple instances.

register_pcmcia_driver

```
int register_pcmcia_driver(dev_info_t *dev_info, dev_link_t *(*attach)(void),
                           void (*detach)(dev_link_t *));
```

register_pcmcia_driver informs driver services that a client driver is present and ready to be bound to sockets. When driver services receives a DS_BIND_REQUEST ioctl that matches this driver's dev_info string, it will call the driver's attach() entry point. When it gets a DS_UNBIND_REQUEST ioctl, it will call detach().

unregister_pcmcia_driver

```
int unregister_pcmcia_driver(dev_info_t *dev_info);
```

This informs driver services that it should no longer bind sockets to the specified client driver.

The CardBus client interface

The CardBus card interface is designed to be essentially an extension of the PCI bus. CardBus cards are typically designed using standard PCI chip sets. For simplicity in the client drivers, and maximum code sharing with regular kernel PCI drivers, we provide a sort of ``super client" for configuring CardBus cards. This is implemented in the cb_enabler module.

The cb_enabler module is somewhat similar in philosophy to the Driver Services layer for 16-bit cards. CardBus client drivers register with it, and provide a few entry points for handling device setup and shutdown, as well as power management handling. The cb_enabler module takes care of configuring the card and fielding Card Services events. So, all CardBus-specific code is in the enabler rather than the PCI driver.

It is not mandatory for CardBus clients to use the cb_enabler interface. If a particular client requires more direct control over its CardBus configuration than is provided through the cb_enabler module, it can register directly with Card Services and perform Card Services calls directly, just like a 16-bit client.

The cb_enabler module has two entry points: register_driver and unregister_driver. At some point, these functions may migrate into the kernel: hence the generic names.

register_driver

int register_driver(struct driver_operations *ops);

The driver_operations structure is given by:

```
typedef struct driver_operations {
        char            *name
        dev_node_t      *(*attach) (dev_locator_t *loc);
        void            (*suspend) (dev_node_t *dev);
        void            (*resume) (dev_node_t *dev);
        void            (*detach) (dev_node_t *dev);
} driver_operations;
```

The name field is used by cb_enabler when registering this client with Card Services. The rest of the structure describes a set of event handlers for this client. The function returns 0 on success, and -1 on failure.

unregister_driver

void unregister_driver(struct driver_operations *ops);

The ops parameter should be the same structure pointer passed to a prior successful call to register_driver. The client should take care to only call this function when no devices are currently being managed by this client.

The driver_operations entry points

The attach() entry point is used to configure a single device, given a ``device locator" structure describing where to find it.

The dev_locator_t structure is given by:

```
typedef struct dev_locator_t {
```

```
    enum { LOC_ISA, LOC_PCI } bus;
    union {
        struct {
            u_short     io_base_1, io_base_2;
            u_long      mem_base;
            u_char      irq, dma;
        } isa;
        struct {
            u_char      bus;
            u_char      devfn;
        } pci;
    } b;
} dev_locator_t;
```

The attach() function should return either NULL or a valid dev_node_t structure describing the new device. All the other entry points will use this pointer to identify the device to be manipulated. The cb_enabler module will invoke the attach() and detach() entry points in response to card insertion and removal events. The suspend() and resume() entry points will be called in response to power management events.

There is no way for a driver to refuse a suspend() or detach() event. When a detach() event is received, the driver should block any subsequent I/O to the specified device, but may preserve internal data structures until the kernel device is actually closed.

Interface to User Mode PC Card Utilities

Driver services creates a pseudo-device for communicating with user mode PC Card utilities. The major number of the device is chosen dynamically, and PC Card utilities should read /proc/devices to
determine it. Minor device numbers correspond to socket numbers, starting with zero.

Only one process is allowed to open a socket for read/write access. Other processes can open the socket in read-only mode. A read-only connection to driver services can perform a subset of ioctl calls. A read/write connection can issue all ioctl calls, and can also receive card services event notifications.

Card Services Event Notifications

Driver services implements read() and select() functions for event notification. Reading from a pcmcia device returns an unsigned long value containing all the events received by driver services since the previous read(). If no events have been received, the call will block until the next event. A select() call can be used to monitor several sockets for new events. The following events are monitored by driver services:

CS_EVENT_CARD_INSERTION, CS_EVENT_CARD_REMOVAL, CS_EVENT_RESET_PHYSICAL, CS_EVENT_CARD_RESET, and CS_EVENT_RESET_COMPLETE.

Ioctl Descriptions

Most driver services ioctl operations directly map to card services functions. An ioctl call has the form:

int ioctl(int fd, int cmd, ds_ioctl_arg_t *arg);

The ds_ioctl_arg_t structure is given by:

```
typedef union ds_ioctl_arg_t {
        servinfo_t          servinfo;
        adjust_t            adjust;
        config_t            config;
        tuple_t             tuple;
        tuple_parse_t       tuple_parse;
        client_req_t        client_req;
        status_t            status;
        conf_reg_t          conf_reg;
        cisinfo_t           cisinfo;
        region_info_t       region;
        bind_info_t         bind_info;
        mtd_info_t          mtd_info;
        cis_dump_t          cisdump;
} ds_ioctl_arg_t;
```

The following ioctl commands execute the corresponding card services function:

DS_GET_CARD_SERVICES_INFO
    Calls CardServices(GetCardServicesInfo, ..., &arg->servinfo).
DS_ADJUST_RESOURCE_INFO
    Calls CardServices(AdjustResourceInfo, ..., &arg->adjust).
DS_GET_CONFIGURATION_INFO
    Calls CardServices(GetConfigurationInfo, ..., &arg->config).
DS_GET_FIRST_TUPLE
    Calls CardServices(GetFirstTuple, ..., &arg->tuple).
DS_GET_NEXT_TUPLE
    Calls CardServices(GetNextTuple, ..., &arg->tuple).
DS_GET_TUPLE_DATA
    Calls CardServices(GetTupleData, ..., &arg->tuple_parse.tuple). The tuple data is returned in arg->tuple_parse.data.
DS_PARSE_TUPLE
    Calls CardServices(ParseTuple, ..., &arg->tuple_parse.tuple, &arg->tuple_parse.parse).
DS_RESET_CARD
    Calls CardServices(ResetCard, ...).
DS_GET_STATUS
    Calls CardServices(GetStatus, ..., &arg->status).
DS_ACCESS_CONFIGURATION_REGISTER

Calls CardServices(AccessConfigurationRegister, ..., &arg->conf_reg).

DS_VALIDATE_CIS
Calls CardServices(ValidateCIS, ..., &arg->cisinfo).

DS_SUSPEND_CARD
Calls CardServices(SuspendCard, ...).

DS_RESUME_CARD
Calls CardServices(ResumeCard, ...).

DS_EJECT_CARD
Calls CardServices(EjectCard, ...).

DS_INSERT_CARD
Calls CardServices(InsertCard, ...).

DS_GET_FIRST_REGION
Calls CardServices(GetFirstRegion, ..., &arg->region).

DS_GET_NEXT_REGION
Calls CardServices(GetNextRegion, ..., &arg->region).

DS_REPLACE_CIS
Calls CardServices(ReplaceCIS, ..., &arg->cisdump)

The following ioctl commands invoke special driver services functions. They act on bind_info_t structures:

```
typedef struct bind_info_t {
        dev_info_t              dev_info;
        struct dev_info_t      *instance;
        char                    name[8];
        u_char                  major, minor;
        void                    *next;
} bind_info_t;
```

DS_BIND_REQUEST
This call connects a socket to a client driver. The specified device ID dev_info is looked up in the list of registered drivers. If found, the driver is bound to this socket using the BindDevice call. Then, driver services calls the client driver's attach() entry point to create a device instance. The new dev_link_t pointer is returned in instance.

DS_GET_DEVICE_INFO
This call retrieves the name, major, and minor entries from the dev_link_t structure pointed to by instance.

DS_UNBIND_REQUEST
This call calls the detach() function for the specified driver and instance, shutting down this device.

Finally, the DS_BIND_MTD request takes an argument of type mtd_info_t:

```
typedef struct mtd_info_t {
        dev_info_t    dev_info;
        u_int         Attributes;
        u_int         CardOffset;
} mtd_info_t;
```

This call associates an MTD identified by dev_info with a memory region described by Attributes and CardOffset, which have the same meanings as in the card services BindMTD call.

Anatomy of a Card Services Client Driver

Each release of the Linux PC Card package comes with a well-commented skeleton client driver that should be used as a starting point for writing a new driver. Look for it in modules/dummy_cs.c. This is not just a piece of sample code: it is written to function as a sort of generic card enabler. If bound to an IO card, it will read the card's CIS and configure the card appropriately, assuming that the card's CIS is complete and accurate.

Module Initialization and Cleanup

All loadable modules must supply init_module() and cleanup_module() functions, which are invoked by the module support code when the module is installed and removed. A PC Card client driver's init function should register the driver with driver services, via the register_pcmcia_driver() call. The cleanup function should use unregister_pcmcia_driver() to deregister with driver services. Depending on the driver, the cleanup function may also need to free any device structures that still exist at shutdown time.

The *_attach() and *_detach() Functions

The *_attach() entry point is responsible for creating an instance of the driver, setting up any data structures needed to manage one PC Card. The *_attach() function should allocate and initialize a dev_link_t structure, and call RegisterClient to establish a link with card services. It returns a pointer to the new dev_link_t structure, or NULL if the new instance could not be created. The *_detach() entry point deletes a driver instance created by a previous call to *_attach. It also breaks the link with card services, using DeregisterClient.

The *_attach() entry point is called by driver services when a PC Card has been successfully identified and mapped to a matching driver by a DS_BIND_REQUEST ioctl(). The *_detach() entry point is called in response to a DS_UNBIND_REQUEST ioctl() call.

The *_config() and *_release() Functions

The *_config() function is called to prepare a PC Card for I/O. Most drivers read some configuration details from the PC Card itself, but most have at least some built-in knowledge of how the device should be set up. For example, the serial PC Card driver reads a PC Card's CFTABLE_ENTRY tuples to determine appropriate I/O port base addresses and corresponding configuration indices, but the driver ignores the interrupt information in the CIS. The *_config() function will parse relevant parts of a PC Card's CIS, then make calls to RequestIO, RequestIRQ, and/or RequestWindow, then call RequestConfiguration.

When a PC Card is successfully configured, the *_config() routine should fill in the dev_name, major, and minor fields in the dev_link_t structure. These fields will be returned by driver services in response to a DS_GET_DEVICE_INFO ioctl().

The *_release() function should release any resource allocated by a previous call to *_config() and blank out the device's dev_name field.

The *_config() and *_release() functions are normally called in response to card status change events or from timer interrupts. Thus, they cannot sleep, and should not call other kernel functions that might block.

The PC Card Event Handler

The *_event() entry point is called from card services to notify a driver of card status change events.

Locking and Synchronization Issues

A configured socket should only be released when all associated devices are closed. Releasing a socket allows its system resources to be allocated for use by another device. If the released resources are reallocated while I/O to the original device is still in progress, the original driver may interfere with use of the new device.

A driver instance should only be freed after its corresponding socket configuration has been released. Card services requires that a client explicitly release any allocated resources before a call to DeregisterClient will succeed.

All loadable modules have a use count that is used by the system to determine when it is safe to unload a module. The convention in the PC Card client drivers is to increment the use count when a device is opened, and to decrement the count when a device is closed. So, a driver can be unloaded whenever all associated devices are closed. in particular, a driver can be unloaded even if it is still bound to a socket, and the module cleanup code needs to be able to appropriately free any such resources that are still allocated. This should always be safe, because if the driver has a use count of zero, all devices are closed, which means all active sockets can be released, and all device instances can be detached.

If a driver's *_release() function is called while a device is still open, it should set the DEV_STALE_CONFIG flag in the device state, to signal that the device should be released when the driver's close() function is called. If *_detach() is called for a configured device, the DEV_STALE_LINK flag should be set to signal that the instance should be detached when the *_release() function is called.

Using Existing Linux Drivers to Access PC Card Devices

Many of the current PC Card client drivers use existing Linux driver code to perform device I/O operations. The card services client module handles card configuration and responds to card status change events, but delegates device I/O to a compatible driver for a conventional ISA bus card. In some cases, a conventional driver can be used without modification. However, to fully support PC Card features like hot swapping and power management, there needs to be some communication between the PC Card client code and the device I/O code.

Most Linux drivers expect to probe for devices at boot time, and are not designed to handle adding and removing devices. One side-effect of the move towards driver modularization is that it is usually easier to adapt a modularized driver to handle removable devices.

It is important that a device driver be able to recover from having a device disappear at an inappropriate time. At best, the driver should check for device presence before attempting any I/O operation or before handling an I/O interrupt. Loops that check device status should have timeouts so they will eventually exit if a device never responds. The dummy_cs driver may be useful for loading legacy drivers for compatible PC Card devices. After binding dummy_cs to a card, the legacy driver module may be able to detect and communicate with the device as if it were not a PC Card. This arrangement will generally not support clean hot swapping or power management functions, however it may be useful as a basis for later developing a more full-featured client driver.

Where to Go for More Information

The Linux Kernel Hackers' Guide, written by Michael Johnson, is a good source of general information about writing Linux device drivers. It is available from the usual Linux FTP sites.

The genuine PC Card standard is only available from the PCMCIA association itself, and costs a significant amount of money. To contact PCMCIA:

Personal Computer Memory Card International Association
1030 East Duane Avenue, Suite G
Sunnyvale, CA 94086 USA
(408) 720-0107, (408) 720-9416 FAX, (408) 720-9388 BBS
http://www.pc-card.com

Chapter 10: PC Card Development Utilities

While the purpose of most client drivers is to support or manage a PC Card, another role a card services client can perform is that of a utility or tool. This section illustrates some possible utility functions a client can perform without managing the function of a PC Card. The sample code and executable files for these programs are available via the publisher's ftp site at **ftp.peer-to-peer.com/pub/pc-card**.

The first sample program parses the CIS of a PC Card. CSINFO is a DOS or full-screen OS/2 version, CSINFOW is the Windows 3.1 version, CSINFOPM runs under OS/2 Presentation Manager, and CSINFW32 runs under Windows 95/98 and Windows NT. The program determines how many sockets are present on the system, then proceeds to interrogate the CIS on cards that are inserted into these sockets. The program then displays the tuple information contained on the PC Card.

The second sample program has two names: CARDMGR for Windows and PCCARDPM for OS/2 Presentation Manager. These two programs demonstrate the methods for coding callback handlers from an application program in a particular environment. Each program registers a callback handler and, when a PC Card is inserted into a socket it simply displays the Level 1 Version/Product Information Tuple for that card. The programs also demonstrate how simple launching of an application based on a card services event can be.

The third utility program is called DEVCHG and works under Windows 95/98 and Windows CE. According to preliminary information, this program should work on the forthcoming Windows NT 5.0. This program demonstrates how a Win32 program can receive the WM_DEVICECHANGE message when PC Cards are inserted and removed from the system.

The fourth utility program, UARTTYPE, can be built to run either under DOS or OS/2. The program determines the type of UART present on a PC Card modem card. This is useful in determining if the modem card has a buffered or nonbuffered UART, as discussed in chapter 2.

This chapter finally ends with some utility programs to interrogate the socket controller. They do not use Card Services and are dependant on the type of socket controller used in a system.

Table 10-1 shows the assemblers, compilers, and toolkits required to build the code.

Sample Program	Assembler	Compiler	Toolkit
CSINFO.EXE (DOS)	N/A	Microsoft C 6.0	N/A
CSINFO.EXE (OS/2)	N/A	Microsoft C 6.0	N/A
CSINFOW.EXE	N/A	Microsoft C 6.0	Microsoft Windows 3.1 SDK
CSINFOPM.EXE Nmake -f csinfopm.mak	N/A	IBM C Set/2 1.0 or IBM C Set++ for OS/2	IBM Developer's Toolkit for OS/2 Warp
CSINFW32.EXE	N/A	Microsoft Visual C++ 5.0	N/A
CSDRVR.VXD	MASM 6.11	Microsoft Visual C++ 5.0	Microsoft Windows 95 DDK
UARTTYPE.EXE (DOS) Nmake -f uarttype.dos	N/A	Microsoft C 6.0	N/A
UARTTYPE.EXE (OS/2) Nmake -f uarttype.os2	N/A	Microsoft C 6.0	N/A
CARDMGR.EXE	N/A	Microsoft C 6.0	Microsoft Windows 3.1 SDK
PCCARDPM.EXE	N/A	IBM C Set/2 1.0 or IBM C Set++ for OS/2	IBM Developer's Toolkit for OS/2 Warp
DEVCHG.EXE	N/A	Microsoft Visual C++ 5.0	Microsoft Windows CE Toolkit for Visual C++ 5.0 (for Windows CE version; not needed for 95/NT version)
DOSPCIC.EXE	N/A	Microsoft C 6.0	N/A
PMPCIC.EXE	MASM 5.1 (for .DLL)	IBM C Set++ for OS/2	IBM Developer's Toolkit for OS/2 Warp
WINPCIC.EXE	MASM 6.11 (for .VXD)	Microsoft Visual C++ 5.0	Microsoft Windows 95 DDK Microsoft Windows NT DDK

Table 10-1: Required Program Template Software Tools

A Utility For Parsing the Card Information Structure (CIS)

CSINFO

This utility program can be built for either DOS or OS/2. It displays both card services information as well as the CIS for each PC Card present. Every socket on the system is scanned. The information is written to the screen; however, it may be directed to a file. A sample output for a PC Card system with both Token-Ring and Ethernet PC Cards is shown in Figure 10-1.

```
Card Services Information
-------------------------
Number of Sockets=2  Revision=0110  Level=0200
Vendor String:
IBM OS/2 PCMCIA card services Device Driver Version 1.11.

(C) Copyright IBM Corporation 1992, 1993, 1994.

All Rights Reserved.


Socket 1
--------
Card State=00C1  Socket State=0001

  Configuration Information
  -------------------------
  Handle=0698
  Attributes=0002
  Intface Type=02
  Card Config Base=00000800
  Assigned IRQ=9
  IRQ Attr=00
  Base Port1=0A20
  Number of Ports=04
  Attrributes=00
  Base Port2=0000
  Number of Ports=00
  Attrributes=00
  I/O Address Lines=16

  Card Tuples
  -----------
  Tuple Code=01
    Tuple Length=7
    Tuple Data:
      01 05 19 02 D9 3A FF      .....:.
  Tuple Code=15
    Tuple Length=33
    Tuple Data:
```

```
      15 1F 04 01 49 42 4D 00  ....IBM.
      54 4F 4B 45 4E 20 52 49  TOKEN RI
      4E 47 00 30 39 33 33 39  NG.09339
      32 39 00 4E 4F 4E 45 00  29.NONE.
      FF                       .
  Tuple Code=1A
    Tuple Length=8
    Tuple Data:
      1A 06 01 21 00 08 0B FF  ...!....
  Tuple Code=1B
    Tuple Length=24
    Tuple Data:
      1B 16 E1 81 7D 11 55 36  ....}.U6
      FC 0B B0 60 20 0A 07 30  ...` ..0
      FF FF 11 20 00 00 01 FF  ... ....
  Tuple Code=20
    Tuple Length=7
    Tuple Data:
      20 05 A4 00 1E 00 FF      ......  Tuple Code=21
    Tuple Length=5
    Tuple Data:
      21 03 06 03 FF           !....
  Tuple Code=14
    Tuple Length=2
    Tuple Data:
      14 00                    ..
  Tuple Code=10
    Tuple Length=8
    Tuple Data:
      10 06 AA FF 56 00 84 FF  ....V...

Socket 2
--------
Card State=00C1  Socket State=0000

  Configuration Information
  -------------------------
  Handle=06BC
  Attributes=0002
  Intface Type=02
  Card Config Base=00020000
  Assigned IRQ=5
  IRQ Attr=00
  Base Port1=0120
  Number of Ports=10
  Attrributes=00
  Base Port2=0130
  Number of Ports=10
  Attrributes=00
  I/O Address Lines=16

 Card Tuples
  -----------
  Tuple Code=01
    Tuple Length=7
    Tuple Data:
      01 05 D4 0A 53 E9 FF     ....S..
  Tuple Code=17
    Tuple Length=5
    Tuple Data:
      17 03 53 09 FF           ..S..
  Tuple Code=20
    Tuple Length=6
```

```
    Tuple Data:
      20 04 A4 00 02 00          .....
  Tuple Code=21
    Tuple Length=4
    Tuple Data:
      21 02 06 03                !...
  Tuple Code=15
    Tuple Length=59
    Tuple Data:
      15 39 04 01 49 42 4D 20    .9..IBM
      43 6F 72 70 2E 00 45 74    Corp..Et
      68 65 72 6E 65 74 00 30    hernet.0
      39 33 33 34 39 35 00 50    933495.P
      43 2D 4E 49 43 20 45 4E    C-NIC EN
      43 43 20 39 39 30 30 31    CC 99001
      30 37 35 39 2D 30 30 31    0759-001
      41 00 FF                   A..
  Tuple Code=1A
    Tuple Length=8
    Tuple Data:
      1A 06 02 01 00 00 02 0B    ........
  Tuple Code=1B
    Tuple Length=21
    Tuple Data:
      1B 13 C1 81 7E 19 55 15    ....~.U.
      26 01 0E FC 33 45 70 FF    &...3Ep.
      FF 48 40 10 01             .H@..
  Tuple Code=18
    Tuple Length=7
    Tuple Data:
      18 05 00 00 89 B8 FF       .......
  Tuple Code=19
    Tuple Length=5
    Tuple Data:
      19 03 89 B8 FF             .....
  Tuple Code=14
    Tuple Length=2
    Tuple Data:
      14 00                      ..
  Tuple Code=10
    Tuple Length=7
    Tuple Data:
      10 05 84 FF 82 00 48       ......H
```

Figure 10-1: CSINFO Output

This sample program illustrates two concepts: how a utility program can gather information about a PC Card in a socket, and how a utility program can retrieve all of the tuples from a card, starting with the first and ending with the last.

Card services maintains a wealth of information about the configuration of a PC Card in a socket, when the card has been configured by card services. PC Card data, such as the interface type, base address of the configuration registers, assigned I/O ports and IRQ, are maintained on a per-socket basis. The card services request **GetConfigurationInfo** is used to retrieve this information. Only the socket of interest is needed to make this request. CSINFO fills in the GETCONFIGURATIONINFO structure with the socket number that the information is required for and then makes the card services request **GetConfigurationInfo**. If the socket has a configured card in it, the client handle that was used to request this configuration is returned in the Handle argument and the structure is filled in with the card configuration information. For a complete list of the card configuration information returned, see the program diskette included with this book.

The second concept demonstrated is how to loop through all of the tuples on a PC Card. The card services requests **GetFirstTuple/GetNextTuple/GetTupleData** are traditionally used by client drivers to parse a particular tuple, such as the Level 1 Product/Version Information Tuple for the product ID or the function extension tuples for serial port information. These requests can also be used to parse the entire tuple chain on a PC Card. The structure used for the **GetFirstTuple** request contains the field DesiredTuple. A client would usually fill in the value for the tuple desired. The value 0xFF is special and is used to locate the very first tuple found on a card. Subsequent calls to **GetNextTuple** will continue through the tuple chain until a return code of NO_MORE_ITEMS is returned. Figure 10-2 shows a typical tuple processing sequence.

```
//  Now get the Tuple data and print it.
fpGetTuple->Socket = iSocket + BaseSocket;
fpGetTuple->Attributes = 1;
fpGetTuple->DesiredTuple = 0xFF;
fpGetTuple->TupleOffset = 0;
rc = CardServices(GET_FIRST_TUPLE,
                  NULL, NULL, 18, fpGetTuple, NULL);

if (rc != 0)
   if (rc != NO_CARD)
      printf("  Cannot get First Tuple.  rc=%4.4X\n", rc);
   else
      ;
else
{
   printf("  Card Tuples\n  -----------\n");
   while (rc == 0){
      if (fpGetTuple->s.GetFirstNextTuple.TupleCode == 0xFF)
         break;
      printf("  Tuple Code=%2.2X\n",
             fpGetTuple->s.GetFirstNextTuple.TupleCode);
      fpGetTuple->s.GetTupleData.TupleDataMax = 256;
      rc = CardServices(GET_TUPLE_DATA, NULL, NULL, 256,
        fpGetTuple,NULL);
      if (rc != 0)
         printf("  Cannot get Tuple Data.  rc=%4.4X\n", rc);
      else
      {
         printf("    Tuple Length=%d\n",
                fpGetTuple->s.GetTupleData.TupleDataLen);
         printf("    Tuple Data:\n");
         memset(bigbuf, ' ', 512);
         len = hexdump(fpGetTuple->s.GetTupleData.TupleData,
                       fpGetTuple->s.GetTupleData.TupleDataLen,
                       bigbuf, 8, 1);
         //  The returned string has embeded CRLF.  Print the
         //  string one character a a time so that the start of
         //  each line can be indented 4 spaces.
```

```
            printf("        ");
            for (i=0; i<len; i++)
            {
               printf("%c", bigbuf[i]);
               if ((bigbuf[i] == '\n') && (i != len-1))
                  printf("        ");
            }
         }
         rc = CardServices(GET_NEXT_TUPLE, NULL, NULL, 18,
            fpGetTuple, NULL);
      }
}
```

Figure 10-2: Sample Tuple Processing Code

CSINFOW

This utility program is a Windows 3.1 version of CSINFO. It displays card services information and PC Card information for every card found. The first window displayed will be information about card services. The initial window is shown in Figure 10-3.

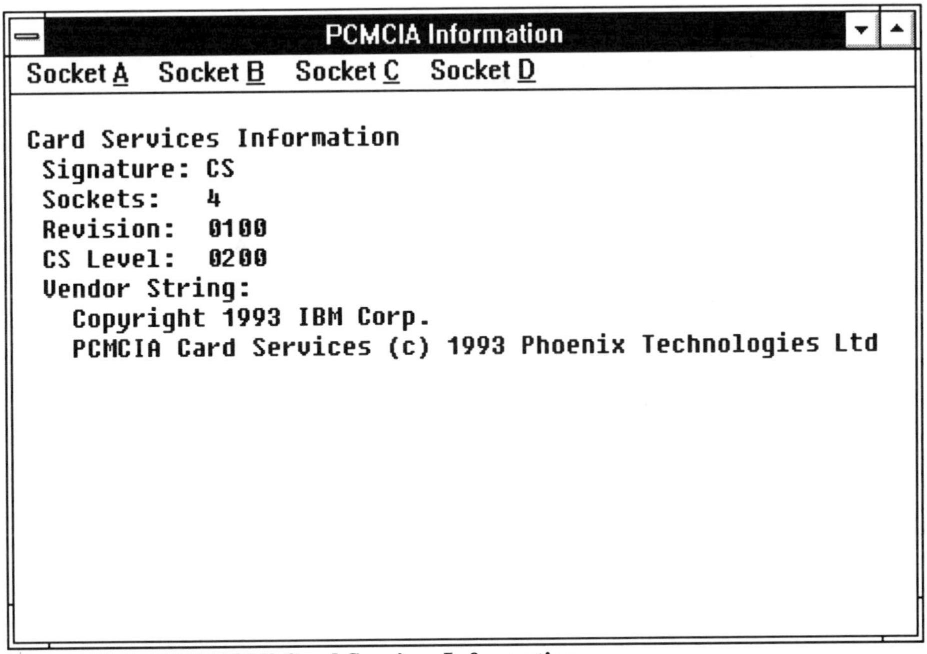

Figure 10-3: CSINFOW Card Services Information

Selecting a Socket option causes information about the PC Card in that socket to be displayed. There are two selections in the drop down menu: Configuration Info and Tuple Data. By selecting Configuration Info, if a card is in the socket and configured by a driver, the configuration information for the card will be displayed. A sample display for a modem card is shown in Figure 10-4.

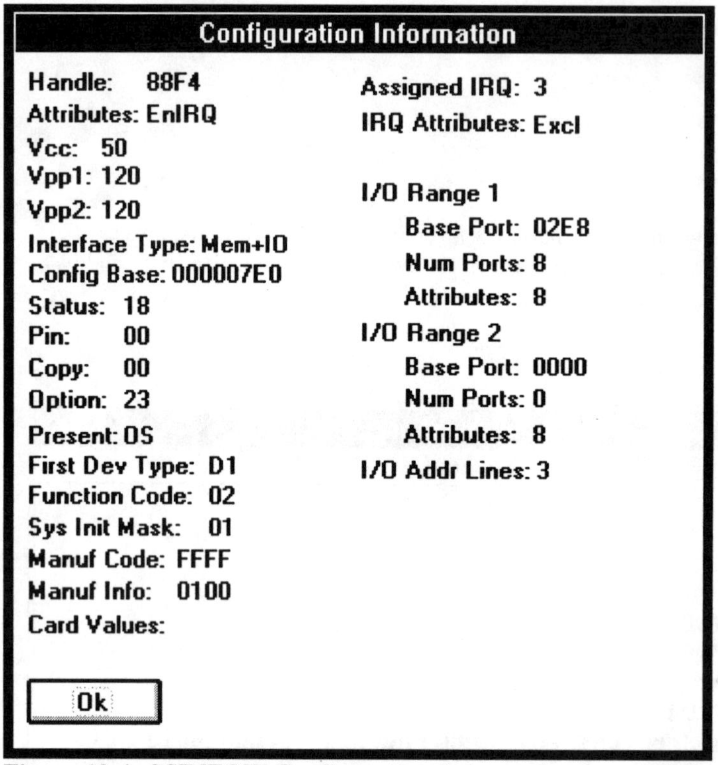

Figure 10-4: CSINFOW Configuration Information for a Modem

Select Tuple Data to see a list of the tuples found on the card. To view a hexadecimal dump of the tuple data, double-click on the listbox entry and a window will appear. Figure 10-5 shows a sample list box of tuples found on a modem card. Figure 10-6 and Figure 10-7 are sample hexadecimal displays of tuple data stored on the card.

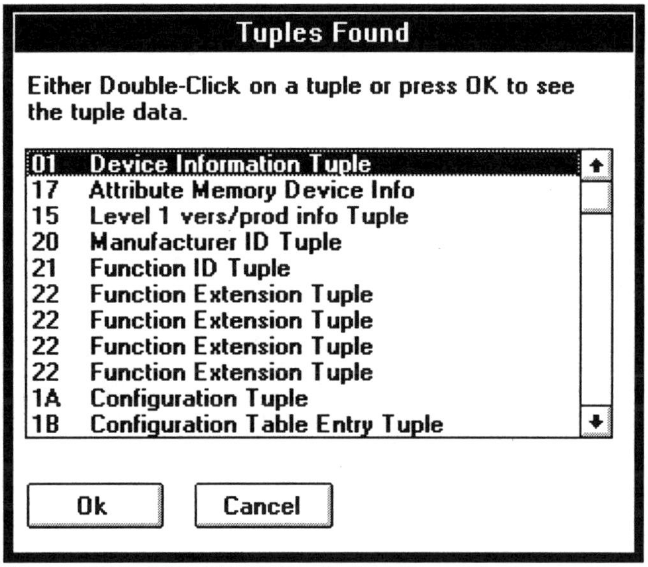

Figure 10-5: CSINFOW Tuple List for a Modem

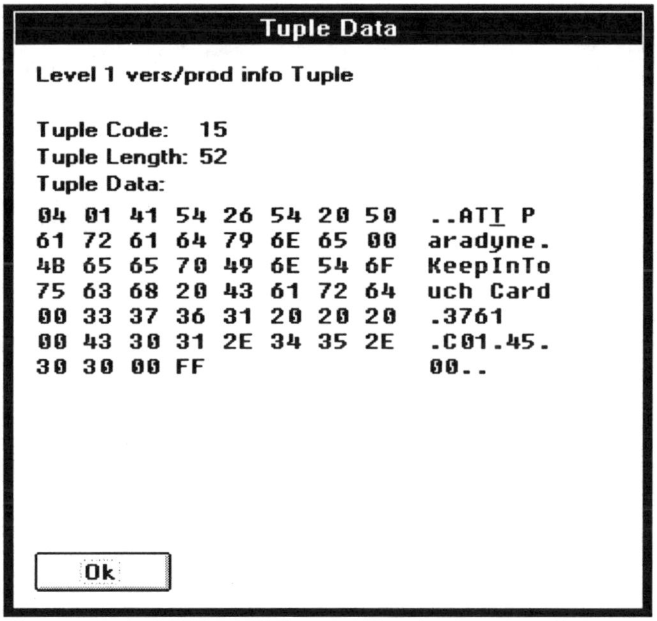

Figure 10-6: CSINFOW Level 1 Version/Product Information Tuple

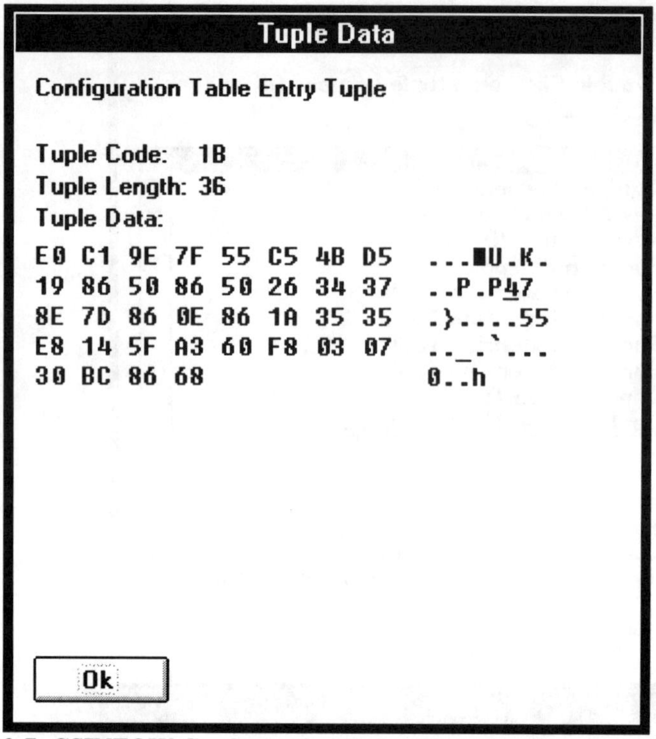

Figure 10-7: CSINFOW Configuration Entry Tuple hex data for a Modem

The main concept illustrated by this sample program is that a Windows utility program cannot simply call card services through the INT 1Ah binding because card services is usually implemented as a real mode device driver that loads during CONFIG.SYS time. In a Windows 3.1 environment, card services functions run in a Virtual-86 mode but appear to applications as if they were running in real mode. Windows programs do not run in real mode; they run in protect mode. Because of the differences between real and protect modes, a protect mode program cannot call the real mode card services functions. DPMI is the mechanism used for a Windows protect mode program to make requests.

DPMI provides a wealth of services. The only service used here is *Simulate Real Mode Interrupt*. This function takes an interrupt value and a pointer to a structure containing the register values for the interrupt, and transfers control to the address specified by the real mode interrupt vector. The function of the interrupt is performed and a return is made to the calling program with the structure modified by the function of the interrupt. Figure 10-8 is a code excerpt from the CSCALL.C program which accomplishes this task.

```
struct _DPMI_REGS
{
   unsigned int    _DI, _DI1;
   unsigned int    _SI, _SI1;
   unsigned int    _BP, _BP1;
   unsigned long   _BP2;
   unsigned int    _BX, _BX1;
   unsigned int    _DX, _DX1;
   unsigned int    _CX, _CX1;
   unsigned int    _AX, _AX1;
   unsigned int    _FL, _ES, _DS, _FS, _GS, _IP, _CS, _SP, _SS;
}  DpmiRegs;
                    .
                    .
                    .
DpmiRegs._AX = 0xAF00 | Function;
DpmiRegs._DX = Handle;
DpmiRegs._DI = FP_SEG(Pointer);
DpmiRegs._SI = FP_OFF(Pointer);
DpmiRegs._CX = ArgLength;
DpmiRegs._ES = FP_SEG(ArgPointer);
DpmiRegs._BX = FP_OFF(ArgPointer);
_asm
{
    mov   ax,SEG DpmiRegs
    mov   es,ax
    lea   di,DpmiRegs
    mov   ax,0300h
    mov   bx,01ah
    mov   cx,0
    int   31h
}

if (DpmiRegs._FL & 0x01)
   return DpmiRegs._AX;
else
{
   if (RetHandle)
      *RetHandle = DpmiRegs._DX;
   return 0;
}
```

Figure 10-8: DPMI Interface Routine

CSINFOPM

The next program is an OS/2 2.1 Presentation Manager version of CSINFO. It displays card services and PC Card information for every card found. The PC Card information is initially dumped in hexadecimal format. If the program can convert the tuple into ASCII readable text, a Format button is available for displaying the tuple in this manner. Figures 10-9 through 10-12 show sample displays from this program.

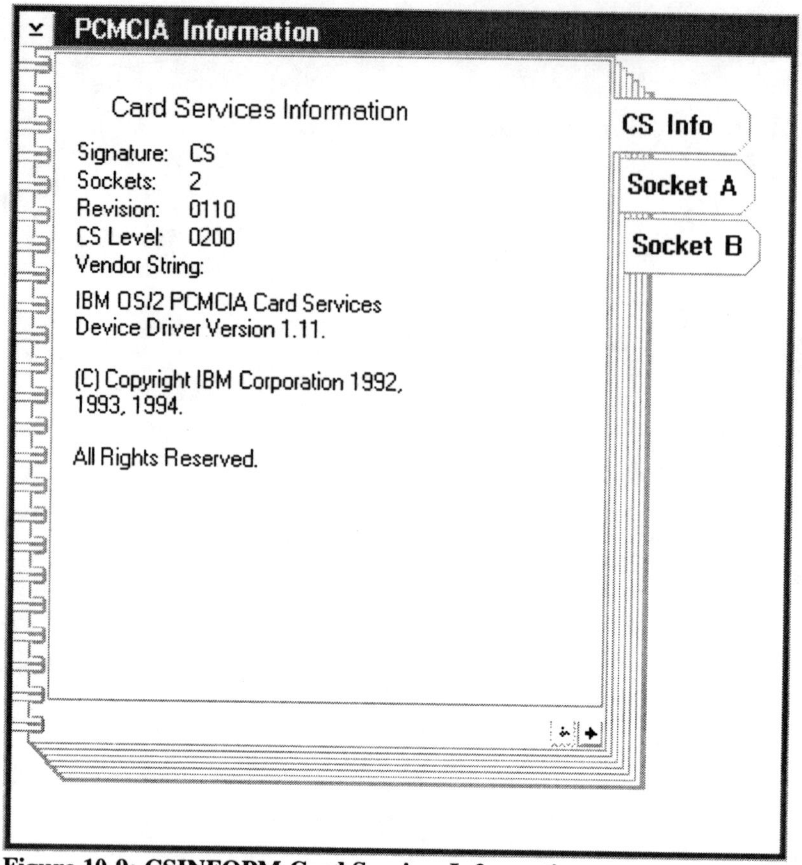

Figure 10-9: CSINFOPM Card Services Information

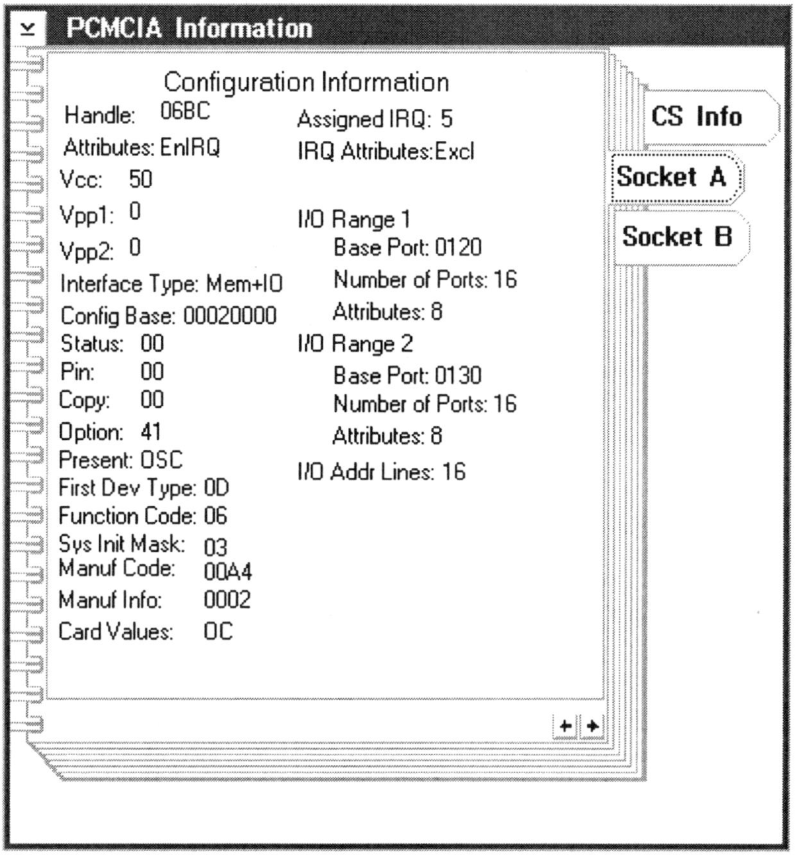

Figure 10-10: CSINFOPM Configuration Information for an Ethernet PC Card

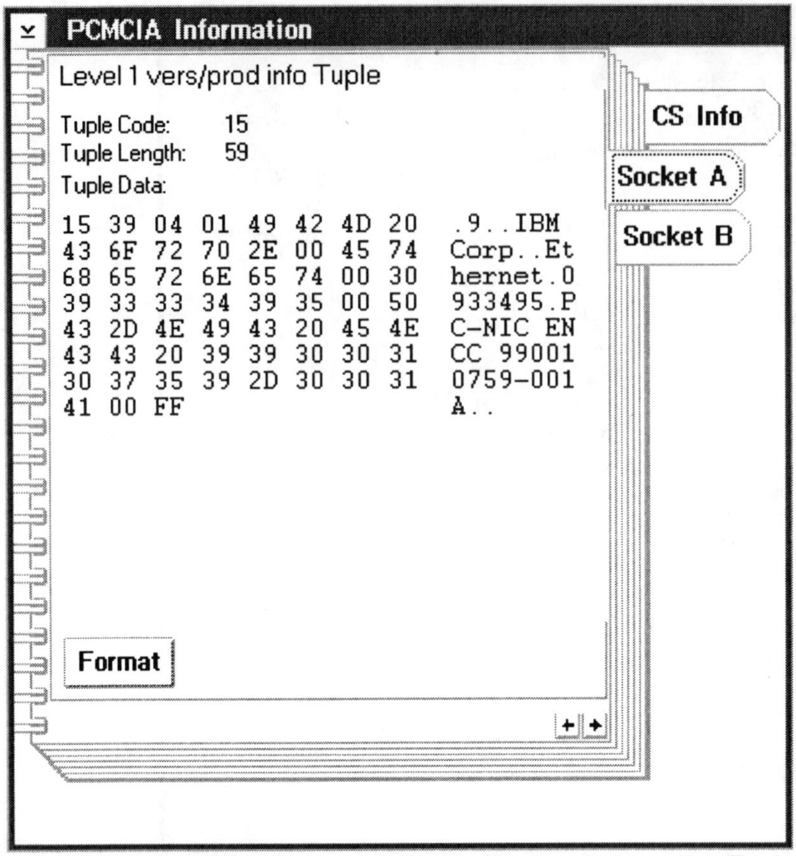

Figure 10-11: CSINFOPM Level 1 Version/Product Information Tuple hex data for an Ethernet PC Card

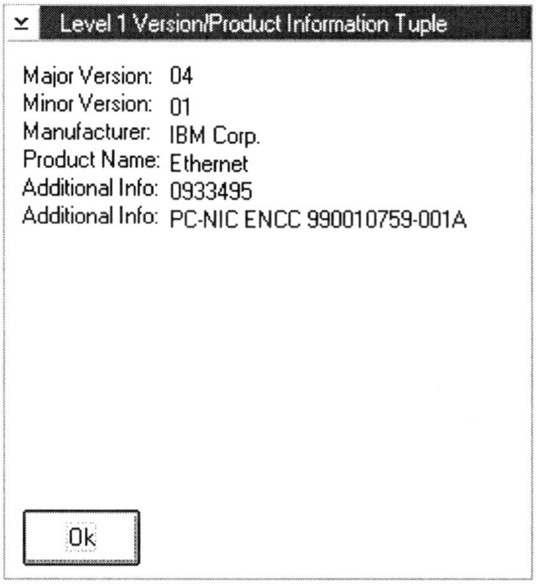

Figure 10-12: CSINFOPM Interpretation of the Level 1 Version/Product Information Tuple

The concept illustrated by this sample program is how an OS/2 application program can make card services requests. For a device driver, the binding is register based: AL contains the function, CX contains the socket, and so on (the PC Card Standard Card Services Specification contains the complete processor bindings). This binding cannot be used under OS/2 since the registers cannot be accessed easily from a program. To solve this problem the OS/2 card services device driver provides a set of IOCtl functions for an application program to use to make card services requests. Rather than fill in registers with values, the application program fills in a structure and then uses the OS/2 function DosDevIOCtl to perform the card services function.

To use the IOCtl interface a program must first issue the OS/2 function DosOpen for the PCMCIA$ device to obtain a file handle to use for DosDevIOCtl. Afterwards the application program fills in a structure that contains all of the arguments that would normally be passed to card services via the register interface, and then calls DosDevIOCtl with a pointer to the structure as the parameter packet, Category 13, Function 4F. For more information on the DosXXXXX calls, see the on-line documentation files that are packaged with the OS/2 Toolkit. Figure 10-13 is a code excerpt from the file CSCALL.C demonstrating the DosOpen and DosDevIOCtl calls.

```
struct _PARMPACK
    {
       USHORT      Function;
       USHORT      Handle;
       ULONG       EventSemHandle;
       USHORT      ArgLength;
       CHAR        ArgPacket[256];
    } parmPacket;


    if (hFile == 0)
    {
       rc = DosOpen("PCMCIA$", &hFile,, 0L, FILE_NORMAL, FILE_OPEN,
                    OPEN_ACCESS_READWRITE | OPEN_SHARE_DENYNONE, 0L);
       if (rc != 0)
          return -1;
    }

    parmPacket.Function = Function;
    parmPacket.Handle   = Handle;
    if (Pointer)
       parmPacket.EventSemHandle = *(ULONG *)Pointer;
    else
       parmPacket.EventSemHandle = NULL;
    parmPacket.ArgLength = ArgLength;
    memcpy(parmPacket.ArgPacket, ArgPointer, ArgLength);
#ifdef OS2_32
    parmLen = 0;
    rc = DosDevIOCtl(hFile, 13, 0x4F, &parmPacket, ArgLength+10,
                       &parmLen, NULL, 0, NULL);
#else
    rc = DosDevIOCtl(&status, &parmPacket, 0x4F, 13, hFile);
#endif
    if (rc != 0)
       rc = parmPacket.Function;
    else
    {
       memcpy(ArgPointer, parmPacket.ArgPacket, ArgLength);
       if (RetHandle)
          *RetHandle = parmPacket.Handle;
    }

    return rc;
```

Figure 10-13: OS/2 DosOpen and DosDevIOCtl calls

CSINFW32

The final program in the CSINFO series is a Win32 application that works on Windows 95/98. It also has limited functionality on Windows NT 4.0 (there is no Card Services available, but PCMCIA.SYS has an undocumented DeviceIoControl that shows tuple data).

Just like all the other CSINFO programs, this one starts with a window that shows Card Service information. A sample window is shown in Figure 10-14.

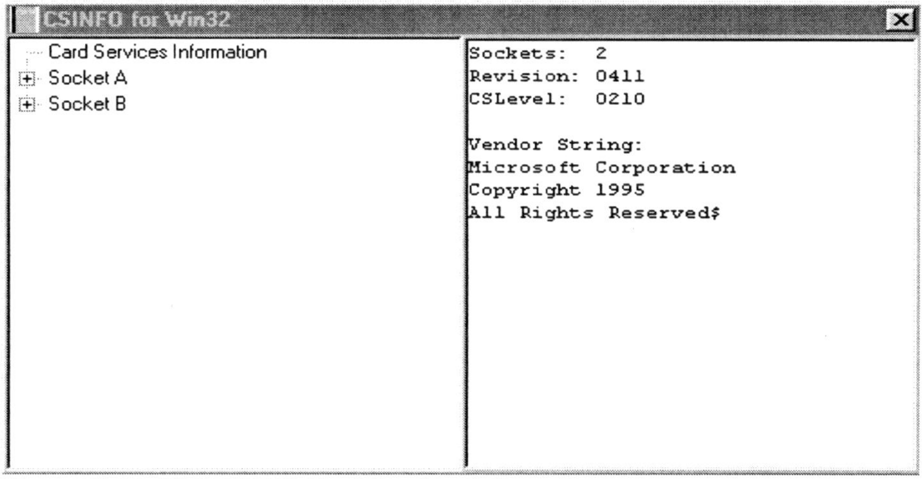

Figure 10-14: CWINFW32 Card Services Information

Expanding on a Socket will show entries for Card Status, Configuration Information, and Tuple Data. Selecting any one of these in the left window will cause the corresponding data to be displayed in the right window. Figure 10-15 shows the Configuration Information for a modem PC Card.

Expanding on Tuple Data shows a list of tuples on the PC Card. Selecting any tuple will cause the tuple data to display in the right window. Figure 10-16 shows the Level 1 Version/Product Information Tuple for the same modem PC Card.

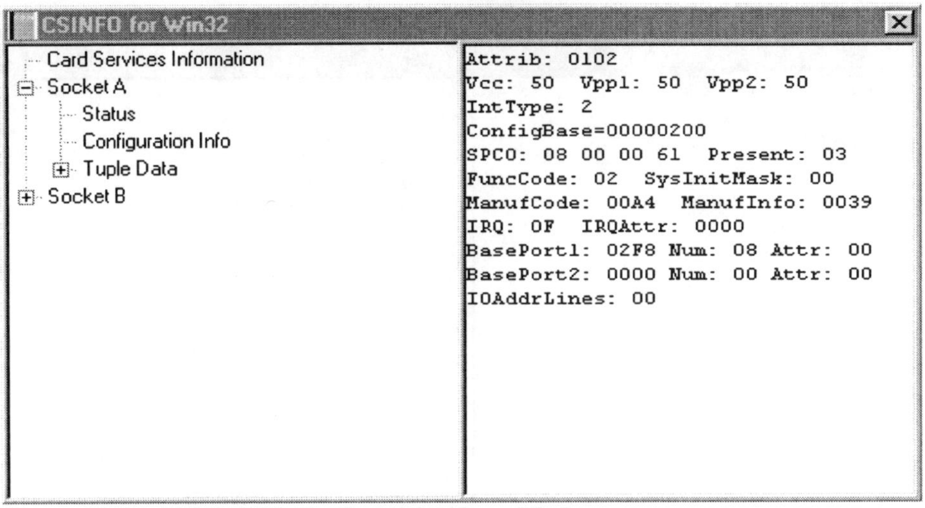

Figure 10-15: CSINFW32 Configuration for a Modem

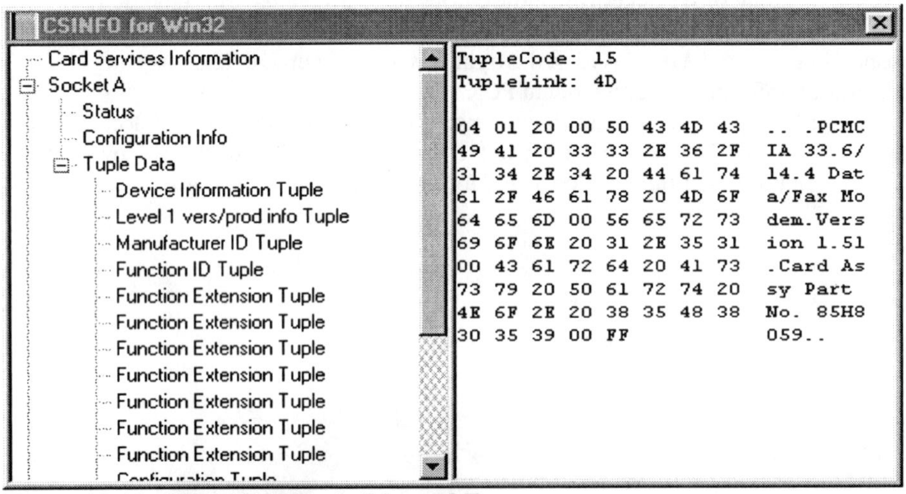

Figure 10-16: CSINFW32 Tuple List and Entry

Since Windows 95/98 only lets device drivers call Card Services, a driver had to be written for this program to work. The driver is called CSDRVR.VXD and must reside in the C:\WINDOWS\SYSTEM subdirectory. It provides applications a DeviceIoControl interface and makes Card Services calls for applications.

Card Services calls cannot be made until all drivers are loaded, therefore the first call must be made during the Init_Complete driver entry. The first call should always be PCCARD_Get_Version to make sure PCCARD.VXD is loaded. This is shown in Figure 10-17. A driver uses the VxdCall macro to make Card Services calls.

```
;*************************************************************************
*
;
;   CSDRVR_Init_Complete
;
;   DESCRIPTION:
;       This routine gets called at INIT_COMPLETE.  All static drivers
have
;       been loaded.  Check to see if PCCARD.VXD is loaded.  If not, its
an
;       error so return an error.
;
;*************************************************************************
*
BeginProc CSDRVR_Init_Complete

        Trace_Out       "CSDRVR: Init_Complete"

        VxdCall PCCARD_Get_Version
        jc      NoCS
        mov     CS_Present,1
        clc
NoCS:
        ret

EndProc   CSDRVR_Init_Complete
```

Figure 10-17: CSDRVR Init_Complete Entry

The assembler language code that makes the Card Services calls is shown in Figure 10-18. The bindings are documented in the Microsoft Windows 95 DDK and also in the PC Card Standard – Card Services Specification for 1995 or 1997.

```
BeginProc CSDRVR_CardServices

        pushad
        Trace_Out       "CSDRVR_CardServices"
        popad
;
;  Save ESI since it points to the DIOC Structure
        push    esi
;
;  Make sure CS is present.
        cmp     CS_Present,1
```

```
        je      CS_Found
        mov     CS_Return,R_GENERAL_FAILURE
        jmp     CS_Exit

UnsuppFunc:
        mov     CS_Return,R_UNSUPPORTED_FUNCTION
        jmp     CS_Exit

CS_Found:
;
;  Make sure we support this function.
;       int     3
        mov     edi,[esi].lpvInBuffer
        mov     ax,[edi].CSDRVR_Function
        mov     edi,OFFSET FunctionTable
        mov     ecx,FunctionTableLen
        repnz   scasb
        jnz     UnsuppFunc

        mov     edi,[esi].lpvInBuffer
        mov     dx,[edi].CSDRVR_Handle
        mov     cx,[edi].CSDRVR_ArgLength
        lea     ebx,[edi].CSDRVR_ArgPacket
        VxdCall PCCARD_Card_Services
        mov     CS_Return,ax

CS_Exit:
        pop     esi                     ; restore DIOC pointer
        mov     edi,[esi].lpvOutBuffer
        mov     ax,CS_Return
        mov     [edi],ax
        mov     edi,[esi].lpcbBytesReturned
        mov     DWord PTR [edi],2
        ret

EndProc   CSDRVR_CardServices
```

Figure 10-18: CSDRVR Card Services Function Call

This driver only supports a limited number of functions; only the functions that request information. This driver cannot request or release resources since that can only be done in a configuration handler. This was explained in Chapter 7.

The DeviceIoControl interface was designed similar to the OS/2 interface. A parameter packet contains the Card Services function, any pointers, and any data structure lengths. The W32_DEVICEIOCONTROL entry into the driver simply verifies the integrity of the data passed in and then calls CSDRVR_CardServices. Figure 10-19 shows the data structure defined for a C-program. On return from DeviceIoControl, the data parameter points to the Card Services return code.

```
struct _CSDRVR_Struc
    {
        USHORT   Function;
        USHORT   Handle;
        ULONG    Pointer;
        USHORT   ArgLength;
        UCHAR    ArgPacket[256];
    } CSDRVR_Struc;
```

Figure 10-19: CSDRVR Data Structure for DeviceIoControl Call

To make the DeviceIoControl calls, an application must first open the CSDRVR.VXD device using the Win32 **CreateFile** call. Afterwards, the application only has to fill in the CSDRVR_Struc with the proper Card Services data and then call **DeviceIoControl**. A code fragment is shown in Figure 10-20.

```
hFile = CreateFile("\\\\.\\CSDRVR.VXD", GENERIC_WRITE | GENERIC_READ, 0,
                    NULL, OPEN_EXISTING, FILE_FLAG_DELETE_ON_CLOSE, 0);

CSDRVR_Struc.Function = Function;
CSDRVR_Struc.Handle   = Handle;
CSDRVR_Struc.Pointer  = Pointer;
CSDRVR_Struc.ArgLength = ArgLength;
memcpy(CSDRVR_Struc.ArgPacket, ArgPointer, ArgLength);
rc = DeviceIoControl(hFile, 0x83E00001, &CSDRVR_Struc,
izeof(CSDRVR_Struc),
                      &CSRet, 2, &dwRet, NULL);
```

Figure 10-20: CSDRVR DeviceIoControl to call Card Services

On return from DeviceIoControl, the dwRet variable will contain the return code from Card Services.

Since Windows NT 4.0 does not have Card Services, another method had to be employed to get CSINFW32 to partially work. The device driver PCMCIA.SYS has an undocumented DeviceIoControl entry point that will read the CIS of a PC Card in a socket. Microsoft ships a utility program, PCMCMD.EXE, with Windows NT 4.0 that uses this undocumented DeviceIoControl. You can find PCMCMD.EXE in the \SUPPORT\DEBUG\I386 subdirectory of your Windows NT 4.0 CD-ROM. A code fragment below shows how to open the device driver and perform the DeviceIoControl:

```
//
//  Open up the PCMCIA device.
hPcmcia = CreateFile("\\\\.\\Pcmcia0", GENERIC_READ,
                     FILE_SHARE_READ, NULL, OPEN_EXISTING,
                     FILE_ATTRIBUTE_SYSTEM | FILE_FLAG_NO_BUFFERING,
                     NULL);
if (hPcmcia != INVALID_HANDLE_VALUE)
{
```

```
                    .
                    .
fNoErr = DeviceIoControl(hPcmcia, 0x42EE0L, &iSocket, 2,
                         pBuffer, 1024, &dwRet, NULL);
                    .
                    .
```

The *iSocket* parameter contains the socket number (0, 1, etc.) while the *pBuffer* parameter will receive the contents of the CIS for the card in the socket. If there is a card in a socket, the return value *fNoErr* will be TRUE. If there is a socket without a card inserted, the return value *fNoErr* will be FALSE and the Win32 function **GetLastError**() will return ERROR_GEN_FAILURE. If there is no socket at *iSocket*, the return value *fNoErr* will be FALSE and the Win32 function **GetLastError**() will have an error other than ERROR_GEN_FAILURE.

With this information, code was written to return data from a few Card Services calls. The code can retrieve the number of sockets, card status, and tuple data. A simulated Card Services was written for CSINFW32 to work on Windows NT 4.0. This simulated Card Services is made up of a daemon program, CSNTD.EXE, and a dynamic link library, CSCALLNT.DLL.

The daemon program allocates a shared memory area where it keeps card status. It then opens device \\\\.\\Pcmcia0 and looks for sockets with or without cards. If a card is in a socket, the CIS is read into the shared memory area. Finally, the daemon enters a loop where it checks periodically if a card has been inserted or removed and updates the shared memory accordingly.

The dynamic link library simply provides a Card Services-like interface into the shared memory area. When a process attaches to the DLL, the DLL opens the shared memory area and maps it to the process address space. Then, when a program makes any of the Card Services calls GET_CARDSERVICES_INFO, GET_STATUS, GET_FIRST_TUPLE, GET_NEXT_TUPLE, or GET_TUPLE_DATA the DLL will gather the data from the shared memory region and return it as if a real Card Services is present. Any other Card Services calls to the DLL result in the UNSUPPORTED_FUNCTION return value.

To run CSINFW32 under Windows NT 4.0, you must first start the daemon CSNTD. Then, make sure CSCALLNT.DLL is either in the current directory or in the system directory with other DLLs. Finally, you can start CSINFW32 to look at the CIS of any cards inserted in the system.

A Utility to Display Card Insertion/Removal

CARDMGR

This Windows utility program simply displays the Level 1 Version/Product Information Tuple when a card is inserted into a socket, or the word empty when a card is removed from a socket. A sample display from this program is shown in Figure 10-21.

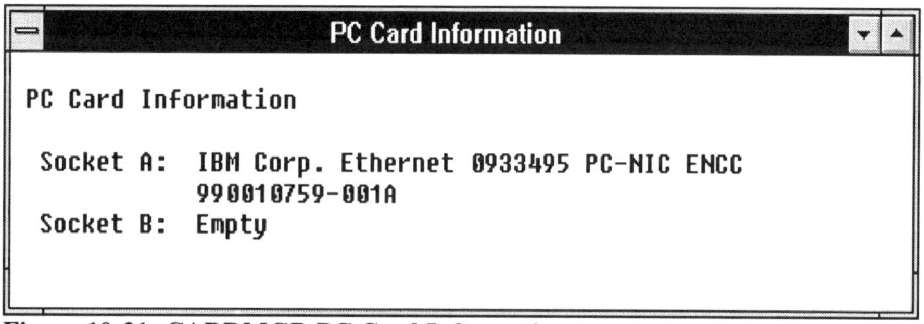

Figure 10-21: CARDMGR PC Card Information

There are two concepts demonstrated by this sample program. First, a Windows 3.1 application program must use DPMI services for coding a callback handler. Second, a Windows 3.1 application program can launch another program based on an event such as CARD_INSERTION. This sample program contains the code to perform the second function, but it is commented out so that the program remains a generic example, not performing a specific function.

Once again, since card services runs in a Virtual-86 mode and a Windows application program runs in protect mode, the services of DPMI are needed to cross the boundaries of the modes. In the previous sample code there was only a one-way call — from protect mode to real mode to perform a card services function. Now, with a callback handler, the call is made the other way — from real mode to protect mode when card services sends events to a callback handler. Card services runs in real mode while the application program callback handler runs in protect mode.

To receive card services events, a program must register a callback handler with a CS **RegisterClient** request. However, a problem exists in that the callback handler will be a protect mode subroutine, while card services is expecting a real mode address. To solve this problem the DPMI function *Allocate Real Mode Callback Address* is used to create a real mode address for the protect mode callback handler address. This DPMI function takes two arguments: the SELECTOR:OFFSET of the protect mode callback handler, and the SELECTOR:OFFSET of a data structure that contains the real mode register values passed to the callback handler. On return, the CX:DX registers contain the SEGMENT:OFFSET of the real mode callback address. The code that issues the DPMI request is shown in Figure 10-22.

```
case  WM_CREATE:
//  Use DPMI to allocate a real mode address for the
//  callback handler.
    segread(&sregs);
    inregs.x.ax = 0x0303;
    p = &ProtCSCallback;
    sregs.ds    = FP_SEG(p);
    inregs.x.si = FP_OFF(p);
    p = &rRegs;
    sregs.es    = FP_SEG(p);
    inregs.x.di = FP_OFF(p);
    int86x(0x31, &inregs, &outregs, &sregs);
    if (outregs.x.cflag) {
       MessageBox(HWND_DESKTOP, "DPMI Allocate Real Mode Callback
               Address failed.", NULL,MB_OK | MB_ICONSTOP);
       PostQuitMessage(0);
    }
    else
    {
       FP_SEG(RealCSCallback) = outregs.x.cx;
       FP_OFF(RealCSCallback) = outregs.x.dx;
    }
```

Figure 10-22: DOS/Windows Code to Issue a DPMI Request

After a real mode address is obtained for the protect mode callback handler, a memory segment below the 1M address is allocated to hold the arguments for the **RegisterClient** request. The argument packet structure is filled in with the standard arguments (Attributes, EventMask, and Version). Then the request is made to card services with the real mode callback handler address, not the protect mode address. After the call completes, the memory segment used for the argument packet is freed. Figure 10-23 demonstrates this procedure.

```
//  Allocate a DOS memory segment for the RegisterClient call.

CSBuffer = GlobalDosAlloc(256);
BufferSeg = HIWORD(CSBuffer);
BufferSel = LOWORD(CSBuffer);

fpRegClient = MAKELP(BufferSel, 0);
fpRegClient->Attributes = RC_ATTR_IO_CLIENT |
                          RC_ATTR_CARD_INSERT_SHARED |
                          RC_ATTR_CARD_INSERT_EXCL;
fpRegClient->EventMask = RC_EVENT_CD_CHANGE;
fpRegClient->Version = 0x0201;
rc = CardServices(REGISTER_CLIENT, 0, RealCSCallback, 14,
```

```
                    MAKELP(BufferSeg, 0), &Handle);
if (rc != 0)
{
   MessageBox(HWND_DESKTOP, "Cannot RegisterClient.", NULL,
              MB_OK | MB_ICONSTOP);
   PostQuitMessage(0);
}

//  Free the DOS memory segment.
GlobalDosFree(BufferSel);
```

Figure 10-23: DOS/Windows RegisterClient Source Code

The protect mode callback handler is entered with DS:SI pointing to the caller's stack and ES:DI pointing to the real mode register structure mentioned earlier. The structure ES:DI points to contains the register values a standard real mode callback would receive: AL=Event, CX=Socket, an so on. It is the responsibility of this routine to exit with an IRET with the address of the real mode register structure in ES:DI and any return register values modified within the structure ES:DI points to. Also, the callback routine must extract the return address from the real mode stack and move it into the CS:IP fields of the real mode register structure. After the callback handler sets up the return registers and stack, it simply posts an event corresponding to the card services event received to the event queue of the main program and exits. The event posted is the Windows User Message offset WM_USER added to the card services event. The word parameter is the socket value for which the event occurred. The entire callback handler is shown in Figure 10-24.

```
void interrupt far ProtCSCallback(WORD es, WORD ds, WORD di, WORD si,
                                  WORD bp, WORD sp, WORD bx, WORD dx,
                                  WORD cx, WORD ax)
{
 WORD far        *pStack;
 REALREGS far    *pRegs;

 // On entry, DS:SI points to caller's stack.
 //           ES:DI points to registers set.
 FP_SEG(pStack) = ds;
 FP_OFF(pStack) = si;
 FP_SEG(pRegs)  = es;
 FP_OFF(pRegs)  = di;

 //  Set DOS return address in the return registers.
 pRegs->RealIP = *(WORD far *)pStack;
 pRegs->RealCS = *(WORD far *)(pStack+1);
 pRegs->RealSP += 4;

 // Send the event to the main loop; the socket is in the WORD param.
 PostMessage(hwndMain, WM_USER+(pRegs->regs.w.RealAX & 0x00FF),
                    pRegs->regs.w.RealCX, 0);

 // Exit with return code in AX and reset CF.
 pRegs->regs.w.RealAX = 0;
 pRegs->RealFL &= 0xFFFE;
}
```

Figure 10-24: DOS/Windows Callback Handler

The main program only responds to two card services events: CARD_INSERTION and CARD_REMOVAL. This sample program redefines the events as Windows message loop events WM_CARD_INSERTION and WM_CARD_REMOVAL. Instructions in the insertion event loop simply retrieve the PC Card's Level 1 Version/Product Information Tuple, save it in an array, then invalidate the window rectangle so that a WM_PAINT message is issued to display the new information. The processing for the removal event simply changes the string to empty and invalidates the window rectangle. Extending this example to support other events such as INSERTION_REQUEST, INSERTION_COMPLETE, EJECTION_REQUEST, and EJECTION_COMPLETE is simple. By adding support for these events, security programs could be implemented on systems that support locking mechanisms restricting PC Card insertion and removal through the use of a password.

When the program terminates, the callback handler is deregistered and the callback handler real mode address is released. This is a very important order to follow. If the real mode address is released before the callback handler is deregistered, and a card services event is posted, the address is no longer valid and may cause system integrity problems. Always remember to deregister the client first. Real mode addresses must be released since there are only 16 per DPMI client and they are a valuable system resource.

The second concept this program demonstrates is how an application program can be launched as the result of a CARD_INSERTION event. The code is commented out so that the sample program remains generic. In the sample code under the WM_CARD_INSERTION event, just before exiting, the code checks if the card inserted is the AT&T Paradyne KeepInTouch modem. If it is, the Windows program TERMINAL.EXE is launched. Even though this is only two lines of code the concept is very powerful. Imagine an application launching various other programs based on the function identification tuple. For example, communication programs launching as the result of a modem or serial port PC Card being inserted, or a LAN application launching when a LAN PC Card is inserted. An .INI file can be maintained to keep a profile of applications launched when a particular card, or group of cards that perform a particular function, is inserted.

PCCARDPM

This is the OS/2 Presentation Manager version of CARDMGR. It performs the same function, namely, to display the Level 1 Version/Product Information Tuple of a card when it is inserted into a socket, or *empty* if a card is removed from a socket. Figure 10-25 shows a sample display for a computer that has an Ethernet card in the first socket and a Modem card in the second socket.

Figure 10-25: PCCARDPM PC Card Information

The main concept illustrated by this sample program is how a callback handler is coded under OS/2. Since card services is implemented as a Ring-0 device driver and an application program callback handler runs with a Ring-3 privilege, a problem exists: a Ring-0 driver cannot call a Ring-3 application. The solution is to use an event semaphore. An event semaphore can be used by both device drivers and application programs. Rather than register a callback handler with the card services **RegisterClient** request, the application program creates an event semaphore and creates a thread that waits for the events to be posted, then registers the event semaphore with card services. Figure 10-26 shows the code that performs this function.

```
case   WM_CREATE:
       //  Create an event semaphore.
       rc = DosCreateEventSem("\\sem32\\regcli", &hevRegClient, 0,
             FALSE);

       //  Start the callback thread.
       rc = DosCreateThread(&tidCallback, CallbackThread, hwnd,
                            0, 4096);

       //  Register a semaphore with card services.
       rcl.Attributes = RC_ATTR_IO_CLIENT | RC_ATTR_CARD_INSERT_SHARED |
                           RC_ATTR_CARD_INSERT_EXCL;
       rcl.EventMask = RC_EVENT_CD_CHANGE;
       rcl.Version   = 0x0201;
       rc = CardServices(REGISTER_CLIENT,
                         0,
                         &hevRegClient,
                         14,
                         &rcl, &Handle);
       break;
```

Figure 10-26: OS/2 Semaphore and Thread Creation for the RegisterClient Call

The callback thread issues the OS/2 call DosWaitEventSem to wait for the event semaphore to be posted. Whenever a card services event occurs, the semaphore is posted by the PCMCIA.SYS (card services) device driver. When an event is posted, the callback thread is awakened. The thread then uses the card services request **VendorSpecific** to retrieve the event that caused the thread to awaken. By the time the thread is awakened, several card services events may have occurred, so it is the responsibility of the thread to continuously call **VendorSpecific** until all events have been retrieved. As each event is retrieved a message is posted to the main window queue that corresponds to the event. Just like the Windows program, the User Offset message is added to the card services event to form an OS/2 PM version of the event. CARD_INSERTION becomes WM_CARD_INSERTION and CARD_REMOVAL becomes WM_CARD_REMOVAL. The socket value is posted as the first parameter. After all card services events have been consumed from the queue, the application program issues the DosResetEventSem call to clear the semaphore and then goes back into waiting for more events with DosWaitEventSem. The complete callback thread is shown in Figure 10-27.

```
void CallbackThread(HWND hwnd)
{
    ULONG     ulPostCount;
    int       rc;

    struct _VS
    {
        unsigned short     InfoLen;
        unsigned char      FuncCode;
        unsigned char      SubFunc;
        unsigned short     Handle;
        unsigned char      Event;
        unsigned short     Socket;
        unsigned short     Info;
        unsigned short     Misc;
    } vs;


    while (TRUE)
    {
       rc = DosWaitEventSem(hevRegClient,SEM_INDEFINITE_WAIT);

       //  Get the event.
       while (rc == 0)
       {
          vs.InfoLen = sizeof(vs);
          vs.FuncCode = 2;
          vs.SubFunc  = 1;
          vs.Handle   = Handle;
          rc = CardServices(VENDOR_SPECIFIC, 0, NULL, 13, &vs,
               NULL);
          WinPostMsg(hwnd, WM_USER+vs.Event, vs.Socket, 0);
       }

       rc = DosResetEventSem(hevRegClient, &ulPostCount);
    }
}
```

Figure 10-27: OS/2 Event Handling

The WM_CARD_INSERTION event in the main program simply reads the PC Card's Level 1 Version/Product Information Tuple and saves it for later display. It then invalidates the window so that a WM_PAINT is generated to display the new data. The WM_CARD_REMOVAL event replaces the above information with the word empty and also invalidates the window. As in the Windows program, when this program terminates it must deregister the client, terminate the callback thread, and then close the event semaphore. Failure to deregister the client will cause the semaphore to still be owned by the device driver and any subsequent attempts to start the program again will cause a failure upon attempting to create the semaphore again. Terminating the thread before deregistering the client could cause unpredictable results if a card services event arrives.

In this sample program, the code is remarked out. However, the code could be used in some interesting ways. When uncommented and compiled, it performs a check to determine if the PC Card inserted is a Token-Ring card. If so, it launches the LAN Services program LOGON.EXE to log the user onto the LAN. However, it could be modified to launch any other desired application, such as a modem application if a modem card is inserted, or a virus check program if a hard disk card is inserted. The possibilities are endless.

A Utility That Shows Application Notifications

Windows 95/98/CE and, from Beta literature, Windows NT 5.0, applications can receive a broadcast message when devices are added or removed from the system. The message is WM_DEVICECHANGE and can only be received in the message loop of a Win32 application. This message is broadcast when a PC Card is inserted, queried for removal, and finally removed from the system. It behaves similarly to a call back handler.

In a Win32 program message loop there are two parameters passed in with the message: wParam and lParam. For the WM_DEVICECHANGE message the wParam is an integer value that represents the event while the lParam is a pointer to a structure with more information about the event. Figure 10-28 shows several events and device types.

Event	Description
DBT_DEVICEARRIVAL	A device has been added to the system.
DBT_DEVICEQUERYREMOVE	A user wishes to remove a device from the system. For example, the user selected the PC Card icon and wants to "stop" using the card.
DBT_DEVICEQUERYREMOVEFAILED	Another Win32 application returned "FALSE" to a DBT_DEVICEQUERYREMOVE. The device cannot be removed.
DBT_DEVICEREMOVEPENDING	All Win32 applications returned "TRUE" to a DBT_DEVICEQUERYREMOVE.
DBT_DEVICEREMOVECOMPLETE	The device has been removed from the system.

Type	Description
DBT_DEVTYP_DEVNODE	A new device node has been added to the hardware tree. Not available on Windows CE.
DBT_DEVTYP_VOLUME	A new hard drive has been added to the system. One example is an ATA PC Card inserted or removed.
DBT_DEVTYP_PORT	A new COM port has been added to the system.
DBT_DEVTYP_NET	A network has been added.

Figure 10-28: WM_DEVICECHANGE Events and Types

When a PC Card is inserted in a Windows 95/98 system, several WM_DEVICECHANGE messages are generated depending on the type of card. A modem PC Card is the simplest case since only two WM_DEVICECHANGE messages are sent. The first is a DBT_DEVICEARRIVAL event for the COM port added to the system, DBT_DEVTYP_PORT. The second is a DBT_DEVICEARRIVAL event for the device node added to the hardware tree, DBT_DEVTYP_DEVNODE. Figure 10-29 shows a sample display for a modem added to a system.

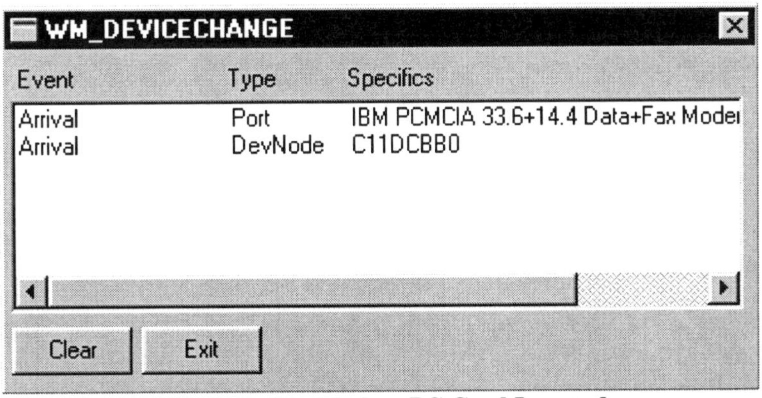

Figure 10-29: Windows 95 - Modem PC Card Inserted

The DBT_DEVTYP_PORT type includes the string that has the name of the modem. This is displayed in the "Specifics" column. The DBT_DEVTYP_DEVNODE contains the binary device node that is added to the hardware tree. This value is formatted and displayed in the "Specifics" column, too.

Even more information can be gathered with the device node. There is an area in the registry called the Dynamic Data area and contains the list of device nodes that make up the hardware tree. It is found at HKEY_DYN_DATA\Config Manager\Enum. Each subkey is a device node. Given a device node, a programmer can use the Win32 registry calls to gather more information about a PC Card as it is inserted to or removed from the system. Figure 10-30 shows a sample registry dynamic device area. The selected device node is for an Ethernet PC Card.

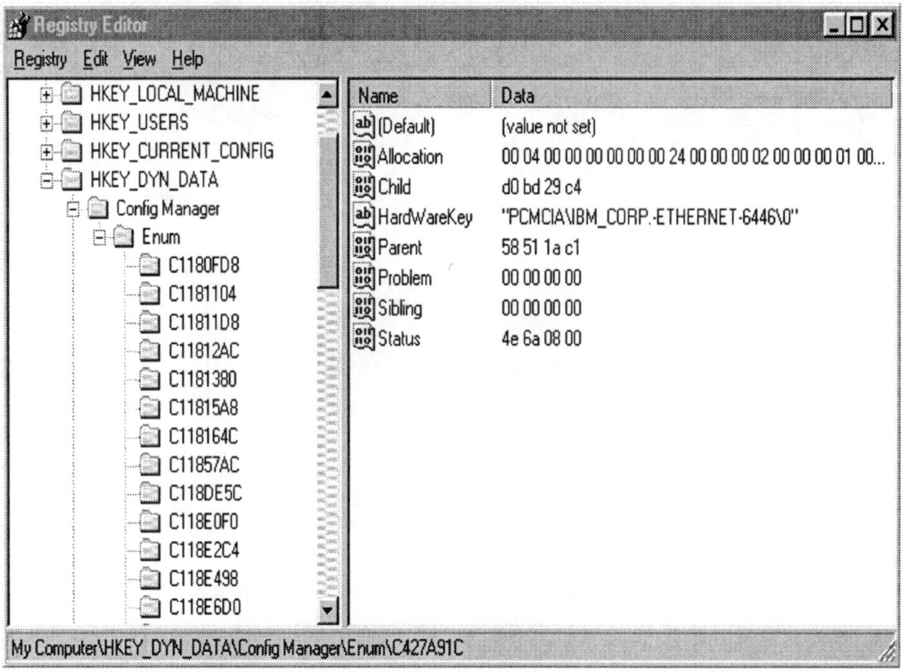

Figure 10-30: Windows 95 Dynamic Data Registry Key

The Allocation subkey contains the values used to configure the PC Card. The data includes the I/O port range, IRQ, memory allocation, and values used in the RequestConfiguration call. Refer to the Windows 95 Device Driver Kit for more information on the Configuration Manager calls used to configure a device. The HardWareKey can be used to access other areas of the registry to gather information about the driver and type of driver.

Under Windows CE there is no DBT_DEVTYP_DEVNODE type. Therefore, when a PC Card is inserted or removed, only the other device type messages will be received. Figure 10-31 shows the display on an Ericsson MC12 HPC when an Ethernet PC Card is inserted.

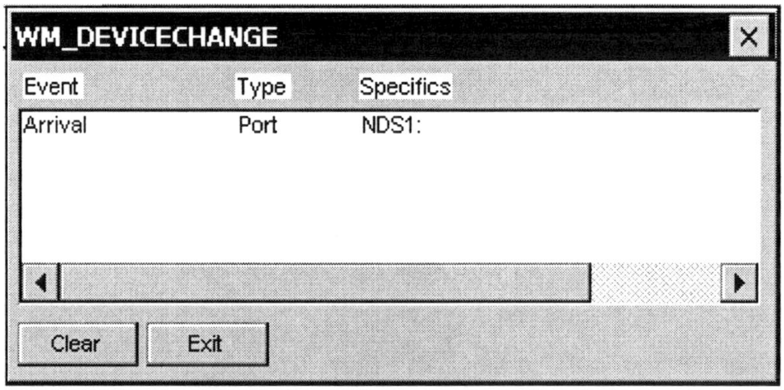

Figure 10-31: Windows CE - Ethernet PC Card Inserted

The code written for this sample program is relatively straightforward. A main window is created and made visible. The message loop associated with the window simply has a WM_DEVICECHANGE case that formats the data appropriately and sends it to the window. A code fragment is shown in Figure 10-32.

```
LRESULT CALLBACK WndProc (HWND hwnd, UINT message, WPARAM wParam, LPARAM
                               lParam)

{
                         .
                         .

    struct _DEV_BROADCAST_HEADER     *pDBHeader;
    DEV_BROADCAST_OEM                *pDBOem;
    DEV_BROADCAST_DEVNODE            *pDBDevNode;
    DEV_BROADCAST_VOLUME             *pDBVolume;
    DEV_BROADCAST_PORT               *pDBPort;
    DEV_BROADCAST_NET                *pDBNet;

                         .
                         .

    switch (message)
    {

                         .
                         .
       case WM_DEVICECHANGE:
            if ((wParam >= DBT_DEVICEARRIVAL) && (wParam <=
                               DBT_DEVICETYPESPECIFIC))
            {
               //
               //  Get the device event.
               lstrcpy(szLine, szEvent[wParam-DBT_DEVICEARRIVAL]);
```

```
//
// Get the device type.
pDBHeader = (struct _DEV_BROADCAST_HEADER *)lParam;
lstrcat(szLine, TEXT("\t"));
if (pDBHeader->dbcd_devicetype > DBT_DEVTYP_NET)
   lstrcat(szLine, TEXT("Unknown"));
else
   lstrcat(szLine, szType[pDBHeader->dbcd_devicetype]);

//
// Parse out information based on the device type.
switch (pDBHeader->dbcd_devicetype)
{
   case DBT_DEVTYP_OEM:
        pDBOem = (DEV_BROADCAST_OEM *)lParam;
        wsprintf(szTemp, TEXT("\tid=%X suppfunc=%X"),
                 pDBOem->dbco_identifier,
                 pDBOem->dbco_suppfunc);
        lstrcat(szLine, szTemp);
        break;

   case DBT_DEVTYP_DEVNODE:
        pDBDevNode = (DEV_BROADCAST_DEVNODE *)lParam;
        wsprintf(szTemp, TEXT("\t%8.8lX"),
                      pDBDevNode->dbcd_devnode);
        lstrcat(szLine, szTemp);
        break;

   case DBT_DEVTYP_VOLUME:
        pDBVolume = (DEV_BROADCAST_VOLUME *)lParam;
        wsprintf(szTemp, TEXT("\tunit=%X flags=%X"),
                 pDBVolume->dbcv_unitmask,
                 pDBVolume->dbcv_flags);
        lstrcat(szLine, szTemp);
        break;

   case DBT_DEVTYP_PORT:
        pDBPort = (DEV_BROADCAST_PORT *)lParam;
        lstrcat(szLine, TEXT("\t"));
        lstrcat(szLine, pDBPort->dbcp_name);
        break;

   case DBT_DEVTYP_NET:
        pDBNet = (DEV_BROADCAST_NET *)lParam;
        wsprintf(szTemp, TEXT("\tres=%X flags=%X"),
                 pDBNet->dbcn_resource,
                 pDBNet->dbcn_flags);
        lstrcat(szLine, szTemp);
        break;
}

//
// Add the line to the listbox.
ListBox_AddString(hwndList, szLine);
```

```
        }
        break;
                    .
                    .
```

Figure 10-32: DEVCHG Window Loop

A Modem Detecting Utility

UARTTYPE

This utility program will either search all sockets or a specified socket for a modem card and determine the UART type based on the function extension tuple. From the DOS or OS/2 command prompt, enter UARTTYPE to search all sockets for a modem card. Enter UARTTYPE socket, where socket is a value from A-H if the modem card is known to be in a specific socket. Entering any other value will cause the following to be displayed:

```
Usage: uarttype <socket>
        <socket> is optional and is A-H.
                 By labeling sockets A-H there is no confusion
                 between card services 2.0 which labels sockets
                 starting with 1 and card services 2.1 which
                 labels sockets starting with 0.  If not specified,
                 uarttype loops over all available sockets looking
                 for a modem and deterring the UART type.
```

The key concept shown in this program is that specific tuples can be scanned to determine the type of card and its capabilities. The function identification tuple, if present on a card, contains information about how the card functions. A partial list of functions includes memory, serial port, modem, parallel port, network LAN, and SCSI card. Refer to the PC Card Standard for a complete list of functions.

Following this tuple are usually the function extension tuples. For serial ports or modems these tuples contain information such as the type of UART (8250, 16450, or 16550), number of stop bits supported, parity supported, flow control methods, data compression protocols, and so on. The complete list of function extensions is very long and takes up several pages in the PC Card Standard. This program simply looks for the function identification tuple, checks if the card is a modem card, loops over all function extension tuples searching for the extension that contains the UART type, and displays the UART type along with a string from the Level 1 Version/Product Information Tuple.

Debugging Tips and Techniques

Debugging card services client applications is similar to debugging any other application program; any debugger can be used. Since these sample programs were built using Microsoft C, IBM C Set++ for OS/2, and Microsoft Macro Assembler, the corresponding debuggers were used to debug the programs, namely, CodeView (including CodeView for Windows) and IPMD for OS/2. Well-behaved applications should examine the card services return codes and act appropriately. These sample programs have minimal error handling since they are a foundation for readers to modify and use as a learning tool. For example, they could be modified so that a DOS or full-screen OS/2 program could display an error if a card services request returns in failure. Likewise, a Windows or OS/2 PM program could pop up a message box with the card services error code.

Because these programs do not actually configure or manage PC Cards, they do not request resources from card services. Once a program endeavors to configure a card, it may be necessary to acquire resources as well as interrogating the PC Card registers to ensure that they are set correctly. The programmer must understand how the PC Card operates and how it interfaces to the computer. For example, the Intel 82365sl PC Card adapter interfaces via two I/P ports, 0x3E0 and 0x3E1. If a program configures a card with **RequestIO** to have four I/O ports starting at 0xA20 and the programmer wants to make sure the I/O range was successfully set, from the CodeView debugger command line, the programmer could enter:

```
>o 0x3e0 8
>i 0x3e1
```

to see the low start byte of the I/O address. The port 0x3E0 is the PC Card adapter index register address; the value written, eight, represent the adapter register the programmer wants to look at. Any PC Card adapter register can be written. In this example the value eight is the low start byte of the I/O address. To see the high byte, write the value nine. The port 0x3E1 is the data I/O address. Values read from or written to this port are actually read from (>I 0x3e1) or written to the PC Card adapter register specified in the out instruction to port 0x3E0 (>o 0x3e0 8). This example assumes the card is in the first socket supported by the controller. If the card was successfully configured with the **RequestConfiguration** request, the programmer would expect to see the following sequence. The commands appearing in **boldface** indicate the commands entered by the programmer, the nonbold entries represent the responses from the in (>I) commands.

>o **0x3e0 8**
>i 0x3e1
>20
>o **0x3e0 9**

>i 0x3e1
>0a

From the CodeView debugger, and from the DOS debugger DEBUG, a programmer can issue various IN and OUT instructions to these two ports to verify that a card is configured properly. For more information on the Intel 82365sl PC Card adapter refer to the Intel document *82365sl PC Card Interface Controller (PCIC)*.

To access PC Card adapters from other vendors, the programmer should obtain a hardware/software specification from the corresponding vendor. Generally, utility applications rarely require this level of debugging. On the other hand, when it comes to debugging a device driver or a new kind of PC Card adapter, the IN and OUT instructions and hardware/software specifications are usually mandatory, as shown in the chapters that discuss writing card services client device drivers.

A Socket Controller Examination Tool

When you are developing software for a PC Card, it is important to know that the hardware has been configured properly and the resources (I/O ports, IRQ, and Memory Windows) are configured as desired.

A PCIC software tool is used for this purpose. It gives you the settings of the Socket Controller that sits between the PC Card and the internal system bus. This allows you to tell what resources are enabled for a PC Card . There is a PCIC software tool for DOS, OS/2, Windows 95/98 and Windows NT. DOSPCIC is for a DOS system. PMPCIC is for an OS/2 system. WinPCIC is used for both Windows 95/98 and Windows NT. PCIC stands for PC Card Interface Controller. This is the original name that Intel gave to the 82365SL socket controller. These initials have become synonymous with the socket controller and are used to refer to it.

The PCIC software tools display the registers on a per socket basis in a machine. Typically, there are two sockets in a machine and it allows you to select between them. The PCIC software tool assumes that you are using an Intel 82365 or compatible socket controller in your machine. This is the standard socket controller type for most PC Card systems. This tool does not support the DataBook TCIC socket controller. There are 40H (64) registers for each socket. Socket A starts at register 0 and extends to register 3FH. Socket B starts at register 40H and extends to 7FH.

To use this tool effectively, it is necessary to have some knowledge of the hardware in a PC Card system. Here is the basic layout of a PC Card based system:

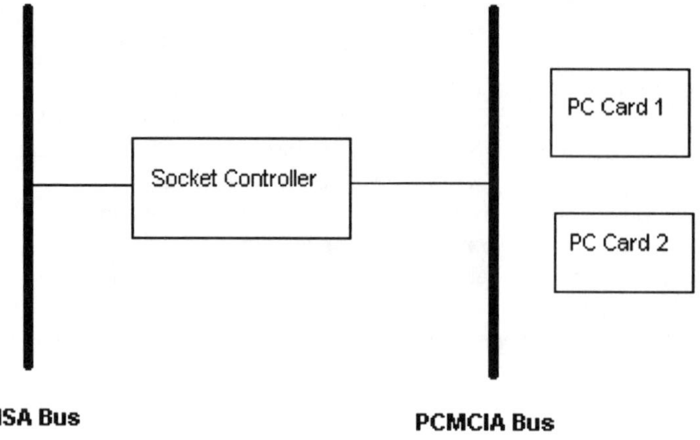

The most important thing to note is that the socket controller is a gate or bridge between two different buses in a machine. A bus contains the address, data, and control lines for various devices in a system. The socket controller bridges the machine's internal bus and PC Card bus and controls any signal, timing, or power differences between the two busses. Before any power gets to a PC Card, the socket controller must be enabled. This is done by software that writes to the registers of the socket controller and configures it. This can be done by a dedicated enabler as in some DOS systems or by Card and Socket Services. Socket Services is the software that actually writes to the hardware socket controller in most modern systems including Windows 95.

Standard Information provided by the PCIC Tools

It is recommended that you obtain the hardware specifications for the socket controller in any system you are developing software for. There are many different makers of socket controllers and while most are Intel 82365 compatible, manufacturers have extended the register definitions introducing incompatibilities. These registers have individual bit definitions and it is important that you are aware of the bit settings and what they mean. Most registers can be written to change their settings if you desire.

The DOSPCIC program prompts the user for the socket that information is desired from and dumps the register contents to the screen. This information can be directed to a file if desired. Figure 10-33 shows a sample output from the DOSPCIC program. Socket 1 was selected; the PC Card inserted in the socket requires one I/O port range, one IRQ, one attribute memory window, and one common memory window. To change any bit values, a debugger such as DEBUG could be used. This program does not allow any keyboard input to change the bit values.

```
General Setup Registers
  40 ID/REV         83  Memory && I/O Supported;  PCIC Rev=3
  41 I/F STATUS     7F  !GPI;  PWR;  RDY;  WP;  IN;  Bat Good
  42 PWR/RESET      91  PWR;  Vpp1_ENO
  44 CRD STS CHG    00  !GPI_CHG;  !CD_CHG;  !RDY_CHG;  !BAT_DEAD
  46 ADRS WND ENAB  43  MEMCS16# -> A23-A17
  47 IO CONTROL     0B  1 MORE WS;  > 0 WS;  IOIS16#;  16-BIT
  56 CD/GEN         C0  16-BIT DLY
  5E GLOB CTRL      00  !PWR DOWN
IRQ Registers
  43 INTR/GEN       79  !RS;  IO;  !INTR#;  PC-CARD IRQ=9
  45 CSC INTR CNFG  00  CSC IRQ=0;  STSCHG INTR DIS
IO Registers
      Window Start Stop
  48 *I/O 0  0120  013F  1 MORE WS;  > 0 WS;  IOIS16#;  16-BIT
  4C  I/O 1  FFFF  FFFF  0 MORE WS;  > 0 WS;  DATA SIZE;  8-BIT
Memory Registers
      Window     Start Stop  Offset
  50 *MEMORY 0  00CA  C0CA  7F36  8-BIT;  > 0 WS;  AWS=3;  !WP;  ATTRIB
  58 *MEMORY 1  80CC  C0CF  3F45  16-BIT;  > 0 WS;  AWS=3;  !WP;  COMMON
  60  MEMORY 2  0000  0000  7F50  8-BIT;  > 0 WS;  AWS=0;  !WP;  ATTRIB
  68  MEMORY 3  0FFF  0FFF  0000  8-BIT;  > 0 WS;  AWS=0;  !WP;  COMMON
  70  MEMORY 4  0FFF  0FFF  0000  8-BIT;  > 0 WS;  AWS=0;  !WP;  COMMON

Enter a socket number or press ENTER to quit:
```

Figure 10-33: DOSPCIC Output

WinPCIC and PMPCIC provide a GUI interface that allows a user to select a socket and display information about the socket. The examples below show WinPCIC as the example program but PMPCIC functions the same way.

Without going into each bit definition, here is the information WinPCIC will provide you that will help you the most:

1. Has the PC Card been detected by the system?
2. Has power been applied to the PC Card?
3. What is the IRQ setting for the PC Card?
4. Are any I/O port windows enabled and what are the settings?
5. Are any memory windows enabled and what are the settings?
6. How are CardBus PC Card settings determined?

Question 1: Has the PC Card been detected by the system?

There are two hardware control lines that a PC Card must have. These are CD1 and CD2. When a PC Card is inserted into a socket, these lines pull the corresponding socket controller lines to ground. The socket controller now should detect the presence of the PC Card. This can be determined by looking at the I/F Status register of the socket controller on the first tab of the tool. The status string should have the word "IN" shown for this register.

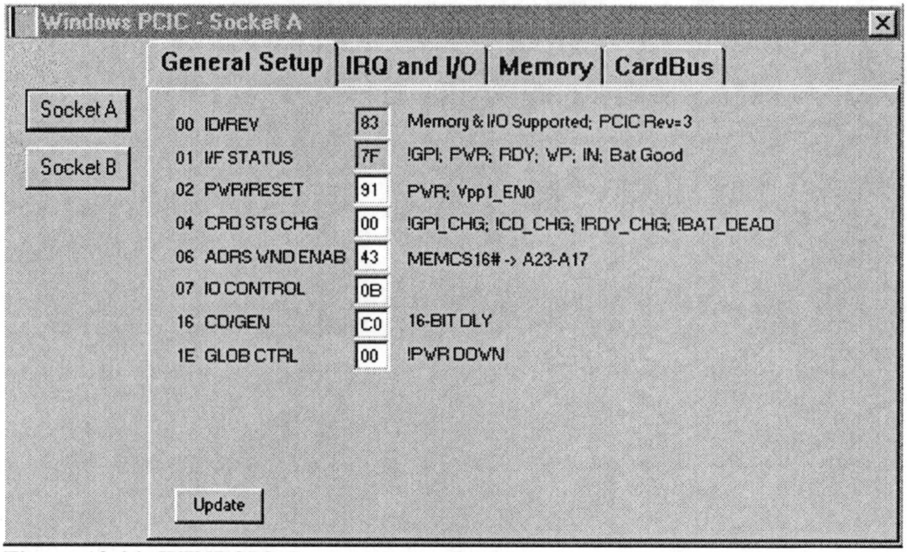

Figure 10-34: WINPCIC General Setup Registers

Question 2: Has power been applied to the PC Card?

After a PC Card is detected, to determine if power has been applied to the PC Card, look at the I/F Status register string again. If you see the word "PWR", power has been applied to the PC Card. See Figure 10-34 above.

Question 3: What is the IRQ setting for the PC Card?

There is only one interrupt line coming from a PC Card. The socket controller redirects this line to the system IRQ line set in the socket controller. By selecting the tab "IRQ and I/O", this setting can be determined by the INTR/GEN CNTL (Interrupt and general control) register. The IRQ is determined by the lower nibble bit definitions. In register CSC INTR CNFG (Card Status change, interrupt), you can determine whether card insertions or removals are reported by an interrupt or polling mechanism. In the example in Figure 10-35, the socket register must be polled to determine if a card's status has been changed.

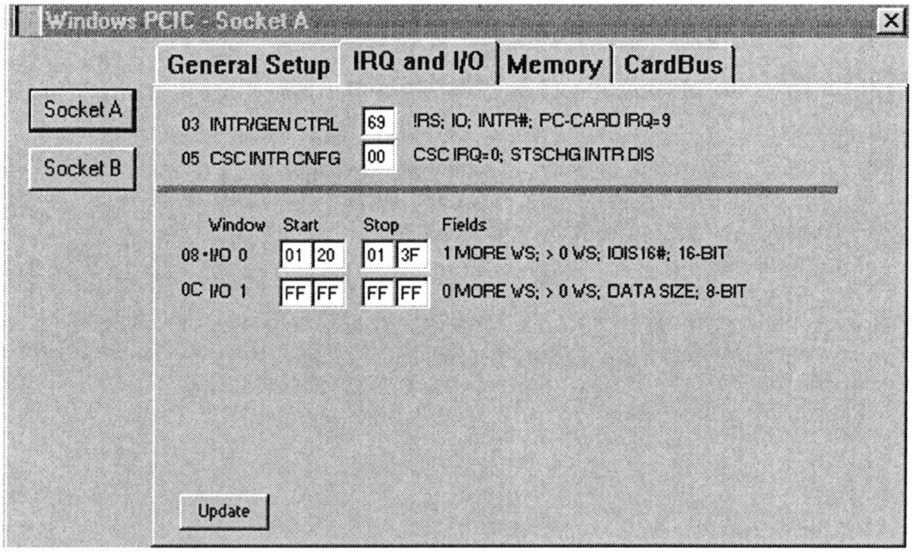

Figure 10-35: WINPCIC IRQ and I/O Registers

Question 4: Are any I/O port windows enabled and what are the settings?

There are usually two I/O port windows available to a PC Card in a socket. By selecting the tab "IRQ and I/O", these settings can be examined. When an I/O port window is enabled, an asterisk will appear between the register number and it's label. I/O ports can be 8 bits wide or 16 bits wide. A PC Card can also signal the socket controller when an I/O port access is 16 bits wide via the IOIS16 bit. The number of wait states for an I/O cycle can be altered by a bit setting. See Figure 10-35 above.

Question 5: Are any memory windows enabled and what are the settings?

There are usually five memory windows available to a PC Card in a socket. By selecting the tab "Memory", these settings can be examined. When a memory window is enabled, an asterisk will appear between the register number and it's label. Memory windows can be 8 bits or 16 bits wide. Memory windows can be for common memory or attribute memory. Multiple wait states can be set for memory windows.

Memory window registers allow you to set address bits 12 through 23 of a physical address only. This leaves a minimum memory window of 4K. In the example in Figure 10-36 below, there is an Attribute memory window configured in register 10 (Memory 0). This is indicated by the "ATTRIB" word on the status line. It is 8 bits wide with 3 additional wait states added to the memory access bus cycle. This is indicated on the status line as "8-bit" and "AWS=3". The starting address is D0000H in the machine's address space. The stop address or ending address would be DOFFFH. This is the memory range or window that the machine would use to access the attribute memory of the PC Card. The Offset registers allow an offset to be added to a memory window address. This offset can be positive or negative (2's complement number). If the incoming memory access is within the memory window defined by the Start and Stop registers, the memory address is added to the Offset registers value. The resulting value is the memory address that is presented to the PC Card on it's bus. In the case below, any address between D0000H and D0FFFH in the machine's address space will be shifted down to address 0H to FFFH in Attribute memory in the PC Card's address space. If the offset registers are set to 0, no address shifting occurs.

Memory Window 1 is configured for common memory starting at D4000H to D7FFFH. This is a 16K memory window that is 16 bits wide and has 3 additional wait states added to each memory cycle. The offset register shifts any machine memory access between D4000H and D7FFFH down starting at 11000H in the PC Card's address space.

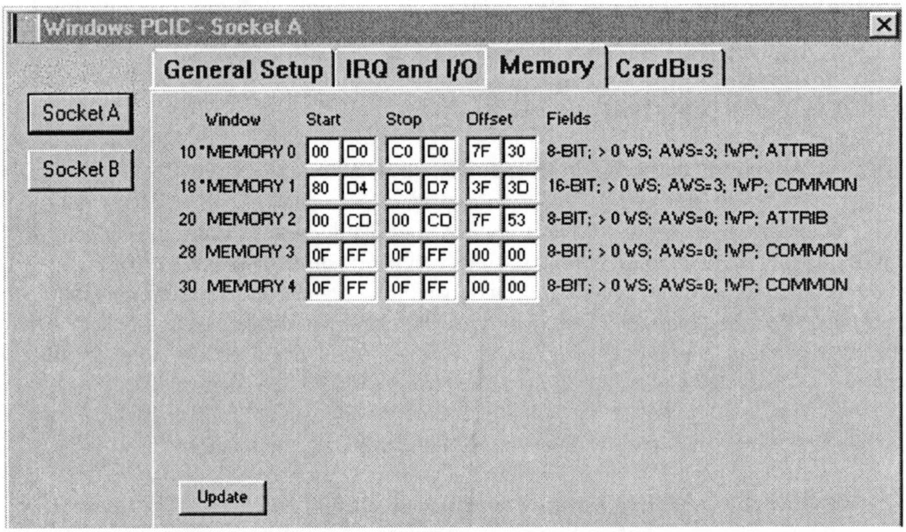

Figure 10-36: WINPCIC Memory Registers

Question 6: How are CardBus PC Card settings determined?

The CardBus socket controller or bridge provides the interface between the internal PCI bus and the PCMCIA socket. The CardBus bridge has resources for each socket. These are referred to as it's configuration space. Every PCI or CardBus device has a configuration space. The CardBus bridge has resources assigned to it by the operating system. In Figure 10-37 below, we can see the resources assigned to a CardBus bridge for socket B in a Windows 98 system:

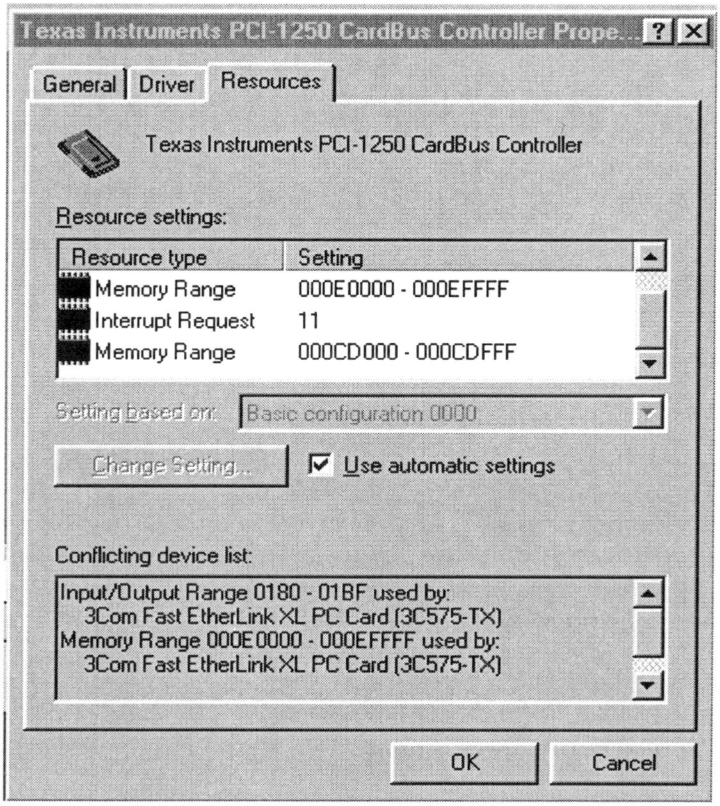

Figure 10-37: TI-1250 PCI CardBus Controller Resources

It shows four different resources: two memory windows, one interrupt Request (IRQ) and if the scroll bar was moved up, you would see an I/O port window. Currently, there are two memory windows. One is 4K in size and extends from CD000H to CDFFFH. The other is 64K in size and extends from E0000H to EFFFFH. The I/O ports mapped from 0180H to 01BFH. The IRQ is set to 11. In this particular socket, we have placed a CardBus Ethernet LAN PC Card. Figure 10-38 shows the settings in the system:

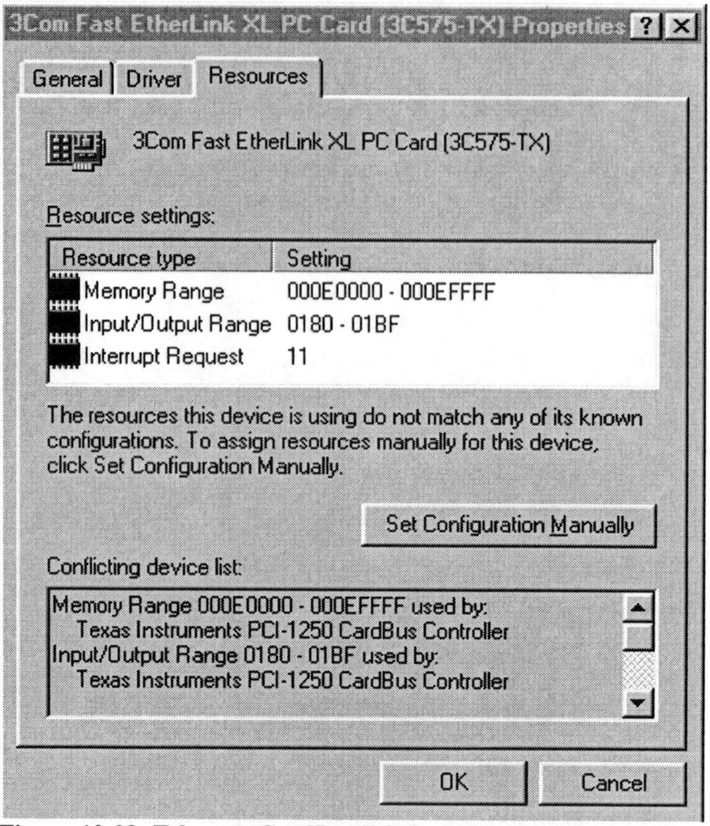

Figure 10-38: Ethernet CardBus PC Card System Resources

This shows a memory window extending from E0000H to EFFFFH, an I/O port window extending from 0180H to 01BFH, and an IRQ of 11. These are the actual resources that this LAN card uses to function. If you look back at the CardBus bridge settings, you will notice that three of the four resource settings match the LAN PC Card. The memory range from CD000H to CDFFFH is a block of PCI memory address space assigned to the socket interface registers. At offset 0 in this address space, the Cardbus socket interface registers are defined. At offset 800H, the ExCA socket interface registers are defined.

The CardBus socket interface registers are,

1. Socket Event Register (offset 00h)
2. Socket Mask Register (offset 04h)
3. Socket Present State Register (offset 08h)
4. Socket Force Event Register (offset 0Ch)
5. Socket Control Register (offset 10h)

These registers are defined in the PC Card Electrical Standard for CardBus.

The ExCA socket interface registers are the 82365 socket controller compatible registers. At offset 800H, register 0 is defined. At offset 801H, register 1 is defined and so on.

If the CardBus Legacy register (44H) is set to 0x3E1h, then the socket controller registers can be examined with other existing tools that utilize I/O operations at 03E0H and 03E1H to gather this data. The value in the CardBus Legacy register is the starting I/O port to map the ExCA registers.

Figure 10-39 shows CardBus bridge values for Socket B when an Ethernet CardBus PC Card is inserted.

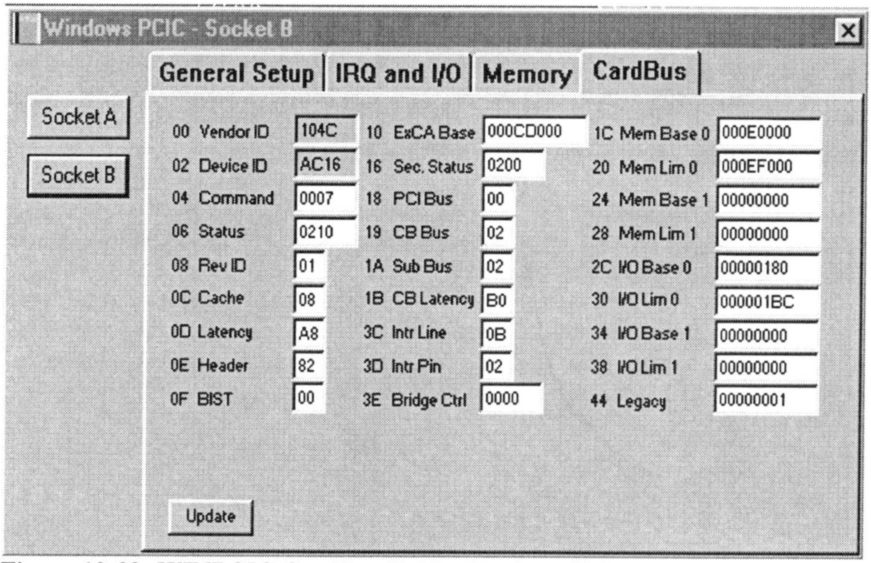

Figure 10-39: WINPCIC CardBus Bridge Register Values

In order for these tools to work, some device drivers needed to be written. Windows 95/98 does not allow an application program to query the PCI registers so the device driver PCIDD was written to make PCI BIOS calls on behalf of an application. Windows NT does not allow I/O port access to applications so PCICDD was written to gain access to I/O ports starting at 3E0h. The interfaces to these device drivers are through the Win32 **DeviceIoControl** function. The file REGIO.C contains all of the interface definitions to these device drivers.

To use the Windows 95/98 device driver PCIDD.VXD, an application would load and open the device with the Win32 **CreateFile** function. The application would then fill in the REGS32 data structure with the values required for a PCI BIOS call and finally use the Win32 **DeviceIoControl** function to have he driver make the PCI BIOS call. A sample code fragment is shown in Figure 10-40.

```
//
//  Install the Win95 device driver for PCI BIOS calls
//  pcidd.vxd.
hPcic = CreateFile("\\\\.\\PCIDD.VXD", GENERIC_WRITE |
                   GENERIC_READ, 0, NULL,
                   OPEN_EXISTING, FILE_FLAG_OVERLAPPED, 0);
                                   .
                                   .
regs32.eax = READ_CONFIG_BYTE;
regs32.edi = iOffset;
regs32.ebx = pcbInfo->pciBusDevFun;
regs32.ecx = 0;

rc = DeviceIoControl(hPcic, IOCTL_PCIDD_BIOS, &regs32,
     sizeof(REGS32), NULL, 0, NULL, NULL);
if (rc)
   pcbInfo->regs.ByteValue[iOffset] = (UCHAR) regs32.ecx;
```

Figure 10-40: PCI BIOS Call to Read a Byte Using PCIDD.VXD

The REGS32 structure will contain the results of the PCI BIOS call on return.

To use the Windows NT device driver PCICDD.SYS, an application would have to start the device driver like a Service. The subroutines InstallDriver and StartDriver, and the Win32 functions OpenSCManager and CreateFile are used to get the device driver loaded and started. Afterwards, the Win32 function DeviceIoControl is used to query the PCIC registers or the PCI CardBus bridge registers. A code fragment is shown in Figure 10-41 that writes an entire socket of PCIC registers and reads a PCI register.

```
//
//  Write a socket of PCIC registers.
DeviceIoControl(hPcic, IOCTL_PCIC_WRITE_REGS, pPcicSocket,
                       sizeof(PCIC_SOCKET), pPcicSocket,
                       sizeof(PCIC_SOCKET),
                       &dwRet, NULL);
                                   .
                                   .
//  Read a PCI configuration register.
regs32.eax = READ_CONFIG_DWORD;
```

```
regs32.edi = iOffset;
regs32.ebx = pcbInfo->pciBusDevFun;
regs32.ecx = 0;
DeviceIoControl(hPcic, IOCTL_PCI_READ_DWORD, &regs32,
                       sizeof(REGS32),
                       &regs32, sizeof(REGS32), &dwRet, NULL);
pcbInfo->regs.LongValue[iOffset/4] = (ULONG) regs32.ecx;
```

Figure 10-41: Writing PCIC Registers and a Reading PCI Register (PCICDD.SYS)

Summary

First, this chapter demonstrated how application programs can be card services clients under DOS, Windows 3.1, and OS/2. The differences in accessing card services functions under the three environments was described. Table 10-2 summarizes these differences.

Operation	DOS	Windows 3.1	OS/2 2.1 Application
Call card services	INT 1Ah	Simulate INT 1Ah using DPMI services	OS/2 DosDevIOCtl function call
Callback Handler Interface	Far Call/Return	DPMI services that switch from real mode to protect mode	Event Semaphore Wait/Post/Reset and dequeuing the events with VendorSpecific

Table 10-2: Methods for Accessing Card Services Based on Operating System Environment

Second, this chapter demonstrated how Windows 95/98/CE application programs can get notifications when PC Cards are inserted, removed, or queried for removal.

Finally, this chapter presented tools to interrogate the PCIC registers for a socket controller when a PC Card is inserted in a socket.

Appendix A: Where To Go For More Information

PCMCIA Standard

International Headquarters
2635 North First Street
Suite 209
San Jose, CA 95131
USA
Tel +1 408-433-CARD (2273)
Fax +1 408-433-9558
http://www.pc-card.com

European Chapter
Avenue Marcel Thiry 204
B-1200 Brussels
Belgium
Tel +32 2-774-9620
Fax +32 2-774-9690

Honk Kong & China
Honk Kong Productivity Council
Contact: K.Y. Leung
HKPC Building, 78 Tat Chee Ave.
Kowloon Hong Kong
Tel +852-788-5778
Fax +852-788-5770

Taiwan
Texas Instruments, Taiwan Ltd.
Contact: Jenny Huang
Tel +886-2-376-2848
Fax +886-2-377-1460

Australia & New Zealand
Advanced Portable Technologies
Contact: Peter Maurer
Unit 4, 6 Campbell St.
Artarmon, NSW 2064 Australia
Tel +61-2-906-3800
Fax +61-2-439-4329

Books

This book, as well as the following, are available for purchase through your favorite bookstore.

PCMCIA System Architecture: 16-Bit PC Cards, Anderson, Don and Shanley, Tom
(ISBN 0-20140991-7)
This book contains both software and hardware 16-bit PC Card information.

CardBus System Architecture, Anderson, Don and Shanley, Tom
(ISBN 0-201-40997-6)
This book contains both software and hardware CardBus PC Card information.

PCI System Architecture, Shanley, Tom and Anderson, Don
(ISBN 0-201-40993-3)
This book contains PCI bus architecture up to the 2.1 standard.

Inside PC Card: CardBus and PCMCIA Design, Haque, Faisal
(ISBN 0-750-69747-4)
This book contains examples of designs with trade-offs and recommendations.

The PCMCIA Developer's Guide, Mori, Michael T.
(ISBN 0-9640342-0-4)
This book contains information geared towards the hardware developer.

Designing With FLASH Memory, Dipert, Brian and Levy, Markus.
(ISBN 0-929-39217-5)
This book contains information geared towards the memory PC Card hardware developer.

Writing OS/2 Device Drivers In C, Mastrianni, Steven J.
(ISBN 0-442-01729-4)
This book contains a chapter on writing PC Card device drivers for OS/2.

Software and/or Development Kits (SDK):

American Megatrends Incorporated
http://www.ami.com
AMIBIOS® Mobile 98 (OEM BIOS)

Phoenix Technologies Limited
http://www.phoenix.com
Card Executive 2.0 for NT (hot swap PC Cards in NT 4.0)

SystemSoft Corporation
http://www.systemsoft.com
System Wizard
Card Works

Cirrus Logic
http://www.cirrus.com
Socket Controller Chipsets

Internet

Source	Address	Content or Focus
Worldwide Web Sites	http://www.phoenix.com	Phoenix Technologies, Ltd.
	http://www.ibm.com	IBM Information and Support
	http://www.compaq.com/	Compaq (See "Additional Information", "White Papers" for PCMCIA articles)
	http://www.apresearch.com	PC Card market research and competitive analysis, including a PC Card supplier database
	http://www.microsoft.com	Microsoft Information and Support
	http://www.simpletech.com	Memory and PC Card Manufacturer
	http://www.synchrotech.com	PC Card Information
	http://www.accurite.com	Developer of PC Card peripherals, controllers, development, and diagnostic tools
	http://www.pacificrimsystems.com	Designs and manufactures PC Card disk drives
	http://www.sycard.com	Portable system development and test tools
	http://www.linux.org	Linux WWW Home Page
	http://www.linuxhq.com	Linux Headquarters Home Page
	http://hyper.standford.edu/~dhinds/pcmcia/pcmcia.html	David Hinds PCMCIA Linux documentation
	http://www.cs.utexas.edu/users/kharker/linux-laptop	Linux on Laptops Page
FTP sites	address: ftp.microsoft.com directory: developr/drg/Plug-and-Play/Tests/PCMCIA file: DTPL.ZIP	Microsoft Developer's FTP Site; the display tuple program
	address: metalab.unc.edu directory: pub/Linux/kernel/pcmcia/SUPPORTED.CA	Linux PCMCIA list of supported cards

	RDS address: ftp.intel.com directory: /pub/IAL/software_specs	PC Card utilities for Intel compatible controller chips, DPMI specifications
USENET Newsgroups	alt.periphs.pcmcia	Questions and discussions about PC Card systems, cards, and software
	comp.sys.laptops	Portable computer questions and discussions, including PC Card topics

Glossary

2.X
A notation used in this book to denote both release 2.0 and 2.1 of the PC Card Standard.

802.2
IEEE standard for Logical Link Control.

Adapter
A traditional adapter card that typically connects to the host system bus (ISA, EISA, PCI, Mico channel) of a desktop type computer.

ADD
Adapter Device Driver. An OS/2 base device driver (BASEDEV) that provides hardware specific services for a physical device. By convention, ADD device drivers have an .ADD filename extension.

AIMS
Auto Indexing Mass Storage, a standard for storing large data sets, such as multimedia or image data files.

Aliased Memory
PC Cards that implement attribute memory space within common memory.

Allocate Real Mode Callback Address
A DPMI function that returns a segment:offset real mode address that will transfer control from real mode to a protected mode procedure.

API
Application Programming Interface. Card and socket services are PC Card APIs.

APM
Advanced Power Management.

Artificial Insertion
Insertion events generated for PC Cards inserted in sockets before the client registered. For example, if a card is present in a socket prior to a client registering with card services, the client will be notified of this via an artificial insertion event

ATA
AT attachment, a standard interface for mass storage peripherals, defined by ANSI X.3T9 subcommittee.

AttachDD
An OS/2 DevHlp call that returns the address of a device driver's Inter-Device Driver Communication (IDC) entry point.

Attribute Memory
The physical composition (RAM, ROM, or EEPROM) of memory housing attribute memory space.

Attribute Memory Space
One of three PC Card address spaces. Attribute memory is unique in that it is read-only and can only be accessed in byte widths. Additionally, it contains the CIS which, in turn, describes the *attributes (*functions and features) of the PC Card.

Bandwidth
A measurement used to describe a device's ability to transfer large amounts of data quickly. A higher bandwidth device is capable of transferring large amounts of data quickly.

Base Address Registers (BARs)
A set of up to eight registers used by CardBus cards in place of configuration registers. Each BAR is capable of responding to either an I/O or memory access in the host system address space.

BASEDEV
An OS/2 CONFIG.SYS statement which loads a base OS/2 device driver. Base device driver that performs I/O during the OS/2 kernel boot sequence in order to provide IPL support. Base device drivers load prior to DEVICE CONFIG.SYS statements. Base device drivers are loaded according to the file extension type. They are loaded in the following order: SYS, BID, VSD, TSD, ADD, I13, FLT, and finally DMD.

BAR
Base Address Register
Registers that exist in the PCI Configuration space. They are used to determine the address space requirements for a CardBus PC Card.

Basic Compatibility Layer
The first of four layers in the CIS. This mandatory layer denotes essential information about the PC Card.

BIOS
Basic Input/Output System. Microcode, generally located in system ROM, that responsible for abstracting basic hardware input/output operations, such as interaction with the diskette drive, from other software programs. The BIOS provides a set of functions other software may invoke to perform operations without concern for the details of the underlying hardware.

Block
An OS/2 DevHlp call to block the current thread. The current thread is removed from the run queue until it is released by the DevHlp Run call.

Buffered UART
A UART that contains a FIFO input character hold register capable of storing up to 16 characters before any data is overrun. The 16550 is an example of a buffered UART.

Bus Enumerator
In Window NT, this is a collection of software drivers that manage the I/O buses in the system. Each bus has its own enumerator that is responsible for determining what devices are installed on the bus and the resources it requires. The bus enumerator reports its information back to the configuration manager. See also Bus Manager.

Bus Manager
In the IBM Power PC operating system, this is a collection of software drivers that manage the I/O buses in the system. Each bus has its own bus manager that is responsible for deterring what devices are installed on its bus and the resources it requires. The bus manager reports its information back to the hardware resource manager. See also bus enumerator.

Bus Master
A means for transferring control of system bus between multiple devices.

Callback Handle
The address of a subroutine of a client that receives control from card services when a registered event occurs.

Callback Handler
The client driver subroutine that receives control from Card Services when a registered event occurs. This subroutine demultiplexes the event mask to determine which event or set of events triggered the invocation.

CardBus
A standard that first appeared in the February 1995 PC Card Standard defining a 32-bit, 33Mhz local bus architecture.

Card Configuration Option Registers (CCOR)
Eight bit, read/write registers defined by the architecture that are used by PC Card software to control the electrical interface, I/O address space, interrupt request signal, and power requirement settings of a PC Card.

Card Configuration Status Register (CCSR)
A register required only by PC Cards that support audio, share interrupts, or report other status information implemented within the register's description. This register is used both to configure specific card behavior and to return status.

Card Configuration Table
A table made up of one or more Card Configuration Registers.

Card Information Structure (CIS)
A data structure, defined by the architecture, that is physically stored on a PC Card which contains information about the card, such as its capabilities and the system resources required to support the card. The content of the CIS varies depending on the PC Card function. For example, a modem PC Card and a LAN PC Card will not have identical card information structures. The CIS resides in attribute memory.

CARD_INSERTION
A card services event indicating that a PC Card has been inserted in a socket, or a client has just registered for insertion events and card services is creating artificial insertion events for PC Cards already in sockets.

CARD_REMOVAL
A card services event indicating that a PC Card has been removed from a socket.

Card Services (CS)
The entity responsible for coordinating and managing system resources among PC Card clients. Card services can be incorporated into the operating system or it can be implemented as a device driver. Card services interfaces to socket services.

CCR
See Card Configuration Registers

CDD
See Client Device Driver.

CIS
See Card Information Structure.

Client Device Driver (CDD)
A program that interacts with card services in order to support a PC Card device.

Cold Ejection
The process of requiring power to a system to be turned off prior to removing a PC Card from the system.

Cold Insertion
The process of requiring the PC card to be inserted into the slot prior to applying power to the PC Card system.

Combo cards
See multi-function PC Card.

Common Memory
One of three PC Card address spaces. Common memory is generally used to store application data. As such, it supports both read-only and read/write operations, including DMA.

Configuration Manager
In Windows NT, this software component calls the resource arbitrator with information to obtain resources required for a device detected by a bus enumerator.

Configuration Option Register (COR)
A mandatory register that is used to configure the PC Card to reset the card, select between pulse or level interrupt mode, or program the card into either I/O or memory mode.

Configuration Server
In OS/2 for PowerPC, the configuration server is the component responsible for the configuration of the system overall. The configuration server is started at system boot time and remains active during the entire life of the system.

Context Hook
OS/2 events that are processed at task time.

Credit Card Adapter
Another name for a PC Card.

CS
See Card Services.

Data Organization Layer
The second of four layers in the CIS. This layer denotes the manner in which the data on the card is formatted: disk-like or memory-like.

Data Overrun
The process of an incoming character displacing another character, such as a character in a UART incoming hold register being overwritten by another incoming character.

Data Recording Format
Sequences of bytes that are updated or accessed by a single, logical operation.

Data Recording Layer
The third of four layers in the CIS. This layer denotes how data in a memory card partition is organized: DOS file systems, Microsoft Flash file system (FFS), vendor specific, or application specific. See Data Recording Format.

Device Helper (DevHlp)
An OS/2 operating system kernel service provided to physical device drivers. The service performs functions on hardware memory, interrupts, semaphores, and queues.

Direct Memory Access (DMA)
The process of bypassing the CPU to transfer data directly to or from computer system memory.

Docking Station
A device that portable computers connect, or dock, to that contains additional features, such as PC Card slots and multimedia capabilities.

DPMI
DOS Protected Mode Interface. DPMI defines an interface for protected mode DOS applications to manage memory, interrupts, exceptions, debugging registers, and coprocessor emulation in the presence of a true protected mode operating system.

EEPROM
Electrically-Erasable Read-Only Memory. Non-volatile memory in which individual bytes can be erased.

EISA
Extended Industry Standard Architecture is an expansion bus that is a 32 bit extension of the 16 bit USA bus.

EPROM
Erasable Read-Only Memory. Memory which can be erased in bulk, usually by exposure to ultra-violet light.

Events
A set of PC Card states that can be reported to registered clients. Events include such activities as card insertion, card ejection, or a dead or low battery. A client requests notification of specific events via the card services **RegisterClient** function.

Event Semaphore
In OS/2, a semaphore that enables a thread to signal a waiting thread that an event has occurred. The waiting thread can then perform an action that is dependent on the completion of the signaled event.

Execute In Place (XIP)
A standard outlining a method for a host system to execute a program directly from common memory on a PC Card.

FIFO
First-In-First-Out. A queuing method whereby the first element added to the queue is the first element removed from the queue.

Flash
A Microsoft trademark used to describe a file system designed for use with either Flash EPROM or
ultraviolet erasable memory cards.

Flash EPROM
A type of EPROM that is electrically erasable. It generally requires an entire block of memory to be erased at once.

Flash Memory
Non-volatile memory that is electrically rewritten and erased in either bulk or block mode.

Free Real Mode Callback Address
A DPMI function that releases a real mode callback address previously allocated with Allocate Real Mode Callback Address.

Handheld PC
A small personal conputer that can fit in your hand.

Hardware Name Space (HNS)
In OS/2 for PowerPC, the HNS is the hierarchical tree that depicts every device available in the system.
See also Hardware Tree.

Hardware Resource Manager (HRM)
In OS/2 for PowerPC, the HRM is the component within the configuration server that is responsible for creating and maintaining entries in the hardware name space (HNS). The HNS is also responsible for fairly allocating system resources among all devices in the system. The resource arbitrator is also responsible for preventing resource conflicts between hardware devices. See also Resource Arbitrator.

Hardware Tree
In Windows NT, the hardware tree is a hierarchical tree that depicts every device present in the system. See also Hardware Name Space.

Hot Ejection
The process of removing a PC Card from a system while power is active to the system.

Hot Insertion
The process of placing a PC Card into a system while power is active to the system.

HPC
See Handheld PC

IC
Integrated Circuit.

IDC
See Interdevice Driver Communication.

IEEE
Institute of Electrical and Electronics Engineers. A leading standard-making body in the United States, responsible for the 802 standards for local area networks.

Independent Addressing
A PC Card that decodes only some of the address lines (A0 through A25) of the adapter. It relies on the adapter to decode the remaining lines.

Initial Program Load (IPL)
The action of loading programs into computer memory for execution. Typically these are the programs, such as device drivers, that are listed in the CONFIG.SYS file. Also known as, Initial Machine Load (IML).

Interdevice Driver Communication (IDC)
A process where one OS/2 device driver calls another OS/2 device driver, usually to obtain information or to request a function to be performed.

Interrupt Service Routine (ISR)
The part of a device driver or program that is responsible for handling interrupts from a physical hardware device.

I/O
Input/Output.

I/O Address Space
A region that is shared amongst all PC Cards in a system. This single 64-megabyte address space is used to map card resources into host system memory.

I/O Mapped
A register or area on a PC Card that is accessed using I/O cycles. For example, a modem register, or port, on an Intel-based machine is accessed by a program using in/out instructions. I/O mapping is typically used to access small areas on a device.

IPL
See Initial Program Load.

IRQ
Interrupt Request.

ISA
Industry Standard Architecture.

ISR
Interrupt Service Routine.

JEDEC
Joint Electron Devices Engineering Council.

JEIDA
Japan Electronic Industry Development Association.

Legacy Device
A hardware device, such as an adapter card, with DIP switches, jumpers, or other mechanisms that require user intervention in order to be configured.

LIFO
Last-In-First-Out. A queuing mechanism whereby the last element added to the queue is the first element taken off of the queue.

Locking Mechanism
A PC Card socket that has hardware, such as a motor-driven mechanism, that can insert and remove PC cards. The motor is started to insert and release the card. Once inserted, a PC Card is locked in place until the motor can be started again to release it.

Logical Link Control
The upper portion of the data link layer, defined by the IEEE 802.2 standard.

Logical Socket
The socket number that card services passes to the callback handler when an event occurs.

Mapping
The process of associating a PC Card address to a host system address. See I/O Mapping and Memory Mapping.

Memory Mapped
A register or area on a PC Card that is accessed using memory cycles. For example, a LAN card typically has at least one memory mapped region. On an Intel-based machine this region is accessed by a program using load/store instructions. Memory mapping is generally used when the area to be accessed is large, as in the case of a LAN card.(for example, a 64k SRAM region).

Memory Technology Driver (MTD)
An embedded or loaded element of card services that performs the device-specific read, write, copy, and erase algorithms required for PC memory cards.

Metaformat
The CIS contents, architecture, definition, and interpretation.

MTD
See memory technology driver.

Multi-function PC Card
PC Cards that can perform multiple functions, such as an Ethernet/Modem card.

NDIS
See Network Driver Interface Specification.

NetBIOS
See Network Basic Input/Output System.

Network Basic Input/Output System (NetBIOS)
A network protocol used on LANs to provide message, print server, and file server functions.

Network Driver Interface Specification (NDIS)
A specification developed by 3Com and Microsoft for developing network device drivers. NDIS is divided into two components: a device driver that controls access to the hardware network card; and a protocol driver that links to the application programs.

Null Modem Cable
A serial port cable designed to pass data between two serial ports.

ODI
See Open Data-Link Interface.

Open Data-Link Interface (ODI)
Data link services specifications for Novell NetWare device drivers.

One Time Programmable
A ROM which can be programmed only once and cannot be erased.

Overlapped Addressing
A PC Card that decodes all the address lines (A0 through A25) of the adapter.

Page
A 16Kbyte portion of a window. Some windows may contain more than one page.

PC Card
A prefix used to refer to the hardware components of the standard. By itself, the term generally refers to a lightweight, low-power adapter card that meets the PC Card Standard.

PC Card Adapter
The chip, typically mounted on the planar of the PC Card system, that performs the system-to-PC Card bus conversion. For example, ISA-to-PC Card or Micro Channel-to-
PC Card.

PCI
See Peripheral Component Interconnect

PCMCIA
Personal Computer Memory Card International Association. This term is used to describe the standard's body.

PCMCIA$
The logical device name, used on the ATTACHDD command, for the OS/2 card services device driver.

PCMCIA.SYS
The file name used for the point enabler in Windows NT. Also used on the DEVICE= statement in the CONFIG.SYS file, for loading the OS/2 card services device driver.

Peripheral Component Interconnect
A high performance bus specification that defines the PCI bus. This bus is intended to define the interconnect and bus transfer protocol between highly-integrated peripheral adapters that reside on a common local bus on the system board or add-in expansion cards on the PCI bus.

Plug and Play (PnP)
A set of architectural standards that attempts to achieve automatic installation and configuration of computer hardware and software without requiring end-user intervention.

Port Replicator
A device that duplicates the ports of the mobile computer. A port replicator is typically used to connect printer, LAN, and other cables. The mobile computer is then quickly and easily detached for times away from the office without having to disconnect cables. Port replicators are sometimes equipped with PC Card slots.

PPC
Power PC.

Processor Bindings
The register definition and other host specific environment programming issues. The host environment is defined by the operating system and the architecture (example: Intel 80386) of the host platform. The bindings tell a programmer how to detect the presence of card services, issue requests and pass arguments to card services, how the binding-specific arguments and services are defined (example: Intel register usage), and how arguments are passed to and from the callback handler.

Program Segment
The lowest available address that DOS assigns to a program.

Program Segment Prefix
The first 256-bytes of a program starting at offset 0 in the program segment.

Protected Mode
The natural 32-bit environment of the 80386, or higher, CPU. In this mode the CPU offers multitasking, virtual memory, and advanced protection facilities.

RAM
Random Access Memory.

Real Mode
In real mode, the 80386 and higher CPU is essentially a fast 8086 and is fully compatible with existing DOS applications.

Reader/Writer
A PC Card device that is designed to replace an existing full-sized floppy drive bay. The reader/writer device comes with either one, two, or four PC Card sockets. This device is a means for retrofitting an existing system to support PC Cards.

REGISTRATION_COMPLETE
A card services event that indicates a **RegisterClient** request has been completed.

Resource Arbitrator
In Windows NT, a software component that is responsible for fairly allocating system resources among all devices in the system. The resource arbitrator is also responsible for preventing resource conflicts between hardware devices. See also Hardware Resource Manager.

Resource Manager
In the PC Card specification, a software component that is responsible for identifying system resources that are unavailable. The resource manager can be implemented as part of the operating system or as a device driver. The resource manager builds a resource map.

Resource Map
A map of all the system resources that are available and an indication of which resources are unavailable.

Ring-0, Ring-1, Ring-2, Ring-3
Levels of privilege in the 80x83 CPU. Ring-0 represents the greatest privilege, Ring-3 the least privilege. Operating systems and environments that run in protected mode, such as OS/2 and Windows 3.1, run their kernels and device drivers at Ring-0. Application programs typically run at Ring-3.

Run
An OS/2 DevHlp call that starts a blocked thread. The thread is put on the run queue.

SCSI
Small Computer System Interface, a standard for connecting peripherals to a high-speed parallel data bus.

Simulate Real Mode Interrupt
A DPMI function that transfers control to the address specified by the real mode interrupt vector.

Slot
The receptacle, typically appearing on a system, where a PC Card is inserted for operation. Also known as a *socket*.

Socket
The receptacle, typically appearing on a system, where a PC Card is inserted for operation. Also known as a slot.

SS
See Socket Services.

Socket Services (SS)
The entity responsible for abstracting the adapter from card services. It is responsible for managing the PC Card system slots and interfacing to card services.

Static RAM
Volatile memory that does not require refreshing to maintain its memory contents.

Super Client Driver (SCD)
A collection of client drivers that are bundled together. Oftentimes, the super client driver performs generic rather than specific functions. For example, a super client modem driver may be capable of enabling a variety of modems in a generic configuration as opposed to a specialized modem client driver that may take advantage of key features of a particular modem.

SYS
An OS/2 base system device driver file extension. A system device driver provides generic system level services for a class of physical devices.

System Specific Layer
The last of four layers in the CIS. This layer is used to contain information specific to a particular operating environment.

Terminate-Stay-Resident (TSR)
A DOS program that stays in memory, allowing other DOS programs time to execute, thus giving the impression that the system is multitasking. Client driver TSR programs are awakened by card services invoking the callback handler routine.

TSR
Terminate-stay-resident. A DOS program that stays in memory, giving the impression that the system is multitasking.

Tuple
A data structure used to describe PC Card information. Tuples are linked together to form the CIS.

Type I
A PC Card that conforms to the memory-only interface portion of the specification. SRAM and Flash cards are typical examples of Type I PC Cards.

The card dimensions are 3.3mm thick and 54mm wide. There is no raised substrate area on a Type I card.

Type II
An I/O PC Card that conforms to the PC Card specification. LAN and modems are typical examples of Type II PC Cards. The PC Card dimensions are 5.0mm thick, 54mm wide, with a raised substrate area of 48mm wide.

Type III
An I/O PC Card that conforms to the PC Card specification. Hard drives are a typical example of Type III PC Cards. The card dimensions are 10.5mm thick, 54mm wide, with a raised substrate area of 51mm wide.

Type IV
A proposed PC Card that is 14mm thick. The PCMCIA committee declined to endorse this proposal; however, a consortium of companies may release a card conforming to this specification.

Type I Extended
A C Card that conforms to the Type I thickness and width dimensions, but contains a 40mm extension off the back of the card which protrudes out of the PC Card system socket.

Type II Extended
A PC Card that conforms to the Type II thickness and width dimensions, but contains a 40mm extension off the back of the card which protrudes out of the PC Card system socket.

UART
Universal Asynchronous Receiver Transmitter. A chip that contains all the software programming control required for processing data, typically off of a system serial port. Similar to the system CPU, UARTs are referred to by chip nomenclature, such as an Intel 8250, 16450, and 16550.

Unbuffered UART
A UART that contains a single character input hold register. The Intel 8250, 16450, 82C50, and 16C50 are all examples of unbuffered UARTs.

Universal Address
A value stored typically on a LAN adapter (or LAN PC Card) that uniquely identifies that card. Also known as the burned-in address.

Universal Installer
See super client driver.

Virtual-86 (V86) Mode
In this mode of the 80386 and higher CPU one or more 8086-compatible programs can be running at the same time, each in its own private address space called a *virtual machine*. Each virtual DOS machine appears to be a complete real mode DOS environment to the program running with it.

Virtual Machine
In the DPMI specification, a DOS address space and all of the DPMI clients which share access to that DOS address space.

Window
A region of host system memory or I/O space through which a PC Card in a socket may be addressed. Windows are allocated (**RequestWindow** or **RequestIO**) and deallocated (**ReleaseWindow** or **ReleaseIO**) via card services.

X86
Refers to a family of Intel Central Processing Units (CPUs).

XIP
See Execute In Place

Index

A

adapter. *See* PC Card hardware
address space
  accessing, 83
  attribute, 58
  common, 58
  decoding, 86, 116
    CardBus, 61
  I/O, 58
applications
  launching, 307, 310
attribute memory, 58, 113
  card information strucutre (CIS), 64

B

base address register (BAR), 61

C

callback handler
  Intel protect mode, 307
  OS/2, 311
card information structure (CIS), 64
  CardBus, 61
  generating, 68
  layers, 64
    basic compatibility, 65
    data organization, 66
    data recording format, 66
    system-specific standards, 66
  parsing, 81
  parsing, sample programs, 287
card services (CS)
  accessing, 331
  application programming interface (API), 35
    function categories, 36
      advanced client services, 36
      bulk memory services, 36
      client services, 37
      client utility services, 37
      resource management services, 37
    function codes, 41
  detecting presence of, 41
  events, 47
    artificialcard insertion, 44
    card insertion, 38, 48
    event mask, 44
    registration complete, 44
  return codes, 36
CardBus
  address decoding, 61
  software impact of, 63
client device driver (CDD)
  callback handler, 34
  callback handler, 46
  compared to point enablers, 30
  definition, 30
  deregistration, 43, 49, 310, 313
  event handling
    client information, 126
    request exclusive, 129, 130
  functional overview, 35
  initialization routine, 33
  interrupt service routine (ISR), 34
  programming model, 33, 44
  purpose, 29
  registration, 43, 44, 45, 108
  types
    I/O, 31
    memory, 31
    MTD, 31
    super client driver (SCD), 30, 31
common memory, 58
configuration registers, 262
  card configuration and status, 262
  card configuration option registers (CCOR), 122, 262
  CardBus BARs, 61
  pin replacement, 263
  socket and copy, 264

D

DOS
  sample programs, 287, 319
DOS client device driver (CDD). *See* terminate stay resident (TSR)
  acquiring resources, 116, 117, 118
  application program, 32
  client data (GetClientInfo), 126
  debugging, 133
  event handling
    card ejection, 124
    card insertion, 112, 133
    registration complete, 109, 112
  header, 95
  interrupt service routine (ISR), 98
  RequestExclusive, 100
  terminate stay resident (TSR), 98
  terminate stay resident (TSR), 33
DOS protected mode interface (DPMI)
  allocate real mode callback address, 307

E

event handling
  DOS, 109
  Linux, 265
  OS/2, 145, 311
  Windows, 309
  Windows, 307, 310
events. *See* card services (CS)
execute in place (XIP), 66

I

interdevice driver communications (IDC), 141
interrupt request (IRQ)
  obtaining, 86
interrupt service routine (ISR), 34

J

Japan Electronic Industry Development Association (JEIDA), 6
Joint Electron Devices Engineering Council (JEDEC), 6

L

Linux, 209
logical socket, 42, 113

M

memory
  mapping, 83
memory
  mapping, 119, 156
memory cards
  Flash, 10
  SRAM, 9
  SRAM/Flash, 10
memory technology driver (MTD), 31
metaformat
  CardBus, 63

O

OS/2, 135
  sample programs, 287, 295, 310, 319
  Warp, 138
OS/2 client device driver
  debugging, 163
OS/2 client device driver (CDD)
  AttachDD to CS, 142
  callback handler, 139, 146
  context hook, 148, 159
  event handling
    card ejection, 145
    card insertion, 145, 147
    registration complete, 143, 147
  interdevice driver communications (IDC), 141
  strategy, 140
    INIT_COMPLETE, 140, 141

P

PC Card
  adapter

functions, 83
advantages, 10, 11, 26
disadvantages, 28
evolution, 22
functional overview, 26
incompatibilities, 16
Type I
Flash, 10
SRAM, 8
SRAM/Flash, 10
Type II
LAN, 11
modem, 11
Type III
hard drives, 12
using
ejecting, 18
inserting, 18, 20, 22
PC Card
extended, 13
multifunction, 14, 61
Type IV, 13
PC Card devices
docking stations, 16
port replicators, 16
PC Card hardware
adapter, 21
CardBus, 61
functions, 21
socket, 18
PC Card software
card services, 23
client drivers, 24
socket services, 23
PC Card Standard
goals, 6
organization
software, 7
releases, 22
Releases
latest enhancements, 61
versions, 14
PCMCIA, 13, 22
association, 5, 6, 22
JEIDA, 6
membership, 6
point enablers, 30
processor bindings, 100, 299

R

resource manager, 23
resource map utility (RMU), 135
retrofitting systems, 17

S

sample programs
debugging tips, 320
OS/2
client device driver, 139
utilities, 295
super client driver (SCD), 30
super client drivers, compared to point enablers, 30
system resources
assigning, 88, 121, 123, 153, 157
I/O ports, 116, 153
IRQ, 118
managing, 91
memory window, 121
releasing, 124, 125, 126, 160

T

terminate stay resident (TSR), 33, 95
tuples, 64
(CISTPL_CFTABLE_ENTRY)
configuration table entry, 72, 115, 123, 158
(CISTPL_CONFIG) configuration, 71, 115, 158, 252
(CISTPL_DEVICE_A) device information, 68, 250
(CISTPL_FUNCID) function ID, 70, 259
(CISTPL_VERS_1) version/product information, 151
(CISTPL_VERS_1) version/product information, 69, 145, 251, 290
(TPLMID_MANF) manufacturer ID, 70
function extension, 71, 319
function ID (CISTPL_FUNCID), 319
parsing, 81, 113, 115, 145

U

UART
  detection of, 319

V

virtual-86 mode, 294

W

Warp. *See* OS/2 Warp
windows
  memory and I/O, 83
windows
  memory and I/O, 57, 84, 119, 155
  releasing, 125
Windows
  sample programs, 307
Windows (Microsoft) sample
  programs, 291
Windows '95
  card services, 173

About the Authors

Steven M. Kipisz is a Senior Staff Engineer with Ericsson in Research Triangle Park, North Carolina. His interest in PC Card development started at IBM in Research Triangle Park where he designed and developed OS/2, Windows 95, and Linux device drivers for various LAN, modem, and multi-function PC Cards. He has instructed developers at the 1993 OS/2 Device Driver Conference on writing OS/2 PC Card client drivers. Currently, his work at Ericsson involves software development for multi-mode cellular PC Cards. Steven holds a B.S. in Computer Science and a B.S. in Mathematics from Wayne State University in Detroit, Michigan.

Brian E. Moore is a Software Engineer with IBM. His career has included software development in Modems, Terminals, and LAN adapters. He has developed device drivers for DOS, Windows 95, and Windows NT for Token-ring PC Cards. Currently, he is working in a JAVA applications group. He holds a B.S.E. from the University of North Carolina - Charlotte and an M.S.E.E. from Georgia Tech.

Dana L. Beatty is a Software Engineer with IBM. Her career has included opportunities working as a developer on LANs and device drivers with OS/2, PCMCIA and CDPD modem product development and, most recently, a stint at Lotus which lead to her current involvement with e-Business Integration Test at IBM in Austin, Texas. Dana has filed several patents relating to this body of development work. She holds a B.A. from the University of Texas, Austin.

Windows 2000 vs. Windows NT 5.0

As this book was going to press, Microsoft changed the name of Windows NT 5.0 to Windows 2000. Windows NT 5 Beta Release 1 was available during the development of this book. As a result, the software utilities developed run correctly on that platform. For more information on this name change, Microsoft has provided a web site explaining the name change. It is:

www.Microsoft.com/windows/news/October1998/win2000.asp

As soon as Windows 2000 is available, it is our intention to test the utilities and update any code that does not function properly. The software will then become available on the Peer-to-Peer Web site via FTP. The address is ftp.peer-to-peer.com/pubs/pc-card.